PONTIFICAL INSTITUTE OF MEDIAEVAL STUDIES

STUDIES AND TEXTS

4

THE LITURGICAL DRAMA IN MEDIEVAL SPAIN

RICHARD B. DONOVAN, C.S.B.

St. Michael's College, University of Toronto

Pontifical Institute of Mediaeval Studies

Toronto, 1958

244.7
D719

165598

Printed in the Netherlands by Royal Van Gorcum Ltd., Assen

PREFACE

U NLESS otherwise indicated, the Spanish liturgical texts presented in this study have been edited from the original sources, and previous editions are mentioned where there have been such. Pointed brackets are used to indicate editorial additions.

A special word might perhaps be said about the bibliography. Amongst the list of manuscript sources are included not only works consulted for this monograph, but also other codices which I was unable to locate. Many of the latter are of the type that frequently contain liturgical plays or information about them. They are therefore important, and their discovery would doubtless increase our knowledge of the liturgical drama in medieval Spain. The bibliography should thus serve as a helpful guide to those who wish to do further research in the subject. As the reader must realize, the list of manuscripts was by no means easy to draw up, since catalogues or inventories of many Spanish ecclesiastical libraries and archives have not as yet been published. Consequently, in many cases, only personal investigation could disclose what manuscripts have been preserved. At present the *Consejo Superior de Investigaciones Científicas*, under the able direction of D. Tomás Marín and Mr. G. Fink, is actively engaged in drawing up and publishing inventories of the manuscript collections of ecclesiastical libraries in Spain. The volume on the cathedral of Tarazona, I believe, has already appeared, and that on Seville will soon follow. Dom A. Olivar, O.S.B., of the monastery of Montserrat, has recently announced the proximate publication of a general inventory of all Catalan liturgical manuscripts still extant in Catalonia or elsewhere (*Hispania Sacra*, VIII, 1955, 439). This work will be anxiously awaited by all investigators of medieval liturgy.

It would be difficult to acknowledge adequately my indebtedness to the many persons whose encouragement and assistance have made this monograph possible. My thanks must be extended, first of all, to the eminent scholar and charming gentleman, Professor Erich Auerbach of Yale University, whose stimulating lectures first aroused my interest in the subject of the medieval religious drama. This work had its origin in a paper written for one of his courses, and with his encouragement it was subsequently presented, in its developed form, as a dissertation for the degree of Doctor of Philosophy at Yale University.

Anyone writing upon the liturgical drama of the Middle Ages must realize the debt he owes to the late Karl Young, whose crowning achievement

PREFACE

in the field, *The Drama of the Medieval Church*, is recognized by all as a masterpiece of modern scholarship. How constantly this book was my companion in the preparation of this study is amply shown by the innumerable references made to it in the ensuing pages.

Special mention must also be made of the many masterful volumes which have been devoted to medieval Hispanic music and culture by Msgr. Higinio Anglès of the Pontifical Institute of Sacred Music in Rome. His *La Música a Catalunya fins al segle XIII* in particular represents years of research and constitutes a treasury of information and directives for subsequent investigators. I am indebted to Msgr. Anglès not only for the fund of knowledge which he has made public in his written works, but also for his personal counsel as well.

The favours granted me in Spain by librarians and archivists are far too numerous for detailed acknowledgement. Even a mere list of them would be prohibitive. Throughout the entire country, save in two or three isolated instances, access to manuscripts, early-book collections, and other library resources was most readily given. I must, however, refer at least to the special kindness shown to me by the following: Msgr. Eduardo Junyent, director of the Museo Episcopal of Vich, Juan Rivera Recio, archivist of the cathedral church of Toledo, Jaime Marqués, archivist of the cathedral of Gerona, Pedro Llado, archivist of the cathedral of Palma de Mallorca, and Dom Marcos Taxonera, O.S.B., librarian at the monastery of Montserrat. Special thanks are also due to Manuel Casares Hervás, archivist of the cathedral of Granada, who kindly transcribed some manuscript passages for me, to Dr. Martín de Riquer of the University of Barcelona, who gave me generously of his time and learning in the interpretation of some old Catalan texts, and to the late Luis Constans and the editors of *Cuadernos del Centre de Estudios Comarcales de Bañolas* for permission to reprint parts of an article on a thirteenth century Sibylline chant. Not soon to be forgotten are the countless pleasurable hours spent in conversation with these distinguished scholars and with many others, all of whom showed me that charming courtesy for which the Spanish are so renowned.

I could not fail to include amongst my acknowledgements the gratitude I owe to one of the outstanding scholars of the United States, Professor Henri M. Peyre of Yale University, for his constant encouragement and for his assistance in helping me obtain a scholarship which made the research for this study possible. Finally I must also express my debt of thanks to the late Reverend Alexander J. Denomy, C.S.B., of the Pontifical Institute of Medieval Studies of Toronto, for his prudent advice during the preparation of this work for print, and to Robert McKinnon, C.S.B., for drawing the excellent map which illustrates this monograph.

R.B.D.

St. Michael's College of the University of Toronto
October, 1957

TABLE OF CONTENTS

CHAPTER 1	Introduction	1
CHAPTER 2	The Origin and Development of Liturgical Drama	6
CHAPTER 3	The Coming of the Roman Rite to Spain	20
CHAPTER 4	Liturgical Drama at Toledo	30
CHAPTER 5	Other Liturgical Plays West of Catalonia	51
CHAPTER 6	Reasons for the Scarcity of Liturgical Plays West of Catalonia	67
CHAPTER 7	Liturgical Plays in Catalonia: Vich and the Seo de Urgel	74
CHAPTER 8	The Liturgical Drama at Gerona	98
CHAPTER 9	Plays at Mallorca	120
CHAPTER 10	Valencia and the Liturgical Drama	139
CHAPTER 11	Further Examples of Liturgical Drama in Catalonia	157
CHAPTER 12	A Brief History of the Dramatic Monologue of the Sibyl	165
	Conclusion	168
	Appendix	172
	Bibliography	198
	Index	221
	MS 105, Vich, Biblioteca Capitular, fol. 58^v	96
	MS 118, Vich, Biblioteca Capitular, fol. 159	97

CHAPTER I

INTRODUCTION

A STUDY devoted to the medieval liturgical drama of Spain has been long overdue. The subject of the liturgical drama is not only fascinating in itself, but is of importance for the history of the theater. Almost all historians see in the dramatic compositions employed by the medieval church in western Europe one of the principal origins of modern drama. For years now scholars have been investigating the liturgical plays of the rest of Europe, and the number of texts which they have collected and published mounts into the six or seven hundreds. However practically none of these works gives more than a fleeting reference to Spain. C. Lange's collection of 224 liturgical Easter plays, for example, contains but two Spanish texts.[1] The admirable work of the late Karl Young, the classic on the subject, gives but two more.[2]

In Spain itself little has been written on the topic. As a result, the beginnings of the Hispanic theater have been left shrouded in almost complete obscurity. Literary historians have been unanimous in pointing out this lack. In the first volume of his *Historia general de las literaturas hispánicas* (1949, p. 432), Diaz-Plaja declares: "No existe un trabajo sistemático y moderno sobre los orígenes del teatro peninsular, ni siquiera trabajos monográficos de la envergadura de los que Gustave Cohen, por ejemplo, ha criado para alumbrar tan interesante aspecto en la literatura francesa medieval... Las numerosas lagunas que se observan en este período de la evolución del género dramático dificultan... la hilación entre las distintas obras, y por lo tanto, la presencia de conclusiones historiográficas." González Palencia, one of the foremost literary critics of Spain, says much the same, pointing out that even the information provided by the few articles which have been published has never been effectively brought together in a single study: "En España no están todavía sistematizados estos estudios ni reunidos siquiera los materiales dispersos para historiar los orígenes de nuestro teatro."[3]

In order to understand what likely took place in the Hispanic peninsula in the field of medieval liturgical drama, almost all scholars who have treated the problem have considered themselves obliged to study what occurred in other European countries, and then conclude that a similar development must have taken place in the region beyond the Pyrenees. It has been repeatedly

---

[1] *Die lateinischen Osterfeiern*, 1887.
[2] *The Drama of the Medieval Church*, 1933.
[3] J. Hurtado y A. González Palencia, *Historia de la literatura española*, 6th ed., 1949, p. 92.

affirmed that in all probability the drama in Castile developed within the liturgy of the church, exactly as it did in France and England, that the plays were first sung in Latin, and then evolved gradually into the vernacular. The one major exception to this rule is perhaps E. K. Chambers, who concluded, because of the scarcity of known plays from Spain, that the drama in that area must have known a somewhat different evolution: "If the influence of the Sarum use and the havoc of service-books at the Reformation may between them help to account for the comparative rarity of the play in these islands [British Isles], no such explanation is available for Italy and Spain. The development of the religious drama in the peninsulas... seems to have followed from the beginning lines somewhat distinct from those of north-western Europe." [4]

Most have declared that it was the monks of Cluny who brought the liturgical drama from the monasteries of France into Spain: "Estos dramas litúrgicos franco-latinos, compuestos durante los siglos XI y XII... fueron traidos a España por les benedictinos de Cluny."[5] This, they reason, must have taken place when the Mozarabic rite in Spain was replaced by the Roman in the eleventh century. No one has ever done much more than *surmise* that the liturgical drama entered the peninsula in this way. There has been no attempt to investigate the matter, with a view to ascertaining just what role the Cluniac monks did play in the development of the early Hispanic theater.

How is one to account for this lack of studies on the early liturgical drama of Spain? Is it because literary historians believed that liturgical plays were rare in Hispanic churches? This is not the opinion of González Palencia who states (p. 94), "Que en España fué abundantísima y extensa esta literatura es incuestionable." Almost everyone who has touched upon this matter has expressed the same view. Is it because the manuscripts do not exist? This is the reason generally put forth by literary critics. J. P. Crawford, for example, begins his monograph on the *Spanish Drama before Lope de Vega* [6] as follows: "Material is almost entirely lacking for a study of the liturgical drama in Spain."

However one may ask the question, is the material lacking for this study because the manuscripts do not exist, or because no one has ever systematically searched for them? González Palencia has wisely left room for this latter possibility (p. 94): "Nos faltan los textos, que o se perdieron, *o están todavía por descubrir en el fondo de nuestros archivos.*"

Strangely enough, the exact whereabouts of certain Hispanic manuscripts which contain liturgical plays, or references to them, has been known for over one hundred years, and these texts have never been edited. To give but one example, as early as 1832 Fr. de La Canal spoke of descriptions of liturgical plays in a fourteenth century *consueta*, or ceremonial, found in the capitular archives of the cathedral of Gerona, and suggested that the passage be publish-

---

[4] *The Medieval Stage*, II, 27.
[5] A. Bonilla y San Martín, *Las Bacantes, o del origen del teatro*, p. 68.
[6] Rev. ed., 1937, p. 1.

ed.[7] In 1935, indicating the available material for a study on the Hispanic liturgical drama, A. A. Parker was still obliged to say vaguely that the Gerona manuscript "apparently gives some account of these dramatic performances."[8] González Palencia speaks of "el inapreciable códice *gerundense* del año 1380, que tantas y tan curiosas noticias nos ha conservado de representaciones sacras" (p. 94).

It seems, then, that lack of curiosity, more than anything else, has been the leading cause of the dearth of studies upon the liturgical drama of medieval Spain. This is surprising when one reflects how painstakingly investigators have been searching for years in the libraries of the rest of western Europe, oftentimes in the same places where others have searched before them.

J. Villanueva, I think, is the only one who has ever looked more or less systematically for the church plays of Spain. At the beginning of the nineteenth century, the learned and indefatigable Dominican consulted all the medieval manuscripts he could discover in the ecclesiastical archives of Catalonia, Valencia, and Seville, and recorded from them whatever he considered of major interest for Spanish history, both ecclesiastic and secular. Some of his findings were reported in the twenty-two volume *Viage literario a las Iglesias de España*, published at intervals from 1803 to 1852. Frequently in the course of his work Fr. Villanueva stated that the liturgical manuscripts of the various church libraries gave valuable information about medieval drama, but he reserved the majority of his notes for the treatise on medieval Spanish liturgy which he planned eventually to publish. Unfortunately, owing to unfavorable political circumstances this great work was never realized, though the notes collected for it assumed grandiose proportions. These notes lay untouched in the Real Academia de la Historia in Madrid – MS 64 (12-19-4) – until H. Anglès edited the plays among them in 1935 in his *La Música a Catalunya fins al segle XIII*. The chapter on the liturgical drama in this latter work is the most important single contribution on the subject that has appeared in Spain. Sometimes, however, Villanueva did not transcribe literally the passages of his sources, so that the plays which Msgr. Anglès has edited from the Villanueva collection do not always correspond with the text of the original manuscript. Anglès tells us, moreover, that he did not have time to ascertain whether these manuscripts were still extant or not (p. 282): "No hem tingut temps ni ocasió per comparar les còpies del pare Villanueva amb els manuscrits respectius de les consuetes assenyalades, ni tan sols podem dir si les tals consuetes es conserven avui iguals al temps del pare Villanueva."

A comprehensive study on the liturgical drama of the Hispanic peninsula is therefore sorely needed to help dispel some of the mystery overhanging the nebulous beginnings of the medieval Hispanic theater. Such questions as the following must be answered. Are medieval liturgical plays lacking in Spain

---

[7] *España Sagrada*, XLV, 13-24.
[8] 'Religious Drama in Medieval Spain', p. 172.

because almost all liturgical manuscripts of this period have been lost or destroyed? Did the drama develop in the same way in every part of the peninsula? What were the relations between the Hispanic kingdoms and France? Did the drama come to Spain from France in the eleventh century, and if so, what role did the monks of Cluny actually play ? . . .

A study on the Hispanic liturgical drama is also needed to complete our knowledge of the medieval theater of other countries. Perhaps nowhere do the principles of comparative literature have better, or more necessary, application than in the field of medieval liturgical drama. This drama was international in character, and influences moved back and forth constantly from one country to another. What was practised in one land very often reflected the customs and usages of another. For this reason, then, no country may be left aside in a history of the drama of the medieval church, especially since so many medieval manuscripts have been lost. Spain is no exception. G. Girot says very well: "Le drame religieux a partout la même provenance: la liturgie chrétienne; il a pour domaine tout l'ancien monde catholique. On ne peut laisser en dehors aucune partie comme *incognita*, telle l'Espagne. C'est pourtant bien un peu ce qu'on fait quant on étudie cette importante branche de la littérature européenne."[9]

The following study has been undertaken in an endeavor to fill to some extent the lacuna in the history of the medieval liturgical drama exposed in the preceding paragraphs.

An analysis of the sources of the church plays edited by Young gives a rather clear indication of the types of manuscripts to be examined in preparation for such a study, and the historical period which investigation of this question must necessarily embrace. Rather surprisingly perhaps, such an analysis reveals that of the total number of plays studied by Young – roughly some five or six hundred – approximately one-half are plays of the fifteenth or sixteenth century! This figure shows the inexactitude of the traditional way of presenting the liturgical drama as a practice that more or less began to die out in the twelfth century in order to give way to the semi-liturgical and vernacular drama. Research into this problem must consequently have as its scope the whole medieval period, from the tenth century when the plays began, until at least the sixteenth century; or better, until 1568, the year of the papal reform of the Roman breviary.

As for the *type* of manuscripts which contain the plays, a scrutiny of the edited texts proves equally revealing. No less than one out of three plays was discovered in a breviary, and one out of five in an *ordinarium* (an *ordinarium* is a manuscript indicating the order and content of the various church ceremonies; it is known by a variety of names depending on the usage of the locality: *liber consuetudinum, directorium, agenda, consueta,* etc.). The rest of the liturgical plays appear chiefly in *processionaria*, tropers, *libri responsales*, and

[9] 'Lacunes de l'histoire du drame religieux en Espagne', p. 61.

various other books of chant. These are the principal types of manuscripts, therefore, which require examination.[10]

The study which follows presents the results of research in the libraries of Spain, France, and the British Museum in London. It is devoted chiefly to the publication of the dramatic texts themselves, the majority of which have not been previously edited. Texts previously edited are also included, in the hope that a convenient and relatively complete *corpus* of Spanish liturgical plays will thus be provided. There is an attempt, in addition, to focus these plays in their international setting, and to describe the liturgical background in Spain in which these plays grew, or could have grown; an understanding of the origins of Spanish drama, and of its relations with that of France, would be impossible without a knowledge of this element. We shall see that repeatedly the new Hispanic texts throw light on the drama of France and other countries, concerning such points as the manner in which certain liturgical plays were performed, the role conceded to the vernacular in the performance of these plays, etc.; in several instances the Spanish texts reveal new types of dramatic ceremonies which probably had a vogue throughout all Europe. Findings in Castile, moreover, may possibly have important implications for the history of the medieval vernacular drama in France.

---

[10] The medieval capitular statutes, account books, and sacristans' manuals still extant in the archives of some cathedral and collegiate churches, though they would not give us the texts of the religious plays themselves, doubtless contain information about their performance. Systematic investigation of such sources, however, would require much time, and would constitute a special undertaking.

CHAPTER 2

THE ORIGIN AND DEVELOPMENT OF LITURGICAL DRAMA

IN ORDER to have a full appreciation of the Hispanic liturgical plays and their significance, one must be able to picture them in their proper international perspective. For this, at least a general knowledge of the history of the liturgical play itself is necessary: what is meant by a liturgical play, how and when it developed, and the different types of plays it produced. These points have all been treated at length in the monumental two volume work of the late Karl Young, *The Drama of the Medieval Church*. We shall only touch upon the main aspects of these problems here, referring the reader who may desire further information to the excellent study of Young.

The liturgical ceremonies of the Catholic Church, as everyone knows, are for the most part very ancient, and consequently offer in themselves an extremely rich and interesting subject. The heart of the sacred cult, the consecration of the Mass, goes back to the time of Christ, and most of the ceremonies which surround it, to the first centuries of the Christian era. From the beginning many of the elements of this liturgy presented an aspect which one might call *dramatic*, and certain writers have not hesitated to apply the term *drama* to the Mass and to the Catholic cult in general. These writers were thinking of such elements as: the re-presentation of Christ's Sacrifice in the Mass, the procession on Palm Sunday and the services of Holy Week, the mystical symbolism, the sacred chant with its responsories and antiphonal singing, and so forth.

However in a study such as this, it is necessary to define what one means by *drama*. Hence it must be observed that, despite their evidently theatrical aspect, such traits of the liturgy as we have mentioned do not constitute drama in the more limited, and strictly literary, sense of the word: there is lacking the essential element of impersonation whereby an *actor* plays the role of another person, real or fictitious. Young defines a drama as "a story presented in action, in which the speakers or actors impersonate the characters concerned."[1] For him, and we believe that he is right, it is the word *impersonate* which is all-important; a ceremony without this quality is not a play. We shall adopt this view in the following study, considering as drama only those ecclesiastical ceremonies which clearly involve impersonation.

The word *liturgical* itself is not devoid of certain difficulties, inasmuch as it is not always easy to determine just which ceremonies fall into this category.

---

[1] I, 80. Unless otherwise indicated, all references to Young are to his work, *The Drama of the Medieval Church*.

In the Middle Ages the "official liturgy" of the Church, if one may so speak, was limited to the essential part of Catholic worship, such as the Canon of the Mass, etc.; in the more secondary portions, usage varied considerably from diocese to diocese. The liturgical plays were one of these secondary items. Frequently as these plays expanded with time, their strictly "devotional" spirit diminished, and their evident attachment to the liturgy grew constantly slighter. Just when a given play ceased entirely to be *liturgical*, however, is often difficult to decide. Such writers as Meyer,[2] Creizenach,[3] Lange,[4] and others, have endeavored to establish very distinct criteria for determining such cases, but Young has shown that their efforts have not proved very satisfactory.[5] It is a point which bears re-studying, because many writers have failed to note that, if in may cases the expanded plays left the church for the public squares, in many other instances they continued to develop in the very same part of the church services which they originally occupied.[6] In our study of plays from the Hispanic peninsula, without endeavoring to define the term with any absolute precision, we shall consider as *liturgical* any ceremonies which were performed in the church, with a devotional spirit, and in close connection with some liturgical office.

One of the most ancient works describing in detail the ritual of the early Catholic Church is the celebrated document known under the title, *Peregrinatio Etheriae*, generally considered the work of a fourth century Galician woman.[7] The book is of special interest to us because the authoress comments at considerable length upon the ceremonies of the Church at Jerusalem at that time: the manner in which canonical hours were recited, the role of ecclesiastics and lay persons in the ceremonies, the processions to the holy places where Christ suffered His Passion, and especially the liturgical rites of Holy Week. Doubtless the ceremonies described by the Spanish pilgrim do not constitute dramas. Nevertheless they give us a rather distinct idea of the liturgy of the Church such as it was practised in the fourth century at Jerusalem, and show us how an entire dramatic program could easily evolve from the realistic framework depicted, and from the manifest desire of clerics and people to recall and re-create the notable scenes in the life of Jesus Christ; there was a common wish to relive in spirit the events recounted by the Evangelists. It was to be precisely this same desire which would inspire the liturgists some centuries later to reproduce the scenes in a distinctly dramatic manner. In

---

[2] *Fragmenta Burana*, pp. 59, 79, 80-81, 92.
[3] *Geschichte des neueren Dramas*, I, 84.
[4] *Programm*, 1-35.
[5] I, 411-412.
[6] Evidence for this is to be had, for example, in the directions for the lengthy vernacular play from Erlau: *Visitatio Sepulcri in nocte resurrectionis. Post versum, Et valde.* The verse referred to is the third responsory of Matins. The text of the play is given by E. Hartl, *Das Drama des Mittelalters*, II, 205. The rubrics of the Benediktbeuern play begin, *Cantatis Matutinis*; text in Young, I, 432.
[7] See Cabrol, *Les Eglises de Jérusalem: la discipline et la liturgie au quatrième siècle*.

the fourth century all the faithful participated in this renewal of the Gospel incidents; in the Middle Ages some ecclesiastics would re-create them for the edification of their co-religionists: since they did not live in Judea, they would represent the scenes which had taken place there. The exact moment at which these ceremonies were brought from Asia Minor to the West is not known, but it must have occurred rather early; the majority of them were known in Europe before the seventh century.

The attempts to relate the Western medieval theater with the dramatic forms which developed in the Orient have attained but little success. Discovery has been made of a rather peculiar Greek play, *Christos Paschon*, which dates from the fourth century according to some critics, from as late as the eleventh or twelfth according to most. This play borrows heavily from works of Euripides and other classical Greek authors, but in the opinion of Professor Grace Frank, it is an example of a strictly literary drama, that is, one not intended to be acted.[8] Miss Maria de Vito seems to affirm that one of the Western types of plays, the *Processio Prophetarum*, proceeds from the Byzantine theater;[9] however she offers no evidence that the pseudo-Augustinian sermon, which eventually became a play in the West, was ever dramatized in the Orient. On the whole, evidences of a close relationship between the Occidental liturgical drama and Byzantine theater are very few. An examination of the oldest texts of the *Visitatio Sepulchri*, generally regarded as the earliest form of liturgical drama to develop in the West, seems to indicate rather clearly that the Easter play, as a dramatic creation, is of Occidental origin.

Among the ceremonies which played a central role in the Holy Week rites during the Middle Ages were the *Depositio* and the *Elevatio*. Both of these ceremonies were eventually to bear a close relationship to the liturgical drama. The former took place on Good Friday after the celebration of Mass and before the chanting of Vespers, and consisted of a solemn procession, followed by the placing of a cross in a *sepulchre* to commemorate the death and burial of Christ. Sometimes instead of a cross, a consecrated Host or an image of Christ was used, or sometimes both a cross and the Host. Many of the medieval service-books contain a résumé of the ceremony, the following from Rouen illustrating the close relationship between the *Depositio* and the Adoration of the Cross:[10]

> Quando Crux adorata fuerit a clero et populo, eleuet eam sacerdos alte, et incipiat cantor hanc antiphonam:
>
>> Super omnia ligna cedrorum, tu sola excelsior, in qua uita mundi pependit, in qua Christus triumphauit, et mors mortem superauit in eternum.

[8] 'Introduction', p. 64; *The Medieval French Drama*, pp. 5-6.
[9] "Cosi un esempio di derivazione sicura dal teatro bisantino è il dramma dei Profeti di Cristo, che fu molto diffuso in Francia" (*L'Origine del Dramma Liturgico*, p. 113).
[10] Paris, Bibl. Nat., MS lat. 904, Grad. Rothomagense saec. xiii, fol. 92^v-93; text printed by Young, I, 135.

Quo uiso, clerus et populus genuflectant, et chorus finiat antiphonam. Qua cantata, Crux paruula in commemoratione sanguinis et aque deflentis de latere Redemptoris aqua et uino lauetur, de quo commemorationem sacram clerus bibat et populus, et ad opus infirmorum reseruetur. Quo facto, sacerdotes et clerici accipiant Crucifixum et portent ad Sepulchrum preparatum cantantes hoc responsorium:

> Sicut ouis ad occisionem ductus est, et dum male tractaretur, non aperuit os suum, traditus est ad mortem ut uiuificaret populum suum. Versus: In pace factus est locus eius, et in Syon habitatio eius. Responsorium: Vt uiuificaret.

Et tunc ponatur in Sepulcro, pedibus uersis ad orientem, et cooperiatur pallio, et incensando illam dicat archiepiscopus uel sacerdos hanc antiphonam:

> In pace in idipsum dormiam et requiescam.

Qua cantata, claudat hostium Sepulchri. Responsorium:

> Sepulto Domino, signatum est monumentum; uoluentes lapidem ad hostium monumenti; ponentes milites qui custodirent illud. Versus: Ne forte ueniant discipuli eius et furentur eum, et dicant plebi: Surrexit a mortuis. Responsorium: Voluentes.

His expletis, ministri Crucis casulis induti afferant ad altare cum uino non consecrato reseruatum Corpus Domini.

In this case, at Rouen, it was a cross which was used. After being carried to the burial place during the chanting of a responsory, it was laid in the sepulchre, covered with a winding sheet, and incensed. Thereupon the door of the sepulchre was closed, and the ceremony was concluded with the chanting of the responsory, *Sepulto Domino*.

The *Elevatio* might be called the complement of the *Depositio*. It took place on Easter morning, and involved the taking up of the cross or Host that had been placed in the sepulchre, thus symbolizing or commemorating Christ's resurrection from the dead. If a Host had been used in the *Depositio*, the ceremony on Easter morning was generally accompanied by a procession; otherwise it was performed, as a rule, in more or less private fashion, the symbolic cross being removed before the people entered the church for the Easter morning services. In this way, the people would be reminded, when they arrived, that Christ was no longer in the tomb, but had arisen. In churches where the Easter play itself was performed, the *Elevatio* was an excellent preparation for it, because the shroud which had been used to envelop the cross was left as a visible sign of the resurrection; in the course of the play, the angels, or the "Three Marys", would triumphantly show the shroud to the people. At Rouen, the *Elevatio* was performed before the regular liturgical office began, that is, just before Matins:[11]

---

[11] The *Liber de Officiis Ecclesiasticis* of Jean d'Avranches; text in Migne, *P.L.*, 147, 51-52, and

Decima hora noctis pauci clerici induti veniant, et Crucifixum cum incenso et thymiamate levantes, antiphonamque *Surrexit Dominus de sepulchro* ‹cantantes›, loco suo honorifice constituant. Post cunctis campanis sonantibus, januas ecclesiae aperiant, et Matutinas incipiant.

The position of this ceremony at Rouen was the ordinary one. Young records but five instances of its appearance after *Matins*, and comments upon one of these texts as follows: "Among the exceptional features of the particular ceremony now before us, the most puzzling is its position in the liturgy – at the *end* of Matins."[12] I point out this fact here, because we shall find that in at least two Spanish texts the *Elevatio* occupies this same position.[13]

If these two Holy Week practices were later associated with the drama, and perhaps even helped to suggest it, it was not from them, however, that the liturgical play first developed. The immediate source of such plays was the phenomenon of trope-singing. Originally the word *trope* was a musical term, but in the Middle Ages it came to be applied more regularly to the words themselves which accompanied the music. In this literary sense, a trope may be defined as a verbal amplification of some passage of the liturgy, either as an introduction, an interpolation, or a conclusion, or any combination of these. For example, the final *Ite, missa est* of the Mass, and its response, were frequently *troped* by the insertion of a phrase between the first and last words of the formula; the following variation is typical:

Ite *nunc in pace, spiritus sanctus super vos sit, iam* missa est.
Deo *semper laudes agite, in corde gloriam et* gratias.

Historians of the liturgy do not know who began the practice of writing these new musical texts in the Middle Ages, but from the ninth century on, they become very numerous. Ordinarily the term is associated with Notker Balbulus (*ca.* 840-912), a monk of the Benedictine abbey of St. Gall, but it seems very probable that the invention belonged to some French monastery. It is Notker himself who gives us this information. According to his oft-told story, in 860, after the sacking of the abbey of Jumièges by the Norsemen, a certain monk fled to St. Gall, bringing with him a service-book which contained several tropes of a rather elementary type. Inspired by this example, Notker applied his literary talents to the composition of more ambitious tropes, and in a short time his monastery became the center of this new custom. Young affirms that the first of these new literary embellishments may have

---

reprinted therefrom by Young, I, 555. For information regarding the nature of the various liturgical offices mentioned here and throughout the course of this study, for example, the office of Matins, one may consult Young, I, 44–75.

[12] I, 131; the italics are Young's. The five instances which he records are: Saint Gall, eleventh century, p. 131; Hungary, fifteenth century, pp. 147-148; Sens, p. 554; and two texts from Soissons, twelfth century, pp. 304, 554.

[13] See pp. 61 and 63 of this study; both of these texts involve dramatization, another rare feature.

been written in the French Benedictine abbey of Saint-Martial at Limoges, or at Saint-Benoît-sur-Loire, a suggestion doubtless proposed because of the important role played by these two monasteries some years later in the dissemination of tropes and liturgical plays.[14]

Of all the new compositions, by far the most important for our consideration was the famous *Quem quaeritis*, sung before the introit of the Easter Sunday conventual Mass; out of this piece was to evolve the earliest recorded play of the medieval Church. The version from Saint-Martial de Limoges, written between 923 and 934, is generally regarded as the oldest extant example:[15]

TROPHI [16] IN PASCHE

Psallite regi magno, deuicto mortis imperio! Quem queritis in sepulchro, o Christicole?

Responsio:

Ihesum Nazarenum crucifixum, o celicole.

Responsio:

Non est hic, surrexit sicut ipse dixit; ite, nunciate quia surrexit. Alleluia, resurrexit Dominus, hodie resurrexit leo fortis, Cristus, filius Dei; Deo gratias, dicite eia!

Like most of the new compositions, the Easter *Quem quaeritis* was divided into question and response, a form which lent itself well to eventual dramatization. All that was required to transform this chant into a play was a direction that the singers of the questions and responses impersonate the historical figures represented. It seems quite probable that this did not take place until the trope was shifted from its position before the introit of the Mass to a corresponding one after the conclusion of Matins. Karl Young knew of but one instance of the *Quem quaeritis* being dramatized before Mass; and

---

[14] I, 184. For further information on the question of tropes, one may consult Gautier, *Histoire de la poésie liturgique au Moyen Age: les Tropes*; Frere, ed., *The Winchester Troper*, introduction; Handschin, 'Trope, Sequence, and Conductus', *The New Oxford History of Music* (1954), II, 128-174; and Young, I, 178-238.

[15] Paris, Bibl. Nat., MS lat. 1240, Trop. Sancti Martialis Lemovicensis saec. x, fol. 30ᵛ, printed by Young, I, 210. For the date of the manuscript, see the arguments advanced by H. M. Bannister, in *Journal of Theological Studies*, II (1901), 420 sqq. Young follows the opinion of Bannister, and adds that the original version of the trope was likely composed by Tutilo at St. Gall around the year 912 (I, 205). Edith Wright, in her fine study, *The Dissemination of the Liturgical Drama in France*, is not always careful to distinguish between a mere trope and a real play. Consequently she appears to consider this trope from Saint-Martial as a liturgical play, and because of its early date concludes: "(Saint-Martial) seems to have been the true creator of the liturgical drama in France and perhaps in Europe" (p. 31; see also p. 41. Recently Grace Frank seems to have accepted this view; see *The Medieval French Drama*, p. 66). This affirmation is seriously open to question, first of all, because the original form of the *Quem quaeritis* may have come from St. Gall, and secondly, because we do not really know if the present Saint-Martial text was actually dramatized.

[16] Trophi] Trophum (?MS).

since this occurs in a late fifteenth century text, he sees in the example merely an "imitation of the plays which . . . had been common for centuries at the end of Easter Matins." [17]

Curiously enough, the earliest evidence of dramatization of the *Quem quaeritis* is found in a manuscript, not from France, but from England. The text is the celebrated *Regularis Concordia*, composed between 965 and 975 by an English Benedictine, Saint Ethelwold, bishop of Winchester. This precious document, which was to serve as an appendix to the Rule of St. Benedict for the English monks, devotes many folios to the liturgical rites which the bishop wished to be observed in his country. In the portion of the work which discusses the ceremonies of Holy Week, we find not only a description of the *Depositio* of Good Friday, but explicit directions for the staging of an Easter play "for the edification of the faithful." It is none other than our trope, now become an authentic play. Instead of the choir, it is the individual monks who sing the various parts of the text, one monk becoming the angel at the tomb, and pronouncing the lines befitting his "role", while three others represent the Marys who have come to anoint the Body of their Master. The simplicity of the directions adorns the text with a charm and freshness which it will never lose: [18]

> Dum tertia recitatur lectio, quatuor fratres induant se, quorum unus alba[19] indutus ac si ad aliud agendum ingrediatur, atque latenter Sepulchri locum adeat, ibique manu tenens palmam, quietus sedeat. Dumque tertium percelebratur responsorium, residui tres succedant, omnes quidem cappis induti, turribula cum incensu manibus gestantes ac pedetemptim ad similitudinem querentium quid, ueniant ante locum Sepulchri. Aguntur enim hec ad imitationem Angeli sedentis in monumento, atque Mulierum cum aromatibus uenientium, ut ungerent corpus Ihesu. Cum ergo ille residens tres uelut erraneos, ac aliquid querentes, uiderit sibi adproximare, incipiat mediocri uoce dulcisone cantare: [20]
>
>   Quem queritis ‹in sepulchro, o Christicolae›?
>
> Quo decantato fine tenus, respondeant hi tres uno ore:
>
>   Ihesum Nazarenum ‹crucifixum, o coelicola›.
>
> Quibus ille:

---

[17] I, 222. Outside of Spain, I have come across only one other example of an Easter play put on before Mass, a twelfth or thirteenth century version from the Benedictine monastery of Fruttuaria in Italy; text in Albers, *Consuetudines Monasticae*, IV, 74-76. This piece, too, is probably based on the plays at Matins, because in the middle of the ceremony one finds the rubric, *Tunc canant illi tres responsorium, Dum transisset Sabbathum*; this reference is to the third responsory of Matins, which in this case, is borrowed for the morning festivities.
[18] London, Brit. Mus., MS Cotton Tiberius A. III, fol. 21-21ᵛ; in Young, I, 249.
[19] alba] abba (MS).
[20] It is to be remembered that this play, like almost all the medieval Church performances, was sung; musicologists tell us that the music, though simple, was strikingly beautiful.

Non est hic, surrexit sicut predixerat; ite, nuntiate quia surrexit a mortuis.

Cuius iussionis²¹ uoce uertant se illi tres ad chorum dicentes:

Alleluia, resurrexit Dominus, ‹hodie resurrexit leo fortis, Christus, filius Dei.›

Dicto hoc, rursus ille residens uelut reuocans illos dicat antiphonam:

Venite et uidete locum ‹ubi positus erat Dominus, alleluia›.

Hec uero dicens surgat, et erigat uelum, ostendatque eis locum Cruce nudatum, sed tantum linteamina posita, quibus Crux inuoluta erat. Quo uiso, deponant turribula, que gestauerant in eodem Sepulchro, sumantque linteum et extendant contra clerum, ac ueluti ostendentes, quod surrexerit Dominus et iam non sit illo inuolutus, hanc canant antiphonam:

Surrexit Dominus de sepulchro, ‹qui pro nobis pependit in ligno, alleluia.›

Superponantque linteum altari. Finita antiphona, prior congaudens pro triumpho regis nostri, quod deuicta morte surrexit, incipiat hymnum *Te Deum laudamus*. Quo incepto, una pulsantur omnia signa.

Because early in his work St. Ethelwold speaks of his intention to adopt certain usages practised at the continental monasteries of Fleury and Ghent, many critics have concluded that the Easter play found in the *Regularis Concordia* was one of these usages. Some have even felt justified in attributing to Fleury the invention of the liturgical drama.[22] This assertion, however, has still to be proved. On this whole question of the origin of the English play, at least until new evidence is uncovered, one must adopt the sound and conservative position held by Young: "The general probability would seem to be that these ceremonies were brought into the *Regularis Concordia* from the Continent; but of this, there is no proof."[23]

We know, in any case, that by the year 1000 the new Easter play was flourishing in France, England, and Germany. Before long, other scenes associated with the Resurrection began to appear in the piece: the Marys on their way to the merchant's shop to purchase ointments, the race of Peter and John to the tomb, the apparition of Christ to Mary Magdalen. On Easter Monday a play was introduced commemorating the appearance of the risen Christ to the disciples on the road to Emmaus, a dramatic production which came to be known as the *Peregrinus*.[24]

After the monks had adopted the custom of presenting liturgical plays on Easter morning, it was natural that the enthusiasts of the new drama should

---

[21] iussionis] iussimus (MS).
[22] See especially Cohen, *Le Théâtre en France au moyen âge*, p. 9.
[23] I, 583.
[24] A respresentative text of the *Peregrinus* play is given in the Appendix.

turn their thoughts to the creation of plays for the other great season of the liturgical year, that of Christmas. What invited drama more readily than the story of the miraculous birth at Bethlehem, with its account of the angelic apparition, and the visit of the shepherds to the crib? Or the journey of the three Wise Men following the miraculous star? Accordingly the cathedral and monastic churches were soon the scene of new plays on Christmas night and on the morning of January 6th.

For Christmas day the medieval liturgists composed a trope which they clearly modelled after the Easter *Quem quaeritis*. One glance at its content reveals the close relationship:[25]

AD DOMINICAM MISSAM

Quem queritis in presepe, pastores, dicite?
Saluatorem Christum Dominum, infantem pannis inuolutum, secundum sermonem angelicum.
Adest hic paruulus cum Maria matre sua, de qua dudum uaticinando Isaias dixerat propheta: Ecce uirgo concipiet et pariet filium; et nunc euntes dicite quia natus est.
Alleluia, alleluia! Iam uere scimus Christum natum in terris, de quo canite omnes cum propheta, dicentes:
Psalmus: Puer natus est.

Just as the Easter composition involves a kind of imaginary dialogue between the angels and the Marys at the sepulchre, the Christmas piece presents a similar exchange of utterances between the shepherds and certain persons stationed at the manger. The similarities of the two are put in sharp relief by the juxtaposition of several of the key lines:

Quem queritis in sepulchro, o Christicolae?
Quem queritis in praesepe, pastores, dicite?

Jesum Nazarenum crucifixum.
Salvatorem Christum Dominum.

Non est hic.
Adest hic.

Ite, nuntiate quia surrexit.
Nunc euntes dicite quia natus est.

. . . illud quod olim ipse per prophetam dixerat ad Patrem taliter inquiens.
. . . de quo canite omnes cum propheta dicentes.

That the Christmas composition was the debtor is indicated by the fact that it first appears in texts of the eleventh century, whereas examples of the *Quem quaeritis in sepulchro* are numerous from as early as 923.

[25] Paris, Bibl. Nat., MS lat. 887, Trop. Lemovicense saec. xi, fol. 9^v; text given by Young, II, 4.

The number of cases in which the new trope evolved into a play at Matins, as had the Easter form, are actually very few. Young gives only five examples of it, and three of these are from Rouen.[26] There were perhaps two principal reasons for this rarity. Very frequently the scene of the shepherds at the manger was incorporated into the longer Epiphany play; to present the same scene on Christmas Day would have been unnecessary duplication. Secondly, the dramatic element for Christmas was often supplied at Lauds rather than at Matins. In this position it was not the *Quem quaeritis* trope which formed the core of the play, but the antiphon *Quem vidistis, pastores, dicite*, or another similar to it, *Pastores, dicite, quidnam vidistis*. Well aware of the dramatic promise of these antiphons, Karl Young has discussed at great length, in his study on the *Officium Pastorum*, the manner in which the office of Lauds was sung. Nevertheless, aside from one example of impersonation in a text from Rouen, no other cases of dramatization had come to his attention; even at Rouen the "shepherds" who sing the antiphons at Lauds have already appeared in the Christmas play presented after Matins, and their presence in the second office seems to be merely a carry over from the earlier play. Accordingly Young concludes: "The available evidence indicates that this promising dramatic element was neither widely used nor extensively developed in liturgical drama. Aside from its modest part in the *Officium Pastorum* of Rouen, it seems to have played no part in the true drama of the Christmas liturgy." [27] Evidence we have been able to gather, however, proves that the custom of singing Lauds with the choir-boys dressed up like "shepherds", as at Rouen, was quite common in France throughout the Middle Ages.[28] This was true even when there was no play at Matins. This practice, as we shall see, spread also into Spain, and flourished there in some places until the nineteenth century.

Since frequent reference will later be made to the liturgical hour of Lauds, it might be well at this point to indicate briefly the manner in which this office was conducted. The first part of Lauds consisted of five psalms and five antiphons, each of the latter being sung twice, once before, and once after, the corresponding psalm. Generally the antiphon employed with the first or fifth psalm was one of the following two:

> Quem vidistis, pastores, dicite? Annuntiate nobis in terris quis apparuit? Natum vidimus in choro angelorum Salvatorem Dominum, alleluia, alleluia.

> Pastores, dicite, quidnam vidistis, et annuntiate Christi nativitatem. Infantem vidimus pannis involutum, et choros angelorum laudantes Salvatorem.

---

[26] See his *Drama of the Medieval Church*, II, 9-20; the remaining two versions are from Clermont-Ferrand and Padua.
[27] 'Officium Pastorum', p. 347; the Rouen text is found, *ibid.*, p. 387, and in *The Drama of the Medieval Church*, II, 12. The same view is expressed in the latter work, II, 22.
[28] See *infra*, pp. 34-37.

In many churches it became customary to repeat either of these two texts in dialogue form three or four times during the chanting of the psalm. The question would be asked by the choir, and the answer sung by two or three choir-boys, generally from behind the altar. It may be that these boys were regarded as representing the shepherds. Obviously it would not take much to convert these liturgical compositions, like the *Quem quaeritis in praesepe* trope, into a small play. The following text from Clermont-Ferrand is a good example of the manner in which this festal practice was carried out:[29]

> Et finita Missa usque ad complendam, sacerdos qui cantat Missam alta uoce incipiat antiphonam:
>
>> Pastores, dicite ‹quidnam uidistis, et annunciate Christi natiuitatem›.
>
> Deinde chori provisores alta uoce psalmum:
>
>> Dominus regnauit, decorem indutus est: indutus est Dominus fortitudinem, et precinxit se.
>
> Chorus dicat antiphonam:
>
>> Pastores, dicite, quidnam uidistis, et annunciate Christi natiuitatem.
>
> Tres pueri retro altare respondeant excelsa uoce antiphonam:[30]
>
>> Infantem uidimus pannis inuolutum et choros angelorum laudantes Saluatorem.
>
> Chori prouisores:
>
>> Etenim firmauit orbem terre, qui non commouebitur.
>
> ‹Chorus dicat antiphonam:›
>
>> Pastores, supra.
>
> Pueri iterum cantent antiphonam:
>
>> Infantem.
>
> Chori prouisores:
>
>> Parata sedes tua, Deus, ex tunc a seculo tu es.
>
> Chorus antiphonam:
>
>> Pastores, supra.
>
> ‹Pueri antiphonam:›
>
>> Infantem.

---

[29] Bibl. Nat., MS lat. 1274, Breviarium Claromontense saec. xiv, fol. 40ᵛ-41ᵛ. I follow the edition given by Young, 'Officium Pastorum', pp. 359-360.
[30] The custom of singing back and forth across the altar was also frequently followed in chanting the *Quem quaeritis* introit tropes at Easter and Christmas. In the Easter ceremony the altar symbolized the sepulchre. It may be that at Christmas the altar was regarded as representing the *praesepe*; too, in some churches the crib itself was erected behind the main altar (e.g., at Rouen).

Antiphona:
> Quem uidistis? (Followed by four verses of the psalm and a final repetition of the antiphon; the rest of Lauds proceeds regularly.)

In the manuscript before us, no express provision is made for impersonation.

The oldest known example of dramatization at Lauds is a twelfth century version from Rouen.[31] The same codex also contains the oldest *Officium Pastorum* for Matins which has come to light. It seems, nevertheless, that Christmas plays must have developed earlier than this, because the text of at least one eleventh century Epiphany play is composed in part by the Christmas scene of the shepherds.[32] Judging from available evidence, it appears that the Christmas and Epiphany pieces both developed in the eleventh century, approximately one hundred years after the Easter *Visitatio*.[33]

An additional reason, perhaps, for the small number of texts with the *Officium Pastorum*, is that in some churches an entirely different type of play was presented on Christmas Day, giving competition, so to speak, to the shepherds. This was the famous piece known as the *Ordo Prophetarum*, or the *Procession of the Prophets*. Of unique origin, this play did not develop from tropes or antiphons, as did the other Christmas productions, but from a sermon. Presumably written in the fifth or sixth century, and falsely attributed during the Middle Ages to St. Augustine, this sermon was employed in the Christmas office of Matins, generally as the sixth lesson, although its position varied, and sometimes it was recited on other days, such as January 1st. In the course of the sermon, various figures of the Old Testament were summoned to come forth and give testimony concerning the divinity of Christ. Jeremias, Daniel, Moses, and others made an appearance. Finally, as conclusive proof, prophetic passages from Virgil, Nabuchodonosor, and even the Erythraean Sibyl were quoted. With their fondness for drama, the medieval liturgists soon realized how easily this text could be turned into an effective play, and before long the Biblical personages themselves were speaking the lines instead of the *lector*. Isaias was given a beard, Virgil writing materials and a crown of ivy, the Sibyl feminine attire and an inspired look, and the *Procession of Prophets play* was born.[34]

In France, at least one of the personages of the new piece also appeared as the leading character in individual dramatic creations, namely, the prophet Daniel. Thus far, two Daniel plays have been discovered.[35] It was Sepet's

---

[31] Edited by Young, II, 12-13.
[32] The text is from Freising, and is printed by Young, II, 92-97.
[33] As regards the *Three Kings* play itself, or the *Ordo Stellae* as it was frequently called, there are many eleventh century examples. The earliest, to my knowledge, is the one found in a Nevers ritual of 1060; Compiègne, Rouen, and Bilsen also produced the play about the same date. Representative examples of the Christmas and Epiphany plays are given in the Appendix.
[34] The text of the prophet play from Laon may be found in the Appendix. The sermon is given by Migne, *P.L.*, 42, 1117 *sqq.*; it is now attributed to Quodvultdeus, bishop of Carthage (437-453); see *Sacris Erudiri*, III (1951), no. 404.
[35] Texts in Young, II, 276 *sqq.*

theory that all the Old Testament plays composed in the Middle Ages, developed first within the *Ordo Prophetarum*, grew in length, and then were detached as separate productions. This highly conjectural theory has led to much discussion on the part of dramatic historians. It cannot be proved that even the plays about Daniel evolved in this way, and as for the other two known Old Testament plays, there seems to be no connection between them and the *Ordo Prophetarum*.[36] That Sepet's conjecture was perhaps quite close to the truth in regard to one of the characters in the *Ordo Prophetarum*, however, new evidence from Spain will bear ample testimony.[37]

Such were the chief types of liturgical plays that flourished during the Middle Ages: the representation of Christ's resurrection on Easter Sunday, the *Peregrinus* on the following day, and during the Christmas season, the *Officium Pastorum* and the *Procession of Prophets* on Christmas Day itself, and the play of the Magi on the feast of the Epiphany. There were other popular types of dramatic performances, for example, the miracle plays of St. Nicholas, but since no plays in honor of this saint have as yet been found in Spain, these need not be discussed here.

To single out which of the French monasteries and churches played the most prominent role in the dissemination of the liturgical drama from its beginning up until the year 1100 would be a rather difficult task. It appears quite certain that the plays originated in the Benedictine monasteries, but they spread very quickly to the cathedral and collegiate churches. In the latter two the Easter *Visitatio Sepulchri* was probably the rule rather than the exception by the year 1100. We know with certainty that the monastery of St. Martial of Limoges was one of the most important early propagators of the *Quem quaeritis* tropes. Because of this fact, and because one of the most famous medieval playbooks written in France is reputed to have been composed at this monastery (*ca.* 1100), St. Martial has usually been considered one of the earliest disseminators of liturgical plays.[38]

The one other French monastery most commonly associated with the early production of these plays is that of Fleury. Two reasons are at the basis of this. In the tenth century the author of the *Regularis Concordia*, the work which contains the first known church play, spoke of his intention to imitate the customs of Fleury; secondly, two centuries later a playbook with some of

---

[36] *Isaac and Rebecca*, and *Joseph and His Brethren*.
[37] For M. Sepet's theories, see his *Prophètes du Christ*.
[38] The playbook was always attributed to St. Martial without question until very recently. In 1955 Jacques Chailley affirmed that the manuscript was not written at the monastery of Limoges, but at some other unidentified abbey, and that it was brought to Limoges sometime before the thirteenth century ('Le Drame liturgique médiéval à St.-Martial de Limoges', *Revue de l'Histoire du Théâtre*, VII, 1955, 127-144; see also his article 'Les Premiers troubadours et les *versus* de l'école d'Aquitaine', *Romania*, LXXVI, 1955, 213). At the present writing, his book, *L'Ecole musicale de Saint-Martial* (Cercle du Livre), has not yet appeared. Until more evidence has been gathered in support of Chailley's affirmation, we shall continue to accept the traditional view.

the most highly developed liturgical plays known was written for this monastery.[39] We shall have occasion again to refer to these two important monasteries, especially to St. Martial of Limoges.

What was taking place in the Hispanic peninsula all this time? Did the new custom of liturgical plays spread there also? And if so, at what time, and to what extent? It shall be our endeavor to answer these questions in the ensuing pages.

[39] Curiously enough, within the past few years the attribution of this playbook to Fleury has also been questioned; see Solange Corbin, 'Le Manuscrit 201 d'Orléans, drames liturgiques dits de Fleury', *Romania*, LXXIV (1953), 1-43. While Miss Corbin's arguments merit serious reflection, and probably throw light on the type of play represented in the codex, they do not establish necessarily that the plays were compiled elsewhere than at Fleury.

CHAPTER 3

THE COMING OF THE ROMAN RITE TO SPAIN

BEFORE turning our attention directly to the Hispanic liturgical plays, an important historical factor must be given some attention, namely, the different liturgical rite observed in Spain during the *Arab* domination. The new religious plays which developed in such countries as France and England around the year 950 were products of the Roman-French rite. In the land south of the Pyrenees the liturgical rite followed under Arab rule was the Mozarabic. The question is automatically raised: did the liturgical drama develop in the Mozarabic liturgy as well? If it did not, then it could only have entered the Hispanic peninsula when the Mozarabic rite was replaced by the Roman. In the latter case, it is of utmost importance that we know when the Roman-French rite entered Spain, and what persons were chiefly instrumental in introducing it.

The expression *Mozarabic rite* in itself is somewhat misleading. Whereas *Mozarab*, precisely speaking, refers to those Christians who lived and practised their traditional religion under the Arabs, the liturgy which the term designates had been in usage in the Hispanic peninsula long before the coming of the Arabs. An expression such as *Hispanic rite* would be more exact, for according to scholars who have studied the question, this liturgy represented the practice which had been implanted in Spain by the first preachers of the Gospel, and which had developed in the Visigothic period under the guidance of such renowned leaders as St. Isidore of Seville and St. Leander. The Mozarabic rite did not differ from the other recognized liturgies of the Catholic religion in the main points of its worship, but in such matters as the selection of prayers, the music, and the ceremonies, the differences were considerable. As far as the liturgy itself is concerned, the liturgical drama *could have* developed in the Mozarabic rite as readily as in any other, because it was based on the same Gospel narratives and traditions, and celebrated the same major feasts. Certain historians of the drama have not failed to point out this possibility. Graf[1] and Hartmann[2] affirm that the twelfth century *Auto de los Reyes Magos* may have evolved from the Mozarabic liturgy, and Miss Sturdevant, after her examination of probable sources of this same piece in 1927, still felt required to leave room in her conclusion for this possibility, although she appears to disfavor it.[3] G. Baist, on the other hand, rejects the view of Hartmann,

---

[1] *Studii Drammatici*, pp. 251-277.
[2] *Ueber das altspanische Dreikönigspiel.*
[3] *The Misterio de los Reyes Magos*, pp. 46-48, 78.

declaring: "In such different soil as the so-called Mozarabic and the Gallican rite, similar plants could not grow."[4]

The question is properly one for liturgists. Today, I believe that most liturgists will agree that it is safe to hold that *de facto*, the liturgical drama was not known in the Mozarabic rite. In the first place, no examples of it have ever been found in the liturgical manuscripts of this rite, and quite a few of them are still extant. Secondly, it would have been a rather rare coincidence, if at approximately the same time, the identical phenomenon appeared in two different liturgies. The basic materials were the same, but it took 950 years for the process to evolve in the Roman rite. Of all modern scholars, Msgr. H. Anglès has probably devoted most attention to this point. After some hesitation in his early works, he has reached the definite conclusion in his more recent studies that "en la liturgia visigodomozárabe no se habían practicado propriamente las formas literariomusicales conocidas con el nombre de *tropos, secuencias y dramas litúrgicos.*"[5]

The date of the introduction of the Roman-French rite, then, takes on added importance. It is common knowledge that in Castile the Mozarabic rite was *officially* abolished at the Council of Burgos around the year 1080. The exact date of this Council has been controverted, and opinions have varied from 1076 to 1085, but almost all modern scholars hold for either the year 1080 or 1081.[6] However what has not been generally realized until recent years, and even today some historians still err in regard to this point, is that in Catalonia the Roman rite did not appear for the first time in 1068 or 1071, as had for a long time been held, but more that 250 years earlier following the Reconquest by Charlemagne! One begins to surmise already the effects which this fact was to have upon the history of the drama in Catalonia.

Since the liturgical change occurred at widely divergent periods in the two regions of Catalonia and Castile, it is necessary to consider the change in these two regions separately.

The Change of Rite West of Catalonia

The abolition of the Hispanic rite in Castile was brought about by papal authority. This desire of the popes to substitute the Roman rite for the Mozarabic is easy to understand. It was prompted mainly by the desire

---

[4] Review of Hartmann's dissertation in *Zeitschrift für Romanische Philologie*, IV (1880), 444.
[5] *La Música española desde la edad media hasta nuestros días* (1941), p. 14; the same view is expressed in *La Música en la España de Fernando el Santo y de Alfonso el Sabio* (1943), pp. 7-8. In his latest article written for *The New Oxford History of Music* (1954), II, p. 90, Anglès remarks that, in a certain wide sense, one might speak of tropes and sequences in the Mozarabic rite, but these do not represent the same practice known in the Roman liturgy; trope-writing and sequence-writing, as a movement, was unknown to the Spanish rite, and no such manuscript books as tropers or prosers were ever composed.
[6] See Pierre David, *Etudes historiques sur la Galice et le Portugal du VI au XIIe siècle* (1947), pp. 417-419.

for ecclesiastical reform, and this, in the eyes of the popes, could only be effectively achieved by unity. To this outlook was joined a distrust of the Spanish rite, which had passed through centuries of Arab rule, and which for that reason was suspected of having suffered heretical influences. As one can imagine, this latter attitude was not at all pleasing to many Spanish monks and bishops who venerated their liturgy as the heritage of the great saints of Spain. Consequently previous to the formal abolition, it was only little by little, and after a great resistance, that the new rite was implanted.

The movement towards Europe began with King Sancho the Great of Navarre, who came to the throne in 1004. The channels through which European influence came to his kingdom were twofold: Catalonia and Gascony. On the one hand Sancho corresponded with, and became a friend of, Oliva, the influential and revered abbot of Ripoll, who in turn was an admirer of Cluny and a propagator of monastic reform. On the other hand he was related to the counts of Gascony, also great promoters of monastic reform in their own kingdom; it was these leaders who brought him into contact with such powerful figures as William, the Duke of Aquitaine, the King of France, the Duke of Angoulême, Odon of Champagne, and others. In this new circle Sancho heard constantly about the monks of Cluny. We know that about the year 1020 a whole group of Spanish monks lived at the Burgundian monastery. One of these monks was from Sancho's kingdom, a certain Paterno. Reputed for his sanctity, he returned to Navarre in 1024 and was made abbot of San Juan de la Peña. This was obviously no accidental choice. In the same year he introduced the usages and customs of Cluny in his monastery, thus founding the first Cluniac house in Spain west of Catalonia.

It has been said that after introducing the reform in San Juan de la Peña, Sancho the Great extended it to the other monasteries of his kingdom, but Pérez de Urbel discredits this view, declaring, "Todo parece indicar que el caso de San Juan de la Peña fué único."[7] Furthermore the Mozarabic rite had not as yet been disturbed, for the usages adopted in Paterno's abbey *did not include those concerning the liturgy*. It appears that this was the case in all the religious houses where the Cluniac reform was adopted before 1071. Nevertheless the French ecclesiastical influence had begun, and some forty-seven years later, in the year 1071, the Roman-French rite was accepted in this region for the first time, in the same monastery of San Juan de la Peña.[8]

This movement was greatly intensified by the successors of Sancho. Moreover whereas he had introduced monastic reform through Spanish monks, the rulers who came after him did not hesitate to place the monasteries directly in the hands of the French. With the increase of Cluniac activity, the papal agitation for the suppression of the Mozarabic rite grew, especially from the

---

[7] *Sancho el Mayor de Navarra* (1950), p. 316.
[8] See Pérez de Urbel, *op. cit.*, p. 308; Florentino Pérez, 'San Gregorio VII y la liturgia española', *Liturgia*, III (1948), 108.

time of Alexander II (1061-1073) and Gregory VII (1073-1085), the latter, himself, a monk of Cluny. We need not concern ourselves here with the actual events which immediately preceded the abolition of this rite, often interesting enough in themselves. Suffice it to say that it occurred in 1080, during the reign of Alfonso VI of Castile, and with his assent. All those who have studied the question thoroughly affirm that this suppression was effectual almost immediately throughout the entire kingdom:

> De acuerdo con el Rey, abolió solemnemente esta asamblea el rito mozárabe, estableciendo se adoptara inmediatamente en todas las Iglesias el romano. El Papa lo aprobó, y el rito tradicional pasó a ser poco más que una venerada reliquia ... Los obispos españoles, a pesar de todas sus repugnancias, se vieron obligados a someterse. Poco a poco, con más o menos resistencia, fueron adoptando en su diócesis el rito romano. Pero la fecha que señala *la completa romanización de España* fué el año 1085, en que Alfonso reconquistó la importante plaza de Toledo y en que se nombró arzobispo de dicha ciudad el cluniacense Bernardo, abad de Sahagún.[9]

With the consecration of Bernard as Archbishop of Toledo, or even somewhat prior to it, there began, in the words of Pérez de Urbel, "a veritable invasion of Cluniac monks in the peninsula."[10] Inasmuch as historians of the drama have always asserted that it was probably the Cluniac monks who brought the liturgical drama to Spain at this time, it is important that we notice from just which monasteries these monks came, insofar as that is known.

Bernard himself was, of course, by far the most important of the newcomers. A native of Salvetat in Aquitaine, he had been a member of the monastery of Saint-Orens, in the diocese of Auch, a priory of Cluny since the year 1068.[11] After leaving Saint-Orens, upon the invitation of Hugh of Cluny, to enter Cluny itself, he went to Spain where he was soon made abbot of Sahagún, the monastery which King Alfonso wished to make "the Cluny of Spain". In 1085 he was chosen as archbishop of the newly reconquered city of Toledo, an important post which established him as the arbiter of the ecclesiastical destinies of Spain until his death in 1124.

A few years after his consecration, Bernard undertook the reorganization of his cathedral. For this purpose he brought from France a great number of clerics, almost all of them natives of Aquitaine like himself, and upon their arrival entrusted to them the chief canonical functions of his church. From their new positions, almost all these ecclesiastics soon went forth as bishops of the various dioceses of Castile, León, and Galicia.

Gerald, who was eventually canonized a saint, was brought to Toledo

---

[9] F. Pérez, p. 112 (italics are mine); see also L. Serrano, *El Obispado de Burgos y Castilla primitiva* (1935), II, 393; David, pp. 419, 424-426, 557.
[10] *Los Monjes españoles en la Edad Media* (1933-34), II, 428.
[11] There are no records of liturgical plays from this priory.

precisely for the purpose of organizing the ecclesiastical chant. He came from the monastery of Moissac, a religious house which, like Saint-Orens, was a priory of Cluny.[12] After carrying out his functions at Toledo, Gerald was elevated to the see of Braga, where he served from 1095 to 1109.

Along with Gerald, Bernard appointed another chanter to his cathedral, Bernard of Agen, whom he later consecrated as bishop of Sigüenza. These appointments to the positions of chanter indicate that the archbishop was personally concerned about the type of Gregorian music to be established in his cathedral. Since the new rite was being put into effect there, Bernard must have been obliged to obtain some liturgical books from France in order to copy them for use in his church, and this must have been the case in all the Spanish dioceses. Fortunately we are not left entirely in the dark by any means concerning the manuscripts used at Toledo following the reconquest, for the Cathedral library still contains a number of them. One of these, an antiphonary and responsory catalogued number 44.1, is especially informative. Even a hasty scrutiny of the feasts reveals the French origin of the codex, or at least of its original. More important still, one of the saints especially honored is St. Orens of Auch, and the rite followed is *monastic*, not secular. Since a manuscript written for the diocese of Toledo would hardly follow the monastic rite, the codex in question is in all probability one of the originals brought to the Castilian city from some French monastery. That this monastery was Saint-Orens of Auch is almost certain, inasmuch as this saint is given an important place in the manuscript, and Bernard himself had been prior there. The Benedictine author of the treatise *Qué es canto gregoriano*[13] appears to be of the same opinion:

> El 44.1 es de fines del siglo XI o principios del XII; su rito monástico y el hecho de contener los oficios de santos extranjeros, como S. Orencio, obispo de Ausch, S. Medardo, S. Arnulfo, S. Sinforiano y otros, quizás insinúen fuese traído a Toledo por D. Bernardo.

No one has ever made a thorough study of the late eleventh and early twelfth century manuscripts from Toledo. There is no doubt that such an examination would supply us with further information concerning the relationships between reconquered Toledo and individual monasteries and churches in France.[14]

Thanks chiefly to the thirteenth century archbishop of Toledo, Rodrigo Jimenez de Rada (1208-1247),[15] we know the identity of many others who came to the Castilian capital with Bernard: Pierre de Bourges, who had been a

---

[12] One eleventh century manuscript from Moissac possesses the *Quem quaeritis* Christmas trope; the codex may antedate Cluniac control (1047). There are no plays from this monastery.
[13] (Barcelona, 1905), p. 122; the author is a Benedictine Father from the monastery of Silos.
[14] A dissertation written by Ireneo García Alonso for the University of Salamanca on the Toledo rituals of this period will be published in the near future by the Consejo Superior de Investigaciones Científicas.
[15] *Rerum in Hispania gestarum chronicon* (sometimes called *Historia Gothorum*), edited by Andreas Schottius, S. J., in *Hispaniae Illustratae Scriptores*, II, 107-108.

monk with Bernard at the Cluniac priory of Saint-Orens; in 1101 he became
bishop of Burgo de Osma; three came directly from Cluny: Raymond, a
native of Salvetat like the archbishop (he succeeded Pierre at Burgo de Osma
in 1109, and then was archbishop of Toledo from 1126 until 1150), another
Pierre who later became bishop of Palencia, and Dalmatius, who was raised
to the important see of Santiago de Compostella; Pierre of Agen, later bishop
of Segovia; Maurice of Limoges, eventually bishop of Coimbra (1099-1109)
and the successor to St. Gerald at Braga (1109-1118).[16] Lastly one cannot
forget the bishop of epic fame, who fought beside the Cid, Jerome of Périgueux; sent by Hugh of Cluny to introduce monastic reform at San Pedro of
Cardeña, he later became bishop of Valencia and Zamora.[17]

This list gives us some idea of the grandiose proportions of the Cluniac
influx into Spain during the reign of Alphonse the Sixth and his successor.
What took place in the dioceses also took place in the monasteries. The
annexation of Spanish houses to the monastery of Cluny continued on a large
scale until the middle of the twelfth century, and innumerable religious houses
which did not become priories of Cluny, accepted their customs. Cluniac
influence was thus a predominant feature in Castilian ecclesiastical life from
1060 to 1150. If other French Benedictine houses also played an active role
in Spain during this period, it was on a much smaller scale. Their influence was
felt more in the far north of Spain. In that region the French monasteries of
Sainte-Foy de Conques and Saint-Pons de Thomières were in close relationship
with many Spanish houses.[18]

The question which now remains is, did these monks bring liturgical
plays with them into Spain?

The Change of Rite in Catalonia

The political and liturgical situation in Catalonia was quite different.
For the two centuries dating from the conquests of Charlemagne (768-814), unlike Castile, the *Marca Hispánica*, as it came to be called, was closely linked
with France in every way. Moreover it was isolated from the rest of Spain,
for Zaragoza, Lérida, Barbastro, and even Huesca far to the north, were in the
hands of the Arabs until the waning years of the eleventh century or even
later, thus forming a solid wall between northeastern and central Spain. In
Catalonia, after the ninth century, French script was used. From that time
on, the Spanish system of dating by the Julian *era* (38 B.C.) was practically

---

[16] Most historians, following Jiménez de Rada, regard Maurice and Bourdine as the same person;
Pérez de Urbel considers these names as representing two different people (*Los Monjes españoles*,
II, 431).
[17] Some of the details given here are found in Pérez de Urbel, *loc. cit.*; S. Corbin, *Essai sur la
musique religieuse portugaise au Moyen Age, 1100-1385* (1952), p. 83; Núñez Márquez, *Guía de la
S. I. Catedral del Burgo de Osma*, pp. 66-69.
[18] See Defourneaux, *Les Français en Espagne aux XIe et XIIe siècles* (1949), p. 24.

unknown, and until 1180 documents were dated according to the reign of the King of France; out of 978 deeds ranging from the years 857 to 1180, all but eight bear the date and name of the French king.[19] Pérez de Urbel summarizes the situation by declaring: "El aislamiento, que es casi completo en las regiones meridionales (Castilla, etc.), puede decirse que no existe para Cataluña."[20]

It is generally accepted by historians, now, that the Roman-French rite was used in the Catalan churches from the time of Charlemagne's reconquest, that is, approximately from the year 800. According to the old theory, advanced by the great historian, Florez, in *España Sagrada*,[21] the cardinal legate of Alexander II, Hugh Candidus, after holding synods at Avignon, Auch, and Toulouse, organized a council in Gerona in 1068, and there put a stop to the practice of the Mozarabic liturgy. As Anglès says, "Nous ne connaissons aucun document qui puisse prouver cette affirmation."[22] Indeed, all the evidence indicates that the Roman-French rite had already been in usage there for centuries.

Charlemagne's liturgical reform, his effort to replace Gallican chant and liturgy in France by the Roman, is a well known historical fact. In view of the importance he and his followers attached to this liturgical reform, it is hardly conceivable that he would have failed to grasp the opportunity to extend the new rite to the principal monasteries and churches of reconquered Catalonia. That this is precisely what happened, it would appear that an ancient medieval lectionary from Barcelona formerly bore explicit testimony.[23]

Early in the ninth century Narbonne became the metropolitan see of all the newly restored Catalan dioceses: Elne, Gerona, Barcelona, Vich, Urgel. We find the Archbishop of Narbonne presiding at the Councils of Urgel in 799 and 892, at the Council of Barcelona in 991, at Vich in 1027; he officiated at the consecration of bishops in the Catalan cathedrals. It would have been a rather strange situation, if the Roman rite were practised in the mother see, and another rite used in the suffragan sees. As early as 830 Catalan prelates began to interchange with those of France and Italy; at about the same date a French canonical system was introduced into the Catalan cathedrals.

The best proof of all that the Roman-French liturgy was used in Catalonia long before the eleventh century is provided by the service books. Manuscripts still exist from the tenth century in which the chant is entirely Roman. Some of these manuscripts are in Aquitaine notation, a form received *in toto* from France; others are in Catalan notation, a system developed from the French, but with reminiscences of Mozarabic. Villanueva, upon finding in the

[19] See d'Olwer, 'La Littérature latine au Xe siècle', p. 184.
[20] *Los Monjes españoles*, II, 263.
[21] III, 303.
[22] 'La Musique en Catalogne aux Xe et XIe siècles. L'Ecole de Ripoll', p. 157.
[23] See Pujades, *Crónica universal del Principado de Cataluña, escrita a principios del siglo XVII*, VI, 17; his lengthy quotation from the Barcelona lectionary, now unfortunately lost, may be found in Anglès, *La Música a Catalunya fins al segle XIII*, p. 31, n. 1.

Cathedral of Vich ten liturgical and ritual manuscripts, all anterior to 1050, and all in the Roman-French rite, expressed his surprise that "no se halle uno siquiera conforme con el rito mozárabe, ni en el orden de la misa, y de los oficios divinos, ni en los ritos de los sacramentos, ni en el número de las fiestas y su rezo."[24]

Inventories of medieval libraries and records of wills are just as enlightening. Already in 960 we find mention in a very obscure monastery of a *prosario*,[25] a type of chant-book closely connected with the dramatic tradition, and found in the French, but not in the Mozarabic liturgy. Even more important for our purpose is the appearance in documents dating from 1050 to 1069 of no less than five references to *tropers*, indicating that at this time the practice of trope-singing in Catalonia, and perhaps of plays, was already widespread. Anglès' comment merits recording: "Ací trobem, doncs, per primera vegada especificat un Troparium; si un simple clergue de la Seu d'Urgell tenia ja el seu tropari a mitjans del segle XI, per força els monestirs i catedrals catalanes en tindrien de la primera florida dels tropus al segle X."[26] One century later (1147), the Seo de Urgel Cathedral library possessed no less than four tropers, no insignificant number for a small library at that date, thus giving us an idea of the popularity which trope-singing had attained in Catalonia by that time. Tropers, it should be recalled, were unknown in the Mozarabic rite.

It can hardly be doubted, then, that the Roman-French rite was established in Catalonia by the tenth century, and there is no reason to oppose the view that it was introduced with the Reconquest. This view is now held by almost all the important historians of the liturgy: Olivar, Brou, the late Msgr. Gudiol, Pierre David, and especially Anglès. David simply declares: "Les Eglises de ces régions qui dépendaient de l'archévêque de Narbonne suivaient le rite romain comme le reste de l'Empire dès le IXe siècle."[27]

The center of cultural and liturgical activity in Catalonia during the eleventh century was the Benedictine abbey of Ripoll. For this reason, and because this monastery, as we shall see, was intimately connected with the development of the liturgical drama in the Middle Ages, it should be given at least brief consideration here as illustrative of the situation of Catalonia at that date.

Santa María de Ripoll was for Catalonia what the monasteries of Saint-Martial de Limoges and Fleury were for France, Saint-Gall for Switzerland, and Reichenau for Germany. Re-established in the year 888, the monastery was soon celebrated as a center of learning. This is well evidenced by the case of Gerbert, who later became pope. A monk of Saint-Gérard of Aurillac

---

[24] *Viage literario a las Iglesias de España*, VI, 92.
[25] *Ibid.*, XII, app. x.
[26] *La Música a Catalunya*, p. 124.
[27] p. 395. For an excellent presentation of this whole problem of the introduction of the Roman-French rite in Catalonia, one should consult Anglès, *La Música a Catalunya*, pp. 23-39.

in the southern part of France, Gerbert went to Vich and Ripoll because he had heard of their excellence as educational centers. He spent three years in study there (967–970). Shortly afterward he was presented to Pope John XIII in Rome, where according to his biographer, Richer, a monk of Reims and the future pupil of Gerbert, he caused quite a sensation by his learning in mathematics, astronomy and music. Returning to France, Gerbert taught at Reims, amongst other subjects, music as he had learned it in Catalonia. Eventually he became bishop of Reims, then of Ravenna, and finally was consecrated Pope as Sylvester II (999–1003). Focillon, basing his arguments chiefly upon manuscripts 46 and 74 of the *Biblioteca de la Corona de Aragón* in Barcelona, assures us that "l'enseignement qui se donnait à Ripoll . . . . était singulièrement plus complet que celui de Saint-Benoît-sur-Loire sous Abbon."[28]

The monastery of Ripoll reached its apogee under Oliva (1002–1046). A member of one of the most powerful families in Catalonia, and distinguished for his sanctity, Oliva entered Ripoll in 1002 at the age of about thirty-one. He was elected abbot in 1008, subsequently being made abbot of Cuxa (1011) and bishop of Vich (1018); he retained all these offices until his death in keeping with the custom of the times, but fulfilled them well. Revered by all, he acted as arbitrator even in political affairs as far west as Navarre. It was under him that the library of Ripoll became one of the richest in Europe. In 979, according to an inventory, the library contained sixty-five manuscripts; in 1046, the time of the death of Oliva, the number had increased to 246, an average of about three a year. Among the list we find certain types of manuscripts not found even in the famous abbeys of Bobbio, Saint-Gall, Lorsch or Reichenau.[29]

Historians have shown that Ripoll had special relations with many monasteries outside of Catalonia: Moissac, Cluny, Saint-Germain-des-Prés in Paris, Fleury, Saint-Martial de Limoges, and Saint-Victor in Marseille. It appears to be no mere coincidence that among these monasteries we find Fleury and Saint-Martial, perhaps the two abbeys in Europe most famous for their dramatic output in the Middle Ages. Moreover their relationship with Ripoll prevailed just at the time the liturgical drama was beginning to flourish in France.

We are told that in 1013 two brothers from Barcelona, of noble rank, left Catalonia to become monks at Fleury. One of these, John, had been a monk at Ripoll and later prior of St. Cecilia's of Montserrat. The abbot of Fleury at that date was the renowned Gauzlin, who was at the same time bishop of Bourges. Gauzlin and Oliva soon became correspondents, and John continued his association and his correspondence with Ripoll. The two monasteries exchanged manuscripts, an inventory indicating that manuscripts of Fleury

---

[28] *L'An Mil* (1952), p. 80.
[29] See d'Olwer, pp. 204-205, and also Beer, *Die Handschriften des Klosters Santa Maria de Ripoll*, I, 110.

were still present at Ripoll in 1046; eventually John became abbot of Fleury in 1029.[30]

By collating the medieval musical texts of Moissac and Saint-Martial with those of Ripoll, Anglès has established that there existed a close link between the three monasteries in the musical field. This is especially true of the tropers and prosers of the respective abbeys, he remarks.[31] Our study of the liturgical plays will substantiate this view, for we shall see that in numerous instances the texts of Ripoll and Saint-Martial present peculiarities common to the two monasteries.

Thus, unlike Castile, where the influence of the rest of Europe began to exert itself in intensity only from about the middle of the eleventh century, Catalonia was in intimate contact with all the European movements from the year 800 onward. Whereas the Roman-French rite, which developed the liturgical play, was introduced in central Spain only around the year 1075, it had been the rite used in Catalonia for over two hundred years. The Catalonian monastery of Ripoll, not to mention others, was already flourishing and famous for its music school, when the practice of liturgical plays developed. Not only was it flourishing, but it was in close relationship with precisely those monasteries commonly associated with the production of these plays. Hence, one might say, Catalonia was a part of that general territory which saw the tradition of the liturgical play begin; at the least, it was in vital contact with the movement, and fully exposed to those influences which passed back and forth on the continent from one monastery to another. It was not necessarily a question, for Catalonia, of a subsequent introduction of the plays from an outside source. Catalonia contained within its own boundaries the same germ which produced the plays elsewhere: the Roman-French rite, prospering monastic musical schools, and the practice of sequence and trope-singing. It would not even be an impossibility that the representation of liturgical plays began in Catalonia at approximately the same time it did elsewhere, or that Catalan monasteries played an important role in the development of these plays. Be that as it may, it is important, in any case, to understand the difference in the position of Catalonia and Castile in the eleventh century. For Castile, it was a question of new influences; for Catalonia, the elements which produced the liturgical plays were already, at that time, an ancient tradition. This difference in situation was to have a profound effect upon the history of the drama in the two regions.[32]

---

[30] See André de Fleury, *Vita Gauzlini*.
[31] *El Còdex musical de las Huelgas*, I, 18.
[32] For studies on the abbey of Ripoll, see the works of Anglès, d'Olwer, and Beer which have been cited, and also Abadal y de Vinyals, *L'Abat Oliva, Bisbe de Vic, i la seva epoca* (1948), and Focillon, pp. 79-134.

CHAPTER 4

LITURGICAL DRAMA AT TOLEDO

THERE is perhaps no more fitting place to begin an investigation of liturgical drama in Castile, than in the archiepiscopal city of Toledo. We have seen its importance as a focal point of French influence in the eleventh century. It was in the library of this church that the twelfth century *Auto de los Reyes Magos* was discovered, one of the oldest medieval vernacular plays which has come down to us in any language. Alphonse the Wise, in the thirteenth century, spoke of the Christmas, Epiphany, and Easter plays put on by clerics, and his court was at Toledo.[1] Did the custom of performing liturgical plays flourish here in the Middle Ages? Most have surmised that it did. Happily we are now in a better position to attempt to give at least a partial answer to this question.

Fortunately the Toledo Cathedral library still possesses one of the richest collections of medieval manuscripts to be found in Spain, even though down through the centuries many of its manuscripts have been moved at one time or another to other libraries. More than sixty of the manuscripts located at the Cathedral library are liturgical, and the majority of them concern local usage. In addition, at least fifteen other medieval liturgical texts written at Toledo are to be found in other libraries scattered throughout Spain.[2]

Since the earliest Toledo manuscripts, as far as could be discovered, do not contain plays, and since one eighteenth century work describing dramatic liturgical ceremonies at Toledo is already known to some students of Spanish drama, we shall present this latter text first, even though it is relatively late. In this way we shall be able to proceed from the known to the unknown, tracing back as far into antiquity as possible the origin of the ceremonies related in the text in question.

The work referred to is a manuscript found in the library of the *Academia de la Historia* in Madrid. Catalogued 2-7-4 MS 75, it contains some 707 numbered pages, and carries the lengthy eighteenth century title, *Memorias i disertaciones que podrán servir al que escriba la historia de la iglesia de Toledo desde el año MLXXXV en que conquistó dicha ciudad el rei don Alonso VI. de Castilla*. The *Memorias* were written about the year 1785 by Felipe Fernández Vallejo, a canon of the Cathedral of Toledo, who in 1798 became Archbishop of Santiago.[3]

---

[1] *Las Siete partidas*, I, 115.
[2] The numerical figures given here represent only those types of liturgical manuscripts likely to contain plays; they do not, of course, include manuscripts of the Mozarabic rite. A complete list of the Toledo *codices* consulted for this study may be found in the Bibliography.
[3] In the past critics have always used his last name, Vallejo, so we shall adhere to the tradition.

The story of what might be called the "re-discovery" of this manuscript, as outlined by Professor J. Gillet,[4] is not without its significance, although it seems that the whereabouts of the manuscript was always known to some. As early as 1862 Manuel Cañete referred to it,[5] declaring the work to be most important, and that he would say more of its contents later. He talked of it again in 1867, this time adding that the study described "la escena u Oficio de Pastores y la Sybila de la noche de Navidad, traducida de versos latinos en castellanos a fines del siglo XIII", and that the author of the manuscript "de ambas escenas litúrgicas da circunstanciada razón, reproduciéndolas íntegras en latin y en romance."[6] Cañete never divulged more information than this, however, much to the disappointment of historians of the theatre. Repeatedly thereafter the manuscript was referred to by dramatic or music critics, but never adequately studied. Many cited Cañete as proof, without verifying his source, that liturgical shepherd and Sibyl plays were performed in thirteenth century Toledo in both Latin and Castilian.

Vallejo's manuscript finally came to rest in the *Real Academia de la Historia* in Madrid. Dom L. Serrano edited a chapter of the original in 1907, pointing out the whereabouts of the manuscript.[7] It seems, however, that Serrano's work received but little notice, for as late as 1921 Professor G. G. King expressed her hopes to see the text in print, "if it can be found by searching the archives,"[8] and González Palencia himself led investigators further astray by declaring in 1921 that the manuscript was in the *Biblioteca Nacional*.[9] The actual location of the manuscript was pointed out by J. B. Trend in 1926,[10] and subsequently the portion of it which treats dramatic performances at Toledo was studied by Professor Gillet.

Two chapters of Vallejo's work concern us especially, the *Disertación V. sobre la música* (pp. 477–586), and the *Disertación VI. sobre las Representaciones Poéticas en el Templo, y Sybila de la noche de Navidad* (pp. 587–643). In the first of these, the author gives the text and a description of a dramatic ceremony performed at Lauds on Christmas Eve at Toledo in the eighteenth century. This ceremony, he informs us, represents an ancient dramatic tradition, and his account of it, he adds, was taken from a manuscript written by Juan Chaves de Arcayos, *tomo 2, de los que gobiernan en el cabildo*.[11]

In the charming little ceremony which Vallejo describes, provisions

---

[4] 'The *Memorias* of Felipe Fernández Vallejo and the History of the Early Spanish Drama', pp. 264-266.
[5] *Discurso acerca del drama religioso español antes y despues de Lope de Vega*, p. 10; reprinted in *Memorias de la Real Academia española*, I (1870), pp. 368-412.
[6] Introduction to Lucas Fernández, *Farsas y églogas*, p. lxxvii, n. 1.
[7] 'Historia de la música de Toledo', *Revista de Archivos, Bibliotecas y Museos*, X (1907, enero-junio), pp. 219-243.
[8] *The play of the Sibyl Cassandra*, p. 17.
[9] *Historia de la literatura española* (Madrid, 1921), p. 125.
[10] *The Music of Spanish History to 1600*, p. 183.
[11] Arcayos was prebendary at the Toledo Cathedral between 1589 and 1643.

are made for the choir boys – the text does not indicate the number – to come out from the sacristy dressed up like shepherds, just as Mass begins. They proceed up to the area immediately in front of the main altar, and there, while Mass is being celebrated, give expression to their Christmas joy, *danzando y bailando*. When Mass has ended, the office of Lauds begins, and all those in choir intone the first antiphon, namely, *Quem vidistis Pastores? Annuntiate nobis in terris quis apparuit*: "Whom have you seen, shepherds? Announce to us Who has appeared on the earth." Thereupon the *pastorcicos*, under the direction of their choir-master, reply in plain-chant from the middle of the choir that they have seen a Child wrapped in swaddling clothes, and choirs of angels praising the Saviour: *Infantem vidimus pannis involutum, et choros angelorum laudantes salvatorem*. Twice more the same question and answer are repeated. At this point certain chanters step forward from the ranks, and taking two of the *shepherds* by the hands, proceed to sing with them a delightful little composition in the vernacular. This song is quite evidently a development of the theme of the Latin antiphon which has just been finished, the chanters welcoming the shepherds and asking them whence they come and what they have seen, the shepherds replying in a graceful lyric that they have come from Bethlehem, where they have adored the new born King. The verse form employed is a delicate arrangement of a choral refrain and a series of rhymed couplets: two heptasyllabic verses, followed by six octosyllabic; the refrain itself has five syllables. Vallejo observes that the ceremony was observed in substantially the same manner in his own day, except for the dance, which had been eliminated because of certain abuses:[12]

> Desde el principio de la Misa salen del Sagrario los Clerizones vestidos de Pastores, y van al Altar mayor por el Postigo, y estan arriba en lo plano mientra se dice esta Misa danzando, y bailando: y acabada la Misa toman Capas los dichos dos Socapiscoles Racioneros para hacer el Oficio de las Laudes, que se empiezan luego en el Coro, a las que habrá tañido el Campanero, segun es costumbre, por la señal que le hizieron, quando se dixere el Hymno *Te Deum laudamus*, con la cuerda del Coro: y dicho por el Preste: *Deus in adjutorium*, desde su silla, se empieza primero la primera antiphona, que es: *Quem vidistis Pastores*: y la dicen toda, y luego los Clerizones hechos Pastores ministrandolos su Maestro Claustrero dicen en el Choro mayor debajo de la Lampara de plata a Canto-llano el verso *Infantem vidimus Pannis involutum, et Choros Angelorum laudantes salvatorem*, y tornan en el Choro a decir toda la antiphona: *Quem vidistis?* y los Pastores responden entre los dos Choros debajo de la Lampara de enmedio el verso *Infantem vidimus, ut supra*, y despues dicen en el Choro tercera vez toda la antiphona *Quem vidistis?* y responden los Pastores desde la Puerta del Coro del Arzobispo el verso *Infantem*, y luego salen los

---

[12] Vallejo's text is found on pp. 492-495; it has been reprinted with some omissions by Serrano, *op. cit.*, pp. 223 *sqq.*, and fully by Gillet, *op. cit.*, pp. 276-277; the initial reference, f. 495, in Gillet's edition is evidently a misprint.

Socapiscoles con las Capas de brocado, y Cetros, y llegan a los lados del Aguila del Choro del Arzobispo, y alli los Cantores a Canto-llano les hacen las preguntas siguientes, y los Capiscoles asen de las manos a dos de aquellos Pastorcicos, y les preguntan juntamente con los Cantores lo siguiente:

Canto-llanistas.	Bien vengades Pastores, que bien vengades. Pastores do anduvistes? decidnos lo que vistes?
Cantores.	Que bien vengades.
Canto-llanistas.	Pastores del ganado decidnos buen mandado.
Cantores.	Que bien vengades.
Melódicos.[13]	Vimos que en Bethlen Señores nasció la flor de las flores.
Cantores.	Que bien vengades.
Melódicos.	Esta flor que hoy ha nascido nos dará fruto de vida.
Cantores.	Que bien vengades.
Melódicos.	Es un Niño, y Rey del Cielo que hoy ha nascido en el suelo.
Cantores.	Que bien vengades.
Melódicos.	Está entre dos animales embuelto en pobres panales.
Cantores.	Que bien vengades.
Melódicos.	Virgen, y limpia quedó la madre que le parió.
Cantores.	Que bien vengades.
Melódicos.	Al hijo, y Madre roguemos les plega que nos salvemos.
Todos.	Que bien vengades.

En la substancia se hace hoy esta Ceremonia como la refiere el Racionero Arcayos. La Danza en el plano del Altar mayor se habra omitido por evitar excesos, por considerarla abuso . . . .

We recognize at once the antiphon which forms the core of this little piece. It is a combination of the two antiphons which were repeated in many churches of medieval France during the chanting of Lauds on Christmas night. These antiphons and a typical Lauds office from Clermont-Ferrand have been quoted on page 16 in an earlier chapter of this study.

In the Toledo version, at least from about 1600 to 1785, the repetition of the antiphon and the singing of the vernacular lyric took place even before the chanting of the first psalm began. The most significant difference from the

---

[13] For information concerning the distinction between *canto llano*, or Gregorian chant, and *canto melódico* also called *canto eugeniano* by Vallejo, see Serrano, *op. cit.*, p. 222, and Rojo y Prado, *El Canto mozárabe*, pp. 148-151.

Clermont text is that at Toledo the liturgical office at Lauds was definitely dramatized. Vallejo's text raises several important questions: how far back into the history of Toledo can this ceremony be traced, how representative of medieval custom is it, and what light does it project on the medieval practices of France and other European countries?

One point is clearly established: irrespective of any dramatization of the *Quem quaeritis* trope at Matins, parts of the office of Lauds were dramatized in certain localities.

An examination of French liturgical texts reveals that a custom similar to that of Toledo was also observed in many regions of France during the Middle Ages, at least in so far as the portion in Latin is concerned. Since these texts have never been included in a study on the drama, and since they help to place the Toledo usage in its proper tradition, we include a few of them here.

Evidence of dramatization at Lauds is had, for example, in a medieval breviary from Dax; it is of significance, perhaps, that this same region of Aquitaine was the part of France most intimately connected with the kingdom of Castile at the time of the introduction of the Roman-French rite. At Dax the little liturgical play was attached to the fifth psalm rather than the first; we have already observed that the repetition of the antiphon usually occurred in one of these two positions. The text from Dax reads as follows:[14]

> Postquam autem perventum fuerit ad *Laudate Dominum in sanctis eius*, in persona hominum de Christi nativitate interrogancium quartus chorus a pueris claras et consonas voces habentibus quasi loqueretur ita pastoribus. Antiphona:
>> Pastores, dicite quidnam vidistis, et annunciate Christi nativitatem.
>
> Et infantes in persona pastorum sint parati respondere excelsa voce se interrogantibus canentes, Antiphona:
>> Infantem vidimus pannis involutum, et choros angelorum laudantes Salvatorem.
>
> Postea chorus dextera sive sinistra incipiat:
>> Laudate dominum in sanctis eius.
>
> Quo finito, incipiat chorus iterum antiphonam. Antiphona:
>> Pastores dicite.
>
> Postea infantes, antiphona:
>> Infantem vidimus.
>
> Postea chorus alter incipiat:
>> Laudate eum in virtutibus eius.
>
> Et ita, reiterata interrogatione et responsione per singulos versus alternatim finiatur Psalmus.

[14] Toulouse, Bibl. Mun., MS 76, Breviarium saec. xv, fol. 26ᵛ-27; the portion which I quote is immediately preceded by the fifth antiphon.

We find a similar ceremony in an entirely different part of France, the church of Saint-Géry in Cambrai:[15]

Qua cantata, cantor incipit (?):

    Pastores dicite ‹quidnam vidistis, et annuntiate Christi nativitatem›.

Respondent pueri parati ad modum pastorum iuxta altare vel ante:

    Infantem vidimus ‹pannis involutum, et choros angelorum laudantes Salvatorem›.

Deinde cantor incipit psalmum:

    Laudate dominum de celis.[16]

To give an idea of the widespread popularity of this usage in France, we give a final brief indication of it as found in a printed breviary of Narbonne:[17]

Sed antequam incipiat psalmus *Laudate dominum in sanctis eius*, dicatur antiphona:

    Pastores dicite quidnam vidistis et annunciate Christi nativitatem.

Alii vero existentes retro altare respondeant tamquam ex parte pastorum:

    Infantem vidimus pannis involutum; et choros angelorum laudantes salvatorem.

Postea unus ex illis qui tenent cappas incipiat psalmum:

    Laudate dominum in sanctis eius.

Et ita fiat per omnes versus eiusdem psalmi: facta eiusdem antiphone repetitione a cantoribus et facta eodem modo responsione aliis finiatur psalmus.

Since the rubrics of the above text only state *ex parte pastorum*, one might question as to whether the shepherds were actually impersonated in this case. This particular example was chosen precisely because it shows how difficult it is to determine in some instances, judging by the text alone, whether impersonation was clearly intended, or whether the participants merely thought of themselves as representing, or symbolizing, the persons mentioned in the ceremony.

The boundary line separating *dramatic liturgy* from *liturgical drama* was thus often very thin. The type of ceremony quoted earlier from Clermont-Ferrand,[18] which gives no indication of having been *dramatized*, is found in many medieval French manuscripts. It is probable that in many of these cases the antiphons were sung by choir-boys dressed up like shepherds in the same

---

[15] Cambrai, Bibl. Mun., MS 40, Ordinarium Sancti Gaugerici Cameracensis, fol. 11ᵛ; the above passage is immediately preceded by the fourth antiphon. The same text is likewise found in Cambrai, Bibl. Mun., MS 202, Ordinarium Sancti Gaugerici Cameracensis saec. xiv, fol. 22.
[16] There then follows a repetition of the antiphon by the cantor and the *shepherds* as at Dax.
[17] Paris, Bibl. Ste-Geneviève, 8° T. 2160, Breviarium Narbonense, 1535, fol. 29.
[18] See pp. 16-17.

manner as at Dax, Cambrai, and Toledo. In fact evidence from an external source seems to establish that this *was* the procedure observed at Clermont-Ferrand. Writing in 1697, Moléon declared that still in his own day clerics put on la *Pastourelle* during Lauds in this French city.[19]

It would appear, therefore, that the conclusion advanced by Professor Young in his study, *Officium Pastorum*, must be considerably modified in the light of such testimonies as these. The eminent dramatic historian wrote:[20]

> In spite of the dramatic character of the dialogue before us (he has been speaking of the *Pastores dicite* antiphon at Lauds), and in spite of the festal appreciation bestowed upon it in the various forms reviewed above, this liturgical element neither created for itself an independent dramatic office nor joined itself to the *Officium Pastorum* developed from *Quem quaeritis in praesepe*.[21]

Not only did the choir-boys frequently dress as shepherds during Lauds to sing the response to the antiphons *Quem vidistis, pastores* and *Pastores, dicite quidnam vidistis*, but in some regions these antiphons developed into a longer play; in other words, Lauds *did* create for itself, around these antiphons, an independent dramatic office. A hitherto unpublished text from the Augustinian monastery of Pleinpied, near Bourges, bears ample testimony to this. A fourteenth century *ordinarium* written at that monastery directs that the liturgical Christmas play be performed between the fourth and fifth antiphons of Lauds, and it designates the ceremony by one of the usual titles accorded the Christmas piece, namely, the *Officium Pastorum*. The antiphon *Pastores dicite*, rather than the trope *Quem quaeritis in praesepe*, figures in the play. In addition to the two choir-boys who dress as shepherds – they wear a cape, a hood, and carry shepherds' staffs – a third assumes the role of an angel, and the content is enlarged from the simple Lauds version, in which an antiphon and its response are repeated several times, to include the announcement of Christ's birth by the angel, and the *journey* of the shepherds to the crib at *Bethlehem* (here the altar):[22]

> Antiphona:
>
> > Facta est cum angelo ‹multitudo celestis exercitus laudantium Deum et dicentium: Gloria in excelsis Deo, et in terra pax hominibus bone voluntatis, alleluia›.
>
> Finitis psalmo, *Benedicite*, et antiphona, sint parati pueri ad peragendum officium pastorum et duo pueri habentes capas, desuper precincti, tenen-

---

[19] Le Sieur de Moléon (Le Brun des Marettes), *Voyages liturgiques en France*, pp. 75-76. The author uses the expression *pastourelle* and *Office des Pasteurs* as synonyms; see p. 217 of his work.
[20] *Op. cit.*, p. 361.
[21] Professor Young was generally careful to avoid categorical statements; he does not repeat the assertion in *Drama of the Medieval Church*.
[22] Paris, Bibl. Nat., MS lat. n. acq. 368, Ordo Plenipedensis saec. xiv (1390), fol. 169-169^v; the opening antiphon given here is the fourth antiphon of Christmas Lauds.

tes capita sua infra capucium, tenentes baculos pastorales et stent ante altare, unus a dextris et alius a sinistris uultibus in sese inuicem conuersis. Tunc unus de aliis pueris, stans retro altare in sublimi ita ut non uideatur, cantet in persona angeli ea que secuntur:

> Nuncium[23] uobis ‹fero de supernis: natus est Cristus dominator orbis in Bethleem Iude; sic enim propheta dixerat ante›.

Quo finito chorus representans chorum angelorum cantet:

> Gloria in excelsis Deo, ‹et in terra pax hominibus bone voluntatis, alleluia›.

Quo finito duo pueri stantes ante altare ut pastores dicant antiphonam:

> Transeamus usque Bethleem, ‹et videamus hoc verbum quod factum est, quod fecit Dominus et ostendit nobis›.

Et cantando eant retro altare quasi in Bethleem, et statim reuertant ante altare et uertant uultus suos ad chorum. Deinde unus uitatorium (?) dicat antiphonam:

> Pastores dicite quidnam uidistis, ‹et annunciate Christi nativitatem›.

Pueri respondeant cantantes:

> Infantem uidimus ‹pannis involutum, et choros angelorum laudantes Salvatorem›.

Quo finito unus de pueris incipiat antiphonam:

> Paruulus filius ‹hodie natus est nobis, et vocabitur Deus fortis, alleluia, alleluia›.

Tunc custodes chori incipiant psalmum, *Laudate dominum de celis*, et tunc pueri eant per ecclesiam ludentes ad modum pastorum.

The eighteenth century Toledo ceremony described by Vallejo was thus quite representative of medieval dramatic tradition. The question remains, when was it introduced at Toledo? Vallejo himself wrote his study about 1785, but declared that he copied the Christmas text from Juan Chaves de Arcayos. Arcayos wrote between 1589 and 1643. In the opinion of Vallejo, the original *Oficio de Pastores* was brought to Spain from *los monasterios Benedictinos*; he meant, presumably, eleventh century French monasteries. He adds:[24]

> Ni tampoco quiero detenerme a probar que las coplas castellanas que se la añadieron en el siglo XIII, y acaso por D. Lope de Loaysa, son una paráfrasis de la Profecia de la Sybila Eritrea que llamó a Christo *flor* conviniendo con Isaias, y de la antiphona *Quem vidistis* que usa la Iglesia en el oficio de aquella noche.

---

[23] Nuncium] Nucium (MS). For the complete text of the hymn, see Young, II, 433.
[24] p. 495.

Either Vallejo had some proof that the vernacular was added in the thirteenth century, a proof which he does not adduce, or else he merely took it for granted; I suspect the latter to be the case. Here we see the basis for Cañete's unqualified declaration that Vallejo's texts were thirteenth century plays. Cañete in turn was cited by J. Ford,[25] Miss G. G. King,[26] and others. One modern writer, basing her view directly an Vallejo's assertion, has also felt justified in accepting the thirteenth century date as a fact: "Although these documents (those used by Arcayos) belonged to an earlier period than the late sixteenth century, it is impossible to know just how much earlier they were. At any rate, we can definitely infer that some sort of *Officium Pastorum* was presented in Toledo in the thirteenth century, if not before."[27] For the present we shall only observe that as yet this point has not at all been proved, especially as regards the part in Spanish. After presenting the second dramatic liturgical ceremony found in Vallejo's text, we shall examine what other manuscripts reveal about the date of the Toledo *Play of the Shepherds*.

Up to this point we have not commented upon two special characteristics of Vallejo's *play*. First of all, there is the dancing of the shepherds. To my knowledge, no other liturgical plays presented thus far by dramatic historians incorporate this feature into the performance. It is well known that on some important feast-days in the Middle Ages ecclesiastics took part from time to time in certain religious dances.[28] Religious dancing was always especially popular in Spain, and the provision for it in the document before us probably represents a traditional Spanish custom. A select group of choir-boys called *seises* performed these dances, and even today the practice is observed in the diocese of Seville. Some have held that this usage dates back to the time of the Mozarabic rite.[29]

Finally the text from Toledo is an excellent reminder that in many localities the liturgical drama flourished as late as the eighteenth century. In France, to mention only a few places, this was true at Angers,[30] Lisieux,[31] and Clermont-Ferrand;[32] in Germany, at Cologne and Munster;[33] Le Lorrain speaks of it for Flanders.[34] Because it is now more or less traditional to approach medieval religious drama by dividing it into three periods: the *liturgical drama*, from its

---

[25] *Old Spanish Readings*, p. 106.
[26] *The Play of the Sibyl Cassandra*, pp. 16-17.
[27] Beatrice Patt, *The Development of the Christmas Play in Spain from the Origins to Lope de Vega* (unpublished Bryn Mawr doctoral dissertation, 1945), p. 61; in making this statement, Miss Patt was thinking of both the Latin and Spanish elements; see p. 92, n. 1.
[28] See Sachs, *Eine Weltgeschichte des Tanzes*, tr. by Kerr, *Histoire de la danse*, p. 157; Yvonne Rokseth, 'Danses cléricales du XIIIe siècle'; Chailley, 'Un document nouveau sur la danse ecclésiastique'.
[29] On this point see Moraleda, *Los Seises de la Catedral de Toledo*, pp. 13 *sqq.*, p. 74.
[30] Moléon, p. 305.
[31] Du Méril, *Origines latines du théâtre moderne*, p. 148.
[32] Moléon, pp. 75-76.
[33] Young, I, 602-603.
[34] *De l'ancienne coutume de prier debout*, II, 392.

origins until about 1200, the *semi-liturgical* drama, from about 1200 to 1250, and finally the *religious* drama, constituted when the plays were completely secularised, students of the subject sometimes tend to forget that liturgical plays continued in many places as long, or longer, than the vernacular religious plays which had evolved from them. It has already been pointed out that of the hundreds of liturgical texts gathered together in Professor Young's treatise, over half are found in works of the fifteenth century or later.

Closely connected with the question of date is that of the vernacular. If a play is late in date, and especially if it makes use of the vernacular, dramatic historians have been inclined to exclude it automatically from the classification *liturgical*, readily concluding that the play must have been put on outside the church, or if within the church, without any connection with the liturgical services. That this is not always a safe criterion is amply shown by our text from Toledo, and we shall find other such examples.

La Sibila de la Noche de Navidad

In the part of Vallejo's manuscript entitled *Disertación VI. sobre las Representaciones Poeticas en el Templo, y Sybila de la noche de Navidad*, we find a description of yet another dramatic, or semi-dramatic, ceremony which took place on Christmas Eve in the Toledo Cathedral, the prophecy of the Sibyl. Here Vallejo does not say that he has copied from the manuscript of Arcayos, but presents the ceremony as it was still carried out in his own day. The practice was nevertheless an ancient and venerable one, he declares, "una ceremonia antiquissima, y venerable, que en lo substancial no ha padecido alteración:[35]

> En nuestra Santa Iglesia la noche de la Natividad de nuestro Señor Jesuchristo, concluido el himno *Te Deum laudamus*,[36] sale de la Sacristia un Seise vestido á la Oriental representando á la Sybila Herophila, ó de Eritrea. Acompañanle quatro Colegiales Infantes: dos que con albas, Estolones, guirnaldas en la cabeza, y espadas desnudas en la mano dicen hacer papeles de Angeles, y otros dos con las ropas comunes de Coro, y con el fin de que por las hachas encendidas que llevan sean mas visibles los tres Personajes. Suben todos cinco á un Tablado que esta prevenido al lado del Pulpito del Evangelio, y colocados como representa la lamina que he puesto por Cabeza de la disertación,[37] esperan se concluyan los Maytines, y principia la Sybila á cantar las siguientes coplas:

---

[35] p. 627; the following text is found in Vallejo's manuscript on pp. 628-631. It has been reprinted by Gillet, *Memorias*, pp. 273-274.
[36] Note of Vallejo: "Quando se seguia el el (*sic*) Breviario antiguo Toledano se hazia esta Ceremonia despues de la 6a Leccion de Maitines."
[37] The manuscript still contains this drawing; it has been reproduced by Gillet, opposite p. 272.

Sybila	Quantos aqui sois juntados ruegoos por Dios verdadero que oigais del dia postrimero quando seremos juzgados. Del Cielo de las Alturas un Rey vendra perdurable con poder muy espantable á juzgar las Criaturas.

Haora los Angeles que han tenido las Espadas levantadas, las esgrimen, y la Musica canta en el Coro:

	Juicio fuerte sera dado cruel y de muerte.
Sybila	Trompetas, y sones tristes diran de lo alto del Cielo levantaos muertos del suelo recivireis segun hizistis. Descubrirse han los pecados sin que ninguno los hable á la pena perdurable do iran los tristes culpados.
Musica	Juicio fuerte sera dado cruel y de muerte.
Sybila	A la Virgen supliquemos que antes de aqueste litijo interceda con su hijo porque todos nos salvemos.
Musica	Juicio fuerte sera dado cruel, y de muerte.

Concluido todo esto bajan todos del Tablado y dando una buelta por dentro del Coro se van.

Thus we find that in the eighteenth century in the Cathedral of Toledo, while Matins were being concluded and the *Te Deum* sung,[38] a choir-boy would come out from the sacristy dressed up in oriental fashion representing one of the ancient Sibyls. Vallejo is not certain which one, perhaps the Herophilan or Erythraean Sibyl, he suggests. The chorister makes his appearance in processional style, accompanied by four *Colegiales Infantes*, two of them vested in alb and

---

[38] Vallejo says, "concluido el himno Te Deum Laudamus", but later on he states that the Sibyl arrives on the improvised stage while Matins are still in progress.

stole, wearing a garland on their head, and bearing an unsheathed sword in their hand. These are said to represent angels. The other two are dressed in *ordinary style*, that is in soutane and surplice, as the drawing of the manuscript indicates; they carry a torch and are present only in order to render visible the other three personages. All five proceed to a kind of stage erected beside the Gospel tribune, and once arrived, wait until Matins have terminated. Then the Sibyl begins to sing, in Castilian, a grave and solemn prophecy about the judgment to come. Three times the song is interrupted by the chanting of an awesome choral refrain, and on each occasion the two *angels* clash their swords together in menacing fashion, evidently to reinforce the awesome character of the words being sung. After the final chorus, the group descends from the platform, takes a turn about the choir, and returns to the sacristy.

Thanks to the drawing included in Vallejo's study, and reproduced by Gillet, we know the exact costume worn by the Sibyl in Toledo in the eighteenth century. The dress, richly embroidered in *oriental style*, has long, wide sleeves and extends to the ground. On her head she wears a kind of peaked coronet, higher in the front than in the back, evidently a symbol of her prophetic powers. She also appears to be wearing a necklace and pendant, and Professor Gillet distinguishes what he interprets to be earrings, but this latter feature is not very clear in the drawing. In her hands the Sibyl holds a scroll bearing the words and music of her chant.

Gillet writes regarding the drawing:[39]

> The appearance of the Sibyl, in a dress more reminiscent of late sixteenth-century fashions than anything oriental, will have to be discussed more fully when the iconography of this figure, together with her literary history, shall have been reliably established. The Sibyl's traditional garland of laurel seems to have been transferred to the sword-bearing acolytes, but she is still adorned with the heavy necklace and earrings which she wears on some ancient bronzes.

The commentator's surmise that the laurel worn by the angel has been transferred from the Sibyl is quite ingenious. Indeed one wonders why the angels should be wearing the garlands, unless they are supposed to represent halos. Happily we possess at least two texts of the medieval *Ordo Prophetarum* which describe the gestures and costumes of the various prophets. In the Laon version the Sibyl is depicted thus: *veste feminea, decapillata, edera coronata, insanienti simillima*.[40] Thus at Laon the prophetess did wear her ivy, but her expression of mad inspiration was not imitated by her Toledo sister. The latter resembled more closely the Sibyl of the Rouen play, concerning whom the rubrics only say: *Sibilla, coronata et muliebri habitu ornata*.[41] We do not know what type of crown the Rouen Sibyl wore; it may have been of ivy as at Laon, or again, it may have been a type of coronet similar to the one used at Toledo.

[39] p. 273, n. 24. [40] Young, II, 145. [41] *Ibid.*, II, 165.

The angels themselves pose a problem. Why are they with the Sibyl, and why do they carry swords? In the known French versions of the liturgical *Ordo Prophetarum*, the Sibyl portion involves neither accompanying angels nor weapons.

An examination of the text of the Pseudo-Augustinian sermon reveals the reason for the swords. Just before the lector reaches the passage concerning the Sibyl's prophecy, *Judicii signum*, he introduces her testimony in the following manner:[42]

> Quid Sibilla vaticinando etiam de Christo clamaverit in medium proferamus, ut ex uno lapide utrorumque frontes percuciantur, Iudeorum scilicet atque paganorum, *atque suo gladio*, sicut Golias, Christi omnes percuciantur inimici. Audite quid dixerit.

These lines no doubt provided the original suggestion for the sword-bearing. At Mallorca, the Sibyl herself carried the sword.[43] If Professor Gillet had been aware of this when he was proposing his interesting suggestion that the garlands were transferred to the angels, he would probably have included the swords in the transaction. As for the angels themselves, they were perhaps introduced into the Toledo ceremony merely to facilitate matters for the Sibyl.[44]

Vallejo, who elsewhere in his work, regards dramatic performances in church with a rather hostile eye, considering them *juguetes pueriles*,[45] speaks of this ceremony with respect, and even declares that he was moved by it: "que es preciso mueva el anima de los oientes una voz delgada, y lamentable, que con pausa, y gravedad predice el dia tremendo del Juicio" (p. 633). Moreover the music is not at all sweet and melodious, but unearthly: "tan patetica, y poco grata a los oientes, que no hay uno que no desee se concluia quanto antes" (p. 637); sung by a shrill childish voice, without bass and without accompaniment, it seemed, in the demi-obscurity of the enormous nave, to come from another world.

Coussemaker, Creizenach, Chambers, Young, and others who have discussed at great length the liturgical drama of the medieval Church, do not speak of such a performance as this one in the Castilian city of Toledo. Does this mean that the ceremony was peculiar to Spanish soil? And what is its relation to the tradition of the liturgical drama?

We have already encountered the Sibyl in the Pseudo-Augustinian sermon and the liturgical play which developed from it, the *Ordo Prophetarum*. In the sermon the Sibyl answers her summons by pronouncing, in Latin of course, her messianic prediction. In most of the plays she recites, or sings, the first few verses of this passage, the first line of which is:

[42] *Ibid.*, II, 130.
[43] See below, p. 125.
[44] Only one other instance of angels with garlands has come to our attention; see pp. 60–62.
[45] p. 631.

Iudicii signum: Tellus sudore madescet.[46]

The theme of the prophecy is the same as that found in the Toledo ceremony: the Judgment to come. Vallejo ventures his opinion that in the Castilian city also, the Sibylline verses were originally delivered in Latin. Proof of this, he affirms, is found in the parchment which the prophetess wears appended to her left shoulder. He observes:[47]

> Bien creo que al principio se haria en nuestra Iglesia como en la de Roam, Paris ó Narbona, y que se cantarian en latin los versos Sybilinos, bien fuese segun la version que pone S. Agustin en la Ciudad de Dios, bien segun lo que pone Eusebio Cesariense en la Oracion de Constantino, ó bien segun la que ponen otros muchos, pues todos convienen en la substancia. La prueba de esta conjetura es que nuestra Sybila los lleva como por adorno escritos en una tarjeta, que se le prehende en el hombro izquierdo, y son como se sigue:
>
> > Judicii in signum tellus sudore madescet;
> > Et Rex Eternus summo descendet Olympo:
> > Scilicet ut carnem, mundum ut Judicet omnem
> > Vnde Deum fidi, diffidentesque videbunt
> > Summum cum sanctis in Secli fine sedentem.
>
> Pero como el fin de esta Ceremonia era instruir ál Pueblo, y cantando los versos en latin, y en el Coro por algun Psalmista las gentes rusticas no entendian la fuerza de ella quisieron sensibilizarla mas vistiendo un Niño á la Oriental, y poniendo en la boca de este unos versos Castellanos, y que en el concepto dixesen lo mismo que los otros. Favorecia á los que pensaron asi el uso de nuestra Iglesia, que desde el siglo XIII. cantaba los milagros de nuestra Señora varios dias, y estos estaban arreglados á Musica, idioma y Poesia de aquel tiempo como se conoce del Libro Cantigas del Rey D. Alfonso que se guarda en nuestra Biblioteca, y tambien les favorecia para tratar en romance los asuntos mas Sagrados, la version de la Biblia, que el mismo Rey Sabio mandó hacer, y las Representaciones de los Misterios de nuestra Religion, que ya eran comunes en los Templos. Como á los fines del Siglo XIII. ó principios del XIV. infiero es la traducion del sentido de esta Profecia Latina ál idioma vulgar, pues aunque hoy parece su estilo, y locucion mas moderna, se dexa percebir la hán ido acomodando ál Siglo presente.

We note at once that the first verse given by Vallejo is almost identical with that of the traditional text quoted above, but the rest, while agreeing in substance, differs considerably in its expression of the individual lines. The *tarjeta* in all likelihood presents a modernized version composed sometime after the beginning of the sixteenth century, and in reality probably has little to do with the early development of the Sibylline verses at Toledo. Actually

---

[46] For the complete acrostic, see Young, II, 130.
[47] pp. 634-636.

breviaries printed for the Toledo diocese as late as 1551 contain precisely the same text of the Sibyl as that given by the medieval Latin service books.[48]

There will be no attempt at this point to draw any conclusions concerning the origins of the Sibyl ceremony and its possible connection with the *Ordo Prophetarum*. These questions will be discussed at length later in the study, when all available evidence on the matter has been gathered together. We shall merely note here Vallejo's belief that the ceremony of the Sibyl originated with the Church Fathers, the "Monges de Oriente", he declares, "pues tambien la observaban varias Iglesias de Africa" (p. 632); the custom passed into Spanish tradition, according to him, when the French Benedictines came to the Peninsula in the eleventh century.[49]

In the library of the *Academia de la Historia* in Madrid is found another unedited work, which contains approximately the same information about the Christmas practices at Toledo as Vallejo's study.[50] It is a folio manuscript composed of two parts, the first of which is entitled *Descripción de la Santa Iglesia Primada de Toledo*, and the second, *Ceremonias particulares de la Santa Iglesia Primada de Toledo*. According to the preface, the volume is a copy of some other work; it was begun in 1773 by the historian, Father Enrique Flórez, and finished that same year by Francisco Mendez. The original of the second part of the volume, the section which interests us, is probably the manuscript found at the Toledo Public Library in the collection *Borbon-Lorenzana*, MS 154. In any case, the Toledo treatise bears the same title, *Ceremonias particulares de la Santa Yglesia Primada de Toledo*, and the text is identical.[51]

An examination of the contents of this work reveals that Vallejo probably made use of it in drawing up his own study. Since both were compiled about the same time, our knowledge of dramatic ceremonies in the Castilian city is not greatly increased by the document at hand. It does, however, add a few significant details. The most important is a reference to the dress of the *pastores*, an item about which Vallejo says nothing. The choir-boys who perform in this capacity are said to wear a kind of white hood which comes down over the shoulders, *capillos de paño blanco*. It is probably not a mere coincidence that the shepherds of the Christmas play at the monastery of Pleinpied in France were attired in the same way:

> Sint parati pueri ad peragendum officium pastorum et duo pueri habentes capas, desuper precincti, tenentes capita sua infra capucium.

We are told that the *pastores* conclude their performance by singing a *villancico*, and then remain in the choir throughout the entire celebration of Lauds, — as

---

[48] A 1551 Toledo Breviary is found at the *Biblioteca Nacional* under the shelf mark, R. 26179.
[49] Rodríguez informs us that the prophecy was last sung at Toledo in 1866 ('El Canto de la Sibila en la Catedral de León', p. 24).
[50] Catalogued, 11-2-7 MS 444.
[51] The copy is signed *M.N.D.Z.*, which is the signature of Mendez. The text, and further information about the manuscripts, may be found in the Appendix.

they did at Rouen in the twelfth century; they retire to the sacristy only after Lauds have been concluded.

As Professor Gillet suspected might be the case,[52] the important Arcayos manuscript is itself still preserved. It resides in the Toledo Cathedral Library under the catalogue number, 42.29, is composed of 616 folios, of which some 576 are used, and in the index of the library is described as follows:

> Libro de los usos, costumbres, y casos extraordinarios acaecidos en esta Santa Iglesia, con las memorias de las instituciones de algunas Dignidades y Prebendas; un tomo folio, papel, y letra cursiva pequeña.

A copy was made of this work in 1765 which modernizes the spelling, and to a slight extent the text; this copy is kept at the present time without a catalogue number, in the entrance-way to the Cathedral Chapter Room.[53]

As Vallejo affirmed, the description of the Christmas ceremony of the shepherds found in his own study is copied from Arcayos, the only major exception being that he has omitted the *villancicos* which the *pastores* sang as a part of their performance; the passage about the Sibyl is not taken from the earlier manuscript, but the two texts agree in substance. In discussing the latter usage, Arcayos adds some significant comments:[54]

> Y luego sale la Sybilla. Nota: que antiguamente ubo unas mugeres sabias en la gentilidad a las quales Dios dio spiritu de propheçia, para que propheticasen la venida de Jhesu Cristo, en carne, y su sancta passion, y Resurection, y la segunda venida al Juiçio. Destas sybillas haçe mençion sant Agustin en un sermon, el qual se solia cantar en los maytines desta fiesta, en la sexta lection, en la qual Sant Agustin reffiere los versos de la Sybilla que comiençan *Judicii signum*. Y en lugar de los versos latinos a sido y es costumbre en esta sancta yglesia, quando se rreçaba el offiçio toledano de que al tiempo que se deçia la dicha sexta lection salia un donçon vestido como Sybilla de buenos adereços de muger. Y cantava otros versos, en lengua castellana, en lugar de aquellos versos latinos que trahe Sant Agustin en la lection que comiença *juyçio fuerte sera dado, y cruel de muerte*, etc. Y despues que çeso el offiçio toledano, y se haçe el offiçio Romano hasta el dia de oy presevera la çeremonia de salir la Sybilla a cantar los dichos versos, dicho el *Te deum laudamus* de los Maytines, y oration, porque no se diçen las lectiones que se solian deçir en lo toledano. Y sale el dicho cleriçon vestido de Sybilla acompañada de otros dos cleriçones vestidos de angeles.

Arcayos' commentary, verifying an observation made by Vallejo, brings us at least one step closer to the original practice. Formerly, he remarks, when the Toledo office was sung instead of the Roman, the chant of the Sibyl took place not after the *Te Deum*, but after the sixth lesson. In the Toledo office the sixth

---
[52] *Memorias*, p. 279.
[53] The relevant passages from Arcayos' work are given in the Appendix.
[54] Fol. 410ᵛ.

lesson was a sermon of St. Augustine, and in the course of this sermon the Sibylline prophecy, *Judicii signum*, was delivered. Arcayos therefore attaches the chant of the Sibyl to the Augustinian sermon.

He declares that in the Toledo office it was a custom to sing the verses of the Sibyl in Castilian, but he does not tell us at what date the Castilian was substituted for the Latin. His usage of the term *Toledo office* is somewhat ambiguous. Frequently this expression is employed to distinguish the Mozarabic rite from the Roman office which was introduced in Toledo in 1085. Here Arcayos is thinking not of the Mozarabic rite, but of the office used at Toledo immediately previous to the second liturgical reform which took place about 1568 under Pope Pius V. At this latter date, many of the local diocesan practices were abolished in order to unify the liturgy, and render it once again more conformable to Roman custom. The practice of singing the Sibylline verses was therefore probably transferred from the sixth lesson of Matins to its position after the *Te Deum* about the year 1568.

A Toledo ceremonial composed near the end of the fifteenth century, or at the beginning of the sixteenth, amply bears out Arcayos' assertion. The manuscript, which is found at the library of the University of Madrid, contains the following version of the Christmas Eve performance:[55]

> An de tañer a maytines a las .X. oras. Cesado el agilon (sic) dizen los maytines muy solenemente.
>
> . . . .
>
> A la quarta leçion a de salir la sybila del sagrario, el pertugero delante y luego dos clerizones con dos hachas. Y tras ellos otros dos clerizones mayores vestidos de angeles con sendas espadas desnudas. Y tras ellos la sibila. An de entrar por el coro del dean y dar la buelta por el coro hasta la escalera que sube a la tribuna de la epistola. Y subase alla, hasta la .VI. leçion. Esta sesta leçion a de leer el arçediano de toledo, o la mas antigua dinidad o canonigo de su coro despues del. Y leyda un poco de la leçion diga el arçediano, *dic tu sibila*. Y luego diga la sibila lo que a de dezir. Y en tanto que ella dize y los cantores responden, lea el sobredicho arçediano rezado[56] hasta que la sibila acabe. Y acabando la sibila,[57] lea en boz desde dende esta notado en el liçionario. Y acabado diga *tu autem*.[58] Y deçiendase la sibila y vayase por donde vino a desnudar al sagrario.

This text obviously represents an older form of the ceremony, one in which

---

[55] Biblioteca Universitaria (Sección de Derecho), MS 149, fol. 2-2ᵛ. Villa-Amil y Castro, in the *Catálogo de los manuscritos existentes en la Biblioteca del Noviciado de la Universidad Central*, Part. 1, describes the manuscript as follows: "Ceremonial de la Santa Iglesia de Toledo (así dice el tejuelo del códice), 132 hojas de papel, con otras 12 en blanco, 150 x 103; debe datar del siglo XV, muy adelantado, ó ya del XVI."

[56] rezado] razado (MS).

[57] I have supplied the punctuation mark after the word *sibila*. I take *sibila* to be the subject of *acabando* rather than of *lea*; this seems to me to be required by the sense of the passage.

[58] In the recitation of Matins, each lesson is terminated by the formula, *Tu autem, Domine, miserere nobis*.

the Sibyl's song is even more intimately connected with the liturgy than in the previous versions considered. Here the prophecy is given, not after the *Te Deum*, which marks the close of one of the liturgical hours, but during Matins itself, as a part of the sixth lesson. Around 1500 there was no special stage built for the ceremony; the Sibyl merely ascended the tribune from which the epistle was usually read. We are informed that after the arch-deacon had read a small portion of the sixth lesson, he turned to the Sibyl and said to her, *dic tu sibila*, the signal for the prophetess to begin her part. Unfortunately the manuscript is very parsimonious in its instructions and only declares: "y luego diga la sibila lo que a de dezir." As a result, we do not know if at this date the chanter prophesied in Latin or Castilian; at any rate her text was enclosed within a Latin introduction and conclusion. The phrase *dic tu sibila* is perhaps the most noteworthy in the text. As we have seen, this was precisely the type of introductory summons used in the Pseudo-Augustinian sermon and in the *Ordo Prophetarum*: *dic tu Moises, dic tu Daniel*, etc. It should be pointed out that the expression *dic tu sibilia* itself does not ordinarily occur in the sermon, but only in the play.[59] The phrase in our manuscript might, therefore, connect the Toledo prophecy in some way with the *Ordo Prophetarum*, perhaps indicating that, at some time in the past, the Toledo custom of chanting the Sibyl's verses was borrowed from a prophet play. Yet, not much of the rest of the sermon is read aloud, and no other prophets are mentioned: "y leyda *un poco* de la leçion diga el arçediano, *dic tu sibila*." Hence, more probably, the expression was merely modelled on analogous phrases in the sermon itself.

To my knowledge, this is the oldest liturgical text discovered thus far which speaks about the impersonation of the Sibyl at Toledo. Doubtless the custom is older, but just how much older we cannot say with certitude. If the Cathedral account books were examined, they would probably divulge valuable information on this point, but unfortunately time was lacking for such an investigation. Older Toledo documents with the text *Judicii signum* are not at all rare, but the text itself does not prove that the ceremony involved impersonation. Many medieval *ordinaria* give instructions that a *group* of cantors sing the words of the prophecy, and although the ceremonies are minutely described, no mention is made of a cleric playing the part of a Sibyl. At Palencia in the fourteenth century, for example, six clerics rendered the Sibylline verses; it is hardly probable that all six would play the role of Sibyls, especially when the ceremonial remains completely silent on the matter.[60]

The same Toledo codex also presents an older version of Christmas Lauds.

---

[59] The usual introduction to the Sibylline chant has already been quoted above, p. 42.
[60] The Palencia text is given in the Appendix. Of the many similar versions, see for example, Vich, Bibl. Episcopal, MS 212, Consueta of San Juan de las Abadesas saec. xv, fol. 103ᵛ; Barcelona, Archivo de la Corona de Aragón, MS San Cugat 46, Liber de Consuetudinibus monasterii Sancti Cucuphatis saec. xiii (1219-1221), fol. 59; Bourges, Processionale, ed. 1517, in Pothier, *Revue du chant grégorien*, III (1894-95), 103.

Instead of the antiphon *Quem vidistis* being dramatized, here it is the antiphon *Pastores dicite quidnam vidistis* which is so honored, and the shepherds appear during the chanting of the fifth psalm, not the first:[61]

> Enpieçan los dos cantores que tienen las capas las laudes absolute, *Natus est nobis*. Y proçeden more solito hasta el verso de *Laudate Dominum de celis* que dize *ut faciant in eis judicium conscriptum*.[62] Acabado este verso digan los cantores el antifana que enpieça:
>
>> Pastores dicite.
>
> Y acabada digan los pastores en la grada mas alta del altar mayor:
>
>> Infantem vidimus ‹pannis involutum, et choros angelorum laudantes Salvatorem›.
>
> Acabado esto dizen los que rigen el coro con las capas *Laudate Dominum in sanctis*[63] *eius*. Y acabado an de tornar a dezir el antifana:
>
>> Pastores dicite.
>
> Y acabada esta antifana, dizen los pastores a la puerta del coro del arçobispo:
>
>> Infantem vidimus.
>
> Luego dizen los cantores que tienen[64] las capas, *Laudate eum in virtutibus eius*. E acabado este verso tornan a dezir los cantores:
>
>> Pastores dicite.
>
> Y acabando tornan a dezir los pastores dentro en el coro:
>
>> Infantem vidimus.
>
> Hecho esto dizen los dos cantores que tienen las capas:
>
>> Bien vengades pastores, etc.
>
> Y responden los pastorçicos las cosas que vieron. Y baylan y cantan un poco. Y vanse a desnudar.

Thus around the year 1500, the office of Lauds at Toledo was conducted in approximately the same manner as it was during the Middle Ages at Dax, Narbonne, and Cambrai in France, exception being made for the vernacular and the dancing. We shall presently see that in almost every diocese of medieval Spain the cantors and choir-boys repeated the antiphon *Pastores dicite* as at Toledo, but in no other instance in Castile have I found a written indication that the boys were costumed as shepherds. The Toledo texts bearing this indication are most numerous, especially from the year 1499 to 1565.[65] The

---

[61] Fol. 3ᵛ-4; the ceremony is followed by the fifth antiphon, *Parvulus filius*.
[62] This is the last verse of Psalm 149, commonly sung as the fifth and last psalm of Lauds.
[63] sanctis] santis (MS).
[64] tienen] tien (MS).
[65] Almost all the missals printed for the Toledo diocese during this period contain the ceremony; the passage from the missal of the year 1499 is given in the Appendix.

transfer of the ceremony from the fifth psalm to the beginning of the office likely took place at the same time the position of the Sibyl prophecy was changed, that is around 1568.

The Lauds practice can fortunately be traced further back into the history of Toledo than that of the impersonated Sibyl. A fourteenth century breviary found in the library of the Benedictine monastery at Montserrat contains provisions for the usage, and designates it by the more dramatic term *Representacio Pastorum*. The passage reads as follows:[66]

> Quintus psalmus, *Laudate*. Si forte iudicaverint (?) expedire quod fiat Representacio Pastorum, qualiter angelus nunciavit eis Christum natum,[67] dicto psalmo, *laudate dominum de celis* usque ad *laudate dominum in sanctis eius*, interim sint parati ad altare pueri induti ad modum pastorum. Et tunc illi duo cantores qui regunt chorum incipiant hanc antiphonam *pastores dicite*. Respondentibus pueris *Infantem vidimus*, deinde dicatur *laudate dominum in sanctis eius*. Et sic in unoquoque versu[68] repetatur antiphona ut supra dictum est usque ad finem psalmi. Et tunc dicatur ad *Benedictus* antiphona *Gloria in excelsis*. Et si non placuerit ista representacio, finitis laudibus sine capitulo et sine hympno cantores statim incipiant hanc antiphonam ad *Benedictus*.

This manuscript makes no mention of the vernacular in the performance, although its silence in the matter does not preclude the possibility that it was used.

Thus far research has produced no Toledo text with liturgical plays earlier than this one. As a result we are still left in considerable obscurity concerning the origins of the medieval dramatic traditions in this city. In review, we find that two types of liturgical plays were known at Toledo: a brief scene of the shepherds during Christmas Lauds, and the dramatic monologue of the Sibyl. The oldest written record of the former has been found in a fourteenth century breviary; evidences of use of the vernacular in this ceremony date from at least the end of the fifteenth century. The practice of costuming choir-boys to represent the Sibyl and angels was in vogue around 1500. We may presume from Arcayos' remarks that, at least from this time onward, the prophecy was delivered in Castilian; we have no proof that it was used before this, although Arcayos, and others after him, presume that the vernacular was employed as early as the thirteenth century. Certainly the chant of the Sibyl was a custom at Toledo at an early date,[69] but there is no record of its dramatization there previous to 1500.

---

[66] Recently acquired, the breviary had not as yet been catalogued at the time of my visit at Montserrat in 1954.
[67] The phrase *qualiter angelus nunciavit eis Christum natum* refers most likely to the second part of the shepherds' responses, *vidimus . . . choros angelorum laudantes Salvatorem*.
[68] versu] versus (MS).
[69] The breviary at Montserrat, for example, contains the complete text of the *Judicii signum* with its refrain.

It is noteworthy that both these practices were attached to the festivities of Christmas Eve. Conspicuous for their absence are the dramatic activities frequently associated in medieval times with the other great feasts of the year, especially Easter and the Epiphany. No instances of the liturgical *Visitatio Sepulchri* or *Ordo Stellae* at Toledo have as yet been discovered. Possible reasons for the dearth of such texts will be advanced after the liturgical plays found in other parts of Central and Western Spain have been presented.

CHAPTER 5

OTHER LITURGICAL PLAYS WEST OF CATALONIA

THE oldest Spanish liturgical play, to our knowledge, is found in two late eleventh century manuscripts written at the Benedictine monastery of Silos, near Burgos. Both manuscripts are breviaries and they contain an Easter *Visitatio Sepulchri* of the elementary type. The following is probably the older of the two, since it presents a simpler form:[1]

> Interrogatio: Quem queritis in sepulcro hoc, Cristicole?
> Responsio: Ihesum Nazarenum[2] crucifixum, o celicole.
> Interrogatio siue responsio, antiphona: Non est hic, surrexit sicut loquutus est; ite, nuntiate quia surrexit Dominus, alleluia. Surrexit.

The second breviary presents the same version with somewhat fuller rubrics:[3]

> Interrogat Angelus et dicit ad Discipulos: Quem queritis in sepulcro hoc, Cristicole?
> Respondent Discipuli et dicant: Ihesu‹m› Nazarenum crucifixum, o celicole.
> Iterum respondet Angelus: Non est hic, surrexit sicut loquutus est; ite, nuntiate quia surrexit Dominus,[4] alleluia.
> Antiphona: Surrexit. Te Deum laudamus.[5]

Both these texts present the singularity of being the only known liturgical plays written in Mozarabic script and with Mozarabic notation. The content of the manuscripts, however, belongs entirely to the Roman-French rite.

The wording of the text presents two slight peculiarites which might be

---

[1] London, British Museum, Add. MS 30848, fol. 125ᵛ. The passage has been previously edited by Lange, *Die lateinischen Osterfeiern*, pp. 24-25, and Young, I, 577. It is preceded by the *Processio ad Fontem* of Easter Vespers, an arrangement which likely proceeds, as Young indicates (I, 573), from exigencies of space in the manuscript. In the other breviary mentioned, the text is found in the ordinary position of the Easter play, that is, after the third responsory of Matins; the manuscript provides music.
[2] Nazarenum] Nazareno (MS).
[3] London, British Museum, Add. MS 30850, Breviarium Silense saec. xi, fol. 106 ᵛ; previously edited by Lange, *Die lateinischen Osterfeiern*, pp. 24-25, and Young, I, 577. The manuscript has music.
[4] *Dominus* (?) in the margin.
[5] The whole passage was added in the margin and at the bottom of the page, and according to directions, was to be sung after the third responsory *Dum transisset*. This addition was inserted some time after the main text had been completed, because the color of ink is different; however it could not postdate the manuscript very much, since both are written in Mozarabic script; the twelfth century liturgical texts from Silos are composed in French script.

of help in eventually establishing the monastery or church from which this little Easter play was borrowed. The Easter play, especially in its simple form, was extremely stereotyped, and the main phrases used were the same throughout almost all Western Europe. One of these phrases was the initial question *Quem quaeritis in sepulchro, o Christicole?* Of the more than five hundred Easter tropes and plays which have been published to date, approximately two-thirds contain this sentence, and the texts from Silos are the only ones which have the word *hoc* instead of *o*. What has happened, in all probability, is that the scribe copied some manuscript such as the troper found at Vercelli in Italy in which the phrase read *Quem queritis in sepulchro ho cristicole?*[6] The three letters *hoc* thus came in sequence, and the scribe, considering *ho* to be an error, concluded that a *c* had been omitted. The text from Vercelli is the only one known which exhibits this reading.

The other singularity is the phrase *sicut loquutus est*. The ordinary expression is *sicut predixerat*, only five out of three hundred texts having the variant shown in the Silos breviaries. Of these five, again three come from Italy.[7]

It is perhaps not without significance that, whereas in other Spanish monasteries such as San Juan de Sahagún, San Millán de la Cogolla, San Pedro de Cardeña, and Nájera, the influence of Cluny was very marked in the eleventh century, no trace has been discovered of such an influence at Silos. This was doubtless because the monastery had already been reformed by the great St. Dominic of Silos, who was abbot there from 1040 to 1073; under his guidance the abbey came to experience the greatest period in its history. Again unlike many of the Hispanic monasteries, Silos possesses no record of French monks at the abbey during the eleventh century.

For other reasons also, it appears that the little Easter play was introduced at Silos from some monastery which did not follow the liturgical customs of Cluny. The monastic breviary used at Cluny had twelve lessons for all feasts, including Easter; the Silos breviaries of the eleventh century have three lessons for Easter.[8]

Apparently the *Visitatio Sepulchri* did not flourish very long at this Spanish monastery, for it is not found in the breviaries written there during the twelfth century, or in any Silos manuscript thereafter.[9] The same type of simple play appears, however, in another part of twelfth century Spain, in a region where one is not at all surprised to find it, at Santiago de Compostella.

The pilgrimage route to the Spanish shrine was long a well travelled one

---

[6] Vercelli, Bibl. Capit., MS 146, Graduale-Troparium Vercellense saec. xi, fol. 109. The text is given by Young, 'The Origin of the Easter Play', p. 14.
[7] These may be found in Young, I, 207, 226, and 571; one of the others comes from Autun (Young, 'The Origin of the Easter Play', p. 21), and the fifth from Germany (Young, I, 569).
[8] This point will be discussed more fully later; see below, p. 69.
[9] See for example the twelfth century Silos Breviary at the British Museum in London (Add. MS 30849); the Easter ceremonies are given on folio 144.

by that date. It is easy to imagine the numerous guests gathered together for Holy Week and Easter services in the great cathedral. They would have been eagerly looking forward to the liturgical ceremonies of this season, and coming from such countries as France and England as they did, where the Easter play had long been a fixture, they no doubt expected some form of it to be presented at Santiago. Their expectations were not disappointed.

The Benedictine, Dom Germán Prado, tells how one day at Compostella, while he was busily engaged transcribing the music of the famous *Calixtus* manuscript, the archivist of the Cathedral library drew his attention to some folios of Gregorian chant which had been taken from the binding of some old manuscripts. Looking over the folios, Father Prado was soon aware that among them he was holding in his hands an ancient Easter play. In his opinion the folio came from a manuscript written at the beginning or the middle of the twelfth century. The musicologist has described the codex in the Galician periodical, *Nos*:[10]

> A mesma notación con unha soia liña e sin clave de moi belidos trazos e oscilando antre a neumática e a aquitana de puntos sobrepostos á distancias proporcionales acusan un orixen de comenzos ou medeados do século XII.

In his article Prado has transcribed the text of the play, and has also reproduced a photograph of it. The little piece, which we here reprint directly from the photographic reproduction, reads as follows:[11]

AD SIGNIFICATIONEM SEPULCRI

Ubi est Christus meus Dominus et Filius excelsi? Eamus videre sepulcrum.
Quem queritis in sepulcro, o Christicole?
Jhesum Nazarenum crucifixum, o celicole.[12]
Non est hic, surrexit sicut predixerat; ite, nuntiate quia surrexit.
Alleluia! Ad sepulcrum residens Angelus nuntians surrexisse Christum.
Te Deum laudamus.[13]

Evidence that the Compostella text before us was really a play is furnished by a fifteenth century manuscript in the Cathedral library. The manuscript

---

[10] 'O Antiguo melodrama pascoal', p. 79.
[11] At the time of my visit to the Cathedral library in 1954, the twelfth century folio could not be located. However the search was not pressed, and it seems probable that it still remains somewhere in the library. Prado's article has escaped practically all notice; only Anglès refers to it in his invaluable *La Música a Catalunya*, p. 269.
[12] Prado reads *celicola*, but the photographic reproduction has the usual *celicole*.
[13] Fr. Prado does not include these last three words in his transcription, probably because they were not a part of the dramatic performance. However the phrase, which is clearly legible in the photocopy, is important, because it manifests that the text was a play and not merely a trope. Since the Easter play was ordinarily performed after the third responsory of Matins and immediately before the *Te Deum*, it became a custom when copying the text of the play to include the hymn as the finale. Subsequently the *Te Deum* became so closely associated with medieval performances that it was sung even after profane pieces.

contains exactly the same liturgical play as the earlier text, and in addition, provides directions for the staging of it. The codex, a beautifully illuminated breviary said to have belonged to the Canon Miranda, is dated about 1450.[14] On folio 94, after the third responsory of Matins, we encounter the following passage:[15]

> Responsorium, *Dum transisset sabbatum*. Hic tres pueri in similitudine mulierum induti uestimentis candidis peragant de choro usque ad altare unus post unum blande cantantes hanc antiphonam:
>
>> Ubi est Christus meus, Dominus, et filius excelsi? Eamus uidere sepulcrum.
>
> Alius puer stans retro altare in similitudine angeli indutus uestimentis candidis: dicat hanc antiphonam:
>
>> Quem queritis in sepulcro, o Christicole?
>
> Et mulieres rendeant blande antiphonam:
>
>> Jhesum Nazarenum crucifixum, o celicole.
>
> Et angelus antiphonam:
>
>> Surrexit, non est hic sicut predixerat. Ite nunciate quia surrexit.
>
> Et mulieres eodem modo quo ante uenerunt, dicant alta uoce cantantes redeundo antiphonam:
>
>> Alleluia, ad sepulcrum residens angelus nunciat resurrexisse Christum. Te Deum laudamus.

The text possesses all the simple charm of the first known Easter play written by St. Ethelwold some five hundred years previously. Substantially the same as the twelfth century version, it demonstrates that in many churches the liturgical plays remained the same for centuries.

As late as 1497 the angel and the three Marys were still a part of the Easter ceremonies at Compostella. A breviary printed at that date reveals that in the fifty years which had elapsed since the composition of Canon Miranda's breviary, two sequences had been added, one before the *Visitatio Sepulchri* began, and the other as a part of it. We give the text here, because in addition to the two sequences, or *proses*, it adds certain clarifications concerning the dress of the participants:[16]

---

[14] For the date and information about the manuscript, see A. Lopez, *Estudios crítico-históricos de Galicia*, p. 49.
[15] The manuscript has no catalogue number.
[16] Brevarium ad ritum et consuetudinem almae Compostellanae ecclesiae, Vlixbonae (Lisbon), Nicolaus de Saxonia, 1497, fol. 63^v. A copy of this breviary is found at the Biblioteca Nacional in Madrid under the shelf-mark Incunables 874, and another at the Real Academia de la Historia, Incunables 148; A. Lopez, *La Imprenta en Galicia, siglos XI-XVIII* (1953), declares that these are the only known copies.

Responsorium: Dum transisset sabbatum Maria Magdalene et Maria Iacobi et Salome emerunt aromata, ut uenientes ungerent Jesum. Alleluia. Alleluia.
Versus: Et ualde mane una sabbatorum ueniunt ad monumentum orto iam sole.
Presa: Ut uenientes. Gloria.
Responsorium: Dum transisset.
Prosa:

> Alta concinite Christo uoce, astantes plebicule.
> Cuius pie liberate feliciter estis cruore.
> Quem tumulo consepultum et humana fragilitate,
> Deus pater resuscitauit hodie.
> Nulla Iesus sic moritur corruptione.
> Ad solemne festum ualde et celebrandum digne.
> In quo diu nobis clausa panditur uia uite.
> Nunc pura psallamus mente.[17]

Hic tres pueri coopertis capitibus amictis candidis in similitudinem mulierum pergant de choro usque ad altare, unus post unum: cantantes blande antiphonam:

> Ubi est Christus meus dominus et filius excelsi: eamus uidere sepulcrum.

Alius puer stans retro altare, indutus uestimentis candidis in similitudine angeli dicat:

> Quem queritis in sepulcro, o Christicole?

Et mulieres respondeant blande:

> Jesum Nazarenum crucifixum, o celicole.

Et rendeat angelus:

> Non est hic; surrexit sicut predixerat. Ite nunciate quia surrexit.

Et tunc pueri redeant ad chorum sicut ante uenerunt unus post unum cantantes altiori uoce:

> Alleluia. Ad sepulcrum residens angelus nunciat resurrexisse Christum.

Hic dicatur prosa,

> Dic nobis, Maria, quid vidisti in via, etc.
> Te Deum.

Breviaries for the diocese of Compostella were printed in 1541-43, but it appears that no copies of this edition have survived.[18] The 1569 breviary does not have the play.

---

[17] This *prosa* is not listed by Chevalier in his *Repertorium Hymnologicum*.
[18] See A. Lopez, *La Imprenta en Galicia*.

CHAPTER 5

The Santiago *Visitatio Sepulchri* presents no unusual dramatic scenes. However the opening lines sung by the three Marys, *Ubi est Christus meus*, etc., appear in only a few other examples of the play, and both Young and Miss Wright, in discussing these other versions, have pointed out the rarity of the antiphon in question.[19] Young records instances of it in only three other places: Saint-Martial of Limoges, Ripoll, and Poitiers.[20] These churches constitute a rather interesting combination. Miss Wright has found reasons for concluding that the phrase was transmitted directly from Saint-Martial to Poitiers, and we have noted that musicologists link Saint-Martial with Ripoll.[21] It would seem, then, that the French monastery played an important role in the dissemination of this particular version of the *Visitatio Sepulchri*.

We shall discover, however, that if the antiphon *Ubi est Christus meus* was rare in France and other European countries, it was not at all uncommon in Catalonia, where on the contrary, it was very popular. In that area the abbey of Santa Maria de Ripoll was most probably the chief disseminator. It may therefore be that the Easter play came to Compostella not via France and Saint-Martial of Limoges, but through the Catalan monastery of Ripoll.

The concluding antiphon, *Alleluia! Ad sepulchrum residens angelus nunciat resurrexisse Christum*, presents almost the same anomaly. Regarding this antiphon, which is found in several early manuscripts from Saint-Martial, Miss Wright declares: "This response is rarely found in other versions of the *Visitatio*, but occurs at St. Martin of Limoges and at Arles, and in Spain, at Ripoll and Huesca."[22] Thus Compostella again falls into a group with Ripoll and St. Martial. Furthermore, except for the *Visitatio* at Compostella, the two antiphons, *Ubi est Christus meus* and *Alleluia, ad sepulchrum residens angelus*, are found *together* only in texts from Ripoll and Catalonia. This appears to link the Galician city with the Catalan monastery rather than with St. Martial. Musicologists have already established that during the twelfth century Compostella and Ripoll were in close contact in the musical field.[23]

In addition to the early liturgical plays from Silos and Santiago, research has brought to light, for the part of Spain west of Catalonia, only two *Quem quaeritis* tropes from the Aragonese city of Huesca. The following example of the Christmas trope is found in an eleventh or twelfth century *Prosarium-Troparium* at the Huesca Cathedral library:[24]

---

[19] Young, I, 271 and Wright, *The Dissemination of the Liturgical Drama in France*, p. 38.
[20] Young, I, 212-213, 271, 570-572.
[21] See above p. 29.
[22] pp. 28-29; the antiphon was also employed at Saint-Augustin of Limoges; see Young, I, 209.
[23] See Anglès, *La Música a Catalunya*, pp. 259-260.
[24] MS 4, fol. 123. The text is mentioned by Young, II, 427, and others; the manuscript provides music.

IN NATIVITATE DOMINI

Quem queritis in presepe pastores dicite?
Saluatorem Christum dominum infantem pannis inuolutum, secundum sermonem angelicum.
Adest hic paruulus cum Maria matre sua, de qua dudum uaticinando Ysayas dixerat propheta: ecce uirgo concipiet et pariet filium; et nunc euntes dicite quia natus est. Alleluia. Alleluia, iam uere scimus Christum natum in terris de quo canite omnes cum propheta dicentes. Puer natus.

On the same folio is found the corresponding Easter trope:[25]

IN RESURRECTIONE[26] DOMINI

Quem queritis in sepulcro, o Christicole.
Ihesum Nazarenum crucifixum, o celicole.
Non est hic, surrexit sicut predixerat; ite, nunciate quia surrexit.
Alleluia, ad sepulcrum residens angelus nunciat resurrexisse Christum.
En ecce completum est illud quod olim ipse per prophetam dixerat ad patrem taliter inquiens:
Resurrexi.

Huesca was reconquered from the Moors only in 1096, so that if the above-mentioned troper was written in Huesca itself, it must have been composed after this date. In 1073 an ecclesiastical council had been held at Jaca, some fifty miles to the north of Huesca. Many French bishops took part in it, and subsequent to it a certain number of French canons came to Jaca. When Huesca was reconquered, they moved to that point. It is the opinion of Fr. Durán Gudiol, the archivist of Huesca Cathedral, that the liturgical manuscripts of the eleventh and early twelfth century now found at Huesca, were probably written in France.

There is no evidence that these tropes ever developed into liturgical plays in this Aragonese city. A fifteenth century Huesca *ordinarium* makes no mention of any, though it gives a complete description of the liturgical ceremonies practised at the cathedral. We do know from references made in the account books that Christmas and Easter plays were performed in the cathedral during the sixteenth century, and plays in honor of St. Vincent, a local martyr, at least a century earlier; but in all likelihood these plays were presented in the vernacular, and apart from any strict association with the liturgy.[27]

The same *Quem quaeritis* Easter trope as the one sung at Huesca is also found in a fifteenth century missal from the shrine of Nuestra Señora del Pilar at Zaragoza.[28] Since this city was reconquered from the Arabs only in

---

[25] The text has been published by Young, 'The Origin of the Easter Play', p. 24; like the Christmas trope, it is accompanied by music.
[26] Resurrectione] Resurectione (MS).
[27] Information regarding these performances may be found in the Appendix.
[28] Zaragoza Cathedral, Bibl. Capit., MS 31-22, Missale Ecclesiae Beatae Mariae Majoris de Pilari, anno 1442, fol. 150ᵛ. I quote the passage in the Appendix.

1118, it is quite possible that the trope was borrowed from nearby Huesca.

In the same city a very valuable manuscript in the archives of the church of Nuestra Señora del Pilar contains the old ceremonials of several Spanish cathedrals.[29] Written in 1606, the manuscript includes a résumé of what it calls the "consueta antigua" of the *Seo* of Zaragoza (ff. 89 *sqq.*). The *Seo*, of course, refers to the cathedral, and the term *consueta* is a word of Catalan origin for *ordinarium*, or ceremonial. Evidently on the feast of Easter at Zaragoza a kind of representation of the Resurrection was enacted by means of statues, but no impersonation seems to have been involved. The ceremony took place before Mass. At the opportune moment figures of the Blessed Mother and the Marys were disclosed at the sepulchre, then, shortly afterward, a mechanical angel with a sword in his hand descended from the upper part of the church, and arriving near the Marys, suddenly revealed an image of the risen Christ:[30]

> Y estando el Arzobispo y ministros frontero y junto a la capilla de nuestra Señora delante el monumento, comiença un tiple con voz alegre y alta a cantar alleluya. Luego se siguio un estruendo y despues del se ronpio un belo blanco y aparecio un altar muy adornado con muchas flores y enrramado alrededor en el qual avia çinco imagines muy lindas de bulto doradas; a saver es nuestra Señora y las Marias y ✱✱✱.[31] Luego los cantores cantaron de alla dento (sic) entre aquellos corredores y ventanajes muy bien enrramados muchos alleluias y cosas al proposito de la Resurection. Luego vaxo un angel con una espada en la mano y rompio un belo de tafetan carmesí y apareçio una figura de bulto de un Christo resucitado, figura muy hermosa y muy dorada; y los cantores se detuvieron un ratillo con muy linda musica de manera que no solo regoçijaron en esta fiesta a la gente que era mui mucha pero aun enterneçieron los animos de todos los presentes.
>
> . . . .
>
> Este dia solo esta descubierta la rresureczion. Acabada esta ceremonia de la Resurrectzion se dixo la missa con mucha solemnidad.

During the time that elapsed between the writing of the *consueta antigua* and a new one in the seventeenth century, the custom apparently developed of putting on a real play instead of using statues. Just what the exact nature of the play was, however, is not very clear from the references:[32]

> Adonde a estado el monumento se previene para celebrar el Misterio de la Resureccion con las insignias y passos de tan santo misterio con muchas luces.

---

[29] Provisional shelf-mark, Arm. 2, Cax. 6, lig. 1, n. 18.
[30] Fol. 111ᵛ.
[31] This space was occupied by one or two words which I could not decipher. The expression may have been *San Juan*.
[32] Zaragoza Cathedral, Bibl. Capit., MS 42-15, Consueta de la Santa Iglesia Metropolitana de Zaragoza, p. 316.

El Sr. Canonigo espanol dexo 100 s. de renta para la representacion deste misterio.

Along with the ancient ceremonial of Zaragoza, the manuscript in the archives of Nuestra Señora del Pilar includes a copy of a liturgical work from the cathedral of Granada. Found on folios 321 to 395, the text is entitled: *Las buenas y loables costumbres e ceremonias que se guardan en la sancta yglesia de granada y en el coro de ella*. The *Costumbres* inform us that even though Granada was reconquered at the late date of 1492, the liturgical Easter play succeeded in establishing itself in this Andalusian city in the first half of the sixteenth century.

The manuscript itself must have been celebrated enough, for I have come upon no less than four copies of it in different European libraries. Beside the one at Zaragoza, transcripts are found in the archives of the cathedral of Granada (*Sección de Libros*, Lib. no. 17), the Bibliothèque Nationale in Paris (*MS Esp.* 342), and the Chapter library at Segovia (without catalogue number).[33] The title of the Segovia treatise is as follows: *Las buenas y loables costumbres y ceremonias que se guardan en la yglesia de Guadix conforme a las que se guardan en la santa yglesia de Granada y en el choro della*. This title indicates one of the many ways in which liturgical plays spread from city to city throughout Europe. The customs of one diocese were simply copied from those of another. Generally the bishop himself was responsible for such a proceeding; in the case of our manuscript, the texts show that two bishops spread the liturgical drama to several cities.

According to the manuscript, at Granada and Guadix near the beginning of the sixteenth century, and likely later at Segovia, a simplified and rather unique form of the liturgical Easter play was celebrated early on the morning of the feast. At Granada it was enacted at dawn, probably at the conclusion of Matins; the Segovia manuscript states specifically, "after Matins". The ceremony was a kind of combination of a processional *Elevatio* and a brief *Visitatio Sepulchri*. Dramatic historians have pointed out that the *Elevatio* rarely occurred after Matins, especially when it was combined with some sort of dramatic activity.[34] Nonetheless, in addition to the present examples, we shall encounter at feast two other cases of this in Spain. Since these Spanish texts are all found in sixteenth century works, however, they cannot be said to represent a primitive tradition.

For the Easter morning ceremony at Granada a special structure was erected to serve as the *sepulchrum*. Adorned with rich hangings, it was large enough to hold two statues of angels which were placed within. The angels

---

[33] Fr. Casares Hervás, the archivist of the cathedral of Granada, kindly informed me that the Granada manuscript is not the original, but a late copy; the presence of the work at the Bibliothèque Nationale was pointed out by Collet in his bibliography to *Le Mysticisme musical espagnol au XVIe siècle*.
[34] See above p. 10.

held in their hands a linen cloth marked with the imprints of Christ's wounds. We recall that a similar linen cloth figured in the *mise en scène* of many medieval *Visitatio Sepulchri*. An imitation stone was placed in front of the *sepulchre*, and around it an enclosure which was made of reeds and adorned with laurel and flowers. During the night, all the pews and benches were removed from the church, doubtless to make room for both the ceremony and the crowds.

As the Easter procession got under way, it moved from the choir directly to the main altar, where the sepulchre had been constructed. Having arrived, two cantors proceeded to sing the Latin verse which served as the opening for many liturgical Easter plays, *Quis revolvet nobis lapidem ab ostio monumenti*.[35] We are not told that the cantors represented the Marys; perhaps this may be assumed, or perhaps in this version the whole group of ecclesiastics taking part in the procession were considered as visitors of the tomb. If the latter is the case, it is a variation not usually found.

As he sang the last word of the opening antiphon, one of the cantors deftly caused the imitation stone in front of the sepulchre to fall. This caused quite a reaction, for at that point the trumpets sounded, a pair of shotguns went off, and two boys dressed like angels came forth from the sepulchre. The fanfare, of course, was meant to emphasize the supernatural character of the Resurrection, and to heighten the dramatic effect of the angelic apparition. In some churches thunder and lightning were used.[36] The angels are dressed as they frequently were in the *Visitatio Sepulchri*, that is, with richly embroidered albs and stoles, and with amices over their heads. The one exception is the garland which they wear; I have met this adornment only in the ceremony of the Sibyl at Toledo.

The usual verses of the *Visitatio*, the *Quem quaeritis in sepulchro, o coelicole*, and its response, were not employed in the Granada play. The angels merely proceeded from the sepulchre, bearing lighted candles in their hands, and advancing to positions on each side of the sepulchre entrance, sang an antiphon proclaiming the Resurrection:

> Jesum quem queritis non est hic, sed surrexit; ecce locus ubi posuerunt eum. Ite vos in Galileam; ibi eum videbitis sicut dixit vobis, alleluya, alleluya, alleluya.

At this point the usual *Te Deum* was sung. The procession subsequently wound its way around the church for the remaining *estaciones*, but it appears that it was not again interrupted by genuine dramatization:[37]

---

[35] Concerning this introductory antiphon, see Young, I, 259.
[36] Young records it for Coutances (I, 410), Benediktbeuern (I, 435), and Klosterneuburg (I, 640).
[37] Fr. Casares very generously transcribed the text for me. The Segovia volume is the only one which presents significant variants. I give these in the footnotes (A), omitting, however, unimportant differences such as variations in spelling. Actually the text from Segovia is older, showing such readings as *fazer* throughout, but the copyist has modified the original in order to adapt it for use at Guadix. The Easter ceremony is found on the following folios: Granada, fol. 90-91ᵛ; Zaragoza, fol. 360ᵛ-362; Segovia, fol. 53-54ᵛ; Paris, pp. 54 *sqq*.

El dia de la sancta resurrecçión.

A el alva del sancto dia de la Ressurrecçión por espeçial devoçión por el Reverendissimo señor don Anton de Rojas arzobispo[38] dotandola, se haze una processión en la qual se hazen çinco[39] estaçiones. Aparejan para ella lo siguiente: tiran el arca do se puso el sacramento y entoldan las andas, y ponen las tablas que estan pintadas como piedras en la delantera de las andas, o de otra qualquier mejor manera que puede, o como lo suelen poner los años pasados.

Estan dentro puestos dos angeles de los dorados que estan puestos en el altar mayor que tengan un paño de lienço en que esten pintadas o señaladas algunas çicatriçes. Estan assi mismo hechos unos setos de cañas en derredor del monumento, entretalladas en ellas algunas verduras flores y laureles: trahen los sacristanes la custodia de la capilla real porque es pequeña y vistosa la qual lleva el hebdomadario en la proçession ayudandole el diacono y el subdiacono y cada estaçión ponenla en el altar y dize alli su oraçión,[40] procurando de buscar algunas personas que sepan hazer música de aves.[41] Aparejan tres altares, uno a la puerta del choro en el qual ponen la ymagen de nuestra Señora de vulto: este ha de estar cubierto con una cortina que se pueda quitar y poner. Aparejan assi mismo otro altar que esta a la puerta del vestuario, o entran en la capilla real, y alli se haze otra estaçión.[42] E assi mismo aparejan otro altar a la puerta del baptismo, con otra ymagen de nuestra Señora: ha quitado el campanero[43] todos los escaños y vancos que ay en la yglesia, y ponelos en el atrio[44] della, porque aquella noche este la yglesia desocupada.

Tienen assi mismo bien estudiado dos niños que tengan muy buenas bozes:

---

[38] Por el ... arzobispo] The name is crossed out in A and in the margin is written, *Martin de Ayala obispo desta iglesia y por la cofradia* (followed by one other word which I could not make out). The phrase *desta iglesia* may refer either to Guadix or Segovia, for Martin de Ayala was bishop by turn in both places. A loose folio in a modern hand inserted within the Segovia manuscript reads: "Codice en pergamino del siglo XVI (1560 a 1566) regalado a la santa Iglesia de Segovia por D. Martin Perez de Ayala, obispo primero de Guadix despues de Segovia y por fin arzobispo de Valencia, donde murió agosto de 1566."

[39] cinco] quarto (A).

[40] de la capilla real ... oraçión] la qual llevan en las andas quatro presbiteros: haziendo las estaciones que suelen hazer en las demas processiones y en cada una digan una oracion con un verso, parandose con reposo y a la estacion postrera dizen *regina celi* con una oracion (A). This has been added in the margin, and the corresponding part in the text crossed out.

[41] música de aves: Villanueva (I, 153) speaks of an ancient custom observed at the cathedral of Valencia which perhaps helps to explain this rather intriguing phrase in the Granada manuscript: "En la misa de la vigilia de la Ascension del Señor conserva esta Iglesia una costumbre antigua, cuyo origen no he podido averiguar. Pónese un barreño con agua al lado derecho del crucero, y juntamente una espuerta llena de silbatos de caña para distribuir a los niños que acuden como a son de campana. El sonido de estos sencillos instrumentos llenos de agua remeda el canto de los páxaros, cuya alegría en dia de tanto gozo para todo el mundo, parece que quisieron recordar los autores de este uso."

[42] en el qual ... estación] Much of this passage has been crossed out, and it is difficult to tell just what the reading should be.

[43] campanero] replaced by sacristan (A).

[44] atrio] replaced by una capilla (A).

> Jhesum quem queritis non est hic sed surrexit ecce locus ubi possuerunt eum. Ite vos in Galileam ibi eum videbitis sicut dixit vobis: alleluya, alleluya, alleluya.

Estos an de estar vestidos como angeles con amitos sobre las cabezas y con alvas de las mas ricas y estolas de brocado que las tengan puestas como presbiteros, y en las cabezas guirnaldas ricas.

Estos han de tener cada uno una hacha en las manos: tiene cuidado de hazer que sepan y hagan esto el sochantre o el maestro de capilla o qualquiera dellos que el cabildo lo encomendare.

Dize las oraciones la dignidad que ha de celebrar que va vestido con una capa; vistesse de diacono el canonigo del evangelio y de subdiacono el hebdomadario; toman las capas dos canonigos; ay quatro acolitos dos que van con la cruz y dos con la custodia; ay turibularios; van dos dignidades y dos canonigos y dos racioneros vestidos que llevan las varas del palio de brocado sobre la custodia como el jueves y viernes sancto.

Hordenasse la procession desta manera; dos horas hantes del alva[45] repican todas las campanas y hazen tres pausas que duran una hora. En tanto vienen todos los clerigos y vestidos todos los que se han de vestir para hazer el oficio; pone el maestro de cerimonias si es de missa ‹u› otro sacerdote el sacramento en la custodia; y acabadas las tres pausas de repicar hordenan la procession que este desde el choro hasta las gradas del altar mayor y assi hordenada salen por la puerta de la sacristia la cruz grande con sus acolitos y cirios delante a los quales preçeda el pertiguero haziendo lugar hasta el altar mayor donde esta la custodia con el sancto sacramento y alli hordenanse todos en proçession y los de las varas tomanlas y hincanse alli los ministros de rodillas y estando todos assi va solamente la cruz con los acolitos que estan con ella y tras la cruz los cantores a do esta el monumento y llegados cantan los cantores a favordon:

> quis revolvet nobis lapidem ab hostio monumenti.

E antes que los cantores digan la postrera syllaba de la diçción *monumenti*, ha de tener cuidado uno de hazer caer la piedra que esta a la puerta del monumento y tañen las trompetas y juntamente sueltan dos escopetas[46] si no hazen daño a los hornamentos; y salen los dos angeles ataviados como se dixo con sendas hachas uno de una parte del monumento, y otro de otra y ponense a los cantos del arco del monumento; y hazen ynclinación al monumento y dizen

> Jhesum quem queritis, etc.

como es dicho; y luego empiezan los cantores *Te Deum laudamus*.

Since medieval Castilian texts with the liturgical Easter play are almost non-existent, it is perhaps somewhat surprising to encounter this late manifestation of one at Granada. The question of its origin arises. Obviously at the late date of 1500-30, a ceremony such as this might have come from almost anywhere. The principal clue to the source is probably found in the statement

---

[45] dos oras . . . alva] en acabando las maytines (A).
[46] escopetas] replaced by arcabuzes (A).

of the manuscript that the archbishop, Anton de Rojas, endowed the performance and in a phrase of the Segovia codex associating the manuscript with Catalonia. In approving the Granada ceremonies for continued usage, Gaspar de Avalos, who was archbishop there in 1530, wrote as follows:[47]

> Avemos visto y con diligencia exsaminado el libro en que se contiene las buenas y loables costumbres y ceremonias desta sancta yglesia, el qual libro llaman la consueta.

The word *consueta*, as has been indicated, is a Catalan term. Investigation reveals that Antonio de Rojas came to Granada in 1508 from Palma de Mallorca, a city which, as we shall presently see, was one of the chief European centers of the liturgical drama in the Middle Ages. De Rojas had been bishop there from 1496 until 1508, a period when the liturgical drama was at its height in the island city.[48] It must be noted, however, that none of the Mallorcan liturgical plays bears much resemblance to the one described here.

The same combination of the liturgical *Elevatio* and a simplified Easter play, if one may call it that, was practised at Palencia from 1500 until at least 1550. In reality the ceremony in this city involved what might be designated as incidental dramatic movement rather than a play. It is described in a manuscript found in the Chapter library at Palencia, entitled, *Copia literal de el Libro titulado Consuetudinario, o Ceremonial de la Santa Iglesia de Palencia, que por los años de 1550, compiló el Doctor Don Juan de Arce, canonigo*; the copyist was Juan Manuel Largo Paredes, who wrote in 1807:[49]

> Domingo de Pasqua a la una hora despues de media noche el sacristan hace el señal a Maytines ... por manera que en dando las dos se comiencen los Maytines.
>
> . . . .
>
> Acabados los maytines que serán casi al Alba la procesion se ordena, y van todos con cirios ardiendo, y otros ocho o diez Beneficiados de los mas nuebos con achas, y seis caperos, dos Dignidades y quatro canonigos, y todos con silencio van en Procesion hasta el Monumento, y puestos todos de Rodillas, el Preste con dos Acolitos con cirios en las Candaleras, y otros dos incensarios, y algunos con achas, y tambien el Sacristan suben al Monumento. Y antes que se quite el velo el Preste que deve de ser el Prelado, ó el Dean, ú otra persona constituida en Dignidad abre el arce, é inciensa el Sacramento, y tomando el Relicario en las manos se buelve al Pueblo, y luego dos niños del coro vestidos a manera de Angeles con achas ardiendo en las manos cantan *Surrexit dominus de sepulcro, allelluya*, y los cantores responden *qui pro novis*, etc. Y esto se canta tres veces, una

---

[47] Segovia manuscript, fol. 109ᵛ.
[48] In its list of the archbishops of Granada, the *Inventario General* at the Chapter library of this city states (fol. 112): "Don Anton de Roxas desde 1509 hasta 23 de julio de 1524 que avisó al cavildo su promoción a Palencia y al Patriarcado." Regarding his dates at Palma and elsewhere, see Villanueva, *Viage literario*, XXII, 90-95, and Florez, *España Sagrada*, XXVI, 418.
[49] Fol. 42-43ᵛ; the original manuscript, it seems, is lost.

> mas alta que otra, y la tercera vez derriban el velo, y el que tubiere el Sacramento le alce con veneración para que mejor se adore, y tocan las trompetas, y otros instrumentos, cantores y organos y campanas, y como ovieren acavado el Sochantre comienza *Te Deum laudamus*.
>
> . . . .
>
> Este sobre dicha memoria de los maytines y procesión con el Sacramento de la manera que dicha es, dotó Dⁿ Christoval de Merodio, Maestre escuela, y canonigo de ella, y comenzose á hacer la primera vez en el año de 1500 – por dotacion de la qual dio al Cavildo 800 (?) maravedis.

A final example of liturgical dramatic activity from regions west of Catalonia concerns the cathedral of León. From at least the fifteenth century onward, the Sibylline prophecy was sung in this cathedral in much the same manner as it was at Toledo. The liturgical books themselves do not speak of any impersonation of the Sibyl. According to a manuscript which R. Rodriguez dates as thirteenth century,[50] after the sixth lesson of the Christmas office, two canons sang the *Judicii signum*; the *Liber Cantorum* of the fifteenth century has preserved the words and the music.[51] In the cathedral account books, however, entries begin to appear in the fifteenth century speaking of the dress of the Sibyl. Rodriguez, who has studied these accounts, writes as follows (p. 23):

> Desde el siglo XV, por los Libros de Cuentas y Rentas de Fábrica, se puede colegir el atuendo o atavío de la Sibila. Llegaba a la Catedral, desde una dependencia de la misma, vestida con gran riqueza, bien pintada y montada en bien enjaezado caballo, con mucho acompañamiento de mozos, tambores, salterios, trompetas, sonajas y rabeles, más los chiquillos y curiosos que no serían pocos.

The same commentator adds that this ceremony must have been suppressed about the middle of the sixteenth century, since the account books speak of a restoration of it a few years later. A decision of the León Chapter, dated December 4, 1581, declares:

> Ordenaron y mandaron que de aquí en adelante la noche de Navidad se cantase la Sibila como se solia hacer, y que el Sr. Administrador tuviese cuidado de que se aderezase, y el Maestro de ceremonias de informarse de Toledo a qué tiempo y hora se ha de cantar, y el Maestro de Capilla tuviese cuidado de instruir un mochacho que mejor la cante.

Precisely as at Toledo, then, evidences of an impersonated Sibyl first appear at León in the fifteenth century. This does not prove, of course, that the practice was not in vogue at León before this time; nonetheless it would appear that the custom was not introduced before the fourteenth century, since until that date two canons sang the prophecy.

---

[50] 'El Canto de la Sibila en la catedral de León', p. 14.
[51] León, Bibl. Capit., MS 23, fol. 5-8; the Sibylline text is in Latin.

Research has proved that there is no shortage of Spanish texts with the *Judicii signum*. Medieval liturgical manuscripts and early printed books attest to its popularity throughout the entire Hispanic peninsula from Pamplona to Seville, and from Mallorca to Compostella. The texts vary from the tenth century to the present day, the oldest having been written in the vicinity of Burgos around 947.[52] When the Sibylline prophecies were delivered on Christmas Eve, probably in many places they were accompanied by impersonation; of this, however, without more definite evidence, we cannot be certain in any individual case.[53]

The same may be said of Christmas Lauds. In many churches the antiphon *Pastores dicite* and its response were repeated several times during the chanting of the fifth psalm, the response often being rendered by choir-boys behind the altar. Villanueva's paraphrase of this ceremony from a medieval Valencian breviary has often been cited by historians of the drama. The same may also be found in medieval manuscripts, or sixteenth century texts, from such places as Orense, Avila, Burgos, Palencia, and Compostella, not to mention other centers in Eastern Spain. In these cities choir-boys may have been attired as shepherds for the Christmas office as at Toledo, but there is no express indication that such was the case.

Here, perhaps, it should be said that the medieval practice of electing a "boy-bishop" for the feast of the Holy Innocents on December 28 was as common throughout Spain as it was in the rest of Europe. It has become a custom, when speaking of the medieval liturgical drama, to devote a few pages to this *episcopellus*, as he was generally called. This is so because on Holy Innocents Day the elected choir-boy engaged in activities which bordered upon drama. He took the place of the real bishop in the liturgical ceremonies, was dressed in episcopal attire, gave the bishop's blessing, and among other things, usually delivered a satirical sermon, in the course of which he pretended to be one of the Innocents who had escaped the persecution of Herod. Such activites as these, and others in which the boy-bishop took part, were further manifestations of the festive Christmas spirit which inspired such productions as the Procession of Prophets, the *Officium Pastorum*, and the Visit of the Three Wise Men. Each rank of ecclesiastic had his special day in the Christmas season. The deacons were honored on December 26, the feast of St. Stephen, the priests on December 27, the feast of St. John, the choir boys, with their "bishop", on December 28, Innocents Day, and the subdeacons on January 1, or January 6. In Spain the boy-bishop and his antics were known at Toledo, Palencia, Zaragoza, Seville, Málaga, Salamanca, Lérida, Gerona, Vich, Mallor-

---

[52] Most now hold that the music for the Burgos text was added in the late eleventh century; see S. Corbin, 'Le *Cantus Sibyllae*: origines et premiers textes', *Revue de musicologie*, XXXI (1952), 6. The manuscript is now found at Córdoba, Bibl. Capit., MS 1 (*olim* 72), the chant on fol. 69b.

[53] The manuscripts containing the chant of the Sibyl are indicated in the list of liturgical sources consulted for this study, pp. 198-213.

ca, and many other places. Perhaps the one place in the world where the custom has continued without interruption down to the present day is the Benedictine monastery of Montserrat; here, however, the ceremony has always maintained a dignified and charming character, and is of a strictly non-liturgical nature.

If the custom of the boy-bishop was sometimes closely allied with the drama of the Christmas season, it must be pointed out with Young (I, 106-111), that it never in itself became a genuine dramatic piece. For this reason a full account of this custom is not included in the present study.[54]

In review, then, in regions of Spain west of Catalonia, we find the following examples of liturgical drama, or of ceremonies closely connected with it. For the Easter season, the *Quem quaeritis* trope at Huesca and Zaragoza, a simple *Visitatio Sepulchri* at Silos and Compostella, and very late plays (sixteenth century) at Granada, Guadix, Palencia, and perhaps Segovia; for the Christmas season, the *Quem quaeritis* trope from Huesca, the Toledo *Representatio Pastorum* during Lauds, and the dramatic monologue of the Sibyl at Toledo and León.[55]

This list of plays is not, indeed, very lengthy. One wonders at once if there were not many more liturgical plays put on in this part of Spain during the Middle Ages. If not, how is the lack to be explained? In the following chapter, some attempt shall be made to provide an answer to these questions.

[54] A few additional observations, along with a bibliography on this practice in Spain, may be found in the Appendix.
[55] The liturgical Easter play, listed by Young (I, 576) as being found in a *Processionale Navarrense*, comes in reality from the Collège de Navarre in Paris.

CHAPTER 6

REASONS FOR THE SCARCITY OF LITURGICAL PLAYS WEST OF CATALONIA

It has been generally held until the present that the liturgical drama *did* flourish in Castile during the Middle Ages, and that it was brought there by the French Cluniac monks at the time of the change of rite. It is conjectured that, once established, the Latin liturgical plays evolved into the vernacular religious plays, as they did in France and elsewhere. At all events many factors point to a rich medieval tradition of religious plays in Spain. If almost no examples of Spanish liturgical plays are given, it is usually pointed out that the medieval liturgical manuscripts have been lost.

This reason, however, can no longer be so facilely advanced. Doubtless, it is only too true that a countless number of Spanish manuscripts have been irrevocably lost, a far greater percentage, it seems, than in neigboring lands. Nevertheless research has shown that in the cathedral archives and the public libraries of Spain, many liturgical manuscripts are still extant, enough, in any case, to give a representative idea of Spanish liturgical usage in the Middle Ages. In all, not taking into consideration numerous Catalan texts, we have personally examined more than 315 such manuscripts and early printed books, all of them the type that contain liturgical plays in other countries. Of this number, 117 were breviaries, and 18 were *ordinaria*, two classes of liturgical works which retain approximately sixty-five per cent of the plays edited by Professor Karl Young. If these manuscripts contain no liturgical plays in Castile, might it not be a strong indication that the tradition never became firmly established there?

The most important manuscript in this consideration is the *ordinarium*. This type of liturgical work describes, generally in minute detail, all the liturgical ceremonies conducted in a certain church or monastery throughout the entire year. If during the Middle Ages liturgical plays were performed in the church or monastery in question, almost invariably some mention of them is made in the *ordinarium*. This is especially true of the Easter play. In the case of the *Visitatio Sepulchri*, only one exception to this rule has come to my attention.[1]

---

[1] The exception is the monastery of Fleury. Although the famous "play-book" from this monastery is of the thirteenth century, an *ordinarium* of Fleury written in the same period (Orléans, Bibl. Mun., MS 129) does not mention the Easter *Visitatio* found in the play-book. It may be noted that recently this fact has been used by Miss Solange Corbin as an argument that the play-book was not in reality written at Fleury; see 'Le Manuscrit 201 d'Orléans, drames liturgiques dits de Fleury', *Romania*, LXXIV (1953), 1-43. Actually this argument probably does not carry too much weight in this particular instance. The plays of this monastery are of

Thanks to the medieval and Renaissance *ordinaria* which have been preserved in Spain, we possess detailed descriptions of the liturgical ceremonies that were observed at Palencia in the fourteenth century; at the Benedictine monastery of San Millán de la Cogolla from the thirteenth to the fifteenth century; at Huesca, Burgo de Osma, Segovia, Toledo, and the Benedictine monastery of Valladolid in the fifteenth century; and at Zaragoza and Seville in the following century. The only signs of liturgical plays in these manuscripts are the Christmas and Sibyl ceremonies at Toledo. This evidence seems to indicate that liturgical plays were not the custom in the cities mentioned during the medieval period, exception being made for Toledo. We can be reasonably certain of this as regards the Easter play, for once this piece had been introduced into the liturgical customs of a certain church or monastery, it generally persisted there until at least about 1500.

The brief Easter performances at Granada and Guadix are found in late sixteenth century manuscripts, and as has been observed, these practices may have been introduced from some region like Catalonia. Compostella presents a unique case because of its peculiarly close relationship with the other countries of Europe from the eleventh century onward. As for the liturgical Latin Epiphany play, no text has as yet been found any place in Spain, nor has the liturgical *Peregrinus* play been found west of Catalonia.[2]

In view of these facts, one is inclined to conclude that the liturgical drama penetrated Castile and non-Catalonian Spain sporadically, and on a very limited scale, rather than as a vast, general movement. Exception might perhaps be made for the ceremony of the impersonated Sibyl, but as yet there is record even of this practice only at Toledo and León. In our estimation it is not a mere coincidence that research recently undertaken by Miss Corbin in Portugal has produced similar, or even less fruitful, results. The distinguished French musicologist writes as follows:[3]

> Par un malheureux hasard, ou plutôt par phénomène singulier, le drame sacré ou mystère est à peu près absent des textes portugais médiévaux, alors qu'il s'est épanoui avec tant d'éclat dans le reste de l'Occident.
> . . . .
> En tout cas, aucune trace ne subsiste, dans les livres liturgiques connus soit dans leur entier soit par fragments, ni de mystères joués à l'église ou sur le parvis, ni de drames sacrés qui prolongent la liturgie dans tant d'églises d'Occident. Les tropes mêmes sont extrêmement rares ...

---

a very developed type, and dramatic historians have had considerable difficulty in ascertaining the relation of many of them to the liturgy. It is quite possible, in my opinion, that these plays were not performed as an integral part of the regular liturgical ceremonies, but as distinct from them, and perhaps even at another time of the day. This would explain why the *Visitatio Sepulchri* does not appear in the *Ordinarium*.

[2] I prescind here, of course, from the Sicilian plays contained in manuscripts at the Biblioteca Nacional in Madrid.

[3] *Essai sur la musique portugaise au Moyen-Age, 1100-1385*, pp. 271-273.

Des savants portugais nous avaient fait remarquer cette lacune avec une trace de mélancolie. Un an de recherches prouve qu'il y a bien en effet lacune.

Actually Miss Corbin did discover one small liturgical Christmas play, a little shepherd ceremony at Lauds, comparable to the one described in the fourteenth century Toledo breviary. The text is found in a fourteenth century breviary from the monastery of the Holy Cross at Coimbra. This monastery, Miss Corbin informs us, was founded in 1132, and from the beginning accepted the customs of St. Ruf of Avignon; it had no relations with Cluny.[4]

How does one account for the failure of the liturgical drama to penetrate Castile as a widespread movement? The most plausible reasons are perhaps threefold. First of all, it must be remembered that the Roman-French rite was brought into Spain as a *reform* of the liturgy. Since this was the case, the monks and clerics entrusted with the establishment of this reform were probably not particularly anxious to introduce such novel and non-essential ceremonies as liturgical plays. This would have been so especially at the outset.

Secondly, a large percentage of the monks actively engaged in the establishment of the new rite came, as we have previously seen, from Cluny and from monasteries akin to it in spirit and custom; many Spanish monasteries in the eleventh and twelfth centuries were submitted directly to Cluny. Those who have asserted that monks from the Burgundian monastery brought the liturgical plays to Spain, have failed to advert to the fact that no such plays have ever been found at Cluny or at any of its priories.[5] At Cluny the monastic breviary with twelve lessons for Easter Matins was used. Extremely rare are the instances of Easter plays, or of any other liturgical plays, found at monasteries which used a breviary of this type. Karl Young has found only two examples of it in all of Europe. Discussing one of these, he states:[6]

> The interest of the *Officium Sepulchri* from this manuscript (a Benedictine *Ordinarium* of German origin), arises not only from the text of the dramatic office itself, but also from the fact that in this case the *Officium* was sung in a monastery where at Easter the monastic *cursus* had not given way to the Roman .... We have before us, then, one of the rare examples of an *Officium Sepulchri* that was sung after the twelfth respond.

---

[4] pp. 91 *sqq*. The manuscript is now located in the Municipal Library of Porto, MS 1151, where it is listed as a psalter. Miss Corbin writes of the ceremony: "Le Psautier . . . nous offre cependant une petite pastorale, qui prend place à Laudes dans la nuit de Noël. S'adressant aux Pasteurs, on leur chante l'antienne classique *Pastores, dicite quidnam vidistis et annunciate Christi nativitatem*. Ici la rubrique indique *respondeant pastores: infantem vidimus, pannis involutum, et choros angelorum laudantes Salvatorem*. C'est alors seulement qu'on chante le psaume *Laudate*" (*op. cit.*, p. 293).

[5] In her book on this monastery, *Monastic Life at Cluny, 910-1157*, p. 107, Miss Evans writes: "I have come across no evidence of religious drama at Cluny itself."

[6] 'Some texts of Liturgical Plays', p. 310; see also *The Drama of the Medieval Church*, I, 312, 547, 596-597.

More recently Dom K. Hallinger, treating this question at considerable length, concludes that because the twelve-lesson office was used at Cluny, the Easter play did not exist there: "dieser Brauch unkluniazensisch ist."[7]

It appears, then, that Cluny itself and the liturgical drama were not intimately linked. As a consequence monks who came to Castile directly from Cluny probably did not bring liturgical plays with them. The same was likely true of those who came from Cluniac priories, and we have seen the important role played by these monks in eleventh and twelfth century Spain. At all events it is a point which calls for reflection. Moreover it is interesting to recall that Santo Domingo de Silos, the one Spanish monastery in which a liturgical play does appear, shows no evidence of having had any direct connection with Cluny.[8]

A final factor which must be considered is the late date of the change in liturgical rite. The official change was pronounced in 1080; Toledo was reconquered even later, in 1085. Precisely at this time another important historical phenomenon was taking place: vernacular literature was beginning to come into prominence.

The eminent scholar, Menéndez Pidal, ascribes the famous Spanish play, the *Auto de los Reyes Magos*, on scribal and linguistic grounds, to the middle of the twelfth century.[9] Certain dramatic historians seem to claim that this play represented, already at this date, an established tradition of vernacular drama.[10] If these estimates are correct, and if one remembers that in the

---

[7] *Gorze-Kluny* (Romae, 1950-51), II, 906-910; see also André Wilmart, 'Le Samedi-Saint monastique', *Revue bénédictine*, XXXIV (1922), 159-163.

[8] The question of abbeys which were reformed by Cluny after the liturgical plays were already a custom there, is a different matter. Miss Wright, in her study, *The Dissemination of the Liturgical Drama in France*, has devoted some observations to this point which should be recorded here: "Evidence that the Cluniac order disapproved of the liturgical drama is chiefly negative (that is, if I interpret Miss Wright correctly, Cluny apparently disapproved of the liturgical drama, but the only "evidence" we have of this disapproval is of a negative nature, for example, the complete lack of plays from Cluniac liturgical manuscripts). Cluny was the product of a reforming spirit and in the beginning at least was characterized by a stricter discipline than the Benedictine order. Moreover, the tendency toward conservatism and uniformity of service was doubtless stronger within this closely-knit body . . . .

At all events, it is a noteworthy fact that there are no extant plays from Cluny itself or from any of its priories, although St. Martial of Limoges and Fleury, perhaps the two most important churches in the history of the liturgical drama, were both reformed by Cluny. Fleury, however, provides no argument either for or against Cluny's hostility to plays, since it never adopted the Cluniac regulations. The case of St. Martial is somewhat different. This monastery was reformed later than Fleury (in 1063) when the Cluniac order was fully developed, and it seems to have been closely associated with Cluny for half a century. Moreover, some of the plays from St. Martial are preserved in manuscripts which post-date Cluniac control. It seems possible that the Cluniac administrators, while not sanctioning the plays in their own priories, allowed them to be retained in this old and powerful abbey, where the *Quem quaeritis*, at least, had been sung from the tenth century" (pp. 9-11). It may be noted that Saint-Martial did not become a priory of Cluny, but retained its title of abbey.

[9] *Cantar de Mío Cid*, I, 144.

[10] Gillet affirms: "The records of the medieval drama in the Peninsula, with the exception of a few tropes, begin in the middle of the twelfth century with the startling *Auto de los Reyes Magos*,

period immediately subsequent to the change in rite there was likely some hestitation on the part of ecclesiastical authorities to introduce liturgical plays, the dates 1085 and 1150 are brought even closer together. Until fairly recently it was the more common opinion that the source of the *Auto de los Reyes Magos* was one of the Latin liturgical plays brought from France.[11] Miss Sturdevant, however, in her excellent study on this play, has shown rather conclusively that the immediate source was *not* a typical eleventh-century Latin liturgical play, but in all probability a *vernacular* work.[12] After carefully comparing the Spanish play with the known versions of the Latin Three Kings play from the point of view of phraseology, dramatic structure, and content, Miss Sturdevant observes as follows:[13] "The conclusion, then, to be drawn from a comparative study of the Latin liturgical plays and the *Reyes Magos*, is that there is *no evidence of any direct relation between them.*"

Proceeding to examine the six main points which differentiate the Spanish piece from the Latin plays in dramatic structure, Miss Sturdevant finds that all but one of these items are common to the vernacular plays.[14] Moreover she shows that the motif peculiar to the Spanish *Auto* – the use of gifts by the three kings not as a sign of adoration, but as *tests* of the Christ Child's divinity – is repeatedly found in another vernacular literary type, the French narrative poems of the Infancy. The similarities in every way between the Spanish play and these narrative poems establish beyond a doubt that there was a direct relation between them; besides the important test of gifts, the Three Kings in both are on a pilgrimage; in both the star has appeared twelve or thirteen days previously; and the verbal resemblances are even more striking:

Poems of the Infancy	Reyes Magos
bien savoient por verité que Dieu estoit en terre né (Bib. Nat. 1526)	bien lo veo que es verdad certas nacido es in tirra
Si c'est or prent de main . . . il serra reis en tere. (Brit. Mus., Cott. Vit. D III)	Si fure rei de terra el oro quera
s'il le prenoit, qu'il seroit rois par le mierre	si fure omne mortal, la mira tomara

entirely in the vernacular and so far advanced in characterization and metrical skill as to imply a considerable previous development" (*Memorias*, p. 266).
[11] See Fitzmaurice-Kelly, *A New History of Spanish Literature*, (Oxford, 1926), p. 7; Morel-Fatio, review of Hartmann's dissertation on the Three Kings play, *Romania*, IX (1880), 467-468; Ford, *Old Spanish Readings*, p. 99.
[12] *Misterio de los Reyes Magos: Its Position in the Development of the Mediaeval Legend of the Three Kings* (Baltimore and Paris, 1927).
[13] pp. 54-55; the italics are mine.
[14] They are found also in the late Latin transitional piece from Benediktbeuern.

>   s'il le prenoit .... disoient
>   que il seroit mortex.
>   (Bib. Nat. 1526)
>
>   que il seroit homme mortal
>   (Bib. Nat. 9588)

In the light of this evidence, Miss Sturdevant concludes (p. 79): "The adoption of a peculiar motif of the legend, and close verbal similarities prove . . . the influence of the French narrative poems of the Infancy as an essential vernacular and non-dramatic source of the Spanish play."

If the date given by Menéndez Pidal is correct, it would mean that the vernacular religious drama was at least beginning by 1150. If there is a close relationship between the *Auto de los Reyes Magos*, on the one hand, and the French plays and poems of the Infancy, on the other, as there seems to be, it would appear that the vernacular religious drama was already in progress *before* 1150. The findings of Miss Sturdevant could have important implications which she does not put forward. To suggest the possibility of an influence of French *vernacular* plays on the Spanish *Auto* is to suggest that the French vernacular drama had developed before the middle of the twelfth century.

The question of the date of the first plays in French is a point seldom broached by dramatic historians. The celebrated *Jeu d'Adam*, generally considered the oldest known example of a play written predominantly in French, is usually dated about the third quarter of the twelfth century.[15] Judging from the content and the skilful dramatic technique of this little masterpiece, however, the play is probably by no means the first to have been composed in French. The only part of the play intimately connected with the earlier liturgical drama is the Procession of Prophets; neither the delightful scene with Adam and Eve, nor the episode of Cain and Abel, is previously found in any liturgical play. In all likelihood plays of a simpler and more transitional nature had prepared the way for the *Jeu d'Adam*. Just when such plays began to be written, however, has been left a moot question.

In the liturgical drama itself, French first appears in the celebrated *Sponsus*. The greatest authority on this play, the late L.-P. Thomas, affirms in his recent critical edition of the text that the manuscript in which the *Sponsus* appears was written during the last few years of the eleventh century.[16] He states, moreover, that the text is only an adaptation from some work composed in the north of France; consequently the original must have been written somewhat earlier.

Could it not be possible that the practice of composing religious plays in the vernacular developed in the same period that vernacular poetry began

---

[15] This is the date assigned to the play in the latest comprehensive work on French medieval drama; see Grace Frank, *The Medieval French Drama* (1954), p. 76. Studer affirmed in 1918: "The date of composition undoubtedly falls within the period 1146-1174, and the probabilities are that it comes much nearer the earlier than the later limit" (*Le Mystère d'Adam*, intro., p. lvi).

[16] *Le Sponsus* (1951), p. 2.

achieving a position of prominence, that is, around the first half of the twelfth century? If that did happen, it would help explain the surprising lack of liturgical plays in medieval Spanish service books. If French and Spanish plays were being written, there would be no need to introduce the earlier and more elementary Latin liturgical play. It would appear from the *Auto* that the vernacular religious plays were performed in Castile in the twelfth century, and a century later Alphonse the Tenth spoke of religious plays as a common Castilian practice. In our opinion, whatever the reason, and whatever the date, when religious plays began to be introduced in Castile on a large scale, they were already in the vernacular.

It should be remembered that, in all probability, proportionately more medieval vernacular plays have been lost than Latin plays. This applies to every country in Europe. The Latin liturgical plays are preserved in great numbers, because they were written in manuscripts which were not composed for the sake of the plays, but for use in the liturgical services. Manuscripts such as these had more chance of survival. The vernacular plays, especially the simpler ones, would have been of a more informal and impromptu nature. For that reason they were no doubt frequently consigned to loose folio sheets which were easily lost, or destroyed once the custom of presenting plays, or the particular play in question, had fallen into desuetude. Often in the presentation of vernacular plays, for the sake of convenience, the parts of each "player" were written on separate folios, and hence could be even more easily lost.[17] The more elementary vernacular religious plays were oftentimes not even put in writing, but were simply transmitted by oral tradition.[18]

All evidence weighed, then, it appears to us that in the parts of Spain thus far considered, the Latin liturgical plays were never introduced in very large numbers. Miss Corbin, it should be remembered, has arrived at the same conclusion for Portugal. Three possible reasons have been suggested for this lack: 1. the introduction of the Roman-French rite as a *reform* of the liturgy; 2. the important role played in the introduction of this rite, and in Spanish ecclesiastical life in general, by monks from Cluny and Cluniac priories; 3. the possibility that the vernacular drama had already developed when religious plays began to penetrate Central and Western Spain as a general practice. That some factors such as these must have been at work, will appear even more probable, I believe, when we discover the remarkable good fortune enjoyed by the liturgical drama in the neighboring region of Catalonia.

---

[17] Evidence of such procedure is found, for example, in the Sulmona Passion Play (Young, I, 701-708), in the famous Shrewsbury fragments (Young, II, 514), and in the plays from Palma de Mallorca; see below, pp. 121-122.

[18] Concerning this point, see the very interesting article of López Santos, 'Autos del Nacimiento Leoneses', pp. 7-32. López informs us that today, in some small villages of León, the religious plays are still performed in the churches after Matins on Christmas Eve. The plays which he describes obviously represent a very ancient tradition, and help us understand what likely took place in some Spanish churches during the Middle Ages. I quote a few significant passages of López's article in the Appendix.

CHAPTER 7

LITURGICAL PLAYS IN CATALONIA: VICH AND THE SEO DE URGEL

EVEN a cursory examination of some of the liturgical documents of Catalonia quickly reveals that this part of Spain was one of the great centers of the liturgical drama in the Middle Ages. Here, unlike Castile, wherever medieval liturgical manuscripts remain in any great number, almost invariably some record of tropes and plays is likewise found. This holds true especially in the cathedral cities and towns. By no means an exception is the city of Vich, situated some forty miles from the French frontier.

The Vich cathedral library possesses one of the richest collections of medieval liturgical manuscripts in Spain. Among these is the Ripoll troper which contains the oldest Catalan tropes and plays which have come down to us. The two most ancient Easter tropes are found together on the second folio of this manuscript:[1]

VERSOS

Vbi est Cristus, meus Dominus et filius excelsi? Eamus uidere sepulcrum.
Alleluia, ad sepulcrum residens angelus nunciat resurrexisse Cristum.
En ecce completum est illud quod olim ipse per prophetam dixerat,[2] ad
Patrem taliter inquiens: Resurrexi.

IN RESURRECIONE

Ora est, psallite, iubet domnus canere, eia dicite!
Quem queritis in sepulcro, cristicole?
Ihesum nazarenum crucifixum, o celicole.
Non est hic, surrexit sicut predixerat;
ite nunciate quia surrexit dicentes: Resurrexi.

The texts before us constitute two different versions of the traditional Easter trope, as is indicated by the first word of the introit of the Mass, *Resurrexi*, which follows each one. The first portion presents a rather striking anomaly:

---

[1] MS 105 (olim 111); the part of the codex in which the tropes appear was written in the eleventh century. The catalogue numbers presently employed at the Vich cathedral library are those of Gudiol, 'Catalèg dels manuscrits de Vich', *Butlleti de la Biblioteca de Catalunya*, VI-VIII (1920-32). The index formerly followed was that of Villanueva, 'Códices e incunables de la Catedral de Vich', *Boletín de la Real Academia de la Historia*, XXV (1894), 320-331. Both tropes have been previously edited by Young, 'Some Texts of Liturgical Plays', p. 308, and the first one only by the same author in *The Drama of the Medieval Church*, I, 570, and by Anglès, *La Música a Catalunya fins al segle XIII*, p. 271. Unless otherwise stated, all future references to Anglès shall be to this work. The manuscript provides music.
[2] dixerat] dixerad (MS).

no other example has as yet been found of the form *Ubi est Christus meus*, etc. as a composition distinct from the usual *Quem quaeritis* trope. Since in a later manuscript, which is probably also from Ripoll, the two tropes appear as a single unit, it seems that at this monastery the compositions were sung first as separate entities, and then were subsequently united.

Young has already pointed out that "the liturgical-dramatic texts contained in this manuscript are of unusual interest."[3] He was thinking chiefly of the plays it retains, of one of which he remarks: "The office ... is unique in the form found here. The latter part ... is especially important in showing an embryonic stage in the development of this office."[3] He might have said the same, I think, of the trope now before us.

In the previous chapters of this study, we have noted that outside Catalonia the antiphon *Ubi est*, etc. has been found only at Compostella, St. Martial and Poitiers. Generally St. Martial has been regarded as its chief disseminator. In actual fact the Ripoll manuscript is the oldest which exhibits the phrase, since the St. Martial play-book in which the antiphon occurs could not have been written before 1096. The date, the embryonic state of the trope in the Ripoll manuscript, and the fact that the trope was extremely popular everywhere in Catalonia throughout the Middle Ages, and rarely elsewhere, suggest that this particular composition originated at the monastery of Ripoll.

The two pieces appear as a single trope in Manuscript 106:[4]

IN DIE SANCTO PASCHE TROPUS

Ora est, psallite; iubet domnus canere; eia dicite!
Vbi est Christus, meus Dominus et filius excelsi? Eamus uidere sepulcrum.
Quem queritis in sepulcro, Christicole?
Ihesum Nazarenum crucifixum, o celicole.
Non est hic, surrexit sicut predixerat; ite, nunciate quia surrexit, dicentes:
Alleluia, ad sepulcrum residens angelus nunciat resurrexisse Christum.
En ecce completum est illud quod olim ipse per prophetam dixerat, ad Patrem taliter inquiens:
Resurrexi.

The popularity of this version of the *Quem quaeritis* trope in Catalonia is shown by its appearance in the service-books of many other cathedral and

---

[3] 'Some Texts of Liturgical Plays', p. 302.
[4] Troparium saec. xii-xiii, fol. 48ᵛ. The provenance of this manuscript is not certain. It has been assigned by some to Ripoll and by others to Vich, and more lately Anglès suggests that it may have been written at the Augustinian monastery of Manlleu. Since Manlleu is only sixteen miles from Ripoll, and since the repertoire of this troper is so similar to that of the previous one, I venture to attribute it provisorily to Ripoll. The trope has been previously edited by Young, 'The Origin of the Easter Play', pp. 33-34, and *The Drama of the Medieval Church*, I, 213; both text and music have been published by Sablayrolles, *Vida Cristiana*, III (1916-17), 366 and Anglès, p. 272. In these editions the codex is listed as MS 31.

monastic churches. It was sung at the cathedral of Vich itself, as no less than three medieval manuscripts give evidence. Exactly the same text as the one given above is found, for example, in a thirteenth century Vich *Processionale*.[5] More interesting for us is the text supplied by two Vich *ordinaria*, or *consuetas*, as they were commonly called in Catalonia. The *consuetas* describe the ceremony that accompanied the chanting of the trope. The older of the two was written in the early part of the thirteenth century by Andreas de Almunia (d. 1234), a canon of the cathedral. He summarizes the Vich practice as follows:[6]

> Episcopus cum ministris eat ad altare Sancte Marie Magdalene,[7] et ibi sedeat, et induat se casullam, et sint cum eo induti .xii. sacerdotes, et .vi. diachoni, et antequam inde exeat, uadat diachonus cum uirga pastorali in manu, et cum uno socio ad altare sancti Petri, et dicat alta uoce:
>
> Ora est, psallite: iubet dompnus canere, eia, dicite.
>
> Et in choro sint induti .vi. clerici cum capis sericis, et stent duo ad altare, et alii duo ex eis ante altare: qui dicant:
>
> Ubi est Christus meus Dominus ‹et filius excelsi? Eamus videre sepulcrum›.
>
> Et illi qui sunt ad altare:
>
> Quem queritis in sepulcro, ‹Christicole›?
>
> Et alii dicant:
>
> Jesum Nazarenum ‹crucifixum, o celicole›.
>
> Et illi qui sunt ad altare leuent pallium altaris dicendo:
>
> Non est hic; surrexit ‹sicut predixerat; ite, nunciate quia surrexit, dicentes›:
>
> Alii uero debent redire ad chorum cantando:
>
> Alleluia! Ad sepulcrum residet angelus, nunciat ressurrexisse Christum. En ecce completum est ‹illud quod olim ipse per prophetam dixerat, ad Patrem taliter inquiens›:
>
> Et in coro dicant submissa uoce officium *Ressurrexi et adhuc*. Et dicant

---

[5] Vich, Bibl. Capit., MS 117 (olim 124), fol. 2ᵛ-3ᵛ.
[6] Vich, Bibl. Capit., MS 134, fol. 17ᵛ-18. The *consueta* follows two other unrelated works and has separate pagination. This passage was copied in the early part of the nineteenth century by Villanueva, and edited in turn from the Villanueva manuscript (Madrid, Real Academia de la Historia, 64: 12-19-4) by Anglès, p. 278. As we have stated in an introductory chapter, Villanueva sometimes did not make a literal copy. Since all his notes are in Latin, it is frequently difficult to know whether he has directly quoted a manuscript, or only summarized it. The various texts which Anglès gives, therefore, do not always represent the reading of the original manuscript, as he himself points out (see *La Música a Catalunya*, p. 283, n. 2). We quote here, of course, from the *consueta* itself.

ad diapason, *Gloria Patri*. Et cum *Gloria* dicitur, episcopus cum sacerdotibus et ministris ueniat in coro.

Since the majority of introit tropes which have been edited thus far by historians of the liturgical drama rarely supply descriptive rubrics, this text is especially welcome. It is interesting above all, because it illustrates how close some of the introit tropes came to true drama. The two clerics at the altar clearly represent, or symbolize, the angels, and the other two who answer their queries are undoubtedly thought of as the "Marys". The former lift the linen cloth of the altar, testifying that Christ is no longer in the "sepulchre". Thereupon the Marys return to the choir, announcing the glad tidings to those present.[8]

The Easter ceremonies of the cathedral were closely imitated at the nearby monastery of Santa Maria del Estany, an eleventh century foundation of the Canons Regular of St. Augustine situated some twenty miles west of Vich. The version there was as follows:[9]

> Ad missam sint iiij. cantores in coro qui incipiant officium. Set primo ueniant ad altare. Et duo illorum abscondant[10] se retro altare. Et alii duo maneant ante altare. Et diachonus ueniat cum baculo pastorali, si prelatus est presens, ad altare et stet in dextro cornu altaris et alta uoce dicat, *Ora est psallite* totum(?):
>
> > Ora est, psallite; iubet[11] domnus canere; eya dicite.
>
> Finito isto versu, illi qui sunt ante altare respondeant, *Ubi est Christus*:
>
> > Ubi est Christus, meus Dominus et filius excelsus? Eamus uidere sepulcrum.
>
> Finito isto versu, illi qui sunt retro altare respondeant uersum sequentem cantando *Quem queritis*:
>
> > Quem queritis in sepulcro, o Christicole?
>
> Et alii respondeant:
>
> > Ihesum Nazarenum crucifixum, o celicole.
>
> Et dum cantatur iste versus, illi qui sunt retro altare reueniant ad altare et stet unus illorum in dextro cornu et alius in sinistro, et leuent pallium altaris dicendo versum:

---

[7] Another hand has added marginal notes giving more explicit directions about the chapel of St. Mary Magdalen and the altar of St. Peter, but these are to a large extent illegible, and in any case, do not substantially alter the sense of the passage.
[8] The fifteenth century *consueta* from Vich contains the same ceremony. The text is given in the Appendix.
[9] Vich, Bibl. Capit., MS 118, Liber Processionarius Monasterii Stagnensis saec. xiv, fol. 85[v]-86[v]; the text is accompanied by music.
[10] abscondant] abscondan (MS).
[11] iubet] iube (MS).

> Non est hic, surrexit sicut predixerat, ite nunciate quia surrexit
> dicentes:

Finito uersiculo, alii debent se girare uersus corum et cantare versum, scilicet,

> Alleluya! Ad sepulcrum residens angelus nunciat resurrexisse
> Christum.

Dum iste versus cantatur, alii duo ascendant[12] corum. Et finito isto versu, totus corus dicat istum versum, *Ecce completum est*. Quibus finitis omnes cantores incipiant submissa uoce officium,[13] *Resurrexi*.

At the Seo de Urgel, likewise, in the far north of Spain, and at the monastery of San Juan de las Abadesas near Ripoll, the *Quem quaeritis* was sung on Easter morning, though in these churches the text used was somewhat different. Finally, medieval choir books found at the Biblioteca Central in Barcelona also include the ceremony.[14]

Thus is northern Catalonia, the festive Easter trope was a traditional part of the church services from the eleventh century, at the latest, until the sixteenth. As we might expect, the trope early became a play in the same region.

The oldest Catalan Easter play known is found, like the first tropes, in the Ripoll troper (MS 105), in the portion of the manuscript written in the early part of the twelfth century. Unfortunately the text is very difficult to read in many places, because part of the original has been erased to make room for later additions; these erasures, in many instances, have resulted in lacerations of the folio:[15]

> VERSES PASCALES DE III M[ARIIS]
>
> Eamus mirram emere
> cum liquido aromate
> ut ualeamus ungere
> corpus datum sepulture.
>
> Omnipotens Pater altissime,   5
> angelorum rector mitissime,
> quid facient iste miserime!

---

[12] ascendant] ascedant (MS).
[13] officium] officum (MS).
[14] These texts are given in the Appendix.
[15] Fol. 58ᵛ-62; in assigning dates to manuscripts of the Vich capitular library, I follow those given by Gudiol, 'Catalèg dels manuscrits de Vich'. The passage has been previously edited by Young ('Some Texts of Liturgical Plays', pp. 303-308, and *The Drama of the Medieval Church*, I, 678-681), and by Anglès, pp. 275-278; the latter also gives the music. In re-editing from the original manuscript, I adopt many of the readings proposed by Young.

Dicxit Angelus:[16]

>Heu, quantus est noster dolor!
>Amisimus enim solatium,
>Ihesum Christum, Marie filium;   10
>iste nobis erat subsidium.
>>Heu, ‹quantus est noster dolor!›

>Set eamus unguentum emere,
>quo possimus corpus inungere;
>non amplius posset[17] putrescere.   15
>>Heu, ‹quantus est noster dolor!›

>Dic tu nobis, mercator iuuenis,
>hoc unguentum si tu uendideris,
>dic precium, nam iam habueris.
>>Heu, ‹quantus est noster dolor!›   20

Respondet Mercator:

>Mulieres michi intendite.
>Hoc unguentum si uultis emere,
>datur genus mirre potencie,
>quo si corpus possetis ungere
>non amplius posset[18] putrescere   25
>neque uermes possent comedere.

>Hoc unguentum si multum cupitis,
>unum auri talentum dabitis;
>nec aliter umquam portabitis.

Respondet Maria:

>O mercator, unguentum libera.   30
>Ecce tibi ‹dabi›mus m‹un›era.[19]
>Ibimus Christi ungere uulnera.
>>Heu, ‹quantus est noster dolor!›

>‹Cuncta, sorores, gau›dia[19]
>deflorent in tristicia   35

---

[16] Dicxit Angelus] For the first word the scribe has written dicx̄. As Young points out, the rubric is obviously out of place here, since an angel could hardly speak ll. 8-12. It may possibly be that the rubric was meant to refer to ll. 5-7, which could quite appropriately be delivered by an angel (the invoking of God as the Lord of angels, and especially the reference to the Marys in the third person). In the three other known versions containing the stanza *Omnipotens* (see Young, I, 285, 439, 670), the stanza is spoken by the Marys, but these texts are all late; the one under discussion is the oldest with the verses, and it could represent the original form.
[17] posset] poscet (MS).
[18] posset] poscet (MS).
[19] In this line the parts within brackets are obscured through laceration of the bottom of fol. 59.

> cum innocens opprobria[20]
> fert et crucis suspendia
> Iudeorum inuidia,
> et principum perfidia![21]
> Quid angemus et qualia! 40
>
> Licet, sorores, plangere,
> plangendo Christum querere,
> querendo corpus ungere,
> ungendo mente[22] pascere
> de[23] fletu, uiso uulnere, 45
> dilecto magno federe
> cor mo‹n›stratur in opere.
>
> Cordis, sorores, creduli
> simus et bene seduli,
> ut nostri cerna‹nt› oculi 50
> corpus Christi, uim seculi.
> Quis uolvet petram tumuli
> magnam siue uim populi?
> uirtus[23] celestis epuli.
>
> Tanta, sorores, uisio 55
> splendoris[24] et lustrascio
> nulla sit stupefatio,
> uobis sit exultatio.
> Mors[23] et mortis occasio
> moritur uita uicio. 60
> Nostra, surge, surreccio.
>
> Hoc, sorores, circuitu,
> lecto, dicite, sonitu
> illis[23] qui mesto spiritu
> et proditio[25] transitu 65

[20] opprobria] obrobria (MS).
[21] perfidia] perfudia (MS).
[22] mente] With the first syllable of this word the musical notation ceases for the remainder of the page. Beginning at line 42, the text for the remainder of fol. 59ᵛ is bunched together as though the writer were trying to save space. What has evidently happened is that the text which originally occupied fol. 59ᵛ and the bottom of fol. 59ʳ (ll. 34-86) has been erased, and replaced by this later version. This is clearly indicated by the lacerations and thin spots in the folio. It is doubtless no coincidence that the lines which bear mark of erasure, (34-86), constitute an independent unit in the piece: all are rhyming eight-syllable verses. The scribe began writing the music for the newly added verses at the beginning of the folio, but he soon realized he could not fit the entire addition with the music in the remaining space. Accordingly he desisted giving the musical notation and proceeded to bunch and abbreviate his words. On the following folio the musical notation begins once again.
[23] Over this word is the letter .a. which no one has been able to explain.
[24] splendoris] This reading is very doubtful.
[25] proditio] The manuscript seems to read *prodium*, but this would impair the meter.

    dux uicto surgit obitu
    querantur lecto strepitu
    . . . scis . . . dux ortitu.[26]

    Quid faciemus, sorores,
    graues ferimus dolores?   70
    Non est, nec erit seculis,
    dolor doloris similis.
    Iesum gentes perimere,
    semper decet nos lugere,
    set ut poscimus gaudere,   75
    eamus tu‹m›bam uidere.

    Tumbam querimus non lento
    corpus ungamus unguento,
    quod extinctum uulneribus
    uiuis preualet omnibus.   80

    Regis perempti premium[27]
    plus ualet quam uiuencium,
    cuius amor solacium
    iuuamen et presidium
    et perenne[28] subsidium   85
    sit nunc et in perpetuum.

  Ubi[29] est Christus, meus dominus et filius excelsi? Eamus uidere sepulcrum.
Respondet Angel‹us›:[30]
  Quem queritis in sepulcro, Christicole?
Respondet Maria:
  Ihesum Nazarenum crucifixum, o celicole.
Respondet Angel‹us›:[30]
  Non est hic, surrexit sicut predixerat; ite, nunciate quia surrexit dicentes.
Respondet Mari‹a›:[30]
  Alleluia, ad sepulcrum residens angelus nunciat resur‹r›exisse Christum.
  Te Deum laudamus.

This is the oldest Easter play with the *mercator* that has been found anywhere in Europe. According to Gudiol,[31] the folios containing this episode were

---

[26] Much of this line is illegible.
[27] perempti premium] perhempti preuium (MS).
[28] perenne] per homne (MS).
[29] The words *Ubi est Christus, meus Dominus* are repeated at the top of fol. 60, and the music is resumed at the same point.
[30] The margin is cut away.
[31] 'Catalèg dels manuscrits de Vich', *Butlletí de la Biblioteca de Catalunya*, XII (1923-27), 131.

written in the latter part of the eleventh century, or at the beginning of the twelfth. Of the seven other known liturgical plays which provide a part for the merchant, the next earliest are the two thirteenth century plays from Tours and Benediktbeuern. Dürre has already pointed out that the scene may be of Catalan origin.[32]

The refrain, "Heu, quantus est noster dolor", recurs in many Latin liturgical productions, and was to be a special favorite in the vernacular plays; the Three Marys of Origny-Sainte-Benoîte, for example, sing while on the way to the merchant, "Heu las! nostre dolour con grans il est."[33] The passage of eight-syllable verses hastily added by our scribe I have found nowhere else, and the opening stanza nowhere outside Catalonia. The final scene, beginning *Ubi est Christus meus*, as we already know, was a traditional feature of Catalan tropes and plays.

Vich cathedral itself was the scene of a *Visitatio Sepulchri* early on Easter morning, but unfortunately we do not possess the text of the play. References to the performance after the third responsory of Matins are made in both the Vich *consuetas* and in a breviary. The earlier consueta simply states as follows:[34]

> Tercium responsorium, *Et valde mane*, cum verbeta,[35] et cum *Gloria*, et verbeta *Christus hodie surrexit ex tumulo*. Deinde fiat representacio de .III. Mariis. Qua facta, episcopus dicat *Te Deum laudamus*. Versus *Surrexit Dominus de sepulcro*. Deinde dicantur Laudes.

The breviary from the same cathedral is not much more informative, though it gives the text of the *verbeta*:[36]

> Responsorium: Et ualde mane una sabbatorum, alleluia, alleluia, ueniunt ad monumentum, alleluia, orto iam sole, alleluia, alleluia.
> Versus: Mulieres emerunt aromata; summo diluculo ueniunt ad monumentum.
> Presa: Orto. Gloria.
> Responsorium: Et ualde mane.

Verbeta.

Christus hodie surrexit ex tumulo,
uicto zabulo, expugnato baratro.

---

[32] *Die Mercatorszene im lateinisch-liturgischen, altdeutschen und altfranzösischen religiösen Drama*, pp. 15-16, 24. The merchant became a popular figure in liturgical plays throughout most of Europe, as the places of origin of Young's texts indicate: Narbonne, Tours, Origny-Sainte-Benoîte, Zwickau, Klosterneuburg, Benediktbeuern, and Prague.
[33] Text in Young, I, 413-419.
[34] Vich, Bibl. Capit., MS 134, Tertia Pars, fol. 17.
[35] *Verbeta* were short proses sung on principal feast days after the various nocturns of Matins. The music for these pieces was generally syllabic, and often featured a refrain sung by the people. We shall frequently meet the work in Catalan manuscripts. For a brief discussion of the term, see Anglès, p. 232.
[36] Paris, Bib. Nat., MS lat. nouv. acq. 903, Breviarium Vicense saec. xiv, fol. 163[v].

> Una sabbati ueniunt summo iam diluculo
> sancte femine unguento satis cum mirifico;
> redeunt sed Christo non inuento.
> Orto iam sole, alleluia, alleluia.
>
> Deinde fiat officium de tribus Mariis. Quo facto incipiat sacerdos *Te Deum laudamus*.[37]

We do know that from at least the thirteenth century onward, an Easter sepulchre was in use at Vich. The ceremonial of this period, after describing the procession to the font on Saturday of Easter week, declares: "Postea ad sepulcrum, antiphona *Surrexit Dominus de sepulcro*" (fol. 19ᵛ).

The cathedral of the Seo de Urgel was not without its play of the Three Marys. Happily the fifteenth century *consueta* composed for the cathedral not only mentions the performance, but gives a brief description of it. The manuscript, which is found in the chapter library of the Seo de Urgel, gives the following version on folio 69ᵛ:[38]

> Est notandum quod dum tercium ‹responsorium› dicitur, succentor debet habere .iij. pueros quos debet facere parari, juxta altare Sancti Odonis ut infra dicetur. Postea sint .iiij. clerici et stent in pavimento altaris, scilicet duo in parte dextra, et duo in sinistra. Et dicant bini: *Adam nouus omnis*.[39] Et precentor vel succentor uocet .iij. Marias dicendo: *Venite*, ter, prima uice alta, secunda alciori, tertia altissima. Pueri habeant facies tectas uelaminibus tenuissimis, et quilibet deferat capam rubeam sicut uicarius Sancti Odonis uoluerit eis tradere; et quilibet portet capssam cum candela accensa, quas debet dare janitor maior. Et cum succentor uocat eas, sint ante hostium cori. Et in prima uocatione ueniant ad primum gradum introitus cori, in secunda uocatione ueniant usque ad pulpitum cori, in tertia uocatione cum dixit, *Venite, nolite timere uos*, ipsi pueri dicant media uoce:
>
> > Ubi est Christus ‹meus Dominus et filius excelsi? Eamus videre sepulcrum›.
>
> sicut notandum est. Et statim sint duo pueri, post altare Sancte Marie, et dicant in suo cantu:
>
> > Quem queritis ‹in sepulcro, o Christicole›?
>
> Et isti cantant. Pueri qui dicuntur Marie accedant ante januam cancellorum, et ibi stantes cantent:

---

[37] The fifteenth century Vich *consueta* gives directions for the same ceremony; the passage may be found in the Appendix.

[38] The manuscript bears no catalogue number. The text has been previously edited by Anglès, p. 274, from the slightly inexact Villanueva copy at the Real Academia de la Historia.

[39] omnis] oms̄ (MS). I have not succeeded in identifying this composition. Perhaps instead of being part of the verse, the word *omnis* indicates that the entire piece is to be sung. In that case, the reference may be to the sequence *Adam novus veterem* which was sung in the Fleury and Coutances Easter plays; see Young, I, 408, 473, for the plays and the text.

Jhesum Nazarenum ‹crucifixum, o celicole›.

Quo finito pueri post altare qui dicuntur angeli, dicant sicut notatur:

Non est hic; ‹surrexit sicut predixerat; ite, nunciate quia surrexit, dicentes:›

Et tunc Marie accedant ad pauimentum altaris, et uertentes facies ad corum dicant:

Alleluya! Resurrexit ‹Dominus, hodie resurrexit leo fortis, Christus, filius Dei›.

Quo finito, pueri qui dicuntur angeli dicant excelsa[40] uoce, *Te Deum laudamus*, et in coro respondeatur et finiatur.

Thus at the Seo de Urgel three boys played the part of the Marys. Our attention is caught by the rubric directing that they wear veils over their faces. This practice was not uncommon in liturgical plays, but it seems that it was especially popular in Catalonia. The boys were attired in red capes, and carried the usual ointment jar, along with lighted candles. The triple invocation *Venite* is rather unusual for an Easter play, being recorded by Young only in pieces from Sicily and in the *Ludus Paschalis* from Tours.[41] The usual *Ubi est Christus meus*, so traditional in Catalonia, is here found once again.

Since the twelfth century ceremonial from the same cathedral does not mention the play, it was perhaps not performed there at that early date:[42]

‹Responsorium› *Et ualde mane una sabbatorum*. Verbeta, *Ortum predestinatio*.[43] Sequntur postea versus, *Adam nouus*, et *Mulieres*.[44] Quibus peractis, et candelis interim omni clero traditis et accensis, omnes in superpelliciis stantes, *Te Deum laudamus* solempniter cantent.

The day after Easter, as well, had its play in Catalonia. As was stated in an earlier chapter of this study, on Easter Monday at Vespers the clerics of many churches dramatized the apparition of the risen Christ to His disciples on the way to Emmaus.[45] That the play was not unknown in Catalonia is shown by its appearance in the Ripoll troper; the text is found immediately after the Easter play, and is entitled, *Versus de Pelegrino*:[46]

---

[40] excelsa] This word is partially blurred in the manuscript.
[41] I, 442, 599. It seems that in certain regions this type of summons constituted a traditional overture for the Epiphany play. We find an almost identical rubric in a piece from eleventh century Nevers: "Finitis lectionibus, iubeat Domnus Presul preparare tres clericos in trium transfiguratione Magorum, quos preparatos terque a presule vocatos ita: *Venite*; pergant ante altare hunc versum dicentes ..." (Paris, Bibl. Mazarine, MS 1708, Lib. Resp. Nivernensis, fol. 81ᵛ; edited by Young, II, 50).
[42] Vich, Bibl. Capit., MS 131, fol. 38.
[43] The text of this *verbeta* may be found in Young, I, 615.
[44] This may be the brief *versus* given by many Catalan breviaries: "Mulieres emerunt aromata; summo diluculo veniunt ad monumentum." For an example of it, see above, p. 82.
[45] See above, p. 13; the text of the *Peregrinus* from Rouen is given in the Appendix, p. 172.
[46] Vich, Bibl. Capit., MS 105, Troparium Ripollense saec. xi-xii, fol. 60-62. The text has been previously edited by Young ('Some Texts of Liturgical Plays', pp. 306-308, and *The Drama of the Medieval Church*, I, 681) and Anglès, pp. 279-281; the latter gives the music.

VERSUS DE PELEGRI⟨NO⟩ [47]

Rex in acubitum iam se contulerat,
et mea redolens nardus spirauerat;
in ⟨hortum⟩ [48] ueneram in quem descenderat,
at ille transiens iam declinauerat.

Per noctem igitur hunc querens exeo;
huc illuc transiens nusquam reperio.

Angeli: Mulier, quid ploras? Quem queris?
Maria: Occurrunt uigiles ardenti studio,
Quos cum transierim, sponsum inuenio.
Ortolanus: Mulier, quid ploras? ⟨Q⟩uem queris?
Maria: Tulerunt Dominum meum, et nescio ubi posuerunt eum.
Si tu sustulisti eum, dicito michi, et eum tollam.
Ortolanus: Maria, Maria, Maria!
Respondet Maria: [49] Raboni, Raboni, Raboni! [50]
Maria rediens dicat: Dic, impie Zabule, quid ualet nunc fraus tua?
Discipuli: Dic nobis, Maria, quid uidisti in uia?
Maria: Sepulcrum Christi uiuentis, et gloriam uidi resurgentis;
Angelicos testes, sudarium et uestes.
Angeli: Non est hic, sur⟨r⟩exit sicut predixerat uobis.
Discipuli: Credendum est magis soli Marie ueraci quam [51] Iudeorum
turbe fallaci. Scimus Christum sur⟨r⟩exisse a mortuis uere:
tu nobis, Christe, Rex, miserere.

Qui sunt hij sermones quos confertis ad inuicem ambulantes,
et estis tristes? Alleluia.
Respondent du⟨o⟩: [52] Tu solus peregrinus es in Iherusalem et non
cognouisti que facta sunt in illa his diebus? Alleluia.
Respondet: [53] Que?
Respondent du⟨o⟩: [54] De Ihesu Nazareno, qui fuit uir propheta, potens
in opere et sermone coram Deo et omni populo, alleluia.
Euouae. [55]

Young has appended the above passage to the Easter *Visitatio Sepulchri*, but the two are doubtless distinct plays. This version of the *Peregrinus* is unique in almost every respect, and seems to be both disordered and fragmentary.

---

[47] The margin has been cut away.
[48] hortum] The word is illegible in the manuscript.
[49] Changed, by a later hand, from *Item responde Maria*.
[50] Raboni] The third *Raboni* supplants, through erasure, *magister*.
[51] quam] quomodo (MS).
[52] This rubric is added above the line in a later hand, replacing the original text: *Respondens unus cui nomen Cleophas dixit ei*.
[53] Respondet] This rubric, added above the line, replaces *Quibus ille dixit*.
[54] This rubric, also added above the line at a later date, replaces the former text *Et dixerunt*.
[55] Euouae] These are the vowels of the closing formula *seculorum amen*. The text is immediately followed by the rubric *Versus de Crismate in Cena Domini*.

The conversation between Christ and the disciples comes to no conclusion, but is interrupted almost as soon as it begins; the scene of Christ's revelation of Himself to His disciples, which usually forms the core of the *Peregrinus* play, is given no place in the performance. In no other play found to date does the episode of the journey to Emmaus follow a scene between Christ and Mary Magdalen, although the reverse occurs once.[56] The opening six verses sung by Mary Magdalen, her first reply to the angels, and her remark, "Dic, impie Zabule, quid valet nunc fraus tua", do not appear in other plays either.[57]

As several historians of the medieval theater have remarked, records of the liturgical *Peregrinus* are not very numerous. In our research in Spain we have come across one other instance of the play. The Vich *consueta*, written in the year 1413, declares that if the clerics of the cathedral so desire, they may present the play at Vespers on Easter Monday, the usual time for the performance:[58]

> In reuersione oratio, *Concede quaesumus*. Et fiat *Oficium Peregrini*, si uoluerint, sicut ordinatum est.

A rather unusual type of liturgical play was performed at Vich on the Sunday following Easter, a day not ordinarily noted for its dramatic activity. One of the ecclesiastics would play the role of Mary Magdalen at Mass during the singing of the prose *Victimae paschali laudes*. The account of the ceremony given by the *consueta* is quite verbose, but since it explains the origin of the practice, we quote it here in its entirety:[59]

> Prosa *Victime paschalis laudes*, que dicatur ad lectricum bini et bini ut moris est. Notandum tamen est quod iuxta ordinacionem domini Poncii de Bruno, quondam doctoris decretorum, precentoris Vicensis, debet fieri hac dominica de biennio in biennium representacio siue hostensio armorum siue eorum que seruierunt ad passionem Domini, qua quidem arma, siue insignia, siue instrumenta, habere habet et custodire beneficiatus per ipsum Poncium institutus in altare Transfixionis Beate Marie, prout constat per instrumentum institucionis ipsius beneficii confectum Vici, die .xii. mensis Aprilis, anno a Nativitati Domini M°CCCC°, et clausum per Nicholaum Mathei, presbyterum notarium publicum Vicensem, auctoritate domini Vicensis episcopi, et tunc dicta prosa incipiatur a Maria Magdalene. Et prosequitur ad lectricum per binos presbyteros, ut est moris. Et dum peruentum fuerit ad versum *Dic nobis Marie*, hostenduntur dicta insignia, siue instrumenta per ipsam Mariam Magdalene seriatim iuxta ordinem quem habent cantores, quibus hostensis, finitur dicta prosa ad lectricum ut est moris.

---

[56] The play is from Sicily; see Young, I, 479.
[57] The verse, *Dic, impie Zabule*, etc., was borrowed from the prose, *Fulgens praeclara rutilat*, sung at Vespers during Easter week in many Catalan churches.
[58] Vich, Bibl. Capit., manuscript without catalogue number, fol. 54ᵛ. The passage is preceded by a description of the procession at Vespers.
[59] Fol. 57 of the fifteenth century consueta.

The plays became increasingly more numerous at Vich towards the middle of the fifteenth century. Long before this time it had become traditional to have certain ecclesiastics dress as Apostles and other Biblical figures for the Corpus Christi procession. In 1463 this custom was adapted for usage on Holy Thursday, the twelve "apostles" keeping watch at the repository where the Sacred Host was reserved until the following day:[60]

> En 1463 a 5 Abril Francisco Terrades, beneficiado de esta iglesia, instituyó que doce presbíteros vestidos "ad modum apostolorum, qui solent indui in repraesentationibus sanctorum in die Corporis Christi", asistiesen al monumento todo el Jueves Santo, cantando salmos "usque in crastinum hora communicandi." No es esta la memoria mas antigua de la solemnidad usada en los monumentos ó como decimos sagrarios: en la iglesia de Ager la hay ya de ello en el siglo XII. Todo esto es de las actas capitulares.

Very early in the region of Vich, the liturgical *Visitatio Sepulchri* evolved into more ambitious productions in the vernacular. The text of one of these vernacular plays was discovered in the early part of this century, but the article in which it was published seems to have escaped all notice. Since few such vernacular plays from the Hispanic peninsula have been preserved, I take the liberty to re-print it here. Though the piece was probably not performed in close connection with the liturgy, it may have been presented in the cathedral after the third responsory of Matins.

The play was first printed in the Catalan review, *Vida Cristiana*, I (1914), 238–240, by J. Gudiol, who states that he found it at the Vich capitular archives in a copy written by Joseph Serra i Campdelacreu, formerly archivist at Vich. Inasmuch as the original which served as the source for Serra's copy has never been found, Gudiol gives the play as he came upon it in the transcription, without beginning or end, and with a lacuna in the middle. He points out that the archaic language, and the very marked Provençal influence, indicate a date of composition considerably earlier than that of November 17, 1445, which Serra has jotted in the margin; in his estimation, the play is probably a fourteenth century text:[61]

Dicat senturio:

> Car ne saps res dir ne far
> Que ja pusque del cel lauar,
> Ne jamays als teus retornar.

---

[60] Villanueva, *Viage literario a las Iglesias de España*, VI, 98. According to Gudiol, the text quoted by Villanueva is found in the Vich capitular archives, Necrologi D., fol. 9v; see 'El Drama sagrat a Catalunya', in *Gazeta de Vich*, 1924, No. 2776, 2-3.

[61] The text, as printed by Gudiol, lacks punctuation, and is obviously corrupt in some places. The majority of emendations which I make were suggested by the well-known medievalist, Dr. Martín de Riquer of the University of Barcelona, who very graciously consented to read the text and recommend improvements. Since Dr. Martín de Riquer did not formally edit the text, and since I have not faithfully followed all his suggestions, any errors in the changes are to be attributed to myself.

>Mas d'ayço los hauem a gardar:
>Que no'l nos pusque hom amblar,
>Sos deixibles, per nuy affar.

Dicat senturio:

>A pas, a pas, companyons meus:
>Aturatz vos, no'us sia greu‹s›!
>No say cal ren mi vey venir,
>Don nos coven[62] tuyt a fugir.[63]
>Mas fugir no porem, so creu,
>Que'l cor mi fall, tal paor hay.[64]

Tunc fiet terre motus cum alio tumulto qui dum fiet angeli venient ad monumentum quorum omnium timore vigiles cadent in terra facie versu pro nimio timore quasi dormientes et judei venient et dicant illis:

>Com stats vosaltres, cavallers?
>Marrits e tristz, com vos pres?
>Par que bataya haiats haüda,
>Mas que no la haiats vensuda.
>Tots vos vahem spauorditz:
>Are ges no paretz ardits.
>Vosaltres tots tremolats.
>Dietz que'us ha 'nderroquats.
>Sabetz si es al monument Jesus?
>Dietz ho, e leuats sus.[65]

Senturio surgente a terra dicat:

>Sapiats, senyor, que'us ho diray
>Com es stat, no'us en mintray,
>Si donques no m'ho[66] tol paor
>Que hay haüda del Saluador
>Que vuy maytin ressuscita
>E del muniment se laua.
>Et si d'ayço mi no creetz[67]
>Per tots aquetz ‹h›o prouaretz
>Qui han lur part en la paor
>E par-lurs ben en la color.

Judei senturio et eius sociis:

>Senyors, axo vos no digats,
>Que fort ne[68] serietz blasmatz;

---

[62] coven] comen (Print).
[63] fugir] tugir (Print).
[64] The faulty rhyme of these last two verses indicates an original in another language or dialect.
[65] For this last line the edition of Gudiol reads: *Diretz no e leauts sus*.
[66] no m'ho] non ho (Print).
[67] creetz] crectz (Print).
[68] ne] na (Print).

> Mas vos poretz aço ben dir:
> Que hauietz voluntat de dormir,
> E'ls dexebles, en durment,
> Lo's amblaren, sertament;
> E si'us plau, axi ho diretz
> E de nos don e gardo n'hauretz.

Tunc veniant Mariae et dicant omnes insimul:

> Eamus mirram emere
> Cum liquido aromate
> Quod valeamus ungere
> Corpus datum sepulture.

Primo dicat Salomee:

> Ay, senyor Deus, ver payre glorios,
> Qui'ns redimist del teu sanc precios,
> Per nos ets mort e leuats en crotz.

Dicat Maria Jacobi:

> Perdut hauem all qui'm solia guiar,
> E en tot loch mon gint aconseyar.
> Marides som; hon lo porem trobar?

Dicat Maria Magdalene:

> Que moutes[69] veus li ausi dir e comptar,
> Cant entre nos solia prediar,
> Que al terç jorn deuia suscitar.

Dicat Maria Salomee:

> Per ço es obs que aneu engüen comprar,
> Perque pusquam les grans nafres untar.[70]
> . . . .
> Deus, qui volguist per nos morir,
> Qui nos pora est vas obrir,
> Que no podem, per nuy affir,[71]
> La pera moura ne'l vas obrir?

Dicat primus angelus:

> Vos qui n'hauetz en Deu sper,
> Qui al sepulcre volch gaser,
> Venitz[72] auant lo loch vaser,
> Que no'us en qual pesor hauer.

---

[69] moutes] montes (Print).
[70] Gudiol remarks that in Serra's copy a few blank lines followed at this point, indicating that there had been a lacuna in the original.
[71] affir] alfir (Print).
[72] Venitz] Vanitz (Print).

Et Marie, flexis molieris, pisat(?) monumentum quoad illum circumcirca.
Et primo (Maria) Jacobi ad eundem soneum:

>> Ay Deus, qui tot lo mon fasist!
>> Hon es lo cors de Jhesu Christ?
>> Lassetes, que tant l'auem quist[73]
>> Et no'l hauem trobat ne vist!

Dicat secundus angelus:

>> Vos qui fetz tal suspirament,
>> E manetz dol e marriment,
>> A qui[74] portats aqueix angüent,
>> E que queretz al moniment?

Dicat Maria Magdalene:

>> Nos querem Deus glorios,
>> Qui en crou fo levat per nos;
>> Pensauem-nos que açi fos,
>> En aqueix vas hon eretz[75] vos.

Dicat primus angelus:

>> L'anuyt[76] mudats de marriment
>> E vostre cor aiats jausent,
>> E'i fetz saber a tota gent
>> Que Deus viu[77] es sertanament.

Dicat secundus angelus:

>> Tornatz-vos-en per lo camin,
>> Sapien-ho vostres vaÿns,
>> Que Deus qui feu e pan e vin,
>> Ressusatat es vuy maytin.

Dicat primus angelus:

>> En Galilee vos n'anatz
>> Per veser Deu que demanats,
>> E aquel poretz vaser assatz,
>> Que aqui es, ço sapiatz.

Mulieres respiciant monumentum. Tunc humiliter sciens Jhesus . . .
Postea recedat in . . . Galilea . . . ad apostolos, et dicat Maria Magdalene
ad eumdem soneum:

>> Senyor, la festa que farem
>> En Deus laudar la despendrem,
>> Que Ell tracs vuy d'infern Adam
>> E altre qui ten son reclam.

[73] quist] quest (Print).
[74] A qui] Aqui (Print).
[75] eretz] Gudiol's edition has the future form *seretz*, but this does not seem to fit the context.
[76] L'anuyt] la nuyt (Print).   [77] viu] vuy (Print).

Dicat primo Maria Magdalena:[78]
> Dic-nos, Maria, que has vist?

The play exhibits features common to many medieval vernacular Easter plays. In keeping with the usual procedure, the rubrics have been given in Latin. It is interesting that the one Latin passage spoken, *Eamus mirram emere*, etc., is the same found in the early Ripoll troper. This is the only other instance of it that has come to our attention. Its appearance here, nevertheless, in a play where all the other verses are delivered in the vernacular, suggests that it was especially well known in northern Catalonia.

Briefly summarizing the play, we find that the fragment, as we have it, begins with the scene of the guards at the sepulchre. Stricken with fear at the tumult caused by the earthquake and at the sudden apparition of the angels, they fall to the ground, "as though sleeping", but the Jewish leaders come and bribe them to say that, while they slept, Christ's disciples came and took away their Master's Body. There follows the scene of the Three Marys on their way to the merchant, but the scene with the merchant is missing. The Marys next appear at the sepulchre, where they meet the two angels, and are informed that Christ has risen. The text terminates with a translation of the verse, *Dic nobis, Maria, quid vidisti in via?*, taken from the prose *Victimae paschali laudes*. The piece probably closed with the dramatization of the prose, like many of the liturgical Easter plays.[79]

Dramatic Activity During the Christmas Season

The Christmas *Quem quaeritis* trope was every bit as popular at Vich and the Seo de Urgel as its Easter counterpart. The oldest record of it is found in Manuscript 106 (olim 31) in Vich's cathedral library.[80]

AD MISSAM MAIOREM TROPUS

> Quem queritis in presepe, pastores, dicite?
> Saluatorem Christum Dominum, infantem pannis inuolutum, secundum sermonem angelicum.
> Adest hic paruulus cum Marie matre sua, de qua dudum uaticinando Ysayas dixerat propheta: Ecce uirgo concipiet et pariet filium; et nunc euntes dicite quia natus est.
> Alleluia, alleluia! Iam uere scimus Christum natum in terris, de quo canite omnes cum propheta, dicentes:
> Puer natus est.

---

[78] This rubric seems to be misplaced; Mary Magdalen usually sings the response to the question, which is obviously directed to one of the Marys.
[79] See, for example, the *Visitatio Sepulchri* of Compostella, p. 55.
[80] Troparium Ripollense (?) saec. xii-xiii, fol. 30; the text has been previously edited by Sablayrolles, 'A la recherche des manuscrits grégoriens espagnols, Iter Hispanicum', p. 243.

Because this Christmas trope was more stereotyped than its Easter model, wherever it is found, it almost always presents the same reading. Thus we encounter an identical text in a thirteenth century Vich *Processionale* and in two prosers of unknown origin at the Biblioteca Central in Barcelona.[81] Other Christmas introit tropes were also sung in Catalonia, for example, those beginning *Quem vates* and *Quem sine matre*; apparently, however, none of these ever developed into a play.[82]

Some of the medieval manuscripts give a description of the ceremonies which accompanied the singing of the trope. Because of their rather extensive rubrics, I give the accounts found in two manuscripts from the monasteries of San Juan de las Abadesas and Santa Maria del Estany. In the former abbey the ceremony was appropriately conducted at the Blessed Virgin's altar:[83]

> Dum hec fient, similiter induant se alii duo cantores seu officiatores clerici de melioribus cantoribus qui sint. Itaque inter omnes in missa dicenda sint octo cantores. Et illi duo maiores stant in intrante chori, ut supra in vesperis et matutinis. Alii sex stent juxta faristollum. Pulsato itaque classico, dicantur tropi, nisi fuerit sermo uel nimis alta dies, quia tunc possunt ommitti. Et dicantur in hunc modum. Duo cantores, scilicet, ultimi de canonici, uadant ad altare Beate Marie, et duo, scilicet, primi, ad altare Sancti Johannis. Et illi qui stant in altare Beate Marie incipiant *Quem queritis in presepio*. Illi duo qui stant in altare Sancti Johannis respondeant, *Saluatorem Christum Dominum*. Et illi de Sancta Maria iterum, *Adest hic paruulus cum Maria matre sua*. Deinde illi de Sancto Johanne uertant se ad chorum, et nuncient eis, *Alleluia, alleluia, jam uere scimus Christum natum in terris*. Et his finitis, illi quatuor cantores qui remanent in choro incipiant officium summissa uoce, *Puer natus est*, et illi qui dixerunt tropos redeant ad chorum.

At Santa Maria del Estany the same introit trope approached even closer to genuine drama. A résumé of the practice as it was observed at that monastery is given by a fourteenth century *Processionale*:[84]

> Ad introitum, antiphona,
>
> > Gloria in excelsis Deo et in terra pax hominibus bone uoluntatis. Alleluia!
>
> Ad missam sint .iiij. cantores in coro qui incipiant officium ad missam. Set primo ueniant ad altare. Et diachonus incipiat in cornu altaris dextro, *Ora est psallite*. Et duo illorum abscondant se retro altare. Et alii duo

---

[81] Vich, Bibl. Capit., MS 117, fol. 1ᵛ-2; Barcelona, M. 298 (39), Cantoral saec. xv, fol. 183, and M. 299 (40), Cantoral saec. xv, fol. 141. In these last two manuscripts, the piece is listed as a *Prosa*.
[82] The trope *Hodie cantandus est* written by Tutilo of St. Gall, and generally considered to be the oldest of the Christmas compositions, I have not found in Spain.
[83] Vich, Bibl. Capit., MS 212, Consueta de San Juan de las Abadesas saec. xv, fol. 115-115ᵛ.
[84] Vich, Bibl. Capit., MS 118, fol. 10-12; the manuscript is provided with music.

ueniant ante altare. Et illi qui sunt retro altare incipiant, scilicet, tropus *Quem queritis in presepe*.

> Ora est, psallite, iubet[85] domnus[86] canere, eya dicite.

Dicant alii qui sunt retro altare:

> Quem queritis in presepe, pastores, dicite?

Respondeant illi qui sunt coram altare:

> Saluatorem Christum Dominum, infantem pannis inuolutum secundum sermonem angelicum.

Illi qui sunt retro altare ueniant ad altare, et stet unus in dextro cornu altaris et alius in sinistro, et leuent pallium altaris dicendo versum, *Adest hic*.

> Adest hic paruulus cum Maria matre sua, de qua dudum vatizinando Ysayas dixerat propheta: Ecce uirgo concipiet et pariet filium; et nunc euntes dicite quia natus est.

Finitis versibus, alii duo girent se ad populum dicentes versum:

> Alleluya, alleluya! Iam uere scimus Christum natum in terris, de quo canite omnes cum propheta, dicentes, Puer natus est.

At Vich itself the usage was the same as at Estany, and a very similar practice was traditional during the Middle Ages at the Seo de Urgel.

Despite the popularity of Christmas tropes, no examples of the *Officium Pastorum* have been found at Vich or the Seo de Urgel. There was other dramatic acitivity on Christmas Eve, however. At Vich, from at least the fifteenth century onward, the Sibyl came forth during Matins to sing her prophecy. We find in the *consueta* written in 1413:[87]

> Lectio .ix. legitur per domnum Episcopum, si fuerit, sin autem, per domnum abbatem Stagnensem si fuerit, in ambone ubi debet accedere precedentibus luminariis cum sollempnitate solita, uel per alium oficiantem, sine luminariis. Et incipit *Castissimum*, et post hunc sermonem continuantur tres sermones, scilicet, *Audite fratres*, *Inter pressuras*, *Set vos inquam*, cum versibus *Judicii signum* quos quatuor clerici bini et bini cantent, uel per Sibillam. Et post versus continuatur sermo *Hec de Christi natiuitate*.

It is noteworthy that the *consueta* distinguishes between two methods of delivering the prophecy: it is rendered either by a group of cantors, "bini et bini", or by someone who actually impersonates the Sibyl. This rubric gives support to our earlier inference that at Palencia in the fourteenth century the

---

[85] iubet] iube (MS).
[86] domnus] domus (MS).
[87] Fol. 10ᵛ; most of this passage has been previously published by Anglès, p. 300.

Sibylline verses were not delivered by a "Sibyl". In the Castilian city the verses were sung "a quatuor vel sex binatim", which seems to correspond to the first alternative mentioned by the Vich *consueta*.[88]

For some reason Anglès has concluded that the Catalan ceremony of the Sibyl was very different from the usage observed at Toledo, and much less dramatic: "Aquesta representació, tan simple, de les Consuetes catalanes, contrasta amb aquella altra, tan dramàtica i tan vistent, de la catedral de Toledo."[89] In our opinion, the Catalan practice was probably very similar, though perhaps the two angels did not appear. Moreover, we shall presently see that in some Catalan cities the Sibyl took part in dramatic productions of a very advanced type.

We know at least one item of the costume worn by the prophetess in fifteenth century Vich. Gudiol has copied the following exerpt from the account books at the cathedral:[90]

> Sibila per Nadal. Ne parlen els comptes de Vich de 1485. En 1518 es parla de dos parells de guants per la Sibila.

As was the case at León, the earlier Vich manuscripts do not refer to the Sibyl. The thirteenth century *consueta* simply states:[91]

> .viiij. lectio, *Castissimum Marie Virginis*. Item alii sermones *Audite fratres*, *Audite Mariam colloquentem nobiscum*, et *Inter pressuras*, et *Set uos inquam conuenio o Judei*. Cum versibus *Judicii signum*. *Hec de Christi natiuitate*. Responsorium, *Gloria in altissimis Deo*, cum uerbetis. His dictis, legatur euangelium, *Liber generacionis*. Quo finito dicat sacerdos *Benedictus qui uenit in nomine Domini*. Tunc uero sit paratus episcopus uel sacerdos, et cum processione eant ad ecclesiam Sancte Marie cum antiphona *O beata infancia*. Et dicatur ibi Missa.

The Seo de Urgel ceremonials provide approximately the same information:[92]

> Lectio .ix. *Inter pressuras* . . . . Et janitor mayor debet sibi tenere lucernam cum candela accensa. *Inter pressuras* legatur tota cum prophetis, et cum *Judicii signum*, cantando responsorium, *Gloria in altissimis*.

Anglès suggests that the Epiphany play was performed at Ripoll in the tenth and eleventh centuries. He bases his opinion on a tenth century fragment at the Archivo de la Corona de Aragón in Barcelona:[93]

---

[88] See above, p. 47.
[89] *La Música a Catalunya*, p. 300.
[90] I take the quotation from the manuscript notes for Gudiol's *Arqueología litúrgica de la provincia eclesiástica Tarragonina*, today located at the Vich chapter library. This monumental work was never published, and unfortunately, after the author's death, considerable portions of the original manuscript were accidently destroyed.
[91] Vich, Bibl. Capit., MS 134, Tertia Pars, fol. 5.
[92] Seo de Urgel, Bibl. Capit., manuscript without catalogue number, fol. 25^v-26. The twelfth century ceremonial gives the same account on fol. 15 (Vich, Bibl. Capit., MS 131).
[93] 'La Musique en Catalogne aux Xe et XIe siècles. L'Ecole de Ripoll', p. 173; see also *La Música a Catalunya*, p. 284. The complete phrase, found on fol. 157^v, is as follows: "Tres

> Quant au drame liturgique nous sommes renseignés par le MS. 74 . . . .
> Ce manuscrit renferme quelques indications: "Tres magi adsunt: Baldasar, Gasbar, Melchior, etc.", qui d'après Beer constitueraient un reste du plus ancien drame sur les rois mages conservé dans la littérature latine hispanique.

It hardly need be pointed out that this one sentence provides very slight evidence in support of such an inference. It does establish, nevertheless, that this triad of names for the Magi was popular long before the date 1158 rigidly assigned to it by K. Hartmann.[94]

A phrase which should be of even greater interest to historians of the Epiphany play is found in another Catalan manuscript. Everyone is familiar with the celebrated advice given by Hamlet to his players: that they should pronounce only the lines set down for them, and that, above all, they should not out-Herod Herod. It is thought with good reason that the latter expression was suggested to Shakespeare by the medieval Epiphany plays. In these pieces Herod early became a comic character, and his rantings and tirades were the joy of medieval audiences. The *New Oxford English Dictionary* (1933) comments upon Hamlet's phrase as follows:

> *To out-Herod Herod*: to outdo Herod (represented in the old Mystery plays as a blustering tyrant) in violence; to be more outrageous than the most outrageous; hence, to outdo in any excess of evil or extravagance. (A casual Shakespearian expression, which became current in the 19th c.).

The expression has generally been considered Shakespeare's own. That it was current already around the year 1200, however, is shown by its appearance in the Vich *consueta* written about that time. The Catalan scribe lists as one of his reasons for not reciting the *Invitatorium* on the feast of the Epiphany:[95]

> Ne Herodidemus Herodes qui dixit Magis, *Ite et interrogate* diligenter de puero . . . et hoc dolose dixit.

Shakespeare in medieval Latin! Here the phrase has the connotation of "seem to outdo Herod in hypocrisy and deceit", but it may well be an indication that as early as 1200 Herod the actor had given special vogue to the expression by his antics and extravagance.[96]

---

magi adsunt, Baldasar, Gaspar, Melchior. Ad adorandum Dominum uenientes, tria munera secum tulerunt."

[94] *Ueber das altspanische Dreikönigsspiel*, pp. 51-79. Hartmann, and several commentators after him, use this date as an argument to prove that the Spanish *Auto de los Reyes Magos* could not have been written before the middle of the twelfth century.

[95] Vich, Bibl. Capit., MS 134, tertia pars, fol. 6ᵛ. Du Cange does not list the word in his *Glossarium Mediae et Infimae Latinitatis*. The *Invitatorium* is a short verse sung at the beginning of Matins inviting the participants to come and adore Christ.

[96] Evidence of Herod's violent conduct in the plays is found in many eleventh and twelfth century texts. Commenting on Herod's character as portrayed in the eleventh century Freising play, for example, Young declares: "Of the violence of this personage, we are left in no doubt. He dashes the book of prophecies to the ground, makes impulsive gestures, and no doubt brandishes his sword . . ., movements abundantly supported by his utterances, which are, as we have seen, superlatively angry and arrogant" (II, 99).

A final testimony concerning medieval plays at Vich during the Christmas season is contained in the *Actas Capitulares* of the cathedral. An entry of the year 1360 reveals that on St. Stephen's and St. John's Day plays were regularly performed within the precincts of the cathedral cloister:[97]

> Statutum fuit quod in processionibus festorum S. Stephani et Joannis Evangelistae, non introducantur in claustrum novum aliqua animalia, videlicet, equi, roncini, muli, asini, boves vel similia, occasione quorumdam ludorum quae in illis festivitatibus in ipso claustro fieri consueverunt.

On other days of the year, tropes modelled after the *Quem quaeritis* compositions were sung at Ripoll on the feasts of the Ascension and St. John the Baptist (June 24th), but these pieces apparently never became plays.[98] Much more dramatic is a charming trope for the feast of the Assumption of the Blessed Virgin (August 15th) found in the fourteenth century *Processionale* from Santa Maria del Estany. Based upon the antiphon *Ubi est Christus meus*, the piece is the only one of its kind which has yet been found:[99]

> Finito isto responsorio immediate nisi uenerit in dominica hoc festum, diachonus incipiat antiphonam ad introitum, scilicet, *Hodie Maria Virgo*. Finita in coro, descendant quatuor cantores qui ueniant ante altare. Duo illorum abscondant se retro altare. Et alii duo maneant coram altari. Et diachonus ueniat ad altare et stet in dextro cornu altaris et alta uoce dicat, *Ora est psallite*, etc. Finito versu, illi qui sunt ante altare dicant versum *Ubi est Mater*. Finito isto versu, illi qui sunt retro altare respondeant, *Quem queritis*. Et alii dicant versum *Matrem Natzareni*. Et dum cantatur iste versus, illi qui sunt retro altare ueniant ad altare. Et stet unus illorum in dextro cornu altaris et alius in sinistro, et leuent pallium altaris dicendo versum *Non est hic*. Finito isto versu, alii duo girent se versus corum et cantent[100] versum *Alleluia! Gaudent*[101] *sancti*. Et dum iste versus cantatur, alii duo ascendant corum et incipiant officium ad Missam submissa uoce, *Gaudeamus*. Ad introitum antiphona:

> > Hodie Maria Virgo celos ascendit[102] gaudere, quia cum Christo regnat in eternum.

> Tropus *Ora est*, require in die sancto Pasche. Illi qui sunt ante altare respondeant dicentes:

> > Ubi est Mater nostri Domini, columpna nostre spei? Eamus uidere sepulcrum.

> Respondeant illi qui sunt retro altare:

> > Quem queritis in sepulcro, o Christicole?

[97] Cited by Anglès, p. 284. These performances, however, would have been of a non-liturgical nature, and were probably performed in the vernacular.
[98] For texts of these tropes, see the Appendix.
[99] Vich, Bibl. Capit., MS 118, fol. 158ᵛ-160; the manuscript provides music.
[100] cantent] canten (MS).
[101] Gaudent] Gadent (MS).
[102] ascendit] ascedit (MS).

Vich, Biblioteca Capitular, MS 105, saec. xi-xii, fol. 58ᵛ, Earliest Easter Play with the Merchant Scene

dicit. ♦. Matrem nazarenu. ♦ dñi
cātaf iste. ℣. illi qi ſt retro altare uenī,
ant ad altare. Et stet una illoȝ i dext.
cornu altaris et alius in sinistro et
leuent pallium altaris dicendo. ℣. Xp̄s
est lux. ¶ Finito isto. ℣. alij duo bi ẽr
serius̄ cor̄ et cantēt. ℣. Illa. Tadet
ta. Et dū iste v̄sus cantat alij duo r
ascendant cor̄ et incipiat offm ad mis
sam sub missa uoce. Gaudeamus.

Hodie maria uirgo celos ascendit

gaudete quia cū xp̄o regnat ineternū

Tropus ante altare
Mariestr xp̄i ẽ ascēdūt
Xc̄ i des dicentes
Sc̄e paſtor
laudabit

Dic est mar

Vich, Biblioteca Capitular, MS 118, saec. xiv, fol. 159, Dramatic Trope
for the Feast of the Assumption

Alii dicant:

> Matrem Natzareni crucifixi, o celicole.

Alii qui sunt retro altare ueniant ad altare. Et stet unus in dextro cornu altaris, et alius in sinistro. Et leuent pallium altaris dicendo:

> Non est hic, ascendit ad celi culmina, super angelorum celica regnans agmina.

Alii cantent uersus corum versum sequentem:

> Alleluya! Gaudent sancti presente Maria, decantent fideles uoce pia, Gaudeamus.

Just as the altar symbolized the sepulchre of Christ in the Easter ceremony at Estany, so on the feast of the Assumption it represented the sepulchre of the Blessed Mother. The whole ceremony is obviously an imitation of the Easter practice.

In review, judging from the texts presented, tropes and liturgical plays were far from a rarity in medieval Vich and its environs. Not only were the clerics and monks of this diocese, and also those of Seo de Urgel, very active in the presentation of plays, but it appears that they employed their talents at writing new types and new forms. Ripoll was probably one of the important disseminators of the liturgical drama in Western Europe. It was closely linked with St. Martial of Limoges, and perhaps some of its monks were influential in bringing the drama to Santiago de Compostella. The dramatic Easter trope *Ubi est Christus meus* first appears there, and the merchant scene is found at the Catalan monastery in a *Visitatio Sepulchri* some one hundred years before it is recorded in an Easter play elsewhere. All the plays performed at Ripoll were also staged at Vich, and dramatic tropes were exceedingly popular at Santa Maria del Estany.

Yet, notwithstanding all this evidence of dramatic productivity, the diocese of Vich, at least from the thirteenth century onward, was probably not the chief center of the liturgical drama in medieval Catalonia. If the clergy from this region played a very important role in the early dissemination of tropes and plays, their dramatic enthusiasm, it appears, was eventually surpassed in churches of other Catalan sees. In the next few pages we shall observe what took place on festive days, by way of dramatic activity, in the medieval cathedral of Gerona.

CHAPTER 8

THE LITURGICAL DRAMA AT GERONA

From earliest times the cathedral of Gerona was famous throughout Catalonia for its numerous and colorful liturgical customs. An examination of the contents of manuscripts originating from this church proved to Villanueva that this reputation was well merited:[1]

> Una de las cosas que mas deben excitar la curiosidad de los anticuarios en esta iglesia de Gerona es la multitud y singularidad de sus ritos antiguos. Yo creo que así por ellos como por la gravedad de los oficios eclesiásticos mereció esta catedral ser llamada "madre de las ceremonias".

The famous fourteenth century Gerona *consueta*, rarely consulted in the original,[2] is fortunately still preserved in the Gerona chapter library. For the history of the liturgical drama, this manuscript is truly an "inapreciable códice", to use Gonzalez-Palencia's expression. Within its pages one finds a description or mention of no less than eight medieval plays, countless tropes, and picturesque résumés of the festive ceremonies which marked the liturgy of St. Stephen's, St. John's, and Innocents Day.

The manuscript, at present without catalogue number, is of large format, contains 272 folios, and is very legibly written. On the wood cover is inscribed, "consueta antiquissima Ecclesie Gerundensis, 1360", and the *incipit* on folio 7 reads: "Hic incipit dominicale et consueta secundum ordinem et morem Sedis Gerundensis."

Turning to the section which treats of the Easter ceremonies, we find first of all, as we might expect, a reference to the familiar *Quem quaeritis* trope. At Gerona it was sung in its usual position before the introit of the Mass:[3]

> Et dicatur tropus, scilicet, *hora est psallite*, a duobus pueris indutis dalmaticis qui stent in medio hostii rexiarum; quo dicto, alii tropi dicantur ad letrilium de duobus[4] clericis, scilicet, *Quem queritis*, cum sequentibus. Sequitur officium *Resurrexi*.

Since the piece began with the words *Hora est psallite*, it may have been the

---

[1] *Viage literario a las Iglesias de España*, XII, 193.
[2] See the initial chapter of this study, p. 2.
[3] Fol. 59ᵛ. The cathedral ceremonial is not the only one still extant at Gerona. A lengthy *consueta* from the collegiate church of St. Felix of Gerona is found at the Seminary library in the same city. It, too, contains many references to plays. On fol. 71ᵛ it gives virtually the same account of the Easter trope as the one here quoted.
[4] duobus] A later hand has added above the line the numeral, .iii.

same as the trope chanted at Ripoll and Vich, though in some churches the verse *Hora est, etc.* was immediately followed by the *Quem quaeritis*.[5]

At Matins the cathedral of Gerona was the scene of a very colorful *Visitatio Sepulchri*. Unfortunately, in keeping with his custom throughout the manuscript, the scribe does not give the text of the play, but only a description of it. The performance took place after the third responsory *Et Valde mane* and the *verbeta* (fol. 58–58v):

> Et ponuntur candele in rotulis. Et etiam accenduntur, per heredem d'En Banyols, .xxxi. cerei quilibet medii quartoni, qui ponuntur in ferris sancti sepulcri. Et comburunt ibi dum durent. Et dicuntur antiphone, responsoria, lectiones, et verbeta, et graduali et alleluia, et omnia alia que dicuntur de duobus in duobus cum superpelliciis. Postea fiet Representacio que fit in ecclesia de Tribus Mariis per nonos de capitulo. Et cantores cum processione clericorum ordinent Tres Marias et Mercatorem sicut ordinatum est in tropierio. Quibus omnibus finitis, cantores incipiant *Victime paschali laudes*. Et ipsam cantando intrent chorum, et hic fit Representacio per Marias ad sepulchrum, dicendo versum *sepulcrum*, prima primum versum, secunda secundum, tertia *surrexit*, et angelus, *dic nobis Maria*. Et postea totus chorus respondeat *Scimus Christum*. Qua finita, domnus episcopus uel sacerdos incipiat *Te Deum laudamus*.

According to the ceremonial, after the third responsory and the *verbeta* of Easter Matins had been chanted, thirty-one candles were placed in the sepulchre by way of preparation for the play. This rubric reveals that, as in numerous other churches in the Middle Ages, a special *sepulchrum* was used at Gerona for the *Visitatio Sepulchri*. Apparently it was in the choir, for a later directive declares: "intrent chorum et hic fit Representacio per Marias ad sepulcrum."[6] The *consueta* also states that the bishop said Mass in the sepulchre: "Postea pulsentur campanelle sepulcri. Et interim domnus episcopus faciat confessionem ... et incipiat officium Misse .... Et finiatur Missa in sepulcro" (fol. 58v).

Since nine ecclesiastics are mentioned as taking part in the performance, there was probably that number of roles in the play – a large cast for a liturgical piece. The Gerona *Visitatio*, then, must have been of a very advanced type. One of these personages, we are told, was the *mercator*. Hence there was a merchant scene in the Gerona play, as at Ripoll. Three of the roles were taken by the Marys, and one, or perhaps two, by the "angels". We are left to conjecture about the identity of the remaining three or four persons: perhaps

---

[5] For an example of the latter, see the text from Apt in France (Young, I, 212).
[6] This was the usual location of the *sepulchrum*, especially in France and England; see Brooks, *The Sepulchre of Christ in Art and Liturgy*, chapter 6. Of course, it is possible that the phrase *hic fit representacio, etc.* refers merely to the title of the play, *Repraesentatio ad Sepulchrum*, without meaning to imply that the actual sepulchre was in the choir. The play doubtless involved the *Quem quaeritis* scene, but we are not informed where that took place.

Christ in the Resurrection scene and several Apostles, or again, the *unguentarius* episode may have been an unusually elaborate one, involving several other personages besides the ointment-seller and the Marys. We shall have occasion to return to this point again.

The first part of the play, which centered around the purchase at the merchant's booth, did not take place in the choir, but in a different part of the church. The cantors and players gained this scene of action by a procession. Later, when this first episode had been concluded, the entire group, with the Marys, returned to the choir for the rest of the play. The scribe speaks of two *repraesentationes*, as though there were two different plays, but he most likely employs the word in the sense of *scene*. Once in the choir, the Marys were asked the usual question, *Dic nobis, Maria, quid vidisti in via*, each one answering in turn with the traditional verses, *sepulchrum Christi*, etc. The choice of an angel as interrogator is unusual, and seems inappropriate, for in the course of the sequence one of the Marys replies that she has seen *angelicos testes* – a rather unlikely response to a questioning angel. Ordinarily the phrase *dic nobis*, etc. is allotted to the chorus, or to clerics acting as apostles. Perhaps the scribe, thinking of the earlier scene at the tomb, wrote the word by mistake.

The phrase, "et cantores . . . ordinent Tres Marias et Mercatorem *sicut ordinatum est in tropierio*", indicates clearly enough the manuscript which contained the text and music of the Gerona *Visitatio Sepulchri*. A scrutiny of bibliographical lists reveals that in recent years no less than three Gerona tropers have been reported extant. Anglès lists the following:[7] 1) Paris, Bibl. Nat., MS lat. nouv. acq. 495, Troparium Gerundense saec. xii; 2) Barcelona, Biblioteca Central, M. 911, Troparium-Prosarium Gerundense saec. xv; 3) Gerona, Collegiata de San Felix, s.n., Graduale-Troparium Gerundense saec. xv. Investigation discloses, however, that the Parisian troper contains no plays; the troper formerly at the collegiate church of St. Felix cannot be found; and the manuscript at the Biblioteca Central in Barcelona, though in part a troper, proves to be more especially a *prosarium*.

Nevertheless, on folio 156ᵛ of the latter manuscript, in the part of the codex devoted to the Credo of the Mass – a section which ordinarily does not treat of liturgical plays – there is pasted a small portion of a folio from another manuscript. This fragment is devoted to the text and music of a liturgical Easter play. The reader's attention is arrested by the rubric *Respondet Mercator*, which stands out in the very center of the text: in all probability the fragment is a part of the missing Gerona troper.

The folio appears to have been written in the thirteenth or fourteenth century, and is composed of six lines of text, three on either side, with music throughout. The portion begins very much *in mediis rebus* with a verse sung by the merchant:

---

[7] *El Còdex musical de las Huelgas*, I, intro., p. xvi *sqq*.

> \<non\> umquam[8] posset putrescere,
> neque uermes possent \<comedere\>.

Sicut supra:

> \<Heu, quantus est noster dolor.\>[9]

Respondet Mercator:

> Hoc unguentum si multum \<cupitis\>,
> \<unum\> auri talentum dabitis;
> nam aliter numquam \<portabitis\>.

At this point the folio has been cut off. On the reverse side we find the Marys already at the sepulchre:

> \<Alleluia, resurrexit\> Dominus, leo fortis, Christus, filius \<Dei\>.

Quo facto, dum mulieres descenderint de sepulcro, incipiant cantores prosa\<m\> hanc, et dicatur a coro sicut consuetum est, usque ad illum versum, *Dic nobis Maria*:

> Victime paschali \<laudes immol\>ent Christiani. Agnus redemit oues, Cristus in\<nocens Patri reconciliavit peccatores\>.

Here the fragment terminates. One notes immediately the striking similarity between the words sung by the merchant in this play, and those used by the ointment-seller in the Ripoll performance.

An examination of the beautifully written *consueta* of the church of St. Felix, a large fifteenth century manuscript of over two hundred folios, reveals that the *Visitatio Sepulchri* was also performed during the Middle Ages at St. Felix; again, however, the scribe says very little about it:[10]

> Et ponuntur candele in rotulo. Antiphona, responsorium, uerbete, gradualia, et alleluia dicuntur de duobus. Postea fiat Representatio de Tribus Mariis. His finitis, dompnus abbas, seu ille sacerdos qui facit officium, incipiat *Te Deum*.

In all probability the *Visitatio* at St. Felix was the same as that of the cathedral, for the ceremonies prescribed by the *consuetas* of the respective churches are very similar throughout.

The play of the Three Marys retained its popularity at the cathedral of Gerona until well past the middle of the sixteenth century. References to the piece here and there in the capitular statutes establish this. On March 15, 1474, for example, it was decided by the cathedral chapter, "Quod honestum

---

[8] umquam] The reading of this word is doubtful.
[9] The music is given for this line, but not the text. However from the context and the music, it is obviously the familiar refrain sung by the Marys. See the text of the *Visitatio Sepulchri* from Ripoll, given above, p. 78. The music is quite similar to that published by Anglès for the same refrain in the Ripoll play.
[10] Fol. 71. The play was presented, as usual, after the third responsory of Matins.

est quod servarentur de cetero omnes laudabiles consuetudines huius alme sedis, et presertim illa qua consueverunt canonici et presbyteri de capitulo facere Representationem Resurrectionis in officio matutinorum in die Sancte Pasce."[11]

What the play had become by 1539 is shown by a chapter decree recorded in that year. By that time not only did the merchant have a role in the play, but his wife also, and in addition to her an apothecary, and the apothecary's wife and son. The statute also refers to a *Representatio Centurionis*, and to plays of Mary Magdalen and St. Thomas:[12]

> Die sabbati X Maii MDXXXVIIII fuit communi omnium tam presentium in Capitulo quam infirmorum consultorum consensu facta sequens ordinacio siue statutum. Licet maiores nostri pia consideratione et ad excitandam populi deuotionem introduxerint, singulosque Canonicos in suo nouo ingressu astrinxerint, ut eorum quilibet secundum ordinem antiquitatis in festo Pasche Resurrectionis Redemptoris nostri Jhesu Christi in presenti Ecclesia Gerundensi in Matutinis singulis annis faciat representationem, que uulgo *Les tres Maries* dicitur; tamen quia experimento compertum est, id quod ad Dei cultum laudem et honorem introductum fuerat, ad ipsius noxam et offensam tendere, multa scandala inde oriri, populi indeuocionem excrescere, et infinita animarum ac corporum pericula insurgere, ac diuinum officium plurimum perturbari, et denique Ecclesie decorem et honestatem inquinari: propterea Capitulum predicte Ecclesie uolens, ut tenetur, tot scandalis et periculis obuiare, omnemque lasciuiam, abusum et turpitudinem ab ipsa Ecclesia extirpare, post uarios tractatus matura omnium deliberatione[13] reformando statuit et ordinauit, quod de cetero dicta representatio non possit fieri nisi in hunc qui sequitur modum. Videlicet: quod, finita verbeta, tres Marie uestibus nigris, ut moris est, indute incipiant canere versus solitos in poste ubi inuitatoria cantantur, et cantando eant ad altare maius, ubi sit paratum Cadafale cum multa luminaria, et ibi sint Apothecarius cum Uxore et Filiolo, necnon Mercator cum Uxore sua, qui non intrent nisi finita tercia lectione, et ibi fiat illa representatio petitionis unguenti ad ungendum sacratissimum Corpus Christi, ut moris est. Quando ipse persone representationem facture uenient ad Ecclesiam, nulla sint tympana siue tabals, neque trompete, nec aliquod aliud genus musicorum, neque niger, neque nigra siue famula, nec crustula, siue flaons aliquo modo projiciantur. Hec enim magis ad ludibrium quam ad Dei cultum populique rissum et indeuotionem ac diuini officii perturbationem tendere dinoscuntur. Representationes Centurionis, que fieri solebat in Matutinis, Magdalene et Thome que fieri consueuerant ante uel post Vesperas, uel in medio, in quibus erat consuetudo, immo corruptela piscandi, omnino extirpari uoluit atque decreuit dictum

---

[11] *Actas Capitulares*, 1474, fol. 14ᵛ.
[12] This passage has been previously published by Villanueva, *Viage literario*, XII, 342-343, and La Canal, *España Sagrada*, XLV, 23-24; Young reprints the passage from Villanueva, II, 504. I here re-edit from the original capitular statutes, 1528-1539, fol. 360-360ᵛ.
[13] deliberatione] delliberatione (MS).

Capitulum, et nihil aliud quam quod supradictum est aliquatenus fieri prohibuit atque prohibet, nisi de expresso consensu ipsius Capituli nemine discrepante.

Wishing to eliminate certain scandalous practices, the chapter here declares what was to be allowed in the future in the presentation of the drama of *Les tres Maries*. As Anglès remarks (p. 275), if it is here a question of a new ordinance drawn up especially to avoid abuses, and the apothecary with his wife and child, and the merchant and his wife still appear, what must the play have been before the reform? The legislators may have had in mind not so much the number of personages in the play, as the manner in which the players and spectators behaved. Still, one wonders what is to be inferred by the prohibition of anyone masquerading as a negro, negress, or servant girl ("neque niger, neque nigra siue famula").

Despite the number and identity of the characters, we need not necessarily conclude that the performance was given in the vernacular, though it likely was. The thirteenth century Latin *Visitatio* from Tours provides roles for two merchants, and the Latin Benediktbeuern play of the same century allots a role to the merchant's wife.[14] It must be remembered that we still have not identified four characters who appeared in the version known at Gerona in 1360. As for the time of the 1539 performance, we know that it was staged, like the Easter plays of the previous years, after the third responsory and *verbeta* of Matins: "in Matutinis . . . faciat representationem, que uulgo Les tres Maries dicitur . . . finita verbeta."

While permitting the drama of the Three Marys, the sixteenth century chapter decree forbade the further performance of the *Repraesentatio Centurionis*, or of the plays of Magdalen and Thomas. The first mentioned piece formerly took place at Matins, presumably along with the *Visitatio*. From the terminology of the statute, it would seem that two different plays were presented at Matins, *Les tres Maries* and the *Repraesentatio Centurionis*, but these were probably two different parts of one long play. The piece may have resembled the vernacular Easter production staged at Vich; in that performance the centurion appeared in the opening scene, and the Marys shortly afterward.

It is more difficult to say whether the *Repraesentationes* of Magdalen and Thomas were one play or two. They were presented "ante vel post vesperas, vel in medio"; this was presumably Vespers of Easter Day. Sometimes the *Peregrinus* was performed during this office. In several texts of this latter play the principal episode of Christ's apparition to His disciples was followed by a second scene between Christ and Mary Magdalen, and a third between Christ and St. Thomas. However if the Gerona play had been of this type, the scribe would probably have referred to it by its usual name. The association of the of the phrase *consuetudo immo corruptela piscandi* with both representations (*in*

[14] Texts in Young, I, 432, 438.

quibus erat consuetudo) suggests that they were two continuous scenes of one play.[15]

The abuse itself mentioned, that of fishing (*piscandi*), is quite intriguing. It is possible that the play with St. Thomas involved the scene recorded by St. John (chap. 21), in which Christ appeared to the apostles after His resurrection as they were fishing in the sea of Tiberias. In that episode the apostles had been fishing all night and had taken nothing, but at Christ's word, they let down the nets, and made an astounding catch. The scene indeed had dramatic possibilities, although the execution of it in church doubtless would have presented the medieval ecclesiastical playwrights with considerable difficulties. Moreover, apart from Christ, St. Peter was the central figure of that scene, rather than St. Thomas. Whatever the nature of the performance, the declaration of the statute that the *repraesentationes* were sometimes enacted "in the middle of Vespers" implies that, at one time at least, they had been liturgical plays.

As in so many places in the Middle Ages, the plays acquired such popularity in Gerona that it was difficult to abolish them. Despite the prohibitions of the cathedral chapter, as late as 1560 the plays of St. Mary Magdalen and the Descent from the Cross were enacted in the church. Finally, however, on April 5, 1566, even the Easter play was abolished forever.[16]

The fourteenth century *consueta* speaks of a *repraesentatio* at Easter Vespers which may have been the Magdalen play (fol. 60):

> Responsorium, *Hec dies*. Et non incipitur ab episcopo, sed a duobus clericis in pulpito. Postea dicunt versum *Confitemini, alleluia*; *angelus Domini*. Prosa, *Clara gaudia*, aut potest hic fieri representatio illius prose, *Surgit Christus cum tropheo*.

The prose *Surgit Christus cum trophaeo* was well known throughout medieval Europe.[17] Composed in dialogue form, the hymn involves a series of questions and answers concerning the Sacred Passion. St. Mary Magdalen is envisaged as the principal figure, and it is she who responds in a very touching manner to the interrogations: *Dic, Maria, quid vidisti contemplando crucem Christi*, etc. These interrogations and the whole form of the composition were almost certainly inspired by the famous sequence *Victimae paschali laudes*.

Impressed by the obvious dramatic possibilities of this sequence, Young makes reference to it in his treatise on the medieval theater (I, 496), but for lack of proof, he hesitates to conclude that it was ever dramatized:

---

[15] A vernacular play on the theme of Mary Magdalen's conversion was staged at Palma de Mallorca in the first half of the fourteenth century. It is not known where the piece was performed, perhaps either in church or at a public square. The fragmentary text of the play has been published by J. Quadrado in *La Unidad católica*, Palma de Mallorca, 1871 (reprinted in Milá y Fontanals, *Obras Completas*, VI, 315-323).
[16] Recorded in the Actas Capitulares for these years.
[17] The most common version of it has been published by Dreves and Blume, *Analecta Hymnica Medii Aevi*, LIV, 365-366.

Because of their imitating the dialogue in the sequence *Victimae paschali* one may draw special attention to the two laments *Surgit Christus cum trophaeo* and *Dic, Maria, quid vidisti contemplando crucem Christi*, in each of which the Virgin,[18] in response to interrogation, recalls successive moments in the Passion. It appears, however, that these two dramatic *planctus* are not directly related to the extant plays.

In 1846, F. Mone printed a version of the same prose from a fifteenth century manuscript found at the monastery of Lichtenthal.[19] This version definitely seemed to involve dramatization, for the questions are preceded by the rubric "angeli", and the replies by the rubric "Maria". Mone accordingly considered the text a play.

Discussing the same text some time later, G. Milchsack observed that when the question *Dic nobis, Maria* figured in the Easter plays, it was ordinarily sung by the choir, or by clerics acting as "apostles", and not by "angels". Suspecting that the author of the Lichtenthal manuscript was not thoroughly acquainted with traditional plays, and that he merely invented the distribution of the roles himself, Milchsack concluded that the prose of the Lichtenthal codex was probably never performed as a play. He writes:[20]

> I am of the opinion that to establish such a theory (viz., that the sequence *Surgit Christus* was dramatized at the German monastery), one needs better proofs than the dialogued form of the sequence and the dubious attribution of the roles . . ., and I believe that a manner of presentation utilizing several choruses . . . is the only one which form and tradition permit us to suppose.

Evidently Young agreed with Milchsack, because he refers to that author's observations, and does not mention the Lichtenthal text published by Mone and others. The passage in our Gerona *consueta*, then, takes on importance, because it supplies the proof that the sequence in question was sometimes presented as a little play.[21]

The text of the prose as it was sung at Gerona is given, with music, though without dramatic rubrics, in the proser at the Biblioteca Central in Barcelona:[22]

---

[18] In one version of the sequence, the dominating personage in the dialogue is the Holy Virgin; see *Analecta Hymnica*, LIV, 364.
[19] *Schauspiele des Mittelalters*, I, 19-20. It appears that the manuscript is no longer at the monastery.
[20] *Die Oster- und Passionsspiele*, I, 94.
[21] In France, according to the editors of *Analecta Hymnica* and Chevalier, *Repertorium Hymnologicum*, 19918-19919, the sequence was traditionally sung at Sens, Bordeaux, Saintes, Arles, Ainay, Nantes, Besançon, Lyon, Rodez, and other cities; in Spain at Segovia and Zaragoza.
[22] M. 911, Prosarium Ecclesiae Gerundensis saec. xv, fol. 70v-73. The sequence is immediately preceded by the prose *Clara gaudia festa paschalia*, listed for Easter Sunday. To give an idea of what the dramatic ceremony may have been like in the Catalan cathedral, I print in square brackets the rubrics furnished by the Lichtenthal codex (these rubrics are *not* in the Gerona manuscript).

ITEM ALIA PROSA

[Chorus:]

    Surgit Christus cum tropheo,
    iam ex agno factus leo
    solemni uictoria.

    Mortem uicit sua morte,
    reserauit seram porte
    sue mortis gratia.

    Hic est agnus qui pendebat,
    et in cruce redimebat
    totum gregem ouium.

    Cui cum nullus condolebat,
    Magdalenam consumebat
    doloris incendium.

[Angeli:]

    Dic, Maria, quid uidisti
    contemplando crucem Christi?

[Maria:]

    Vidi Ihesum spoliari,
    et in crucem subleuari
    peccatorum manibus.

[Angeli:]

    Dic, Maria.[23]

[Maria:]

    Spinis caput coronatum,
    uultum sputis maculatum
    et plenum liuoribus.

[Angeli:]

    Dic, Maria.[24]

[Maria:]

    Clauos manus perforare,
    hastam latus uulnerare
    uiui fontes exitum.

[Angeli:]

    Dic, Maria.

---

[23] Dic, Maria] The music for this phrase is the same as that in the preceding verse of the angels, so doubtless the whole phrase was repeated.
[24] This invitation and the following answer are lacking in the Lichtenthal codex.

[Maria:]
> Quod se Patri comendauit,
> et quod caput reclinauit
> et emisit spiritum.

[Angeli:]
> Dic, Maria.

[Maria:]
> Totum mundum tenebrari,
> terram motam concassari,
> monumenta reserari,
> uelum templi lacerari.
>
> Tracto tartarorum duce
> cruci figitur in cruce
> qui tenebras pellit luce
> uerus sol iusticie.

[Angeli:]
> Dic, Maria, quid uidisti
> quando Cristum amisisti?

[Maria:]
> Matrem flentem sociaui,
> quam ad domum reportaui,
> et in terram me prostraui,
> et utrumque deploraui.

[Angeli:]
> Dic, Maria, quid fecisti
> postquam Ihesum amisisti?

[Maria:]
> Post unguenta preparaui,
> et sepulcrum uisitaui;
> non inueni quem amaui,
> planctus meos duplicaui.

[Angeli:]
> O Maria, noli flere:
> iam surrexit Cristus uere.[25]

[Maria:]
> Certe, multis argumentis
> uidi signa resurgentis.

---

[25] This important transitional verse, and the following, are not found in the German manuscript.

[Chorus:]
> Dic nobis, Maria,
> quid uidisti in uia?

[Maria:]
> Sepulcrum Christi uiuentis
> et gloriam uidi resurgentis.[26]
>
> Dic nobis.
>
> Angelicos testes,
> sudarium et uestes.
>
> Dic nobis.
>
> Surrexit Christus, spes mea;
> precedet suos in Galileam.
>
> Credendum est magis soli
> Marie ueraci
> quam Judeorum
> turbe fallaci.
>
> Scimus Cristum surrexisse
> a mortuis uere;
> tu nobis, uictor
> rex, miserere. Amen.

It is interesting to observe how the dialogue portion of this prose has been combined, somewhat inharmoniously it is true, with that of the sequence *Victimae paschali laudes*. We do not know exactly how the prose was dramatized in the Catalan cathedral, but the ceremony was probably very simple. It is not impossible that the distribution of roles was the same at Gerona as at the German monastery, though Milchsack rigidly holds to the opinion that such an arrangement was impossible: "diese unerklärliche verwechselung der apostel mit den engeln für welche weder früher noch später eine analogie sich findet."[27] It is true that we are somewhat surprised to find angels questioning Mary Magdalen in this fashion, but a careful reading of the text reveals that such an arrangement was by no means unthinkable. It should be noted that the angels do not ask the questions taken from the prose *Victimae paschali laudes* (*dic nobis, Maria, quid vidisti in via?* etc.), which would be far more unfitting; the rubrics assign this role to the chorus. One has to imagine that

---

[26] This is the last verse given in the German codex. The scribe no doubt presumed the remainder of the piece was known.
[27] *Loc. cit.*

after the angels announce the resurrection to Mary (*O Maria, noli flere, iam surrexit Christus vere*), the tone changes from one of sorrow to joy, with Mary hastening to tell the disciples (the chorus) the good tidings. Questioned by them, she tells them what she has seen. Of course, we should not attempt to apply rigorous logic to these ingenuous medieval productions. That angels sometimes did the questioning even in the sequence *Victimae paschali laudes* we are certain, for this occurred at Gerona itself during the Easter play at Matins: "et angelus: dic nobis, Maria."

Not content with the *Visitatio* of Easter morning and the dramatization of the prose *Surgit Christus* at Easter Vespers, the Gerona ecclesiastics continued the dramatic festivities at Mass the following morning. On this day it was the prose *Victamae paschali* which was acted out, a choir-boy taking the role of Mary Magdalen:[28]

> Prosa, *Victime paschali laudes*. Et duo pueri cantent ante letrilium versum, *Dic nobis, Maria*. Et unus puer stans ante altare Sancte Marie induto dalmatica cum alifafa in capite, qui teneat aliquam capçam in manu in representatione resurrectionis Christi. Versa facie uersus chorum respondeat *sepulcrum Christi uiuentis*. Et iterum illi duo de choro dicant *Dic nobis, Maria*. Et ille qui erit ad altare respondeat *angelicos testes*. Iterum illi duo de choro dicant *Dic nobis, Maria* et ille qui erit ad altare respondit *Surrexit Christus spes mea*, et clauiger paret subdiachonem, et diachonus ad euangelium. Postea chorus respondat *Credendum est magis*.

This text throws light upon a question which until now has remained somewhat obscure: whether or not sequences were ever dramatized at Mass. Karl Young knew of but one instance in which the manner of singing the sequence at Mass came close to drama, but he concludes that even in that "isolated case" from Vienne in France, impersonation was probably not involved.[29] The passage from the Catalan ceremonial shows quite conclusively that in some churches the sequence was indeed sometimes dramatized in this part of the liturgy; the similarity of the texts from the two cities also makes it quite certain that the Vienne ceremony was accompanied by impersonation as well. Doubtless it was this type of ceremony which Durandus, the bishop of Mende (c. 1237–96) had in mind when he stated that the *Visitatio* was performed in some communities "ad Missam cum dicitur sequentia illa: *Victimae paschali laudes*, cum dicitur versus: *Dic nobis*, et sequentes."[30] In a later chapter we shall encounter a much more elaborate play at this same point in the liturgy.[31]

---

[28] Gerona, Bibl. Capit., Consueta Gerundensis (1360), fol. 60ᵛ. Virtually the same passage is also found in the margin of an uncatalogued fifteenth century breviary at the Gerona Seminary library.
[29] I, 274-275.
[30] *Rationale Diuinorum Officiorum Guilhelmi Mimatensis Ecclesie Episcopi*, fol. 210ᵛ. See Young's discussion of the bishop's statement, I, 605.
[31] See below, p. 133.

The identical *Repraesentatio* took place at the church of St. Felix, but there it was presented during Vespers of Easter Monday rather than at Mass:[32]

> Prosa, *Victime paschali*. Hic potest fieri Representatio, hoc est quod duo pueri in choro dicant *Dic nobis Maria*. Et alter puer stans in ianua rexiarum indutus dalmatica cum alifafa in capite, qui teneat aliquod in manu in representatione Resurrectionis Christi uersa facie ad chorum, respondeat versum, *Sepulcrum Christi uiuentis*. Et iterum illi duo dicant: *Dic nobis*. Et ille respondeat, *Angelicos testes*. Iterum illi duo dicant *Dic nobis*, et ille respondeat: *Surrexit Christus spes mea*. Postea chorus respondeat, *Credendum est magis*, et sic finitur.

Christmas Plays at Gerona

The dramatically inclined clerics at Gerona were even more active on Christmas Eve than during the Easter season. Of this the fourteenth century *consueta* is a precious testimony. Whereas the ecclesiastics of some churches, such as Rouen, distributed the liturgical plays over different days of the festive season, presenting the *Officium Pastorum* on Christmas Night, the *Ordo Prophetarum* on January 1st, and the *Officium Stellae* on January 6th, the officiants at Gerona seemed determined to present as many as possible on Christmas Day itself.

The first Christmas Mass, of course, as today, commenced at Midnight. Since it was preceded by the three nocturns of Matins, two plays, long responses, numerous *verbeta*, and the singing of the Gospel, *Liber generationis*, the people must have begun coming to church around seven o'clock in the evening; the first play was staged as early as the fifth lesson of Matins. A lengthy description of what took place during these pre-midnight hours, though unfortunately the dramatic texts themselves are not given, is found on folios 23ᵛ–24 of the *consueta*:[33]

> Lectio quarta: Sermo, *Clementissimus Pater*. Responsorium, *Quem vidistis*. Lectio quinta: *Castissimum Marie Virginis*. Et si fiat Representacio Partus Beate Virginis, hec lectio dicitur nona, et lectio *Inter pressuras* que est nona dicitur quinta, et fit in ipsa si uoluerit Representacio Prophetarum. Et postea in nona que est *Castissimum* fit si uoluerint Partus Representacio. Sin autem leguntur lectiones ut ordinate sunt in libro legende. Et hec fiunt propter Dei honorem et laboris alleuiationem. Responsorium *O magnum*. Lectio sexta de homiliario evangelii *Exiit edictum*.

. . . .

---

[32] Gerona Seminary, Consueta Ecclesiae Sancti Felicis saec. xv, fol. 73ᵛ.
[33] This text has been partially edited by Anglès, p. 283, n. 2. As he observes, the Villanueva manuscript gives only a very rapid summary of it. Because of its briefness, the summary is confusing and has led some commentators into error. See Paul Aebischer, 'Un Ultime écho de la *Procession des Prophètes*', p. 268.

Lectio nona: legitur sermo *Inter pressuras atque angustias presentis temporis*. Et fiat hic Prophetarum Representacio si uoluerint. Et eorum quilibet dicat suum titulum ut in legenda continetur de prophetis. Et tunc in letrilio dicatur *Judicii signum* per Sibillam. Et finito primo versu per ipsam, chorus respondeat *Judicii signum*. Quo finito, incipiat ipsa cum quodam alio clerico uel scolari bene cantante versum *E celo rex adueniens* cum sequentibus. Et in fine cuiuslibet versus chorus reiteret *Judicii signum*. Aliter[34] dicatur sicut est terminatum in legendario, a quatuor clericis scilicet bini et bini in truna; et finita lectione dicatur responsorium *Verbum caro factum est*. Et dicitur primus versus *Olim prophete a duobus clericis in choro ante letrilium*. Secundus versus, scilicet *Tamquam sponsus . . . Gloria Patri . . .* Et ponuntur candele in rotulis cori et sepulcri, que debent durare usque quo prima sit finita. Et dicitur verbeta *Sollempnis et leta* a quatuor clericis in letrilio.

Thus at Gerona on Christmas Eve sometimes one, sometimes two, plays were presented during the celebration of Matins. One of these performances, known as the *Repraesentatio Partus Beate Virginis*, was associated with the sermon *Castissimum Mariae Virginis*. Ordinarily this sermon was read as the fifth lesson,[35] but if the play took place, it was transferred to the ninth position, and the piece enacted at that point.

Exactly what this play was, however, is another question, for in keeping with his usual practice, the author of the *consueta* does not give the text; perhaps like the Easter piece, it was contained in the missing troper. From the title we know that the play had for its theme the birth of the Christ-Child. This of course was the central theme of the Christmas performance known elsewhere as the *Officium Pastorum*, and the Gerona play may have resembled one of these. The title *Repraesentatio Partus*, for example, could have been very appropriately applied to the Rouen Christmas play, perhaps the most famous of the *Officia Pastorum* published to date.[36] In that piece a *praesepe* was erected near the altar, and a statue of the Blessed Mother placed within it. When the shepherds had been informed by the angels of Christ's birth, they came to the manger in search of the Child, where they were met by the *obstetrices*. These latter replied to their questions by drawing back a curtain, which revealed the statue of the Mother and Child. At the familiar words, *Adest hic paruulus* (we have frequently seen this antiphon in the Christmas trope), the *obstetrices* pointed to the Divine Child, and at the phrase *Ecce Virgo concipiet et pariet filium*, to the Mother:[37] this scene was an admirable *Repraesentatio Partus*. The shepherds thereupon knelt in adoration, and then turning to the chorus and people, concluded the play by singing the verse, *Alleluia! Iam vere scimus Christum natum in terris*.

---

[34] Aliter] Anglès reads *aliud*; MS: *ali'*.
[35] In Christmas Matins there were nine lessons in all, three in each nocturn.
[36] The text of this play is given in the Appendix, p. 173.
[37] For the complete verse, see above, p. 93.

At Gerona the play was attached in a special way to the lesson *Castissimum Mariae Virginis*, a homiletic piece, which like the sermon *Inter pressuras*, was attributed in the Middle Ages to St. Augustine.[38] When the play was performed, it was presented during the ninth lesson, and the sermon *Castissimum* was moved out of its ordinary position to accompany it. The *consueta* declares: "in nona lectione que est *Castissimum* fit si uoluerint Partus Representatio." This statement raises the interesting question as to whether the sermon itself may not have been dramatized. Such an evolution would by no means have been unique in the history of the liturgical drama, for the sermon *Inter pressuras* had already given the famous *Ordo Prophetarum*.

An examination of the text shows that dramatization would have been possible. The greater part of the sermon is in dialogue form, and provides notable speaking parts for the Blessed Mother, St. Joseph, and the Angel Gabriel. The theme is the Virgin Birth. The substance of its argument, however, concerns primarily the Annunciation and the holy conception rather than the Divine Birth itself; the title given to the sermon in the Migne edition is significant: *De Annuntiatione Dominica*. Most important of all, in the course of the sermon the Christmas scene at Bethlehem is not portrayed, a scene which was almost inevitably a part of any Nativity play. Hence, all things considered, the Gerona *Repraesentatio* probably did not consist solely of a dramatic rendering of the sermon. It is even more likely that the lesson served only as an excellent introduction, and that the play itself was performed after the lesson had been concluded. Still, if the play contained more than one scene, and was of a cyclic nature – on a small scale, of course – it is conceivable that parts of the lesson may have been incorporated into the dramatic performance. Since this may have occurred, we present here the version of the sermon employed as the fifth lesson of Christmas Matins at Valencia:[39]

> Castissimum Marie Virginis vterum, sponse Virginis clausum cubiculum, signatum pudoris cenaculum, merito plenissime collaudarem, si messem meterem, quam non seminarem. De qua dicit apostolus. Quecumque seminauerit homo: hec et metet. Verum est omnimodo, fratres charissimi, verum est hoc: omnem hominem metere quod seminauit. Deus autem potest metere quod non seminauit: sicut ipse Filius Virginis in quadam euangelii lectione dicit. Meto vbi non seminaui, et colligo vbi non sparsi. Dicat dicat, solus dicat natus ex Virgine Filius Marie, dicat sponse

---

[38] The full text of this sermon may be found in Migne, *P.L.*, 39, 2107-2110. The work may have been written by Ambroise Autpert, an eighth century Benedictine monk from Provence who became abbot of the Italian monastery of St. Vincent of Volturno; see Msgr. P. Glorieux, *Pour revaloriser Migne* (Lille, 1952), p. 26.

[39] *Hores de la Setmana Sancta* (Valencia, 1533), fol. 248v-250. I have not seen the sermon as it appears in medieval Gerona lectionaries. A fourteenth (?) century Gerona breviary at the chapter library gives only the first five lines of the lesson, but a longer form than this would have been read in the public recitation of the office at the cathedral; the same breviary presents only the five opening lines of the sermon *Inter pressuras*, and we know that this sermon was dramatized.

Matri sue: meto vbi non seminaui, et colligo vbi non sparsi. Dicat et Maria:

> Et ego te filium generaui, virginitatem meam non violaui. Regnum tenui virginitatis: et Regem genui castitatis. Ingredientem et regredientem habui in palatio ventris Filium Imperatoris; et manibus meis non amisi clauem regii pudoris. Porta facta sum celi: ianua facta sum Filio Dei. Illa porta facta sum clausa, quam in visionem Ezechiel propheta vidit; de qua dicit in me prophetizans: Vidi portam in domo Domini clausam; et dixit ad me angelus: porta hec quam vidisti non aperietur, et homo non transiet per eam, quia Dominus solus intrat et regredit per eam, et clausa erit in eternum.

Sed mirabilior prophetie adimpletio. Que est porta in domo Domini clausa, nisi quod Maria Virgo semper erit intacta? Et quid est homo non transiet per eam, nisi quia Ioseph non cognouit eam? Et quid est Deus solus intrat et regredit per eam, nisi quia Spiritus Sanctus impregnauit eam, et angelorum Deus nascetur per eam? Et quid est clausa erit in eternum, nisi quod Maria Virgo est ante partum, Virgo in partum, et Virgo post partum? Dicat ergo Maria:

> Porta facta sum celi, ianua facta sum Filio Dei. Adimpleuit ventrem meum diuinitate, et vterum meum non euacuauit castitate. Exiuit ex ventre meo gygas cursu magnificus, et venter meus non est pudore euacuatus. Hec in conceptione inuenta sum sine pudore, nec in parturitione inuenta sum cum dolore.

O mira et laudabilis inter feminas que ab angelo salutatur virginitas. Sola impregnata, nec uitiata; exonerata, nec euacuata, quia sic est ab angelo salutata: Ave, inquit, Maria gratia plena Dominus tecum. Considero conceptum tuum Beata Virgo, et expauesco; intueor partum tuum, et contremisco. Adoro Filium tuum, et reuiuisco. Enarra mihi obsecro modo, quomodo meruisti dici Mater Dei, sponsaque Filii Dei? Ignosce mihi quod audeam cum sponsa Domini mei confabulari; tantum indica mihi quomodo poterit per te Filius Dei generari. Audite, fratres charissimi, audite Mariam nobiscum loquentem, carne absentem spiritu presentem:

> Erat, inquit Maria, in domo mea, puella Iudea, ex semine David regis generata. Adulta facta sum, et desponsata. Non interueniente adulterio, sed intercedente Spiritu Sancto. Desponsauit me vir Iudeus, et amauit me Christus Deus. Nam ignoto Ioseph sponso meo, venit ad me paranimphus de celo. Gabriel, Christi archangelus: facie rutilans, veste coruscans, incessu mirabilis, aspectu terribilis; me visitauit et perturbauit. Dixitque mihi:

> Ave, inquit, Maria, gratia plena, Dominus tecum. Dominus, inquit, tecum, sed plusquam mecum. Dominus tecum, sed non sic

mecum. In me enim licet sit Dominus, aliter in te, quia per te nasciturus est Dominus.

Dixitque illi Maria:

Quomodo fiet istud, vt ex vtero grauescam pudico, et inmunis sim a marito, quem penitus non cognosco? Desponsata sum homini iusto; si cum illo non conuenero, vnde erit quod generabo? Sed si potest fieri vt concipiam intacta, et generem clausa, indica mihi modum et paratum inuenies animum meum.

Refert angelus Gabriel modum conceptionis, quod in verbo fieret Saluatoris:

O Maria, inquit, Virgo Dei, Filia Dei et Mater Dei. Si hunc a me modum requiris, quomodo virgo concipies, et virgo paries, et post partum virgo permaneas, vel quomodo fiet in te qui fecit te, audi me et non perturberis in te. Spiritus Sanctus superueniet in te, et virtus altissimi obumbrabit tibi. Ita te virtus altissimi obumbrabit, vt nec estum patiaris libidinis, et Mater sis Creatoris.

Respondit Maria ad angelum:

Ecce ancilla Domini, fiat mihi secundum verbum tuum.

Tu autem, Domine, miserere nobis.

The author of this text was by no means devoid of poetic talent. His piece shows imagination and has considerable charm. If part of this sermon was dramatized, it is a notable addition to the group of liturgical plays known to date.

The ninth lesson of Christmas Matins (or if the *Repraesentatio Partus* was performed, the fifth) was devoted to another, and more celebrated, pseudo-Augustinian sermon, *Inter pressuras atque augustias*. At Gerona it was presented in its most festive form, that is, with the dramatized *Processio Prophetarum*. This type of play has already been discussed at some length in an introductory chapter of this study (p. 17), and a typical version of it has been included in the Appendix (p. 176), so we have an approximate idea of what the Gerona piece must have been like. It is noteworthy that in the Catalan cathedral the play was given as *a part* of the lesson, and not apart from it as in all the examples of the play published to date (at Tours *after* the ninth lesson, at Rouen before Mass).[40] Moreover it seems that at Gerona the text of the play was taken directly from the sermon, just as it appeared in the *legendarium*, or *lectionarium* as it was more commonly called: "Et eorum quilibet dicat suum titulum ut in legenda continetur de prophetis." In other words, it appears that the sermon itself was dramatized, whereas for the plays from Rouen, St. Martial, etc., special verses were composed modelled upon the sermon.[41]

[40] See Young, II, 153, 165.
[41] There is a fourteenth century *legendarium* at the Gerona chapter library, but it is the volume devoted to the feasts of the saints (*sanctorale*) and not the one which gives the lessons for seasonal

In many of the Prophet Plays the Sibyl spoke only several lines, but at Gerona, as in most Spanish churches, she sang her entire prophecy. She was accompanied in her chant by another cleric, whose function it probably was to help the young "prophetess" through the difficult parts.

It is not difficult to discern why, if the two plays were performed at Matins, the *Ordo Prophetarum* was presented first, and the *Repraesentatio Partus* afterward. The former, with its prophecies concerning the birth of Christ, served as an appropriate introduction to the second piece; the reverse order would have been illogical.

The cathedral was not the only scene of dramatic activity in this Catalan city on Christmas Eve. The same two plays were put on at Matins in the collegiate church of St. Felix:[42]

> Lectio quinta, *Castissimum Virginis Marie*. Si fiat Representatio Partus Beate Marie Virginis, hec lectio dicitur nona, et lectio *Inter pressuras*, que est nona, dicitur quinta. Et fit in ipsa si uoluerint Representatio Prophetarum, et postea in nona que est *Castissimum* fit Partus Representatio; sin autem, leguntur lectiones ut ordinate sunt in legendario. Et hec fiunt propter Dei honorem et laboris alleuiationem. Responsorium, *O magnum* . . . .
> Lectio nona legitur sermo *Inter pressuras*, et fiat hic Prophetarum Representatio si uoluerint; alioquin dicitur testimonium per Sibillam, *Judicii signum*, idest, *Al iorn del iudici*, in truna uel in alio decenti. Responsorium *Verbum caro factum est*.

At St. Felix, even if the *Procession of Prophets* was not acted out during the ninth lesson, the Sibyl nevertheless retained her dramatic role; in the fifteenth century she delivered her prophecy in Catalan.

The dramatic activity continued during Lauds, though it is difficult to determine just what took place at this office. During the singing of the psalms, the well-known antiphon, *Infantem vidimus*, was repeated several times by choir-boys stationed behind the altar, as in so many other churches. The scribe does not say whether they were costumed as shepherds: "Et pueri aggregati cum suo magistro retro altare incipientes ad illum locum *infantem uidimus* explicant totam antiphonam." The concluding part of the ceremony is summarized in the *consueta* of the cathedral as follows:[43]

feasts (*proprium de tempore*). Anglès has reproduced a facsimile of one folio of the sermon from an eleventh century Gerona *lectionarium* which has since been lost (p. 151). The facsimile shows the conclusion of the sermon with the words of Nabuchodonosor and the Sibyl, so in all likelihood Nabuchodonosor had a role in the Gerona play; we know that the Sibyl did, because the *consueta* mentions her expressly.

[42] Gerona Seminary, Consueta Ecclesiae Sancti Felicis saec. xv, fol. 34.
[43] Fol. 24ᵛ. This passage has been paraphrased by Villanueva, who obviously also had difficulty in interpreting it, for he has eliminated or added certain words. Anglès repeats Villanueva's summary without comment (p. 283): "Ad Benedictus. Antiphona: *Gloria* dicatur ab Episcopo vel sacerdote si non fiat repraesentatio. At si dicta repraesentatio facta fuerit, et ibi fuerint angeli, recipiunt Jhesuellum in manibus et incipient *Te Deum laudamus*, post finem, Evangelium *Liber*, et *Gloria* ante *Benedictus*."

> Capitulum *Apparuit* ab episcopo uel sacerdote remanente induti ad altare. Responsorium, *Paruulus filius*. Hymnus, *Enixa est*. Versus *Verbum caro*. In euangelio[44] antiphona *Gloria in excelsis*. Et dicatur ab episcopo siue sacerdote, si non fiat Partus Representatio, at non si dicta Representatio facta fuerit et ibi fuerint angeli; recipiunt Ihesuellum in manibus et incipiunt *Te Deum laudamus*. Post finem, euangelium et *Gloria in excelsis Deo* ante psalmum *Benedictus*.[45]

Probably the scribe is referring to the *Repraesentatio Partus* which took place at Matins. If that play was performed, and "angels" had taken part in it, at the point in Lauds where the bishop ordinarily sang the *Benedictus* antiphon, a pause was made and the "angels" took the "Child-Jesus" in their arms (likely a small image that had been used in the Christmas play), and sang the *Te Deum*. This is very unusual procedure, for ordinarily there is no *Te Deum* at Lauds unless a play is performed at that office. Perhaps the *Repraesentatio Partus* was sometimes performed at Lauds. Villanueva interprets the words "post finem evangelium" as referring to the gospel *Liber Generationis*. This gospel had already been sung in the cathedral at the conclusion of the Matins play, and one wonders why it should be repeated at Lauds. If it is a question of a different gospel, the problem still remains, because in normal procedure no gospel was sung at this point in Lauds. The *consueta* from St. Felix does not help us here, since it makes no reference to a play in its summary of this office. However we are enlightened about one feature of the performance: angels sometimes had a role in it.[46]

Along with the plays the ancient tropes were still sung in both Gerona churches:[47]

> Ad Missam duo pueri induti dalmaticis stantes equales in medio rexiarum, uersi ad chorum, dicant tropum, scilicet, *Psallite, fratres mei*. Sequitur tropus: *Quem queritis in presepe*, cum quatuor versibus sequentibus, et dicuntur de duobus in duobus clericis ad letrilium. Officium, *Puer natus est nobis*.[48]

---

[44] euangelio] eg⁰ (MS). The abbreviation may be *cg⁰*. Villanueva has avoided the word by simply writing, "Ad Benedictus". In any case the word probably refers to the *Benedictus* canticle; the antiphon *Gloria in excelsis Deo* was usually sung before it.

[45] The actual punctuation of the manuscript is as follows: "Et dicatur ab episcopo siue sacerdote. si non fiat partus representatio. at non si dicta representatio facta fuerit et ibi fuerint angeli recipiunt ihesuellum in manibus et incipiunt *Te Deum laudamus* post finem euangelium et *Gloria in excelsis Deo* ante ps. *Benedictus*."

[46] As we have seen, the medieval Christmas play usually opened with the "scene of the angels". A choir-boy, garbed as an angel, and stationed somewhere in the upper part of the church, would announce the joyful news to the shepherds: "Nolite timere, ecce enim evangelizo vobis gaudium magnum, etc." Other "angels" representing the heavenly chorus would then join in: "Gloria in excelsis Deo et in terra pax hominibus bonae voluntatis."

[47] Fol. 26 of the cathedral *consueta*; the passage on fol. 35ᵛ of the St. Felix ceremonial is almost identical.

[48] nobis] in nobis (MS).

The final *repraesentatio* of Christmas Day was staged in the afternoon at Vespers. In some respects the record of the piece performed during this office is one of the most important contained in the *consueta*:[49]

> In euangelio[50] antiphona *Hodie Christus* dicatur ab episcopo si ipse fecerit officium, et reiteratur a quodam prelato, uel ab episcopello qui in istis versibus[51] creatur, et sedet se tercio in cathedra episcopali cum duobus sibi contiguis. Et prelati istis diebus cedunt eis. Dicitur oratio ut scriptum. Postea ueniunt cantores et officiatores diachonorum induti capis rubeis. Et faciunt Representationem Martirii Beati Stephani si voluerint. Et ille qui regit cantoriam secundam dat antiphonam Sancti Stephani, scilicet *Preclarus dies*, alicui prelato uel venerabili canonico diachono, et cantores et officiatores dicant *Gloria Patri*. Et in fine antiphone dicitur pneuma, uel si voluerint diachoni dicant responsorium *Sancte Stephane*.

Here we find the Boy-Bishop appearing in the ceremonies. It would have been remarkable if in some way or other he did not find his way into the discussion in this chapter, because at Gerona he was a most popular and active individual. Four pages of the *consueta* are devoted to his privileges (fol. 114^v–116), and he receives equal attention in the St. Felix ceremonial (fol. 132^v–133^v).

At Vespers it was customary to make a commemoration of the saint whose feast day was celebrated the following day. Since December 26th was St. Stephen's Day, a special antiphon and oration were said at the conclusion of Christmas Vespers in his honor. At Gerona the saint was feted not only by an antiphon and an oration, but by a play, a *Repraesentatio Martirii Beati Stephani*. This play took place during the liturgical office, and was probably performed by deacons. Once again the Gerona scribe withholds from us the dramatic text, and the ceremonial from St. Felix does not mention any *repraesentatio*. We know only that the main theme was St. Stephen's martyrdom.

If we can judge from the account books of other Catalan cathedrals, the play was probably realistic enough. Dramatic performances in honor of the protomartyr were extremely popular, it appears, in many parts of Catalonia. A reference to one has already been recorded from a document at Vich,[52] and we shall presently see that the entire liturgy of St. Stephen's Day was dramatized at Mallorca. The play closest to that of Gerona was perhaps the piece regularly enacted in the cathedral of Barcelona. Anglès has published these two items from accounts in the Barcelona capitular archives:[53]

---

[49] Gerona, Bibl. Capit., Consueta (1360), fol. 26^v. Villanueva (*Viage literario*, XII, 195) and Fr. de la Canal (*España Sagrada*, 1832, XLV, 17) have alluded to this passage, and many in turn have cited them. However, to my knowledge, no one has ever published the text of the *consueta*.
[50] euangelio] eg° or perhaps cg° in the manuscript; here the canticle referred to is the *Magnificat*.
[51] Probably at the verse of the *Magnificat*, "Deposuit potentes de sede."
[52] See above, p. 96.
[53] 'Epistola farcida del martiri de Sant Esteve', p. 70.

1413-Dehembre. Item deu que munta la part de la Sacristia les messions[54] qui foren fets per la Representació de Nadal y de Sanct Stheua . . . 13s.[55]

Item deu que pagui a XXIII del dit mes[56] los bastaxs[57] qui apportaren les botas[58] qui seruiran per los cadaffals de la Representacio de Sant Estheua . . . XII & III s. Item deu que compri farine per fer angrut[59] y ayguecuyt[60] y blanch per fer les pedras d'alapidar Sant Estheua y doni a meniar y beure aquells qui ajudaren a tirar la fusta dels cadaffals y tornar y per teytlas . . . XVI s.[61]

Thus the Barcelona *repraesentatio* involved a realistic stoning of St. Stephen with imitation stones. Perhaps the scene was duplicated at Gerona.

Those who have treated the liturgical drama of such countries as France and England, make no mention of St. Stephen plays. Many writers have discussed at length the celebrated "farced epistle" sung half in Latin, half in the vernacular, during Mass on December 26th, and others have informed us about the deacon's part in the three-day "revels" which followed Christmas; but to my knowledge, no one has ever recorded instances of dramatization or impersonation within the St. Stephen's Day liturgy outside of Catalonia.

That such dramatic ceremonies did take place elsewhere is shown by the following passage in an eleventh or twelfth century codex from the cathedral of Cambrai in France:[62]

DE SANCTO STEPHANO

Ante septimam lectionem ueniat diaconus in similitudine Sancti Stephani, dalmatica indutus cum palma in manu, ita dicens:

> Filie Ierusalem, uenite et uidete martyrem cum corona qua coronauit eum Dominus in die sollempnitatis et letitie, alleluia, alleluia!

Chorus:

> Aue, senior Stephane, aue martyr paradoxe qui inter agmina plebis Iudaicae, firmus in Christo fide uelut lampas ardentissima apparuisti Domino, nunc sidus inter sidera celestis aule, succurre huic familie gratissima tua interuentione.

Benedictio:

> Dominus omnipotens benedicat uos; sicut ros in Hermon qui descendit in Sion, sic descendit super uos Dei benedictio.

Mox legat lectionem septimam.

---

[54] messions: expenses.
[55] Comptes de la Sagristia, 1411-1413, without foliation.
[56] December, 1419.
[57] bastaxs: porters.
[58] botas: casks.
[59] angrut: paste.
[60] ayguecuyt: glue.
[61] Comptes de la Sagristia, 1417-1419, without foliation.
[62] Cambrai, Bibl. Mun., MS 78, Prosa-Responsoriale saec. xii, fol. 55^v-56; the manuscript provides music.

Thus at Cambrai, as early as the eleventh or twelfth century, a deacon would come to the choir after the sixth lesson of Matins, wearing a dalmatic and carrying a palm in his hand. He thus represented St. Stephen, triumphant in heaven. Giving expression to his joy in an antiphon, he was greeted by the members of the choir, who beseeched him for a blessing. The blessing was then willingly bestowed in very graceful and flowing language. This beautiful little scene possesses the same charm and touching simplicity of the early liturgical Easter plays, and reveals, in addition, a deep faith in the doctrine of the communion of saints.

Is this text an isolated instance, or were such ceremonies as this common in France during the Middle Ages? This question can only be answered by an examination of the many other unstudied medieval liturgical manuscripts still extant in France.

Finally it would be of interest, I think, by way of conclusion to this chapter, to gather together a few of the principal references made to various religious plays in the capitular statutes of Gerona. In all probability these plays were not strictly liturgical in nature. It is also probable that they were delivered in the vernacular:

> February 16, 1473 (fol. 122):
> Fuit etiam deliberatum quod singulis diebus dominicis fiant honeste representationes de historia dominice, excepta prima dominica quadragesime, in qua occurret festum gloriosissimi Sancti Thome de Aquino, Doctoris egregii et electissimi, in quo sermonem facit de mane ... Postea XVIII Febroarii fuit uisum quod etiam ea die fiant representationes post prandium; et incipientur representationes a temptatione Christi, in qua pauci sufficient et breuiter expedietur et devote.
>
> March 9, 1538 (fol. 313^v):
> Die sabbati VIIII Martii, 1538, ad supplicationem domni Petri Matheu canonici (?) ad quem anno presenti pertinet facere ludos, siue representationes paschales, ... concessum sibi fuit quod cras die dominica possit facere representationem in ecclesia qualiter diabolus tentauit Dominum prout in sancto euangelio continetur.
>
> March 22, 1546 (fol. 378):
> Placuit omnibus quod in ecclesia fiant representationes Passionis Redemptoris Domini Jesuchristi et Septem peccatorum mortalium; sed prius, uideat stilum dictarum representationum Rdus. Dominus Torrent Canonicus et uicarius generalis, sacrarum litterarum doctor egregius, ne quid sit in illis quod aurem omnipotentis Dei offendat.
>
> Feast of Corpus Christi:
> Hacíase su procesión por la mañana, y en ella ademas de los gigantones y otras comparsas, se representaban en las plazuelas de San Pedro y del Vino el sacrificio de Isaac, el sueño y venta de José, y otras historias sagradas, las cuales ejecutaban los beneficiados de la catedral.
>
> (Villanueva, XII, 205).

CHAPTER 9

PLAYS AT MALLORCA

If in the Middle Ages the cathedral of Gerona merited the title of "madre de las ceremonias", its right to this honor must have been seriously challenged by the cathedral of Palma de Mallorca. In few churches of Europe, it seems, were liturgical plays more popular.

Mallorca was reconquered from the Arabs only in the year 1229, hence much later than most of the neighboring region of Catalonia. It is not known with certainty when the Roman-French rite was first brought there. When on the mainland King James the Conqueror entered Valencia in 1238, he found the Mozarabic liturgy still in usage. Msgr. Anglès points out that, although the Balearic cities remained in the hands of the Arabs until the thirteenth century, the churches on the islands were placed under the jurisdiction of the bishop of Barcelona as early as 1060, and in Barcelona of course, the Roman-French rite was practised at that date.[1] The same commentator, nevertheless, seems to be of the opinion that the new liturgy was not completely established at Palma until the reconquest in the thirteenth century (p. 289).

At whatever date the new rite came to the islands, the liturgical drama came with it in triumphant fashion. Three *consuetas* preserved in the Palma capitular archives testify eloquently to this.

As at Gerona, the ceremonies for Christmas began at Palma very early the preceding evening, the opening hour actually being determined by the number of plays to be performed. In a favorable year the Mallorcan church-goers would behold in the course of the evening the shepherds, St. Augustine, the Old Testament prophets, and, to be sure, the inevitable Sibyl. Three different descriptions of Christmas Matins are given by the Mallorcan *consuetas*. The first does not mention the plays:[2]

> Dum dominus episcopus incipiet dicere pro nona leccione legendam *Jube dompne*[3] prelatus aliquis qui sit in choro, uel canonicus aut primicherius, dicat alta uoce *Ora pro nobis, pater*. Et dominus episcopus dicat benedictionem *Sancta Maria Virgo Virginum*. Et dum dominus episcopus dicet leccionem, sex presbiteri ascendant in trunam. Et duo incipiant alta uoce *Iudicii signum*, et chorus respondeat *Judicii signum*. Et predicti sex presbiteri bini et bini dicant omnes alios versus. Et in fine cuiuslibet

---

[1] *La Música a Catalunya*, p. 37.
[2] Palma, Bibl. Capit., manuscript without catalogue number, fol. 19. Villanueva (*Viage literario*, XXII, 176) classifies this codex as mid-fourteenth century. The passage has been partially edited from the Villanueva manuscript by Anglès, pp. 232-233.

versi chorus respondeat *Judicii signum*. Et finitis omnibus versibus, episcopus finiat lectionem. Responsorium *Gloria in altissimis*.

According to this version, six clerics chanted the Sibylline prophecy, alternating two by two, and the chorus sang the refrain. This procedure was identical with that observed at Palencia in the fourteenth century.

The same manuscript contains another account of Christmas Matins which provides for considerable dramatization:[4]

> Ad nonam lectionem assuetum est, si reuerendissimus dominus episcopus Maioricensis facit officium, quando dominacio erit in legendario cum ministris suis et dicet *Jube dompne benedicere*, unus prelatus in cathedra sua uel canonicus respondebit alta uoce *Ora pro nobis, pater*, in sonum lectionis. Et dominus episcopus dicat *Sancta Maria Virgo Virginum intercedat pro nobis ad Dominum*. Et chorus dicat, Amen . . . . Prelatus episcopus procedat ad lectionem *Inter pressuras atque angustias*, usque ad illum locum, *Sancte Augustine, interroga prophetas, Sancte Augustine*. Et episcopus uel canonicus[5] . . . . respondeat unus ebdomedarius uel alius presbiter bonus cantor indutus capa alba stans in peruulo(?) in illo ambone ubi est assuetum cantare epistolam. Et dicat cantando in sonum lectionis, *Adsum, pater*. Et episcopus uel canonicus cantet, *Interroga prophetas*. Et taceat. Et tunc dictus presbiter qui est Sanctus Augustinus procedat ad interrogationes prophetarum secundum suum cartellum. Et dominus episcopus exspectet[6] ibi usque dicte[7] interrogationes fuerint complete. Et finito sermone Beati Augustini cum illis interrogationibus sicut notatum est in legendario, procedatur usque ad conclusionem none lectionis. Verum quando non fiunt interrogationes, neque sermo Sancti Augustini non legitur cum representacione personarum, legitur tota nona lectio continuo more aliarum lectionum usque ad interrogationem Sibille. Et tunc puer ille ornatu pulcre domicelle, uel alii loco eius, cantet illos versus sibillinos qui incipiunt *Iudicii signum*, siue expositionem illorum, scilicet, *al iorn del iudici*, etc. . .[8] Illi presbiteri et clerici de circumstantibus[9] respondeant illi puero induto, sed si non inuenerit, dicatur a duobus primitxeriis in ambone ubi assuetum est cantare responsorium epistole cum capis albis. Et unus dicat unum versum, et alter alium versum usque ad finem. Et immediate dominus episcopus uel canonicus perficiat nonam lectionem dicens *hec de Christi natiuitate*, etc.

[3] dompne] dopne (MS).
[4] Either this second account, which is found on folios 171ᵛ-172, was added at a later date, or else the entire manuscript must be assigned to the fifteenth century. On folio 165 the date 1433 occurs in the body of the text. This does not necessarily mean that the ceremony described postdates 1400; one finds in the second part of the manuscript such expressions as: "Assuetum est ab antiquo quod in ista die . . ." (fol. 174).
[5] There follows an illegible line.
[6] exspectet] exspetet (MS).
[7] dicte] dictas (MS).
[8] There are two illegible words at this point.
[9] circumstantibus] circumtantibus (MS).

Since among the collection of medieval liturgical plays known to date, there are only three complete texts and one description of the *Ordo Prophetarum*, any addition to this number is most welcome. The account from Mallorca not only enlarges our *collectanea*, but also contributes to our knowledge of the manner in which this type of medieval play was sometimes performed.

The *Procession of Prophets* was presented at Palma as *a part* of the ninth lesson. This, we recall, was the same position of the play at Gerona when the *Repraesentatio Partus* was not performed. These two Catalan plays are the only ones discovered thus far which were certainly staged as the lesson itself. Though not older than those edited by Young, they may possibly represent an earlier form of the play. It is commonly accepted that the *Ordo Prophetarum* took its origin from the pseudo-Augustinian sermon, and that for some years this sermon was read as a lesson of Matins before it developed into a play.[10] Did the sermon become a play while it still retained its function as a lesson, with different persons coming forth to deliver the prophetic speeches as they were set down in the lectionary? Or did the sermon become a play only after it had ceased to be a lesson, had been shifted to another part of the liturgical office, and had been rewritten in verse form? The Gerona text suggests that the former may have happened. This point will be discussed more fully in a subsequent chapter.[11]

The Mallorca *consueta* states that the bishop is to read the ninth lesson until he reaches the passage, "Sancte Augustine, interroga prophetas, Sancte Augustine." At this point a cleric, "qui est Sanctus Augustinus", replies to the summons, "Adsum, pater." When the bishop has directed him to interrogate the prophets, "St. Augustine" proceeds to call forth each one as his script indicates. Except for the highly developed Benediktbeuern play,[12] this is the first text of a liturgical *Ordo Prophetarum*, which provides a role for the famous bishop himself. Usually the role of summoner is assigned to vague personages called *Vocatores* (Rouen) or *Appellatores* (Laon). Since the Palma text is found in a manuscript of the fourteenth or fifteenth century, it may have been influenced by the later vernacular Passion Plays, in some of which St. Augustine delivered the opening prologue;[13] on the other hand, it may represent an ancient tradition of the Latin liturgical play.

The player who acted as St. Augustine had his own script of the play (*cartellum*), like the fourth soldier at Sulmona, and the Shepherd at Shrewsbury (see above p. 73). The play, we know, was sung: "et dicat *cantando* in sonum lectionis . . . et episcopus vel canonicus *cantet*."

Once again special provision is made for the Sibyl. As at Gerona, even if the pseudo-Augustinian sermon was not acted out, the Sibyl nevertheless

---

[10] See Sepet, *Les Prophètes du Christ;* Young, 'Ordo Prophetarum', pp. 1-82.
[11] See below, pp. 154-156.
[12] Text in Young, II, 172.
[13] See Froning, *Das Drama des Mittelalters*, II, 340, 379; Chambers, *The Medieval Stage*, II, 77.

appeared to sing her prophecy. The role was played by a choir-boy costumed as a "pulcra domicella", and the verses were delivered in Catalan. If the boy did not sing the prophecy, it was rendered by two clerics who sang the verses alternately.

Brief references to the play in the medieval account books of the cathedral sacristy provide us with a few additional details about the performance. At least four of the personages probably wore a crown of some kind, for an entry in the year 1399 records the following: "Paguí au Guillem Borrell, pintor, per adobar 4 diademes dels profetes ... per la festa de nadal ... 3 sous." These diadems may have been for actors who took the part of kings, since at least two royal figures from the Old Testament, David and Nabuchodonosor, usually appeared in the *Ordo Prophetarum*; the rubrics generally directed that these two personages be dressed in regal attire. Or perhaps at Mallorca most of the prophets wore crowns; a mention of the costumes worn in the Valencian Christmas piece merely refers to "les diademes dels prophetes."[14]

It appears quite certain that one of the roles in the prophet play at Palma was given to Moses. An inventory of the same year speaks of the tablets and golden horns that were provided him: "Item: tabulas Moysi et duo cornua deaurata Moysi." The legislator's appearance in the play is not surprising, since he traditionally had a part in this piece. He was arrayed in much the same way in the Rouen play: "Moyses, tenens tabulas legis apertas, indutus alba et cappa, et cornuta facie, barbatus, tenens virgam in manu." The same entry also speaks of "quinze barbes falses", so apparently there were at least this number of personages in the play. Inasmuch as the cleric who took the part of Daniel was traditionally presented as a youth, and since ordinarily there were some feminine roles in the play (Elizabeth, the Sibyl ...), the number of roles at Palma likely exceeded twenty. As for the beards, the Mallorcan play was again quite similar to others of the period: of the eleven male characters in the Laon play, seven are described as "barbatus".[15]

As late as the sixteenth century, the *Procession of Prophets* was still a part of the Christmas festivities at Palma. The sacristan's hand-book written in 1511 speaks of it in the following terms:[16]

> A las matines, si per uentura volran fer los profetes, tocharan naloy[17] a las sis hores de nit (e si no feran los profetes, tocharan a las set hores de la nit).

. . . .

[14] See below, p. 146.
[15] For the quotations from the account books at the cathedral of Mallorca, see Caimari, 'L'Antiga pietat popular entorn de Nadal', p. 210; for the text and rubrics of the *Ordo Prophetarum* from Laon, see the Appendix, p. 176.
[16] Palma, Bibl. Capit., Sala 1, Armario LXXVI, Tabla I, 2, fol. 6-6ᵛ. Part of this passage has just recently been edited by Caimari, p. 215. An inventory of the capitular library has been published by J. Miralles Sbert, *Catálogo del Archivo Capitular de Mallorca*; I follow his reference numbers.
[17] naloy: the name of a bell.

E anant a la trona, aportera lo dit canonge[18] lo test de argent e un siri blanch ences de pes de mige liure, lo qual siri restera al dit canonge quant haura fet. E deuant lo canonge anira la Sibilla, e deuant la Sibilla les trompes e quatre fedrins del altar, dos ab canalobres d'argent ab siris blanchs, e l'altre ab lo encenser, e lo quart ab la barqueta dels encens. E quant seran a la trona, quant lo qui dira la nouena lectio sera en aquell pas que la Sibilla deura parlar, stroncara lo dir de la lisso. E la Sibilla dira cantant lo *judici*. E acabat lo *judici* lo matex qui dira la lisso procehira la dite lisso lexant lo dit de la Sibilla per que ya sera dit per la dite Sibilla. E dementre que la lisso se dira, posseran al pheristol de la trona una tauayola de sede o domas blanch. E si en dites matines se feran los profetas per semblant, se feran en aquesta nouena lectio, per que Sant Agusti fera les interrogacions en aquell pas que tochara en la dite lisso axi com es dit de la Sibilla. E acabade que sera la nouena lisso e lo noue responsori e la verbeta, lo dit canonge dira lo euangeli, ço [es] *Liber generationis*.

The opening rubric of this text is most enlightening. If the prophet play was to be performed, the bell for the liturgical services of Christmas Eve was rung at six o'clock; otherwise it was sounded at seven. This directive informs us first of all that at Mallorca the rites of Christmas began at an exceedingly early hour – if we reflect that Lauds would not be concluded until early in the morning, we do not wonder that the piety of the faithful was "rewarded" by a play or two. Secondly, the directive reveals that the *Procession of Prophets* lasted approximately one hour – a considerable length of time for an unpretentious liturgical play.

The little procession which accompanies the Sibyl to the pulpit brings to mind the Sibyl ceremony of Toledo. At Palma, though the prophetess had no angels to escort her, she was preceded by trumpeters (*les trompes*), two altar boys with lighted candles, and two others with incense and an incense-boat; she was followed by the canon who was to sing the gospel.[19]

Another Mallorcan manuscript, a fifteenth or sixteenth century *cantorale*, gives a rather unusual rubric for the Sibylline ceremony:[20] "Lo iorn de Nadal, a la novena lisso, *una bona cantora* diu lo *iorn del iudici*." The feminine *una bona cantora* seems to indicate that the prophetess was represented by a woman. Perhaps the manuscript was written for a monastery of nuns; Caimari relates a delightful story about the apprehensions of a sixteenth century religious sister who had been assigned the task of singing the Sibylline chant at the convent of Santa Magdalena in Palma (pp. 216–217).

---

[18] The one who is to sing the gospel, *Liber generationis*.
[19] The trumpeters were evidently a special feature of the rites for Christmas week. They accompanied several of the "liturgical players" to their places of performance, and gave a flourish at the most important parts of the liturgy. The manuscript speaks of the "trompadors de Nadal"; it does not state that they are to play at any time during the Sibyl's performance.
[20] Fol. 84ᵛ; the manuscript is found at the Palma Episcopal Museum.

The chant of the Sibyl did not disappear at Mallorca with medieval times. Though the ceremony was suppressed in 1572 by the bishop, Diego Arnedo, just three years later it was restored at the request of his successor, Vich y Manrique. On different occasions it was prohibited again, but the decrees could not have been very strictly enforced, because the prophecy is still popular at Mallorca today. The Balearic island is the one place in the world where the prophecy is still delivered by a costumed choir-boy.[21] The ceremony has remained not only at Palma, but in almost all of the important towns of the island, the costume of the prophetess varying considerably from parish to parish. According to the description of A. Noguera, the modern attire of the Sibyl in many of the churches is no longer very distinctively feminine:[22]

> En muchas parroquias de la isla se representa la Sibila la noche de la Natividad de Jesu-Cristo. Encárgase de cantarla, inmediatamente después de concluido el *Te Deum*, un muchacho de unos doce años que viste un traje claro de seda profusamente bordado, lleva en la cabeza una especie de gorro armenio del mismo color del traje y sostiene con ambas manos una pesada y reluciente espada. Ocupa el púlpito entre dos monagos y entona el canto de la profecía: canto altamente extraño y original, de sabor marcadamente arcáico a pesar de su tonalidad (que es la moderna).

We note that the sword, which was borne by the escorting angels in the Toledo version, has mysteriously found its way into the hands of the Sibyl; the medieval Mallorcan *consuetas* make no mention of such an instrument.

In other churches the Sibyl's costume is more specifically feminine. At Lluchmaior, for example, it is qualified as "de senyora", or "a la ciutadana", and is composed of "unes faldes de color i a damunt unes de mossolina molt clara que fasse transparent."[23]

Evidently the *Repraesentatio Partus* was not known at Mallorca, but the Christmas festivities were not entirely devoid of a shepherd scene. This was presented at Lauds and resembled the usage of Toledo. The fourteenth century *consueta* describes the ceremony (fol. 19ᵛ–20):

> ‹Precentores› iterent antiphonam *Pastores, dicite*;[24] et chorus respondeat usque ad *Christi natiuitatem*. Et duo pueri induti dalmaticis, uelati, tenentes cereos in manibus, respicientes uersus chorum, stantes prope ante altare Sancte Marie, incipiant in medio antiphone et dicant alta uoce: *Infantem uidimus*; et compleant totam antiphonam. Interim precentores dent antiphonam ab alia parte chori duobus presbiteris; et illa incepta, intonent psalmum *Cantate Domino canticum nouum*. Quo finito usque ad *Laudate Dominum in sanctis eius* sine *Gloria Patri*, iteretur a precentoribus antiphona *Pastores dicite*. Et predicti pueri dicant iterum

---

[21] Miss Corbin informs us that the prophecy is also sung at Braga, Portugal in our time, but without any special dress or *mise-en-scène*; see '*Le Cantus Sibyllae*: origines et premiers textes', p. 1.
[22] *Memoria sobre los cantos, bailes y tocatas populares de la isla de Mallorca*, p. 57.
[23] Pujol, 'El Cant de la Sibilla', p. 217.
[24] It is here a question of the fifth antiphon at Lauds.

> *Infantem uidimus* usque ad finem. Et iterum precentores dent antiphonam *Pastores* duobus presbiteris ad aliam partem chori. Qua incepta precentores intonent psalmum *Laudate Dominum in sanctis eius*. Et finiatur cum *Gloria Patri*. Quo dicto precentores iterent antiphonam *Pastores dicite* et dicti pueri respondeant similiter *Infantem uidimus*. . .

The word *velati* reveals that the boys were considered as representing the shepherds. Appropriately, their verses were sung at the altar of the Blessed Virgin. The sixteenth century sacristan's manual gives the additional direction that the boys were to come to the main altar immediately after the Consecration of the Mass; already at that time they were dressed for their role (fol. 7):

> E quant lo preuera haura alsat lo Corpus Christi en dite missa, dos fadrins de la almoyna, vestits ab domatigues blanchas, ab les cares cubertes ab vels blanchs, pugeran al altar major per a dir la antifona *Infantem uidimus* quant la hora ho requerra . . .

Before the morning Mass the traditional *Quem quaeritis* trope was sung:[25]

> Et duo ex eis, boni cantores, dicant primum versum tropi, scilicet, *Quem queritis*. Et alii duo boni cantores dicant secundum versum, *Saluatorem Christum*. Et finitis per eos omnibus versibus tropi, omnes .xii. submissa uoce incipiant officium, *Puer natus est nobis*.

In the afternoon, dramatic activities for the feast of St. Stephen commenced. At Vespers, and throughout the entire liturgy of the next day, a cleric acted the part of St. Stephen. We have already seen that in many European churches during the Middle Ages, the deacons were traditionally honored on St. Stephen's Day, because the first martyr had been a deacon; and the priests on St. John's Day, because their patron was one of the first priests. Deacons and priests played a dominant role in the liturgical services of these two days. The Mallorcan custom may be ancient, or it may show the influence of the relatively late, but very popular Spanish Corpus Christi procession. In the fourteenth and fifteenth centuries this procession regularly included clerics costumed as St. Peter, St. John, and other saints.[26] The Palma custom must have been fairly ancient, because one of the ceremonials refers to parts of the liturgy of St. Stephen's Day as an "ancient practice no longer in usage."

The ceremony of Christmas Vespers is described in a sixteenth century *consueta*:[27]

---

[25] The *consueta de tempore*, fol. 21.
[26] See above, p. 87.
[27] Palma, Bibl. Capit., Sala 1, Armario LXXVI, Tabla II, 1, fol. 16. Villanueva writes of the manuscript (*Viage literario*, XXII, 177): "Consueta de Sanctis, códice de folio . . . Ordenóse a principios del siglo XVI . . . Yo creo que este es el códice cuya conclusión encargó el Capítulo en acta de 9 de enero de 1516." The copy which Villanueva made of the text here quoted has been edited by Anglès, pp. 284-285; Anglès' declaration that the manuscript was written in 1511 is apparently an error.

> Si fuerint diachones, omnia inferius notata in officio Sancti Stephani fiant per eos . . . .
> In commemoratione Sancti Stephani Prothomartyris fiat ut sequitur. Ad *Magnificat* in Vesperis secundis Natiuitatis Domini, exeat de sacristia beatus Stephanus, scilicet, unus diachonus indutus uestimentis cum dalmatica, velatus facie, tenensque unum cereum album ardentem in una manu, et librum in alia. Et associent eum duo presbiteri tenentes cereum in manu, induti capis purpureis, stantes hinc et inde. Et alii quatuor presbiteri induti capis purpureis teneant et portent super Sanctum Stephanum supercelium, scilicet, unum pannum aureum cum quatuor baculis. Et sic ordinati ueniant omnes intus chorum. Et dum dicitur oratio et *Benedicamus*, duo primicherii officiatores comendent capas octo diachonibus, si fuerint, seu presbiteris bonis cantoribus, qui in processione associabunt Santum Stephanum. Et ibunt coram supercelio. Et dicto *Benedicamus* quatuor precentores induti cum capis, tenentes bordonos, incipiant responsorium *Ecce iam coram te*. Et totus chorus processionaliter cantando dictum responsorium ueniant ante altare Sancti Stephani, et ibi dicti octo diachones vel presbiteri dicant versum *Caritatis gratia*. Et presa finita, dicant *Gloria Patri*. Et dicta presa *Intercedere digneris* a choro, duo pueri cum capis nigris dicant ante altare Sancti Stephani versum *Patefacte sunt*, cum duplici *alleluia*.

Thus at the *Magnificat* of Vespers, "St. Stephen" would come forth from the sacristy, vested in dalmatic, a lighted candle in one hand and a book in the other, and his face covered with a veil (in almost all the liturgical plays at Mallorca the participants wore some kind of veil or mask). On either side of him was a priest with a lighted candle, and he came to the choir under a golden canopy, which was carried by four clerics. When the moment came for the commemoration of St. Stephen, the choir proceeded to the chapel which was dedicated to the saint, the deacon being escorted under the canopy. The sacristan's *consueta*, which also describes the ceremony, informs us that "St. Stephen" took a special part in the rites which took place at the chapel.[28]

At Matins the same evening the honored deacon continued to exercise the same function:[29]

> E quant se dira lo inuitatori se acustumaue en temps passat, e axi es possat en la consueta, que lo qui era Sant Steua se uestia a matines a la sacrastia quant lo inuitatori se deyha, axi propriament com es dit a las primeras vespres. E quant lo ters psalm del primer nocturni se deyha, lo dit Sant Steua ab tots sos ministres partia de là sacrastia, e anaue cantant alguna canso de la Mara de Deu pugant-sen al laginder. E deyha la primera lisso. E quant hauia dita la lisso, deuellaue-sen, e cantant tornaua-sen a la sacrastia per despullarse. Are nos preticha gran temps ha . . . Nota que entigament se acustumaue que quant deyhen la nouena

---

[28] Fol. 75-75ᵛ; the passage is given in the Appendix.
[29] Fol. 76 of the sacristan's *consueta*.

> lisso, lo dit Sant Steua uestit axi com ya es dit al inuitatori anaue al cor, e possaues detras lo pharistol maior e comensaua lo *Te Deum*, e ten prest quel hauia comensat, sen tornaua a la sacrastia per despullarse.

At this office "St. Stephen", dressed in the same manner as at Vespers, entered the church singing some hymn in honor of the Blessed Mother. He then recited the first lesson. When this was concluded, he returned to the sacristy, but reappeared later in the office to intone the *Te Deum*.

Much of the same went on at Mass the following day. The deacon, "velata facie", entered the church in another procession, accompanied the subdeacon to the pulpit for the singing of the epistle, and later did the same for the deacon who sang the gospel. The epistle, of course, was farced: "In die Sancti Stephani ad missam maiorem assuetum est dicere epistolam per duos primixerios in sono de *Veni Creator*; unus dicit latinum et alius post eum dicit uulgare."[30]

St. John was not denied his day. Everything that the deacon did on December 26th was duplicated by a priest dressed as St. John on the following day. The liturgy for the feast of the Evangelist was even more dramatic, as it involved the presence of two impersonated saints, dressed in very realistic attire. The *consueta de sanctis* (1516) describes the ceremonies in the following terms:[31]

> In commemoratione Beati Joannis Apostoli et Euangeliste fiat totum officium sicut ordinatum est superius in commemoratione Beati Stephani. Sed ille qui erit Joannes Euangelista sit indutus vestimentis sacerdotalibus cum casulla. Et alter qui erit Joannes Babtista sit indutus veste pilosa cum agno et cruce argentea. Et ambo sint presbiteri . . . Et dicto *Magnificat*, Sanctus Joannes veniat de sacristia associatus a presbiteris cum supercelicio.

A much better idea of the activities and dress of the two St. Johns is given by the ceremonial of the sacristy:[32]

> E a l'altar de Sant Johan metran lo palis seu, ço es de Sant Johan ab letras entorno. E encortineran la capella de Sant Johan ut moris est, e posseran dos lums al dit altar de Sant Johan, e un missal per dir la oracio.
> . . . .
> E quant diran vespres, lo roder aportera al cor vuyt capes de xemallot blanch per los vuyt preueras qui aniran deuant Sant Johan a la processo, axi de *Magnificat* com a la processo de la claustre . . . .
> E a la sacrastia se vestiran dos preueras la hu per Sant Johan Baptiste vastit ab camis y hamit, ab una esclauina negra pilossa,[33] senyit ab una

---

[30] *Consueta* of the fourteenth century, fol. 174; the passages which summarize the rites of the following day are given in the Appendix.
[31] Fol. 19; the passage has been partially edited by Anglès (p. 285) from the Villanueva copy.
[32] Fol. 77-77ᵛ.
[33] pilossa] palossa (MS).

corde d'espart, descals ab esperdenyes; lo qual aportera ab lo bras esquerra un anyell ab diadema, e ab la ma dreta aportera la creu dels albats conuentuals, e ab la creu sera liguat un titol qui dira *Ecce Agnus Dei*, e una penitencia de pilotes de mar. L'altre preuera se vestira per Sant Johan Evangelista, lo qual anira vestit ab casulla de xemallot blanch, ab un vel blanch de sede deuant la cara, e ab diadema; e ab la ma esquerra aportera una palma, e hun libret, e en la ma dreta aportera hun ciri xich blanch. Los quals preueras lo clauari te carrech de emprar los y de paguar. E aquests dos aniran deuall lo pauallo axi com ya es dit de Sant Steua. E en lo anar deuall lo pauallo, Sant Johan Baptista anira primer vestit axi com ya es dit, e aportera maschare, e apres anira Sant Johan Euangelista vestit com ya es dit, e aportara a cascun costat un preuera ab capade xemallot blancha, e un ciri blanch xich. E aniran al cor en aquella manera, e hora que es dit de Sant Steua, e axi en les vespres com en la missa, com en la epistola e euangeli. E apres dita la oracio a l'altar de Sant Johan, aniran ab la *Salue Regina* a l'altar maior, axi com ya es dit de Sant Steua . . .

One wonders how St. John the Baptist came to be especially associated with the Evangelist, and why on the latter's feast day they did all things in common, both at Vespers and at Mass. The former wore a liturgical amice and surplice, but completed his attire realistically by donning a hairy black mantle (*esclavina*), a cincture of esparto grass and sandals – the people would have had no difficulty recognizing the well-known Gospel figure, so frequently the subject of medieval painters with his "garment of camel's hair and leathern girdle". In his left arm he carried a lamb with a diadem, and in the other some kind of penitential instrument and a small silver cross to which was attached the title, "Ecce Agnus Dei"; like his companion, he was masked ("aportera maschare"). The Evangelist was more simply dressed with a liturgical chasuble (the emblem of the priest), carried a palm and a small book in his left hand, and a lighted candle in the right; he also wore a diadem and had a white silk veil over his face. These two portraits are among the most minutely drawn which have come down to us in medieval liturgical manuscripts. Many years previously in the *Ordo Prophetarum* of Laon and Rouen the holy precursor had also appeared. His dress in those two productions was not unlike that worn by the cleric of Mallorca: "pilosa veste et longis capillis, barbatus, palmam tenens" (Laon); "ipse, nudus pedes, tenens textum" (Rouen).

It is difficult to classify the ceremonies in which the two Mallorcan ecclesiastics took part. They can hardly be said to have participated in a play; strictly speaking, no story was presented in action, and it appears that neither had a speaking role. Perhaps the word *pageantry* best describes their activities. Still, however we define these ceremonies, they are closely allied to liturgical drama.

Apparently at one time at Mallorca the pageantry had been even more elaborate. The text of the *consueta de tempore* which described the Mass of that feast has been erased and replaced by a later version, but enough of the original has been left to disclose that formerly a whole group of ecclesiastics may have been costumed to represent historical personages (fol. 174):

> Assuetum[34] est ab anticho quod in ista die Sancti Johannis ad missam maiorem induuntur duodecim presbiteri sine ebdomedariis, scilicet, in capite[35] . . . XII. et postea VIII. presbiteri boni cantores bini et bini et ultimi gradiuntur duo presbiteri septimanarii et isto modo reuertuntur ad chorum, et similiter quando uadunt ad altare ad dicendum *Benedicamus* et *Verbum caro*, et de altari ad chorum. Et eciam quando ascendunt trunam ad cantandum responsorium et *alleluia* octo presbiteri ex illis ascendunt et quatuor de ultimis remanent ante ambone.[36]

After the phrase *scilicet, in capite*, the original passage must have gone on to describe the costume of the twelve clerics. Since in ordinary liturgical ceremonies these clerics would have worn nothing on their head, I suspect that one of the first words erased was *diadema* or *corona*, and that the group of twelve represented the twelve apostles.[37]

As for the Boy-Bishop of Mallorca, it is safe to say that he outdid all his comrades of other medieval churches. At Palma he was not only bishop, but pope, and his attire included all the vestments befitting his role, even to the tiara! At Matins of St. Nicholas Day he engaged in some kind of ceremony called the *Entrames del Bisbato*, but this probably was not a genuine play.[38]

Liturgical Plays of the Easter Cycle at Palma

After encountering such dramatic enthusiasm on the part of the Mallorcan clerics during the Christmas season, we would indeed be surprised if they did not present some form of liturgical play at Easter Matins. Nor are our expectations amiss. The usage at the Balearic cathedral is described by the *consueta de tempore*:[39]

> Finita uerbeta antequam dicatur *Te Deum laudamus*, tres presbiteri induti uestimentis et dalmaticis, uelati in facie, tenentesque cereos accensos in manibus exeant de sacristia suauiter et morose. Et ueniant ante pauimentum altaris Beate Marie. Et stantes super altiorem gradum altaris, unus post alium, primus ipsorum incipiat et dicat totum uersum prose, scilicet, *Victime Paschali Laudes*, uertendo faciem suam uersus chorum.

---

[34] Assuetum] Asuetum (MS).
[35] After this word four lines have been erased and supplanted by a later text.
[36] At this point a whole column of the original manuscript has been expunged and replaced by a new version.
[37] See below, p. 137.
[38] All three *consuetas* speak of the Boy-Bishop's activities at great length; a brief passage from one of them is quoted in the Appendix.
[39] Fol. 75-75ᵛ. The passage has been previously edited from the slightly inexact copy of the Villanueva manuscript by Anglès, pp. 273-274.

> Et alius immediate post primum dicat secundum versum prose, scilicet, *Agnus redemit oues.* Et tercius dicat tercium versum, scilicet, *Mors et uita.* Et omnes uertant faciem uersus chorum, precentores autem tenentes cereos accensos in manibus stent ad hostium chori uertendo facies suas uersus altare Beate Marie. Et dicant cantando hunc versum, *Dic nobis, Maria, quid uidisti in uia.* Et predicti tres presbiteri ueniant quasi in principio capitis prope tumulum Domini regis, stantes unus post alium. Et primus ipsorum respondeat precentoribus, et dicat versum totum *Sepulcrum Christi uiuentis.* Et precentores iterum dicant versum *Dic nobis, Maria.* Et secundus de eorum trium presbiterorum respondeat et dicet versum totum *Angelicos testes, etc.* Et precentores iterum dicant versum *Dic nobis, Maria.* Et tercius de eorum presbiterorum dicat versum totum *Surrexit Christus spes, etc.* Finito predicto versu, precentores uertentes faciem uersus chorum dicant hunc versum totum, scilicet, *Credendum est magis*[40] . . . et dicat versum totum *Scimus Christum surrexisse, etc.* Dicto isto versu, illi tres prebiteri redeant ad sacristiam. Interim autem dum prosa dicetur, custos sacristie tradat cereos omnibus canonicis presbiteris et clericis existentibus in choro. Et quilibet accendat cereum suum antequam episcopus uel ebdomedarius incipiat *Te Deum Laudamus.* Et debent ardere usque ad finem matutini. Postea custos sacristie reportat eos ad sacristiam. *Te Deum.*

The sacristan's *consueta* also describes this play, and provides some additional information about the costumes. The text is found on folio 25–25^v:

> Lo die de pascho (sic) tocharan per matines a las tres horas . . . . E quant les matines se diran lo roder aparellera a la sacrastia tres domatigues, la una vermella, l'altre blancha, l'altre verde, ab camis, sinyels, y amits, y tres vels blanchs per aportar deuant la care, y tres siris vermells dels xichs, e un professional hahon sera la prosse, ço es *Victime paschali*[41], etc. E quant tot sera aparellat, vestir san tres preueras elegits per los primatxers, e quant diran lo darrer responsori, axiran los dits tres preueras en la forma desus dite ab[42] los siris encessos, e les cares cubertes, e pugeran al terç graho del altar maior; e diran la dite prossa quant tochara a dir la, ab la cara a la volta del cor.

According to these descriptions, at Palma Matins began at three o'clock Easter morning. When the third responsory and the *verbeta* had been sung, three clerics came forth from the sacristy, *suaviter et morose,* their faces covered with a white veil, and a lighted red candle in their hand. Each wore a different colored dalmatic, one red, another white, and the third one green, and an amice, which was doubtless worn over the head. These of course represented the Three Marys. They proceeded to the altar of the Blessed Virgin, where they began the sequence *Victimae paschali laudes,* each one singing a verse.

---

[40] There follow three or four illegible words.
[41] paschali] paschalis (MS).
[42] ab] en (MS).

Instead of the *Quem queritis in sepulchro*, the sequence alone was dramatized at Palma, cantors singing the questions, the Marys, by turn, the answers. It seems that the tomb of a king was used as a *sepulchrum*: "Et predicti tres presbiteri ueniant quasi in principio capitis prope tumulum Domini regis, stantes unus post alium."[43]

The Mallorcans must have been very fond of the hymn, *Victimae paschali laudes*, because they dramatized it again on Easter Tuesday morning at Mass, and in even more impressive fashion. This time only one Mary participated – Mary Magdalen – but she was assisted by an angel, and theatrical stage effects were employed. What is perhaps even more interesting, she sang her lines in Catalan. The following ceremony is quoted from the *consueta de tempore* (fol. 182ᵛ–183):

> Feria tercia ad missam maiorem dicto ultimo *alleluia* quidam presbiter bonus cantor indutus uestimentis femineis coloratis intret chorum cum duobus ceroferariis associatus, qui presbiter representando Mariam Magdalenam in janua primi chori incipiat cantare *Victime paschali*. Et postea chorus procequitur usque ad illum versum *Dic nobis, Maria*. Et tunc illi duodecim presbiteri cum pluuialibus quibus induti sunt cum bordonis in manibus accedant ad januam chori uersus altare et ille presbiter qui representat Magdalenam ascendat ascabellum uel aliud stagnum. Et tunc duo primi presbiteri incipiant cantare, *Are, digues nos, Maria, que as uist en la uia, de Ihesu Christ lo Saluador, q'es de quest mon Redemptor?*[44] Et Magdalena respondeat secundum quod continetur in suo cartello. Et facta responcione per Magdalenam, alii duo presbiteri inmediate sequentes cantent in dicto tono: *Digues nos encare, Maria*. Et sic de singulis. Et finito cartello Magdalene, dicti duodecim presbiteri reuertantur ordinate ad ambonem cantando prosam *Credendum est magis* cum aliis versibus usque ad finem. Quibus completis, diachonus incipiat euangelium.

Thus just before the sequence was to be chanted at Mass, a priest with a good singing-voice entered the choir, an acolyte with a candle on either side of him. He was dressed in a way to represent Mary Magdalen, "indutus femineis coloratis", and began the sequence in the doorway of the choir. When the verses *Dic nobis, Maria* had been reached, the Mary mounted upon a little stool, and the dramatic dialogue then commenced. The use of the vernacular in a play during Mass itself is striking, and as far as I know, this is the first example of it which has yet been found. It appears that the dialogue portion was rendered in Catalan, and the remainder of the prose in Latin. The vernacular verses, which are obviously a free translation from the Latin original, recall the concluding line of the vernacular play from Vich: "Dic nos, Maria, que has vist..."

---

[43] I do not understand the meaning of the phrase, "quasi in principio capitis"; it may refer to the "chapter room". The king mentioned must be either James II or James III; the tombs of both these monarchs are still present in the apse of the cathedral.

[44] The exact punctuation of the latter part of this verse is as follows: *Qes de q'stmō redemptor*.

When we first spoke of the Tuesday morning play, reference was made to an angel and impressive stage effects. These appear in the account of the performance given by the sacristan's *consueta*. Probably this second version constitutes a later form of the play:[45]

> E de mati, ans de comensar les horas, lo ragent fara aportar al altar maior tots los inproperis de Ihesu Crist sagons veura en la consueta de la Maria. E fera aparellar a la sacrastia un vestiment per la Maria, ço es camis ab parament, e una domatigue de vellut vert, e un mantell fet de una capa de vellut vermell, e te esser preuera la dite Maria elegit per lo custos, e doneli un cruat per sos treballs. Mes te hauer lo dit custos un fedri per angell, e donarli ha un sou. E quant lo preuera anira a l'altar per dir la missa, lo sotdiacha aportere lo veronicha, e lo diacha le aportera al euangeli. E quant la missa se comensera, la Maria se vestira, e l'angel per semblant, empero l'angel pugera a la capella de Trinitat per ço que quant haura a cantar stera alt als corradors de la part de Sant Guabriel. E quant la Epistola sera dite, lo ragent ab la dite Maria, e dos fedrins del altar ab sobrepalisos[46] ab los canelobres d'argent maiors ab siris blanchs encessos axiran de la sacrastia per anar al cor. E pesseran fore l'esglesia per lo mirador. Entreran dins la Seu per lo portal de mar, e possarsan prop lo portal del cor per manera que nols puguen veure del cor. E fera encendre los siris si seran apaguats. E axi com acaberan lo *Alleluia Angelus Domini* lo custos ab la Maria e los fedrins deuant entreran al cor. E al repla del cor entre la cadira del Senor Bisbe e del ardiacha, la Maria dira cantant *Victime paschali laudes*, e lo cor reprendra, e dit custos y la Maria ab los dits passeran per lo mig del cor per la part del Senor Bisbe. E aniran a l'altar maior pugant per la part de la capella de Santa Eularia. E deuant l'altar maior sera possat un escabell hahon la Maria pugera ab la cara girade a la volta del cor. E al costat de la Maria a la part dreta stera lo custos per legir la consueta, e per donar los inproperis a la dite Maria. E al corn del altar, a la part hon stera lo sacrista, stera un escola per donar los inproperis al sacrista. E lo dit sacrista los dera a la Maria. E a l'altre corn del dit altar stera un altre escola per a pendre los dits inproperis de la ma de la Maria. E a la porte del cor dins lo cor steran los .XII. preueras ab capes y bordons; los quals interrogaran la dite Maria. E lo custos, legint la consueta, dera lo inproperi a la dite Maria sagons la consueta requerra. E quant vindra en aquell pas que la Maria haura a cantar dels cossos resuscitar,[47] seran aparellats deuall l'altar major set o vuyt fedrins, o tants quants volran, ab camis e cuberts los caps ab amits. E quant vindra lo loch de resuscitar,[48] axiran de deuall

---

[45] Fol. 30-30ᵛ. In the Villanueva manuscript at Madrid, this passage has been noticeably abridged, and except for a few lines, has been translated into Latin; the Latin has been published by Anglès, p. 274. A brief description of the play, with a small part of the text, has also been published in Villanueva's *Viage literario*, XXII, 195.
[46] The scribe first wrote *domatigues*, then replaced it by *sobrepalisos*.
[47] dels cossos resuscitar] Interpreting these words as part of the dramatic text, Anglès has printed them in italics.
[48] resuscitar] Anglès has also printed this word in italics.

> l'altar, e radolant fins baix al darrer graho, anar-sen an a la sacristia.
> E l'angell estera al corrador. Quant vindra lo cas que haura a cantar,
> tindra les ales plenes de candelas encesses. E axint, feran una bombarde,
> o alguna ramor, significant la impetut del seu axir. E quant haura cantat,
> tornar-sen ha, e acabade la consueta la Maria ab lo ragent, e los fedrins,
> aniran a la sacrastia per despullarse. E deuelleran del altar per la part
> de la capella de Sant Guabriel. E dequi hauant, prochiran lo offici.

The Mary wore a richly worked alb ("camis ab parament"), a dalmatic of green velvet, and over the dalmatic a red mantle fashioned especially for the occasion – certainly the costume did not lack color! In addition she probably wore an amice over her head, as the Three Marys did at Palma on Easter morning. She had her own *consueta* of the play – the *cartellum* of the Latin manuscript – and the sacristan prepared the *improperia* according to the directions of this script. The *improperia* were certain items connected with the Sacred Passion which Mary showed to the people at the appropriate moment during the singing of the prose. Villanueva writes of this word: "(Maria) respondebit ut in die Paschae notatum est, ostendens pro se nota populo insignia, sive picta, sive quidpiam consonans (*improperia* vocat consueta)."[49] We have already noted a similar ceremony at Vich: "representacio sive hostensio armorum sive eorum que servierunt ad passionem Domini, que quidem arma, sive insignia, sive instrumenta habere habet ... beneficiatus."[50] If in the Palma performance Mary Magdalen showed many of these articles, as it seems she did, the verses she sang could hardly have been a direct translation from the sequence, for the hymn only mentions the *sudarium et vestes*.

The Mary and an angel began to prepare themselves as Mass commenced. The former remained temporarily in the sacristy, but the angel, an altar-boy adorned with a large pair of wings, proceeded directly to the chapel of the Holy Trinity. This chapel was located in the rear of the church behind the main altar, and in going there the boy followed a route which would prevent his being observed by the people. The Epistle of the Mass was Mary Magdalen's cue. When the Epistle had been concluded, the Mary, and two altar-boys who bore lighted candelabra, made their way to the choir entrance; instead of advancing through the nave, they went outside the church and re-entered by the side door which faced the sea.[51] When the moment came for the sequence, Mary Magdalen entered the choir, intoned the opening verse, and then with her attendants passed through the middle of the choir to the main altar. Here she mounted her stool and turned towards the choir. As she responded to the questions of the twelve priests, she showed the *improperia* suggested by the words of the prose. Evidently in the course of her Catalan song she spoke of

---

[49] Madrid, Bibl. de la Real Acad. de la Historia, MS 64 (12-19-4).
[50] See above p. 86.
[51] If one views the cathedral from the front, this would be the right-hand side; the church, beautifully situated on an elevated site, immediately overlooks the Mediterranean.

corpses being resurrected from the grave (*la Maria haura a cantar dels cossos resuscitar*). At this point, if I interpret the text correctly, seven or eight altar-boys, or even more, all dressed in surplices with amices over their heads, would roll out from beneath the main altar, apparently representing persons rising from the dead.

Shortly thereafter the Mary must have referred to an angel in her song, perhaps in a translation of the verse, *angelicos testes, sudarium et vestes*. In any case the angel, who had been waiting all this time for his cue – doubtless impatiently – suddenly, and dramatically, made his appearance. From the chapel of the Holy Trinity he had gone around to the corridor which extended, high up in the church, along the left side of the main sanctuary. One end of this corridor was just above the chapel of Saint Gabriel, and it was at this spot that the angel fittingly appeared.[52] His entrance was perhaps the most brilliant ever made in a medieval play, for when he came forth from the darkness his wings were all aglow with lighted candles, (one wonders how this feat was achieved); at the same time, as in the Guadix play, a loud noise was made: "una bombarde, o alguna ramor". He sang some verses, too, but just what these were we have no way of knowing. It appears that the angel pronounced the last words of the play, because the *consueta* declares that when he has finished, all return to the sacristy.

At Palma, dramatic activity also marked the liturgical ceremonies of Holy Week. On Good Friday there took place what was known as the *planctus*. This was a lament in verse which undertook to express the sentiments and emotions of one or another of the persons present at the Crucifixion. Most of the *planctus*, and especially the earliest ones, were primarily concerned with the words of the Blessed Mother as she stood beneath the cross witnessing the agony of her dying Son. Hence the frequent title, *Planctus Beatae Mariae Virginis*. Sometimes in the course of her lament, the Holy Virgin would address others who were present at the scene, and on occasion would even evoke a response from them, but it was she who carried the burden of the complaint. In some medieval churches, the *planctus* was acted out by different persons. This was the case at Palma.

The ceremony of the Mallorcan cathedral is described in two different passages of the *consueta de tempore*. These texts are important not only for the history of medieval religious drama in the Hispanic peninsula, but also for the history of the drama in other European countries; though references to dramatization of the medieval *planctus* are not uncommon, descriptions of the *way* in which they were performed are exceedingly rare. Young writes (I, 503):

> For our immediate purpose, however, our curiosity concerning such *planctus* centers less in their content and form than in the manner and

---

[52] A plan of the cathedral as it was in the fourteenth century may be found in Sagristá, *El Enigma de la capilla de la Trinidad*, opp. p. 56.

and circumstances of their delivery. Upon this point, unfortunately, our information is not abundant.

The same writer goes on to say that, according to one medieval text, it seems that the dramatic ceremony took place after Matins on Good Friday.[53] Both descriptions of the Mallorcan practice are very clear on this point, declaring that the *planctus* was performed after the ninth responsory of Matins:[54]

> Item fari [55] dicantur bona hora propter *planctum*. . . . .
> Finito nono responsorio, dicatur *planctus* a tribus bonis cantoribus. Et sint induti uestimentis et dalmaticis nigris uel uiolatis, et uelati faciebus. Et quilibet dicat unum versum *planctus* in eundo. Et in fine cuiuslibet versus omnes insimul flectendo genua dicant, *Ay ten greus son nostras dolors*. Et cum fuerint in truna, dicat ibi quilibet duos versus *planctus*. Finito *planctu*, dicantur laudes.

At Palma the lament was rendered by three singers. We are not told whom the three represent; perhaps the Blessed Mother, another Mary, and St. John. They all wore black or violet dalmatics in keeping with the liturgical season, and of course, as in all the liturgical plays at Palma, the three were veiled. As they proceeded through the church towards the pulpit, each one sang a stanza;[56] when the conclusion of a stanza was reached, all would genuflect together and sing the refrain: *Ay, ten greus son nostras dolors*. We recognize the verse at once: it is a translation of the Latin refrain which was sung in the Vich Easter play, *Heu, quantus est noster dolor*. To our knowledge, this is the first instance of its usage in a dramatic *planctus* which has come to light. Probably the entire lament was delivered in the vernacular at Palma, though of this we cannot be certain. Once arrived in the pulpit, each personage sang two more stanzas, making a total of nine for the complete performance, if my arithmetic is correct. The concluding verse of the *planctus* was immediately followed by the office of Lauds.[57]

---

[53] The text is from Toulouse; see Young, I, 503 and 698.
[54] This first description is found on fol. 72v.
[55] This word here refers to Matins of Good Friday. The more usual term is *farsi*, or *fasi*. Speaking of Matins of Holy Thursday, the author of the sacristan's *consueta* declares (fol. 21): "feran los *fassos*, ço es les matines." Villanueva writes of this term (IX, 148): "Fasos se llamaban en los maitines del Jueves, Viernes y Sábado Santo ciertas preces rimadas (en latin Pharsa) que se cantaban al fin de ellas, como hoy las usa mi orden (Fr. Villanueva was a Dominican); de las cuales vinieron a llamarse asi todos los maitines, y dura hoy esta costumbre en toda Cataluña."
[56] This is doubtless the meaning of the word *versus* in the present context; for use of the word in the same sense in another medieval play, see for example, Hartl, *Das Drama des Mittelalters*, II, 51.
[57] Anglès has referred to this play, but his observations concerning it seem to be incorrect. He writes (p. 231): "Es lliga també amb el cant de les verbeta de matines, el fet que a Mallorca, durant el segle XIV, després del responsori IX, es cantés el *Planctus Sanctae Mariae Virginis* amb lletra vulgar: 'Augats, seyos, qui credets Deu lo payre' amb la represa 'Oy, bels fils cars! Molt m'és lo jorn dolorós e amars!' coneguda ja des del segle XIII." According to our manuscript, this was not the refrain regularly sung in the Mallorcan cathedral. The musicologist cites as

The Good Friday ceremony of Mallorca which has just been quoted represents the practice as it was known in that cathedral in the fourteenth century. As the years passed, the dramatic performance became increasingly more complex. What it was like, perhaps around the year 1440, is shown by the following passage taken from the same *consueta de tempore* (fol. 181–181ᵛ):

> Et postmodum accensis cereis proceduntur ad faros ut in consueta continetur. Et post nonum responsorium fiat Planctus (?) Passionis Domini nostri Ihesu Christi. Prius ueniat unus presbiter indutus cum dalmatica in persona Sancti Petri, et faciat planctum ante crucifixum paratum in medio ecclesie. Et postea ueniat alius sacerdos ex alia parte, et faciat in persona Sancti Johannis. Et immediate alius sacerdos in persona Sancte Marie Matris Saluatoris, et eciam alii presbiteri in persona Sancte Marie Magdalene et Marie Iacobi, etc. Et facta Representacione Planctuum omnes clerici sint in choro et dicant laudes.

In the lapse of time between the composition of these two texts, the number of personages had increased from three to at least six. In the later version the singers of the various laments entered from different sections of the church. They no longer sang their verses in the pulpit, but in the middle of the nave before a crucifix.

The final example of dramatization of the liturgy at Palma de Mallorca is the ceremony which took place at Lauds on the feast of the Assumption. It has been described, without the text, by Villanueva (XXII, 199). The original passage is found in the sacristan's ceremonial, fol. 99ᵛ–100:

> E quant los escolans seran deuellats del campanar, tochades laudes, pendran lo ymatge de nostra Dona qui sera aparellade dins lo capitol sobre un lit ab lo drap de Sant Bernat. E sobre lo lit que los escolans hauran aparellat en la nit sobre lo carner dels canonges, posseran lo cubertor de domas groch que en Jofre dona a la sacrastia, e sobre aquest cubertor posseran lo dit ymatge de nostra Dona ensemps ab lo drap de Sant Bernat, a ab lo bestiment. E cascun corn de lit posseran un canelobre de ferro dels grans, e a cascun canelobre posseran quatre ciris blanchs. E vestir san honse preueras per apostols ab camis y domatigues, acceptat Sant Johan qui aportera casulla blancha ab una palme en la ma. E al costat del dit lit metran un banch[58] a cade part, e sobre los dits banchs un cobribanch a cadehu.

his reference: Villanueva, *Viage literario*, XXII, 193, and J. Masso Torrents, *Repertori de l'antiga literatura catalana*, p. 257. Villanueva merely states: "Había en el siglo XIV la costumbre de decir despues del IX Responsorio el *Planctus* de nuestra Señora, que era una letra vulgar." Torrents speaks of the three known versions of the *Planctus* in Catalan; the first and oldest of these, from Ager, has the same initial verse and the same refrain as those cited by Anglès. Villanueva has published this version in his *Viage literario* (IX, 281). Reading the Dominican's statement that the vernacular *Planctus* was known in fourteenth century Mallorca, Fr. Anglès must have concluded too readily that it was the same composition as that sung at Ager.
[58] banch] blanch (MS).

According to the *consueta*, when Lauds were about to begin, an image of the Blessed Mother was placed upon a bed at the spot where the canons of the cathedral were buried. Just where this burial place was the manuscript does not indicate. Twelve priests then dressed themselves in a manner to represent the twelve apostles, and apparently seated themselves on benches which were placed beside the image, and there recited the office of Lauds.[59] Later in the day, before the High Mass and at Compline, the same twelve clerics accompanied the image of the Virgin in a procession through the church:

> E los .x.(*sic*) apostols aporteran la figura de nostra Dona, e Sant Johan en la palma alta anira deuant la dite figura, e no aportera.

According to a note in the margin the three Marys had once participated in these processions:

> Nota que per la proseso de la claustra ni la proceso depres de uespres no y aura Marias, sino lo subdiacha aportara la ueronica a totes dos prose-sons.[60]

A similar display of pageantry took place on the feast of Corpus Christi. In the procession which wound its way through the city, the onlookers beheld such figures as the twelve apostles, who carried an emblem of their martyrdom, St. Peter in chasuble and tiara, various prophets, etc. Such a ceremony, however, since it took place outside of the church, is to be more properly associated with the late vernacular religious plays than with liturgical drama.

---

[59] This also appears to be Villanueva's interpretation; according to him the bed was placed in the center of the church (*Viage literario*, XXII, 199).

[60] In connection with the Prophet play performed at Palma on Christmas Day, Caimari (p. 210) has cited an item registered in the sacristy account books of the cathedral in the year 1399: "Jo H. Borrell, pintor, atorch a vos senyor Salvador Caselles, sacrista de la Seu, que mi havets dats e pagats 45 sous per fer e pintar 7 parells de ales e 12 diademes e deurar e metrer de fulla ... 10 de agost any dessus dit 1399." Because of the objects mentioned – twelve diadems and seven pairs of wings – and because the date of the entry, August 10th, is closer to the feast of the Assumption of the Blessed Virgin (August 15th) than it is to Christmas, I am of the opinion that this reference had to do with a play for the feast of the Assumption rather than the Procession of Prophets. In some Catalan chruches on August 15th a dramatic performance was regularly given on the theme of the feast (see below, p. 143). In this ceremony actors took the part of the Virgin Mary, the apostles, and a group of angels; these roles would easily explain the need of twelve diadems and wings.

CHAPTER 10

VALENCIA AND THE LITURGICAL DRAMA

LIKE Mallorca, Valencia was not wrested from the Moors until the thirteenth century. Though it had been recaptured by the Cid in the epic battle of 1094, the metropolis had shortly afterward fallen back into the hands of the Arabs; only in 1238 did James the Conqueror take definite possession of this prize city for the flag of Aragon. Historians have been unable to determine with certainty if the Roman rite was brought to Valencia at the time of the Cid's victory; they are sure only that when James made his triumphal entry into the city, he found the Mozarabic rite still flourishing. Because of this situation, the new liturgical drama may not have been known in the Valencian region until the thirteenth century. The relative scarcity of liturgical plays preserved from this district, on the one hand, and on the other, numerous evidences of a prospering vernacular religious theater at Valencia in the fourteenth and fifteenth centuries, both make this possibility appear all the stronger.

None the less, in the city of Gandía, which is situated a short distance south of Valencia, a very picturesque version of the *Visitatio Sepulchri* was celebrated every Easter morning from at least the year 1550 onward. Discovered in a manuscript at the collegiate church of Gandía, the piece has the distinction of being the only liturgical Easter play preserved with polyphonic music, and the added honor of having been composed by St. Francis Borgia. The play was first published, along with the accompanying music, by Mariano Baixauli in 1902.[1] The same author has included a résumé of the play based upon the capitular decree which established the custom. It is fortunate that we possess his article, because in the disastrous Civil War of 1936, all the original documents concerning the performance were destroyed.

According to Baixauli, the religious of the Royal Monastery of Santa Clara at Gandía enjoyed a special papal privilege permitting them to reserve the Blessed Sacrament, exposed in a repository ("expuesto en el *monumento*"), from Good Friday until Easter Sunday Morning. When St. Francis Borgia was about to leave his native city for Rome in 1550, he left behind as a personal remembrance several richly endowed foundations. One of these was the impressive *Quem quaeritis* Easter play which was to take place early in the morning at the monastery of Santa Clara, when the Blessed Sacrament was returned from the "monumento" to the tabernacle of the main altar.

---
[1] 'Las Obras musicales de San Francisco de Borja', pp. 154-170, 273-283.

Since the original manuscript has been destroyed, we reproduce the description of the performance provided by Baixauli:[2]

> El dia de Pascua de Resurrección,[3] a las cinco de la mañana, sale la procesión de la colegial,[4] oficiando de preste el señor deán o el señor capiscol (chantre), y va a Sª Clara, cantando a canto llano el responsorio *dum transisset sabbatum, etc.*[5]
>
> Al llegar la procesión a Sª Clara (aquí comienza el Auto Sacramental, que representa la Resurrección del Señor) las puertas de la iglesia se hallan cerradas, como en la procesión del Domingo de Ramos, y dos ángeles[6] desde dentro preguntan, cantando a duo:
>
>> Quem queritis in sepulchro Christicolae?
>
> Y desde fuera responde la Capilla[7] a cuatro voces:
>
>> Jesum Nazarenum, o coelicolae.
>
> Dicen los angeles:
>
>> Non est hic surrexit sicut praedixerit.
>> Ite, nuntiate quia surrexit a mortuis.
>
> Responde la capilla, *Jesum Nazarenum, etc.*, y los ángeles siguen:
>
>> Venite et videte locum, ubi positus erat Dominus.
>
> Responde el coro, *Jesum Nazarenum etc.*, y entonces se dan tres golpes a la puerta de la iglesia con la cruz, puesta en ella la mano del preste, y al último se abren las puertas y entra la procesión. Los ángeles siguen cantando,[8] *Venite y videte, etc.*, respondiendo la capilla como antes. En llegando al pie del monumento,[9] suben a él las tres Marías (tres infantes vestidos de María), llevando en sus manos los vasos de los ungüentos (unas redomitas de plata) con pañizuelos bordados, mientras cantan a tres voces:[10]

---

[2] Pp. 157-158. A second version of the piece given by Ruiz de Lihory, *La Música en Valencia, diccionario biográfico y crítico*, p. 193, differs somewhat in detail. I present in the footnotes the passages of this second version which provide supplementary information. V. Ripollés has also touched upon this Easter performance in the booklet, *El Drama litúrgico*. The play has been overlooked in almost all general treatises on the liturgical drama. Anglès mentions it (p. 269), and Serís lists it in his *Manual de bibliografía de la literatura española* (no. 2495), but his reference is faulty.

[3] Note of Baixauli: "Del acta de fundación y de las anotaciones de las papeles de música."

[4] "A las cinco de la mañana del domingo, previamente adornadas y enramadas de mirto, laurel y otras hierbas olorosas las calles del curso procesional, salían de la Colegiata el Cabildo y Clero con la capilla y ministriles" (Ripollés, p. 19).

[5] The complete responsory is as follows: *Dum transisset sabbatum, Maria Magdalenae, Maria Iacobi, et Salomae emerunt aromata, ut venientes ungerent Iesum, alleluia, alleluia. Et valde mane una sabbatorum veniunt ad monumentum, orto iam sole.*

[6] "Dos infantes del coro con traje de angel" (Lihory).

[7] Capilla: the choir.

[8] "Al entrar la procesión, mientras se dirige al sepulcro, los ángeles cantan ..." (Lihory).

[9] "Llegan al pie del monumento, y allí se arrodillan y oran" (Ripollés).

[10] "Concluido el verso anterior (*Venite y videte locum, etc.*) suben al sepulcro un ángel, Maria Magdalena y las dos Marias. El ángel lleva corona en la cabeza y palma en la mano, y las tres

Quis revolvet nobis lapidem ab ostio monumenti?

Entretanto la María de la mano derecha se acerca al sepulcro, mira por ambos lados, como quien busca algo, y no encontrando aquello que busca, con ademanes de admiración, puesto en el centro, levanta las manos al cielo, y juntándolas después, hace una profunda reverencia al sepulcro y vuelve a ocupar su sitio. Sube la María de la mano izquierda y repite las mismas ceremonias, y tras ella la de enmedio, que es María Magdalena, quien, después de buscar por ambos lados, descorre, por fin, la cortina que cubre el sepulcro y aparece éste vacío.[11] Entonces, vueltas las tres de cara al pueblo, María Magdalena dice cantando:[12]

Surrexit Christus.

Bajan tres gradas de las nueve que tiene el monumento, y repite lo mismo un tono más alto;[13] bajan otras tres gradas, y subiendo otro punto la voz, canta por tercera vez,

Surrexit Christus.

Y responde toda la capilla a siete voces:

Alleluja, Alleluja.

Se descubre al mismo tiempo el Santísimo y comienza la procesión, que recorre las calles contiguas al Monasterio, cantándose durante el trayecto la Sequentia *Victimae Paschali laudes*, etc., a canto llano, alternando con la capilla, que canta a cuatro voces el verso,

Dic nobis, Maria, quid vidisti in via?

Vuelta la procesión a la iglesia, se reserva el Santísimo, según la rúbrica del ritual, y el cabildo vuelve a su propria iglesia.

The Gandía *Visitatio* displays a marked spirit of decorum and reverence, and is far from devoid of charm. The ceremony began with an early morning procession through the streets of Gandía, and the singing of the responsory *Dum transisset*. When the group arrived at the monastery chapel, the *Quem quaeritis* scene was enacted. This is perhaps the most striking feature of the play. Usually this scene took place at the sepulchre within the chruch. Here it is acted out at the church doors, the procession remaining outside and the angels asking the questions from within. The initial scene concluded, three knocks

---

Marías llevan en las manos vasos llenos de aromas. San Juan y todos los demas personages se quedan al pie del Sepulcro. Mientras el ángel descubre el sepulcro el coro canta a 3 (tiple, 1º, 2º, y bajo)" (Lihory). Baixauli has failed to notice that in the text of the play which he has reproduced, the words *Quis revolvet*, etc. bear the rubric, *Las Marias y San Juan Evangelista*. Baixauli speaks of three Marys, Ripollés of two Marys and St. John, Lihory of three Marys and St. John.

[11] Note of Baixauli: "El Santísimo se sacaba privadamente antes de llegar la procesión."
[12] "Terminado este canto, *Quis revolvet*, el ángel y las Marías vueltos de cara al pueblo entonan al unison" (Lihory).
[13] Lihory adds that the choir responds *Deo gratias* to the first two renditions of "Surrexit Christus".

were given on the door with the shaft of the cross, and at the last of these the doors were opened. The procession then entered the church.

This phase of the performance shows the influence of another church ceremony. On Palm Sunday, when the procession was about to re-enter the church, an identical series of knocks was given. The same also occurred, and in a more dramatic fashion, during the rites for the consecration of a church. Standing outside the main door, the bishop would strike it three times, reciting the verse *Tollite portas, principes, vestras, et elevamini, portae aeternales, et introibit rex gloriae*. One person would respond from within, *Quis est iste rex gloriae?* At the reply *Dominus virtutum, ipse est Rex gloriae*, the doors would open and the procession would enter. This ceremony symbolized the expulsion of evil from the edifice. During the Middle Ages this practice was frequently incorporated into the ritual of the *Elevatio*, a liturgical office observed in many churches on Easter Sunday morning.[14] When it was sung as a part of the *Elevatio*, the antiphon *Tollite portas* usually served to recall Christ's descent into Limbo after His death to redeem the captive souls. Thus a fifteenth century manuscript from the monastery of Saint Gall declares: "Cantant antiphonam, *Attollite portas, principes*, tribus vicibus, pulsantes contra ianuam cum pede crucis in signum redempcionis animarum ex limbo. Ad istum pulsum ianua aperitur."[15]

One such version of the *Elevatio* bears striking similarities to the usage of Gandía, and it is more than likely that Francis Borgia had it before him when he composed his play. The version is found in the famous *Liber Sacerdotalis* written at Venice in 1523 by Alberto Castellani.[16] Young remarks of the Castellani text (I, 624): "The most remarkable feature of this ceremony is the juxtaposition of the formula *Attollite portas* – commonly associated with the theme of the Harrowing of Hell – and the dialogue *Quem quaeritis*." He has found this juxtaposition in no other play. In the Gandía piece, though the words *Attollite portas* are not spoken, the rest of the scene at the church entrance is identical with that of the Venetian performance.

The *Liber Sacerdotalis* could not have been the only source of the Spanish play, however. The former contains neither the verse *Quis revolvet nobis lapidem* nor the sequence *Victimae paschali laudes*, and most important of all, makes no provision for impersonation or costumes. It is the dramatic rubrics which give the Gandía play its special charm: the Marys with their silver ointment jars, the searching of the sepulchre by each in turn (the discovery of course is reserved to Mary Magdalen), the angel with his palm and crown, St. John . . . All of these features are lacking in the Venetian version.

[14] See above, pp. 9-10. The *Elevatio*, we remember, involved the taking up from the sepulchre the Host or cross which had been placed there during the *Depositio* of Good Friday.
[15] The complete text is given in Young, I, 163-164; for a general treatment of the theme of Christ's descent into Limbo, commonly referred to as "the Harrowing of Hell", see Young, I, 149-177.
[16] The relevant passages of the *Liber Sacerdotalis* are quoted in the Appendix.

Once introduced, the *Visitatio* flourished at Gandía over three centuries. Apparently as the years passed the play increased in splendor. Baixauli writes (p. 273):

> Nunca había decaído de su primitivo esplendor, antes recibió éste nuevos impulsos con la piedad de los duques sucesores de su fundador San Francisco, y en especial de Doña Mariana de Borja, que al morir señaló en su testamento la renta anual de cinco libras para más aumento en la distribución.

When the archbishop of Valencia, M. Barrio, visited the city in 1865, the piece was still being performed there. Surprised at the unusual privilege enjoyed by the religious of Santa Clara, the prelate asked to see the papal document which authorized it. When it could not be produced within a space of three years (it had been accidentally burned), he revoked the privilege. This was the last time the liturgical Easter play was performed in Spain.[17]

We have no record of a liturgical *Visitatio* at medieval Valencia; this despite the fact that a printed work of 1494 describes all the liturgical ceremonies conducted at the cathedral on Easter Day.[18] As was stated at the beginning of this chapter, it is probable that the religious plays came to Valencia only in the thirteenth century, and at that date, they would most likely have been already in the vernacular. The capitular statutes and account books of the cathedral speak frequently of plays for the feasts of Christmas, Pentecost, and the Assumption. It is certain that the latter was a vernacular and non-liturgical play, for we possess a portion of the text.[19] In view of the large number of actors and the complicated stage machinery of the others, they were probably of the same type. To give an idea of what the Pentecost performance was like, we present here the description of the play drawn up by Sanchis y Sivera from the medieval expense accounts of the cathedral:[20]

> Construíase un tablado entre el coro y el altar mayor, a la altura del presbiterio. Allí se colocaba el Apostolado, doce hombres ataviados con requísimos trajes, cubiertos sus rostros con caretas, cada una de las cuales reproducía la tradicional cara de los diversos apóstoles, todos ellos ostentando diademas dorados. Entre ellos, o formando grupos diferentes, había varios judíos, también con caretas, representando personajes evangélicos, tres peregrinos vestidos con trajes de rica seda, y varios judíos también elegantemente ataviados, siendo presbíteros los que hacían este papel. Encontrábanse igualmente allí la Virgen, represen-

---

[17] The date, 1565, which appears in Baixauli's study, and which has been repeated by many, is certainly a misprint. Mariano Barrio was archbishop of Valencia from 1861 to 1876, and Baixauli himself declares that the *Visitatio* of Gandía continued in usage "mas de trescientos años" before its suppression (p. 273).
[18] *Hores de la Setmana Sancta*, Valencia, 1494.
[19] See H. Mérimée, *L'Art dramatique à Valencia depuis les origines jusqu'au commencement du XVIIIe siècle*, pp. 45-46.
[20] *La Catedral de Valencia, guía histórica y artística*, p. 467.

tada en estátua, y las piadosas mujeres luciendo vistosos trajes y hermosa cabellera la que desempeñaba el papel de Magdalena. En la parte alta del cimborio hallábanse colocados dos cielos de nubes, uno grande y otro pequeño, formados por diversos lienzos pintados y arreglados de modo especial, donde se veían varios serafines con alas de papel. Las paredes aparecían cubiertas con telas de raso, y se veían, uno enfrente del otro, el sol y la luna, que por un mecanismo especial brillaban y se obscurecían, según lo exigía el curso de la representación. Pero lo notable, al parecer, era el mecanismo empleado para la paloma, que simulaba el Espíritu Santo, desde aquel cielo de telas pintadas que se abría al estruendo de bombardas y otras armas, las que no deberían ser pocas, dada la cantidad de pólvora que se gastaba. Al funcionar "les poliches per tancar y obrir lo cel", y por una combinación de ruedas arriba y abajo, salía velozmente la *palometa* empujada "per lo moviment de un molinet", echando fuego en todas direcciones, producido por varios cohetes en ella colocados, y al mismo tiempo bajaban "cresoletes" encendidos, simulando lenguas de fuego, por medio de una combinación de ruedas "damunt y devall", movidas por el funcionamiento de otras ruedas mayores colocadas no sabemos donde.

Since Sanchis has pieced this account together from many fragmentary bits of evidence, it is quite possible that not all of the elements mentioned figured in the same play. The mechanism of the *palometa*, known elsewhere by the name *colometa*, was popular throughout all of western Europe. During the singing of the hymn *Veni, Creator Spiritus* at Tierce, and sometimes at Mass, the mechanical dove was lowered from the upper part of the church as a symbol of the Holy Spirit. Probably this device was employed at Valencia during one of the liturgical offices, and the actual play performed in the afternoon, or at some other time apart from any liturgical function.[21]

The dramatic spectacle of Christmas Day was every bit as elaborate and colorful, if not more so. Players came and went from "heaven" to "earth", Adam and Eve appeared in the Garden of Paradise, the prophets stepped forth to present their testimony, and no less than twenty-five shepherds journeyed to "Bethlehem" to adore the Christ Child:[22]

Desde el coro, en la parte de la epístola, hasta el púlpito, que estaba en el presbiterio, se construía un tablado de bastante consistencia, sobre el que se colocaba el establo de Betlem, dentro del cual hallábanse representados en figura la Virgen, San José y el Niño Jesús, elegantemente ataviados con trajes de ricas telas, y rodeados de ángeles, serafines y querubines. En sitio no muy apartado veíanse unas torres, simulando la Ciudad Sagrada, y en segundo término contemplábanse las figuras de

---

[21] Concerning the use of a dove, real or artificial, in the liturgy of Pentecost Day, see Young, I, 490-491. In Spain the custom was traditional at Toledo, Palencia, Huesca, Badajoz, Burgo de Osma, Seville, and other places.

[22] Sanchis y Sivera, p. 462.

todos los profetas que anunciaron la venida del Mesías, también ricamente vestidos. Varios personajes de hombres y mugeres, representando pastores y pastoras, aquellos en número de veinticinco, unos en figura y otros de carne y hueso, puesto que cantaban cuando el drama lo exigía, ocupaban el resto del tablado hasta cerca del establo, el cual aparecía iluminado por los resplandores que esparcían veintiocho gruesos cirios colocados entre las nubes que rodeaban los rayos de madera dorada situadas detrás de la imagen de la Virgen. Fuera del tablado, y en el coro, hallábase el árbol del Paraíso con las figuras de Adán y Eva, y encima de dicho árbol aparecía también el Niño Jesús, rodeado de serafines. En lo alto del cimborio colocábase un lienzo pintado que figuraba el cielo, y en la barandilla había vienticinco niños vestidos de ángel con cirios encendidos, rodeando y haciendo la corte á la figura del Padre Eterno. Así todo dispuesto, á un señal convenido abríase el lienzo colocado en lo alto del cimborio y salía una paloma de madera, cubierta de plumas de papel, la que, por medio de un mecanismo especial, llegaba hasta el establo de Betlem despidiendo fuego. Luego bajaba un ángel con un lirio en la mano, mientras otro ángel cantaba, alternando o haciendo coro con él una mujer ó infantillo que la representaba, la cual llevaba la voz de la Virgen.

This play could hardly have been performed as an integral part of the liturgy. The documents tell us, nonetheless, that it was presented "at Matins": "Per manament de capitol font provehit que fes la representació de la nit de Nadal *a les matines* en la millor manera ques pogues fer."[23] In all likelihood it was staged in the vernacular, immediately after Matins and before the *Te Deum*. Many of the German vernacular plays were performed at this moment, and it appears quite probable that the same practice was followed throughout Castile on Christmas night.[24] We recall that Juan del Encina's Christmas Eclogues (1492) were acted out at the Duke of Alba's palace where "el Duque y la Duquesa estaban oyendo maitines"; this suggests that the play was traditionally associated with Matins.

Sanchis does not mention in his résumé a very important item of the stage equipment which figures constantly in the cathedral expense accounts, namely, the "aracoeli". The "aracoeli" was a sort of mechanical lift which moved back and forth between "heaven" and "earth" in spectacular fashion, carrying statues, and at times the actors themselves. It was associated chiefly with the Blessed Virgin. In the final scene of the Assumption performance, it transported her (a statue) to heaven; in the Christmas piece it brought down from the upper part of the church an image of the Virgin and Child.

[23] *Libre de obres*, año 1440.
[24] López Santos tells us that in Leonese towns the Christmas play was presented, and still is, "antes o después de la llamada Misa del Gallo, formando con ella una unidad semi-litúrgica, de tal modo que a veces la misa se intercala entre las distintas escenas del auto" ('Autos del Nacimiento Leoneses', p. 9); a play performed before Midnight Mass would immediately follow Matins.

Still today at Elche the "aracoeli" performs its function in the famous Assumption play, one of the few medieval dramatic productions which has survived to modern times.

Sanchis speaks of prophets in the Valencian Christmas drama, but it seems from his description that he interpreted these to be merely statues. Among the items which have been recorded from the cathedral expense accounts, I have noted but two references to the prophets. The first of these was registered in 1440:

> Item mes compri sis capdells de linyol, tres grossos e tres prims, per obs de la dita representacio, e per les diademes dels prophetes.[25]

These diadems could have been made either for real personages, or for imitation figures. The second entry is no more conclusive: "Pagui per la pintura del rey David y ferli un traje."[26]

When Villanueva examined the medieval manuscripts of the cathedral library at the beginning of the nineteenth century, he remarked that a breviary written in 1464 contained the Sibylline prophecy as a part of Christmas Matins.[27] It was sung in Latin during the sixth lesson, the lesson being the pseudo-Augustinian sermon *Inter pressuras atque angustias*. No mention is made in the breviary of dramatization.

A printed work of 1533 accords much greater prominence to both the prophets and the Sibyl. Whereas in the fifteenth century work only one Old Testament prophet is cited (Isaias), in the latter all the prophets appear. Moreover their names are printed in red before each of their testimonies, as is that of the *Lector* before the other parts of the sermon. These rubrics disclose that the entire sermon was delivered as a dialogue, and perhaps as a play. The *Lector* would introduce the individual prophets, and they in turn would recite the words attributed to them, the part of each one doubtless being assumed by a different cleric. The Sibyl was definitely impersonated. Her song is preceded by the phrase: "la Sybilla deu estar ja apparelada en la trona vestida com a dona." Villanueva comments upon this text as follows:[28]

> En el oficio de esta solemnidad, que se insertó en la semana santa del año 1533, se ve que creciendo la devoción de los Prelados, añadieron todos los testimonios que profetizaron la venida de Cristo; los quales anunciaba el Lector de este modo: "dic tu, Jeremia: dicat et Isaias." Y como se nota con tinta colorada los nombres de estos Profetas, y despues de sus palabras la de *Lector*, es probable que estos testimonios los dixese otro respondiendo a la pregunta del Lector, como lo proviene quando llega a la profecía de la Sibila con estas palabras: "la Sybilla deu estar ja apparelada en la trona vestida com a dona: esto es: la Sibila debe estar ya prevenida en el púlpito en trage de muger."

---

[25] Sanchis y Sivera, p. 463.
[26] *Libre de obres*, 1531, fol. 35.
[27] This codex is now MS 81.
[28] *Viage literario*, I, 134-135.

From the text alone, it is difficult to determine if the clerics actually impersonated the prophets whom they represented, and dressed up to appear like them. Paul Aebischer concludes readily that they did.[29] Basing his interpretation upon Villanueva's presentation of the text, he refers to the sixth lesson of the Valencian Christmas office as "un drame de Noël", and declares, "nous sommes certainement en présence . . . d'une dramatisation du pseudo-sermon de saint Augustin."

Since the publication of Villanueva's work in 1803, many have referred to the liturgical book which contains the dramatic version of the lesson, but no one has ever published the original text. This may be because copies of the volume are relatively rare. In view of the importance of this text, and because there is a serious possibility that it was staged as a play, we here present it in its entirety:[30]

Sermo Sancti Augustini, episcopi. Lectio vi:

Inter pressuras atque angustias presentis temporis nostre seruitutis oficia cogimur, dilectissimi non tacere. Cum potius expediat flere quam aliquid dicere. Verumtamen ne nobis dicatur: serue nequam et piger: quia tu non erogasti pecuniam meam: ego ueniens cum vsuris exigam eam. Peto igitur charitatem vestram: vt que ipse paterfamilias per nos vobis ministrauerit: libenter accipere dignemini. Apostoli Pauli verba sunt. Nox precessit, dies appropinquauit. Deponentes opera tenebrarum induite vos arma lucis. Expulsa itaque noctis caligine: effugatisque tenebris peccatorum: radius veri luminis fulgeat in cordibus nostris. Exigit a vobis ratio: huic congregationi et noctis transacte reddere rationem: et mynisterium Dei de tanto sacramento percepto veram sempiternamque demonstrare salutem. Si enim opera transacte noctis consideremus: et quid egerimus Domino donante explicare valuerimus: inueniemus nos in hac nocte: non opera noctis sed diei peregisse. Quid egimus in hac nocte? Captiuatorem captiuauimus. Quid egimus in hac nocte? Tenebras diabolicas de cordibus nostris excussimus: et lumen verum hauriendum esse demonstrauimus. Quid actum est in hac nocte? Veniens vera fortitudo: alligauit fortem: vt vasa eius diripiat. Quid enim actum est in hac nocte? Stirpata est superbia: introducta est humilitas. Quid actum est in hac nocte? Princeps omnium uitiorum expulsus est: fons omnium bonorum susceptus est.

Vos inquam conuenio o Iudei, qui vsque in hodiernum tempus negastis Filium Dei. Nonne vestra erat illa vox: quando eum videbatis miracula facientem: atque temptantes dicebatis. Quousque animas nostras

---

[29] 'Le Cant de la Sibilla', p. 268.
[30] The full title of the book is as follows: *Hores de la Setmana Sancta: ab una deuotissima oració: preparatoria per a tenir vera contrictio. E una deuotissima contemplacio a nuestra Senyora. E a la fi de dites hores: estan les matines de nadal: ensemps ab la missa del gall* (Valencia, Francisco Romano, 1533). The passage cited is found on fol. 250ᵛ-257. There are two copies of this book at the Biblioteca Nacional in Madrid, and according to Aguiló y Fuster, one at the library of the University of Valencia (*Catálogo de obras en lengua catalana impresas desde 1474 hasta 1860*, p. 37). An earlier edition of the work (Valencia, 1494) does not contain Christmas Matins.

suspendis: si tu es Christus dic nobis palam. Ille autem vos ad considerationem miraculorum inuitabat dicens. Opera que ego facio, ipsa testimonium perhibent de me, vt Christo testimonium dicerent, non verba sed facta. Vos autem non agnoscentes Saluatorem: qui operabatur salutem in medio vestri: adijtientes in malo aistis: Tu de te ipso testimonium dicis: testimonium tuum non est verum. Sed ad hec ille quid vobis responderit aduertere noluistis. Nonne inquit scriptum est in lege vestra: quod duorum hominum testimonium sit verum. Procedant ex lege vestra non duo tantum sed etiam plures testes Christi: et conuincant vos auditores legis: non factores. Dic Esaya testimonium de Christo.

Esayas:
Ecce inquit virgo in vtero concipiet et pariet filium: et vocabitur nomen eius Emanuel: quod interpretatur nobiscum Deus.

Lector:
Accedat et alius testis. Dic et tu Hieremia testimonium de Christo.

Hieremias:
Hic est inquit Deus noster: et non estimabitur absque illo alius: qui inuenit omnem viam scientie: et dedit eam Iacob puero suo: et Israel dilecto suo.

Lector:
Ecce duo testes ydonei ex lege vestra: ex quorum testimoniis non sunt compuncta corpora vestra. Sed alii atque alii ex lege vestra: Christi testes introducantur: vt frontes durissime inimicorum conterantur. Veniat et ille Daniel sanctus: iuuenis quidem etate: senior vero scientia ac mansuetudine et conuincat omnes falsos testes. Et sicut conuicit seniores impudicos: ita suo testimonio Christi conterat inimicos. Dic sancte Daniel: dic de Christo quod nosti.

Daniel:
Cum venerit inquit Sanctus Sanctorum: cessabit vnctio vestra.

Lector:
Quare illo presente cui insultantes dicebatis: tu de te ipso testimonium dicis: testimonium tuum non est verum: nisi quia ipse est qui venerat Sanctus Sanctorum? Si nondum venit sicut vos dicitis: et expectatur vt veniat Sanctus Sanctorum: demonstrate vnctionem? Si autem vt verum est cessauit vestra vnctio: agnoscite igitur venisse Sanctum Sanctorum. Ipse est enim lapis ille abscisus de monte sine manibus conscidentium: idest Christus natus de virgine sine manibus complectentium: qui tantum creuit vt mons magnus fieret et impleret vniuersam faciem terre. De quo monte Esayas propheta dicit.

Esayas:
Venite ascendamus ad montem Domini, et ad domum Dei Iacob.

Lector:
Et de quo dicit Dauid.

Psalmus .lxvii.
Mons Dei mons vber: vt quid suspicamini montes incaseatos? Mons in quo placuit Deo habitare in eo.

Lector:
Hunc cognouit Petrus dicens.

Petrus:
Tu es Christus Filius Dei viui.

Lector:
Agnouit montes: et ascendit in montem. Testimonium dixit veritati: et dilectus est a veritate. Supra petram fundatus est Petrus: vt mortem susciperet illum amando: quem ter negauerat timendo. Dic et tu Moyses legis dator et dux populi Israel testimonium de Christo.

Moyses:
Prophetam inquit suscitabit vobis de fratribus vestris: tanquam me ipsum audite. Omnis anima que non audierit prophetam illum: exterminabitur de populo suo.

Lector:
Prophetam autem dictum esse Christum ipsum audi in euangelio Christum.

Euangelista:
Non est inquit propheta sine honore nisi in patria sua.

Lector:
Accedat autem David sanctus et fidelis testis; ex cuius semine processit ille: cui lex et prophete testimonium dicunt: dicat et ipse de Christo.

Dauid:
Adorabunt inquit eum omnes reges terre: omnes gentes seruient ei.

Lector:
Cui seruient?

Dauid:
Vis audire cui seruient? Dixit Dominus Domino meo: sede a dextris meis. Donec ponam inimicos tuos: scabellum pedum tuorum.

Lector:
Et expresius atque nominatim.

Dauid:
Quare inquit tumultuate sunt gentes: et populi meditati sunt inania? Astiterunt reges terre: et principes conuenerunt in vnum: aduersus Dominum et aduersus Christum eius.

Lector:
Accedat et alius testis. Dic et tu Abacuch propheta: testimonium de Christo.

Abacuch:
Domine inquit audiui auditum tuum et timui: consideraui opera tua et expaui.

Lector:
Que opera Dei iste miratus expauit? Numquid fabricam mundi iste miratus expauit? Absit. Sed audi quid expauit.

Abacuch:
In medio inquit duum animalium cognosceris.

Lector:
Opera tua Deus: verbum caro factum est. In medio duum animalium cognosceris: qui quousque descendisti: expauescere me fecisti. Verbum per quod facta sunt omnia: in presepio iacuisti. Agnouit bos possessorem suum: et asinus presepe Domini sui. In medio duum animalium cognosceris. Quid est in medio duum animalium cognosceris: nisi aut in medio duorum testamentorum aut duorum latronum: aut in medio Moysi et Helye: cum eo in monte sermotinantium? Ambulauit inquit verbum: et exiuit in campis. Verbum caro factum est: et habitauit in nobis. Hoc Baruch ait.

Baruch:
Post hec inquit in terris visus est: et cum hominibus conuersatus est.

Lector:
Ecce quemadmodum conuincunt vos filios falsitatis. Sufficiunt vobis ista o Iudei: an adhuc ad vestram confusionem: ex lege et ex gente vestra: alios introducemus testes: vt illi testimonium perhibeant: cui perdita mente insultantes dicebatis. Tu de te ipso testimonium perhibes: testimonium tuum non est verum? Quod si velim ex lege et prophetis: omnia que de Christo dicta sunt colligere: facilius me tempus quam copia deferet (sic). Verumtamen senem illum ex gente vestra natum: sed in errore vestra non relictum: Symeonem sanctum in medio introducam: qui meruit decrepitus teneri in hac luce: quo usque videret vestram lucem. Quem quidem iam etas compellebat ire: sed expectabat suscipere quem sciebat venire. Tum ipse senex admonitus esset a Spiritu Sancto: quia non ante moreretur nisi videret Christum Dei natum: hunc cognoscens perrexit ad templum. Ubi vero eum portari matris manibus vidit: et diuinam infantiam pia senectus agnouit: tulit infantem in manibus suis. Ille quidem Christum ferebat: sed Christus senem regebat. Regebat qui portabatur: ne ille ante promissum a corpore solueretur. Quid tamen dixit: quem confessus fuit: aduertite o inimici: non Christi sed vestri. Benedicens Deum exclamauit senex ille: et dixit.

Symeon:

Nunc dimittis seruum tuum Domine secundum verbum tuum in pace: quia viderunt oculi mei salutare tuum.

Lector:

Illi etiam parentes Ioannis: Zacharias et Helisabeth: Iuuenes steriles: in senectute fecundi: dicant etiam ipsi testimonium de Christo. Dicant de Christo quid sentiant: et testem ydoneum Christo nutriant. Aiunt enim suo paruulo nato.

Zacharias:

Tu puer propheta altissimi vocaberis: preibis enim ante faciem Domini parare vias eius.

Lector:

Ipsique matri et Virgini Marie Helizabeth sic ait.

Helizabeth:

Unde hoc mihi vt veniat mater Domini mei ad me? Ecce enim vt facta est vox salutationis tue in auribus meis: exultauit in gaudio infans in vtero meo.

Lector:

Intelligens enim Ioannes matrem Domini sui venisse ad suam matrem: inter ipsas angustias vteri adhuc positus: motu salutauit: quem voce non poterat. Qui postea ipse Ioannes precursor et amicus: humilis et fidelissimus seruus: testis ydoneus factus: tanto maior in natis mulierum: quanto estimabatur esse quod non erat. Christum enim eum esse Iudei credebant: sed ille se non esse clamabat dicens.

Baptista:

Quem me esse suspicamini: non sum ego: sed ecce venit post me: de cuius pedibus non sum dignus soluere corrigiam calciamenti eius.

Lector:

O fidelis testis: et amicus veri sponsi: quantum te humiliauisses: si ad corrigiam calciamenti eius soluendam: dignum te esse dixisses. Sed dum ad hoc non dignum te dicis: Iudeis falsis testibus contradicis. Et hec dicta sunt a te: antequam Christum videres. Qui cum ad te ipse venit: humilis implende dispensationis sue gratia: vt a te baptizaretur qui nullum omnino habebat peccatum: quid responderis: quem cognoueris: quale testimonium protuleris. Audiant amici: quia audire nolunt inimici.

Baptista:

Ecce inquit agnus Dei: ecce qui tollit peccata mundi.

Lector:

Et adiecit.

Baptista:

Tu a me venis baptizari. Ego a te debeo baptizari.

Lector:

Agnouit seruus Dominum. Agnouit vinculis originalis peccati obligatus ab omni nexu peccati liberum. Agnouit preco iudicem. Agnouit creatura creatorem. Agnouit paranimphus sponsum. Nam et hec vox Ioannis est.

Joannes Baptista:

Qui habet sponsam sponsus est: amicus autem sponsi qui stat et audit eum: gaudio gaudet propter vocem sponsi.

Lector:

Sufficiunt vobis ista, o Iudei. Sufficiunt vobis tanti testes et testimonia: ex lege vestra et ex gente vestra. An adhuc impudentia nimia audebitis dicere: quod alterius gentis vel nationis homines: Christo debent testimonium perhibere? Sed si hoc dicitis: respondet quidem ille vobis.

Non sum missus nisi ad oues que perierunt domus Israel. Sed sicut vos in Actibus Apostolorum increpat Paulus. Vobis inquit primum oportuerat annunciare verbum Dei: sed quia expulistis illud: nec vos dignos vite eterne iudicastis. Ecce inquit conuertimur nos ad gentes. Demonstremus ergo nos etiam ex gentibus testimonium Christo prolatum: quem veritas non tacuit clamando: etiam per linguas inimicorum suorum. Nonne quoniam ille poeta facundissimus inter sua carmina. Iam noua progenies celo dimittitur alto dicebat: Christo testimonium perhibebat. In dubium hoc veniet: nisi alios ex gentibus ydoneos testes pluraque dicentes: in medio introducam. Illum regem qui vestram superbiam captiuando perdomuit: Nabuchodonosor regem, scilicet, Babylonis non pretermittam. Dic Nabuchodonosor: quid in fornace quando tres viros iustos iniuste miseras: dic quid tibi fuerit reuelatum.

Nabuchodonosor:

Nonne inquit tres viros missimus (sic) in fornacem ligatos?

Lector:

Et aiunt ei. Vere ita est rex.

Nabuchodonosor:

Ecce inquit ego video quattuor viros solutos: deambulantes in medio ignis: et corruptio nulla est in eis. Et aspectus quarti similis est Filio Dei.

Lector:

O alienigena vnde tibi hoc? Quis tibi annunciauit Filium Dei? Nondum quidem mundo nascitur: et similitudo nascentis a te cognoscitur. Unde tibi hoc? Quis tibi istud annunciauit: nisi quia sic te diuinus ignis intus illuminauit: vt cum illic apud te captiui tenerentur inimici Iudei: sic diceres testimonium Filio Dei. Sed quia in ore duorum vel trium testium stat omne verbum: sic ipse Dominus vestram contumatiam confutans. In lege inquit vestra scriptum est: quod duorum hominum testimonium sit verum. Sed iam ex gentibus etiam tertius testis introducatur: vt ei testimonium veritatis ex omni parte roboretur. Quid autem Sybilla vaticinando etiam de Christo clamauerit: in medio proferamus: vt ex vno lapide vtrorumque frontes percutiantur: Iudeorum, scilicet, atque paganorum: atque suo gladio sicut Golias Christi omnes percutiantur inimici. Audite quid dixerit.

La Sybilla deu estar ja apparellada en la trona vestida com a dona.

          Sybilla.

En lo ior del iudici
veuras qui fet seruici.
      E. [31]

Duna verge naxera
Deu y hom qui iutiara
de cascu lo be yl mal
al iorn del iuhi final.
      E.

Mostrar san quinze senyals
per lo mon molt generals
los morts ressucitaran
de hon tots tremolaran.
      E.

Dalt dels cels deuallera
Jesu Christ ys mostrara
en la vall de Iosaphat
hon sera tot hom iutiat.
      E.

Portara cascu scrit
en lo front a sen despit
les obres que haura fet
don haura cascu son dret.
      E.

Als bons dara goig etern
e als mals lo foch dinfern
a hon sempre penaran
puix a Deu offes hauran. [32]

---

[31] This letter indicates that the refrain, *En lo ior, etc.*, is repeated.
[32] An uncatalogued Valencian *consueta* found in the capitular library, and written approximately between the years 1530-1630, contains a similar reference to the Sibyl (fol. 100ᵛ): "Com diguen la sisena liço la Sibilla acompanyada ab lo vedell y dos canalobres va a la trona del evangeli, y quant es hora, diu la Sibilla tres o quatre cobles y tornasen a la sagrestia."

Si de celesti autem natiuitate queritis: beatissimus Joannes Euangelista accedat: et archana nobis reuelet mysteria. Et dicat quid erat: et quando erat: et quid agebat: et vbi venit: et qualiter venit: et qua causa venit. Dic ergo sancte Joannes quid erat:

Joannes:
In principio erat Verbum.

Lector:
Dic et qualis erat:

Joannes:
Et Deus erat Verbum.

Lector:
Et quid agebat:

Joannes:
Omnia per ipsum facta sunt.

Lector:
Ubi venit?

Joannes:
Venit in propria.

Lector:
Et quare venit?

Joannes:
Ut peccata tolleret mundi. Et Verbum caro factum est: et habitauit in nobis.

Credo iam vos: o inimici Iudei: tantis testibus ita obrutos: confutatosque esse ipsa veritate: vt nihil vltra repugnare: nihil querere debeatis. Nos igitur fratres charissimi: inter versutias Iudeorum habentes presidia veritatis: suscipiamus natum Christum: qui nos nascendo: moriendo: et resurgendo redemit: et eterne vite aditum reserauit. Amplectemur fidei brachiis sacra cunabula: veneremur Christum paruulum in presepio: mentibus castis: moribus dignis: et non tam carnali quam spirituali gaudio: diem natiuitatis Domini celebremus. Et si meritis devotis sumus: iungamur vocibus angelorum: et mente deuota sic dicamus omnes pariter. Gloria in excelsis Deo: et in terra pax hominibus bone voluntatis. Tu autem domine miserere nobis. Deo gratias.[33]

In his study of the liturgical drama, Karl Young has come across one other form of the sermon which resembles this. A liturgical book printed for the diocese of Salerno in 1594 divides the lesson into speaking parts in an

---

[33] The text is followed by the responsory, *Sancta et immaculata*.

almost identical manner, the only major difference being that it provides fewer roles for the prophets and says nothing about the dress of the Sibyl. Its author, on the other hand, has taken care to eliminate the rather illogical *inquit* from the prophetic testimonies. Young remarks of this text: "Each testimony is recited, presumably, by a separate person; but there is no evidence of impersonation."[34]

The same dramatic historian refers earlier in his work (II, 126) to three medieval versions of the sermon which are accompanied by curious glosses. All three of these texts are found in lectionaries.[35] In the first two, the names of the prophets appear in the margin opposite the prophetic verses; in the third, the verses themselves are encircled with a red line, and in the margin has been added, *Ia prophecia, IIa prophecia*, etc. Young declares only that the rubrics are "unusual". He does not relate them with the Salerno version.

The *consueta* from Gerona, I believe, throws valuable light upon the meaning of these rubrics. The author of the Catalan ceremonial tells us not only that the *Ordo Prophetarum* was staged in the cathedral during Christmas Matins, but that it was performed according to the text given in the lectionary: "Legitur sermo *Inter pressuras atque angustias presentis temporis*. Et fiat hic Prophetarum Representacio si voluerint. *Et eorum quilibet dicat suum titulum ut in legenda continetur de prophetis.*" In other words, the text of the lectionary itself was used as the basis of the play. It appears quite possible that instead of composing an additional copy of the dramatic text, the Gerona scribes may have followed the more convenient and less expensive course of using the passage already available in the *Lectionarium*. One glance at the length of the lesson which we have reprinted from the Valencian ceremonial makes it clear why a copyist would think twice about transcribing the entire group of prophetic testimonies, if this was not absolutely necessary. In churches and monasteries where the play was of a very advanced and complicated type, the text of the lectionary would obviously have to be completely rewritten, especially if the play was put into verse and sung. It so happens that all the versions of the *Procession of Prophets* presented by Young are of this type – at least those which he considers as genuine plays.[36] Would it not be possible that in some communities the prophetic passages were dramatized simply as they appear in the *lectionarium*, that is, in their unversified form, and in the lesson tone, rather than as a complicated musical piece? It would seem that in its first beginnings at least, the *Procession of Prophets* must have passed through such an evolutionary stage. Young does not discuss this point.

In our opinion the "unusual" rubrics in the three lectionaries mentioned

---

[34] II, 137; he quotes the entire lesson, pp. 133-137.
[35] Paris, Bibl. Nat., MS lat. 1018, Lectionarium Arelatense saec. xii-xiii, fol. 129-132^v; Rome, Bibl. Vatic., MS Vat. Regin. 125, Lectionarium Forcalqueriense saec. xiii, fol. 74-76^v; Oxford, Bibl. Bodl., MS Canon. Liturg. 391, Lectionarium saec. xii, fol. 11^v-14.
[36] Not counting an unusual form sung at the epistle of the Mass, these are only six in number: Rouen, Laon, Einsiedeln, Benediktbeuern, St. Martial of Limoges, and Tours.

above indicate one of three things: 1. the lesson was delivered in dialogue form, as at Valencia and Salerno, and the names Isaias, Ieremias, etc. written in the margin were the cues for the clerics who read these parts; or if they had their own script, for the lector when he reached these points; 2. it was delivered as a genuine play, and the marginal entries served the same purpose (the versions from Salerno and Valencia may well have been plays, as Paul Aebischer thinks); 3. some scribe, using the *lectionarium* as a basis for a new manuscript of the Prophet Play, conveniently indicated the speaking parts by his marginal glosses and encirclings of the text. If our interpretation is correct, the medieval *Ordo Prophetarum* must have been much more popular than the few texts thus far discovered would lead us to suspect. The widespread use of the play as a scene in vernacular pieces also suggests this. In all likelihood an examination of the many medieval lectionaries which are still extant would disclose a considerable number of additional texts of the pseudo-Augustinian sermon with marginal rubrics similar to those of the Arles manuscript (Bibl. Nat., MS lat. 1018). Some of these might also provide valuable information concerning the evolution of the *Ordo Prophetarum*. I suspect that, owing to their very large and awkward format, relatively few lectionaries have been consulted.[37]

---

[37] Villanueva's statement that the testimonies of the prophets were *added* to the Valencian customs in the year 1533 may be incorrect. He comes to this conclusion because, whereas the breviary written in the year 1464 contains only the testimony of Isaias and the Sibyl, the printed book of 1533 accords roles to at least fifteen prophets. However the breviary probably gives an abbreviated version of the lesson, and not the form which would have been followed in the recitation of the office at the cathedral; for this latter service the full-length text of the lectionary would most likely have been employed.

CHAPTER 11

FURTHER EXAMPLES OF LITURGICAL DRAMA IN CATALONIA

IN a manuscript from the collegiate church of St. John of Perpignan are found references to what appears to be a hitherto unknown type of dramatic ceremony for the feast of Pentecost Sunday.[1] According to the manuscript, a fourteenth-fifteenth century ceremonial, at the church of St. John on Pentecost Sunday twelve clerics dressed to represent the apostles, and a child to represent the Blessed Virgin Mary. Each of the apostles wore a diadem, and carried a candle and a script containing the words and music of the *Credo* of the Mass. The Mary wore a crown, also had a candle, and was attired "com una donzella". The upper part of the church, which had already been prepared the day before, was adorned with imitation clouds, and somewhere behind them the *Colometa*, or artificial dove, had been placed in readiness; similar stage machinery, we recall, was employed for the Pentecost festivities at Valencia. When the sequence of the Mass was sung, the "ceremony of the Holy Spirit" took place. The mechanical dove which made its descent from the "heavens", probably came down at this moment. As it did, it brought down along with it a light representing the tongues of fire which had descended upon the Blessed Virgin and the apostles as they prayed in the cenacle on the first Pentecost morning. From this fire the thirteen participants lighted their candles. A few moments later the apostles sang the *Credo*; whether or not their *rotols* carried some special dramatic text, or just the usual words of the Creed, the manuscript does not say. Their chant terminated, the twelve clerics accompanied by the "Blessed Virgin" proceeded to the altar, where they concluded the ceremony by presenting the lighted candles as a part of their Mass offering:[2]

> Item los dits domasers, o saltim lo domaser sepmmaner, en lo jorn de Pentacosta son tenguts, e es tengut, de emprar preueres qui fassen la represantacio dels apostols en lo jorn de Pentacosta e qui sien sufficients en cantar lo *Credo in Deum* a la misa. E mes avant son tenguts, o es tengut,

---

[1] It is by no means out of place to speak of Perpignan in the present study, since during the greater part of the Middle Ages, this city was more closely connected with the Spanish kingdoms than with France. At first the property of the counts of Roussillon, Perpignan later passed into the hands of the kings of Aragon, who ruled over it, except for a period of sixty-three years, until 1462. During the sixty-three year period, the city was the capital of the Kingdom of Mallorca. It was definitively annexed to France by the treaty of the Pyrenees only in 1659. The popular language of the district is, of course, Catalan.
[2] Perpignan, Bibl. Mun., MS 79, Libre de serimonies saec. xiv-xv. The first passage is taken from fol. 7ᵛ, the second from fol. 66ᵛ.

de manar e hauer del obrer de la dita sglesia los rotols en que es scrit e notat lo dit *Credo in Deum*, et donar los als preueres que hauran emprats per fer la dita representacio.

Item los dit domasers, o lo dit sepmmaner, son tenguts, e es tengut, de hauer hun infant que sia abil a fer la representacio de la Maria, e qui sia ab los dits apostols. E lo qual infant deu esser uestit, ligat, e parat axi cum una donzella, e deu portar una corona en lo cap; los quals uestiments, ligars e paraments son tenguts hauer los dits domasers, o lo dit sepmmaner, e aximateys a donar recapte en lo uestir, ligar, e arresar lo dit infant.

Item son tenguts los dits domasers, o lo dit sepmmaner de manar e hauer del damont dit obrer XIII. siris per seruey del dit misteri, e donar aquells a la dita Maria e als dits Apostols segons es acostumat; los quals syris la dit obrer deu hauer de les illuminaries de Sant Johan e de Sancta Maria, segon pus largament es posat en los officis del dit obrer.

Item lo dit obrer es tengut de fer cadaffalchs a totz officis e misteris fahedors en la dita sglesia, o al sementari, e dar e administrar la ornamenta necessaria als regidors dels officis o misteris damont dits.

Item lo dit obrer es tengut donar cascun any en la uigilia de Pentacosta al domaser sepmmaner los dotze rotols en los quals es scrit e notat lo *Credo in Deum*, e mes auant dotze diademes per los dotze apostols, e huna corona[3] per la Maria, e tota la altre ornamenta necessaria al dit misteri.

Item lo dit obrer es tengut cascun any en la dita uigilia de Pentacosta apparellar los cels e la coloma ab dotze candeles. E en lo dia de Pentacosta en la missa maior, quant se diu lo *Veni Sancte Spiritus*, deu fer la serimonia del Sant Sperit, segons es acostumat.

Item lo dit obrer es tengut en lo dit dia de Pentacosta dar e administrar al damont dit domaser sepmmaner, o a aquell qui haura carrech de regir lo misteri dels apostols XIII. siris, los quals deu hauer e pendre de les illuminaries de Sant Johan e de Sancta Maria, e los quals deuen esser donatz a la Maria, e als dits apostols, ço es a saber a cascun hun ciri per pendre del lum que dauallara la dita coloma dels dits cels en remembrança que la Verges Maria e los apostols pregueren[4] e foren illuminats del foch del Sant Sperit. E los quals siris, apres que la Maria e los[5] apostols hauran pres del lum, deuen tenyr en les mans entro que uan a la hufferta, e aquells deuen lixar a la hufferta. E apres deuen sen anar en lo uestiari per despular. E adonchs lo dit obrer deu cobrar los dits ciris, e tornar los en aquells qui regexen les damont dites illuminaryes.

The conclusion recalls the final scene of the Limoges Epiphany play; in the latter the three kings advanced to the altar at the same moment in the Mass to deposit their gifts: "Et vadunt ad offerendam, relinquentes ibi sua jocalia."[6]

---

[3] corona] cora (MS).   [4] pregueren] prengueren (MS).   [5] e los] els (MS).
[6] Text in Young, II, 34-35. During the Middle Ages, after the offertory, the priests and people presented an offering at the main altar known as the *oblatio* or *oblata*. This offering was generally accompanied by a somewhat elaborate ceremonial and by the choral singing of the offertory.

The *repraesentatio* at Perpignan may have been related to an ancient tradition concerning the authorship of the Apostles' Creed. Rufinus of Aquileia (c. 345–410) declares that the Creed was composed by the apostles themselves after the descent of the Holy Ghost on Pentecost Sunday.[7] Since Rufinus begins his article, "tradunt maiores nostri . . .", the tradition was probably already well established by his time. A pseudo-Augustinian sermon written about the sixth century, elaborating upon this view, puts forth as an accepted tradition that each apostle contributed one article, and the author proceeds to identify the contribution of each: "Peter, 'I believe in God, the Father Almighty'; John, 'Maker of heaven and earth', etc."[8] The "apostles" in the Perpignan ceremony probably sang the tenet attributed to them by this old tradition.

This text from the collegiate church of St. John is the first involving some form of dramatization during the Creed and Offertory of Pentecost Sunday which has come to light. Karl Young has already pointed out the rarity of liturgical plays for this feast (I, 491):

> Clearly such ceremonies are not lacking in theatrical effects, and one feels that they ought to have achieved something more positive in the way of impersonation and drama. The disciples, upon whom the Holy Spirit is assumed to be descending, could easily enough have been costumed realistically, and could have sung appropriate sentences, as in the Ascension play from Moosburg. But of such developments the observances under review give no evidence. The impressive theme of Pentecost was not effectually dramatized.

The manuscript at hand makes provision for precisely the type of dramatic ceremony and costuming proposed by Young.[9]

The apostles and the Blessed Virgin Mary were also represented in dramatic Pentecost rites in the city of Lérida. In 1518 a statute was passed by the canons of the cathedral forbidding "misterium illud, quod vulgo dicitur *la Colometa* in memoriam illius Spiritus Sancti in Mariam Virginem Sacratissimam ac Christi Redemptoris Matrem et Apostolos missionis."[10] Commenting on this usage Villanueva remarks (XVI, 91):

---

[7] Migne, *P.L.*, 21, 337.
[8] Migne, *P.L.*, 39, 2190.
[9] The performance of the *Credo* in the Perpignan church may have been related in some way to the type of vernacular Creed play known at York in England. The exact nature of the York play itself has remained a problem, since the text of it has never been found. Apparently it was of cyclic proportions, whereas the Perpignan ceremony, being liturgical in nature, was in all likelihood of quite modest proportions. Nonetheless certain properties of both plays were the same. The French scribe speaks of "los dotze rotols en los quals es escrit e notat lo *Credo* in *Deum*, e mes auant dotze diademes per los dotze apostols"; an inventory pertaining to the English play refers to "xii rotulae nuper scriptae cum articulis fidei catholicae . . . et x diademata pro Christo et apostolis" (see Craig, *English Religious Drama of the Middle Ages*, pp. 334-337).
[10] Recorded by Villanueva, *Viage literario*, XVI, 90.

> Usose esto en todo el siglo XV, en que solían pagarse ochenta sueldos al que dirigía la máquina. También consta el gasto de almuerzo y merienda a los que representaban los Apóstoles, sobre quienes bajaba la paloma.

The ceremony may have been observed in the cathedral of Barcelona as well. An expense item recorded in the account books of that church declares:[11]

> Lo jorn de Pasqua del any de sinch, fonch feta representacio del Sperit Sant que devala com lo *alleluia* se deya entre pólvoro, cordes e trebayes e altres coses, 1 £ 19 s.

Returning to the church of St. John in Perpignan, we find that the *planctus* was sung in dramatic form after Matins on Good Friday, as it was at Palma and Toulouse. At least four roles were involved in the play: the Blessed Mother, St. John, and "les altres Maries". Unfortunately we do not know much about the performance itself:[12]

> Item los dits domasers, o saltim lo domaser sepmmaner, en la Sepmmana Sancta son tenguts, e es tengut, en lo Diuendres Sant, dits e fenits los fas, fer la represantacio de la Maria maior, e de Johan Euangeliste, e de les altres Maries, e fer cantare lo plant que la gloriosa Verges Maria feu del seu car fill Jhesu Christ, e lo plant que feu Sant Johan Euangeliste, e los altres plants que feren les altres Maries, e totes altres coses pertanyents e costumades fer a la dita representacio be e deuotament per persones abils e sufficiens, e qui hauen bones ueus segons es acostumat, e millor si millor fer lo poran.

On Christmas night, of course, the prophetic chant of the Sibyl was heard in almost all the important churches of Catalonia. Villanueva declares, without stating the reason for his opinion, that at Tarragona the ceremony may have included a play (XIX, 96):

> En la noche de Navidad había Sibila, como ya dije de Valencia, aunque acaso aquí mas bien era una representación o escena o comedia.[13]

The oldest vernacular text with the Sibylline prophecy found thus far in Catalonia, or anywhere in Spain, appears to be that discovered by Luis Constans in the parochial archives of the village church of San Andrés del Tor (province of Gerona). Constans estimates that the manuscript was written about 1260.[14] If this date is correct, the Catalan text is about as ancient as

---

[11] Anglès, 'El Cant de la Sibila', p. 71.
[12] Perpignan, Bibl. Mun., MS 79, fol. 7-7ᵛ.
[13] The same writer also speaks of "la función que llamaban Entremesos el día de Santa Tecla, y que consta se representaban en el siglo XV" (*loc. cit.*). Anglès states that these *entremesos* were performed during Matins (p. 232) and gives Villanueva as his reference, but as far as I could determine, the nineteenth century historian says nothing of Matins. In any case, these representations would hardly have been liturgical plays.
[14] 'Un *Dies Irae* en romance catalán del siglo XIII', pp. 7-11. The verses are included in the Appendix.

any that has survived. Only one other thirteenth century version is known: a Provençal text contained in a *lectionarium* located at the Archives de l'Hérault in Montpellier.[15] An additional testimony to the popularity of this vernacular Christmas chant in Catalonia during the thirteenth century is provided by a reference to the verses in a manuscript written for the cathedral of Lérida.[16] None of these works speak about impersonation of the prophetess; the author of the Lérida manuscript merely states:

> Lectio .VI. *Inter pressuras*. Et in ista leccione cantatur versus Siuille a duobus bonis cantoribus. Et scolares cantant *Al iorn del iudici*, etc.

Anglès assures us that the *Sponsus*, or the play of the Wise and Foolish Virgins, was known very early in Catalonia. The eminent musicologist bases his claim on certain mural paintings located at present in the Museum of Barcelona. If his assertion is well founded, it is of great importance for the history of the liturgical drama, since to date only one text of the *Sponsus* has been discovered, that of St. Martial of Limoges. Anglès writes (p. 288):

> Cal no oblidar que el drama *Sponsus* fou conegut ben d'hora al nostre país. Encara que no n'hàgim servat cap rastre musical ni poguem de moment citar res de documentació històrica, tenim el fet de les pintures murals romàniques de Sant Quirze de Pedret servades al present al Museu de Barcelona. Aquestes pintures del segle XII són un document pictòric preciós que ens duu el record de la representació dramàtica de la paràbola de les deu verges folles i prudents a Catalunya.

Finally, we have just enough information from various sources to know that Barcelona was an important center of the medieval religious drama.[17] The play of the Three Marys, for example, was staged in the cathedral on Easter Monday. This was a rather unusual date, the *Visitatio* ordinarily being performed at Matins on Easter Day itself:[18]

> Item lo diluns de Pascha se feu la representació de la Resurrecció, *de les tres Maries*. Pagaren les messions (expenses) entre los Aniversaris e la Obra e la Sagristia. Vench a la part de la Sagristia XXVI sol.

A *sepulchrum* doubtless figured in the staging of this play, since during the Middle Ages one was employed at the cathedral for the liturgical services of Easter week:[19]

> [Ad Vesperas] Finita oratione, dicatur antiphona *Alleluia*. Prosa *In exitu Israel*. Et dicendo, eant ad sepulcrum et ad sanctum Petrum.

---

[15] The manuscript is without catalogue number. The text of the prophecy has been edited by Aude, *Annales du Midi*, xvii (1905), 380 *sqq*.
[16] Lérida, Seminario, MS 6, Consueta secundum usum eccl. Illerdensis saec. xiii, fol. 19^v.
[17] The St. Stephen's Day performance staged in the cathedral of Barcelona has already been mentioned; see above, p. 118.
[18] Comptes de la Sacristia, any 1405; recorded by Anglès, p. 275.
[19] Vich, Bibl. Capit., MS 83, Breviarium secundum usum eccl. Barchinonensis saec. xiv, fol. 87^v.

Parts of two or three medieval *consuetas* describing the usages of the cathedral of Barcelona are yet extant in the capitular library, but the folios pertaining to the important feasts of Easter and Christmas appear to be missing.[20] A fifteenth century Barcelona *consueta*, found at the church of Santa María del Mar in the same city, says nothing of plays. It does inform us, however, that sometime after 1450, a *sepulchrum* was erected at Santa María (fol. 33): "[Ad Vesperas] postea uadat processio ad sepulcrum, postea ad altare majus cantando antiphonam *Regina celi*."[21]

In the year 1494 some kind of Christmas play involving the Sibyl was presented at the Monastery of Santa Ana in Barcelona: "Primo que despengui lo dia de Nadal per la Cibilla entre loguer (renting) de dues cabelleres (heads of hair) qui costaren xvj. diners, hi per lo salari de dita Cibilla iij. sous; es per tot iiij. sous, iiij. diners."[22] Some slight idea of what took place at the cathedral on Christmas night is given by two brief expense items registered for the years 1405–7 and 1419:[23]

> Item lo jorn de Nadal faem representations costa a la part de la sagristia entre totes coses, so es polvoro per focs, refreschs, loguer de fusta per los cadafalchs, e mans, e truyels, e altres coses.

> Deu la dita sagristia a dit candeler per 230 candeles que serviran per lo *Are Coeli* lo dia de Nadal per la representació de la Sibilla amb l'emperador, que pesaren VIII lliures e miga, a rao de 2 souls la lliura. Fonch a XXII de Decembre, 1418.

Noticeable is the plural use of both *representacions* and *cadafalchs*. Since there was more than one stage, the dramatic roles must have been quite numerous. Even more interesting and important is the reference to the *representacio de la Sibilla amb l'emperador*. This play was certainly not the dramatic monologue which we have encountered in so many medieval Spanish churches. The verses of the acrostic, *Judicii signum*, or of its vernacular counterpart, were devoted to the theme of the judgment to come; they contained no reference to an emperor or an *Ara Coeli*. The Middle Ages knew more than one tradition about the ancient oracles. Almost as famous as the Erythraean Sibyl – with whom the *Judicii* is usually associated – was the Sibyl from Tibur. Since in the legend concerning the second prophetess both the emperor and the *Ara Coeli* appear, it was doubtless this story that was dramatized on Christmas night in the cathedral of Barcelona.

The story of the Tiburtine Sibyl and her appearance in art and literature

---

[20] The *consuetas* now form one manuscript (n. 77); since none of the folios are in order, systematic study of the codex is almost impossible.

[21] The original passage, which has been crossed out, was as follows: "Et cantando eum uadat processio coram altari maiori loco altaris Sancti Sepulcri quod in ista ecclesia non est."

[22] Barcelona, Diocesan Museum, *Libre de rebudes y despeses del Monestir de Santa Ana*, any 1494, fol. 25.

[23] Recorded by Anglès, 'El Cant de la Sibila', pp. 71-72, and *La Música a Catalunya*, p. 302.

has been briefly, but masterfully, traced for us in an article by C. A. Thomas-Bourgeois.[24] The theme goes back to early Christian centuries, though the first written record of it is found in the sixth century Byzantine chronicle of Johannes Malalas. Wishing to know if there existed anyone in the world superior to him, the Emperor Octavian consulted the Tiburtine Sibyl. After a three-day wait, the heavens suddenly opened, and the emperor and the Sibyl beheld the following vision:

> Illico apertum est celum et nimius splendor irruit super eum et vidit in coelo quandam pulcherrimam virginem stantem super altare, puerum tenentem in brachiis, et miratus est nimis, et vocem dicentem audivit: "Haec ara filii Dei est."[25]

This striking image was to be known by posterity as the "legend of the Ara Coeli".

The theme became a favorite for medieval painters and miniaturists. M. Thomas has recorded many charming examples. In the beautiful *Livre d'Heures du Duc de Berry* (fourteenth century), for instance, an historiated initial pictures the Sibyl pointing out for the benefit of the emperor, who is wearing a crown, the image of Mary and Jesus in the heavens. On the phylactery which she bears in her hand one reads the inscription, "Hic puer major te est; ideo ipsum adora." In the mural paintings of the cathedral of Amiens discovered in 1937, another young Sibyl appears. She likewise is indicating the sky, where above a wooded hill, evidently the Aventine, the Holy Virgin appears, dressed in blue, with the Infant on her knees; an inscription repeats the words of the legendary prophecy: "Haec ara filii Dei est." At the Sibyl's feet, an old man in royal robes, his scepter and crown on the ground, kneels in adoration; written in letters of gold upon the long red dress of the prophetess are the identifying words: *Sibile tiburtina*.

It was inevitable that the Tiburtine Sibyl should eventually make her way into the medieval Christmas plays. Her sister from Erythraea had been appearing in the liturgical *Ordo Prophetarum* from at least the eleventh century. As the religious drama began to break away from its strictly liturgical setting, and the medieval playwrights came to excercise more originality and freedom, new scenes and characters were introduced in ever growing proportions. In time the episode of the Tiburtine Sibyl and the emperor was added. At just what date, however, no one knows.

In the latter part of the fifteenth century and throughout the sixteenth, the plays which included the scene were numerous. Frequently in these pieces the same Sibyl appears twice, once in the procession of prophets to fortell the coming of Christ, and later to announce to the emperor (or to Herod) that the Messias has already been born; the legends of the two Sibyls were thus

---

[24] 'Le Personnage de la Sibylle et la légende de l'Ara Coeli dans une Nativité wallone', pp. 883-912.
[25] See 'Martini Oppaviensis Chronicon. Imperatores', *Monumenta Germaniae Historica, Scriptorum*, XXII, 443.

focused, as it were, in the one prophetess. This occurs, for example, in the *Mystère de l'Incarnation et de la Nativité* played at Rouen in 1474,[26] and in the *Passion de Sémur*.[27]

If I interpret correctly the article of M. Thomas, the Rouen *mystère* is the oldest play with the scene of the emperor and the Sibyl which he has encountered. The reference to the Barcelona play, then, takes on added importance, since it was written in 1418. M. Thomas visualizes the representation of the scene as follows (p. 911):

> La vision partagée de la Sibylle et d'Octave avait-elle autrefois ou ailleurs provoqué l'entousiasme religieux? Vraisemblablement! Nous avons vu le succès général qui a entouré la légende de l'Ara coeili; et assurément, au théâtre, la miraculeuse apparition céleste devait susciter de l'admiration. Ne se prêtait-elle pas à une mise en scène exceptionnelle? Par un artifice scénique, par une machinerie de tréteaux, la Vierge tenant son enfant devait apparaître un instant aux yeux ravis ou étonnés de la Sibylle et de l'empereur. Sans doute écartait-on un moment le rideau de la mansion céleste où, sur un fond d'obscurité, brillait un autel tout illuminé; là resplendissait une de ces statues polychromées de vierge à l'enfant, couronnée de métal et de pierres précieuses, vêtue de dentelles blanches et de rubans pâles. Peut-être aussi, les personnages étaient-ils vivants . . . .

The picture of the brightly illuminated altar appearing suddenly overhead in the darkness is well imagined. Such a scene must have taken place at Barcelona, for we are told that no less than 230 candles were used for the *Ara Coeli*.

It is unfortunate that M. Thomas was not familiar with the famous Elche and Valencian Assumption plays. These would have given him an excellent idea of the manner in which the emperor's scene was handled in the medieval church performances, because the *Ara Coeli* plays an important function in both of them. In these, of course, the *Ara Coeli* is not employed to represent the emperor's vision, but as a piece of aerial machinery to bring the Holy Virgin to heaven after her death.

Interesting questions are raised by the use of this device in the Assumption plays, questions which may possibly serve as avenues of further investigation for those interested in religious drama. Were the device and the name suggested by the literary theme of the *Ara Coeli*, or were they adapted from Christmas plays, such as the Barcelona piece, in which the Tiburtine Sibyl reveals the heavenly image? The oldest text of the Assumption play, that of Valencia, belongs linguistically to the first years of the fifteenth century,[28] but the play itself is probably much older. Was the scene of the Tiburtine Sibyl with its spectacular aerial machinery already being dramatized in the thirteenth and fourteenth centuries? And last of all, when was it first known in France?

[26] Le Verdier, *Mystère de l'Incarnation de nostre saulveur et redempteur Jesuchrist*.
[27] Roy, 'Le Mystère de la Passion en France du XIVe au XVIe siècle'.
[28] See Shoemaker, *The Multiple Stage in Spain during the Fifteenth and Sixteenth Centuries*, p. 27.

CHAPTER 12

A BRIEF HISTORY OF THE DRAMATIC MONOLOGUE OF THE SIBYL

IN the course of this study treatment of certain questions concerning the dramatization of Sibylline legends has been deliberately postponed, with the realization that these could best be discussed only when all the important Hispanic texts about the Sibyl had been presented. Now that the texts have been brought forward, it would be fitting to present a brief outline of the salient facts known to us about this dramatic phenomenon, and the principal problems concerning it which remain unsolved.

Studies upon the music of the *Judicii signum* have been numerous, but few historians have treated the famous chant expressly from the viewpoint of its relationship to the medieval liturgical drama. The most notable discussions on this latter aspect have been contributed by Anglès (pp. 288–302), Paul Aebischer,[1] and Solange Corbin.[2] The important general treatises on the liturgical drama by Creizenach, Chambers, Young, and others, fail to consider the *Judicii* as a dramatic monologue.

The first attestation of the Sibyl's verses has been traced to Eusebius of Caesarea. In his *Oratio Constantini ad Sanctorum Coetum*, the various prophecies concerning the coming of Christ are cited, and among them, in Greek of course, is the acrostic poem attributed to the Erythraean Sibyl.[3] A century later the prophecy recurs, translated into Latin, in St. Augustine's *City of God*.[4] An author of the fifth or sixth century, perhaps Quodvultdeus, then incorporated the translation into the sermon *Contra Judaeos, Paganos et Arianos*, the work which was to inspire in medieval times the *Procession of Prophets*.[5] After this date historians lose trace of the poem in the West, until it reappears in manuscripts of the ninth century.[6]

It is not known at what date, or in what country, the custom arose of singing the Sibylline poem. The musical accompaniment appears for the first time in three tenth century manuscripts: Saint-Martial de Limoges (Paris, Bibl. Nat., MS lat. 1154, fol. 122a), Lyon (*ibid.*, MS lat. 2832, fol. 123^v), and Ripoll (Barcelona, Archivo de la Corona de Aragón, Ripoll 106, fol. 92^v). The St. Martial text may perhaps be the oldest of the three, since many

---
[1] 'Un Ultime écho de la *Procession des Prophètes*', pp. 261-270.
[2] 'Le *Cantus Sibyllae*: origines et premiers textes', pp. 1-10.
[3] Migne, *P.G.*, 20, 1285-90.
[4] Migne, *P.L.*, 41, 579.
[5] *Ibid.*, 42, 1117-1126; concerning the author, see above, p. 17.
[6] For a list of the oldest manuscripts with the text of the Sibyl, see especially the article of Miss Corbin.

eminent musicologists assign it to the ninth century.[7] It is of note that St. Martial and Ripoll, two monasteries intimately associated in the early development of trope singing and liturgical drama, are here classed together once again.

A tenth century *homiliarium* written near Burgos in Castile contains the poem of the Sibyl as a part of the pseudo-Augustinian sermon, *Inter pressuras*.[8] Because the verses are provided with music, Anglès infers that the Sibylline chant must have originated in Castile, perhaps within the Mozarabic liturgy, that it passed from there to Ripoll, and thence to St. Martial and the rest of Europe.[9] Solange Corbin has shown, however, that this view lacks serious foundation, since the music of the Córdoba manuscript was added only in the eleventh century (p. 5): "Le manuscrit de Cordoue est noté par une main aquitaine, qui ne peut être antérieure à l'arrivée des Bénédictins français dans la région de Burgos (milieu du XIe siècle)."[10]

Historians generally concede that the *Judicii signum* was probably first sung as a part of the pseudo-Augustinian sermon, though it would be difficult to prove this point with any rigorous certitude. For the sake of clarity, it should be remembered that the poem of the Erythraean Sibyl was also known through St. Augustine's treatise, *The City of God*.

P. Aebischer attempts to establish that the poem of the Sibyl was not sung until the Christmas liturgical play, the *Processio Prophetarum*, had already developed within the sermon (p. 267): "En Catalogne (and also in other European countries, the author infers) le chant de la Sibylle dérive, non point directement du sermon faussement attribué à saint Augustin, mais bien de la *Procession des prophetes* dont elle ne serait qu'un dernier écho." His arguments, however, are not convincing. The oldest example of the *Procession of Prophets* dates back only to about the year 1100, whereas the music for the *Judicii signum* begins to appear as early as the ninth or tenth century. As Miss Corbin remarks: "Il me semble difficile à croire que sa présence (that of the Sibylline poem) dès le Xe siècle soit suggérée par un *ordo prophetarum* qui, je crois, n'existe pas encore."[11] In the opinion of the latter critic the influence more probably flowed in the other direction: the recitation or chanting of the Sibyl's prophecy in the middle of the sermon could have encouraged individual recitation of the other prophets' lines.

I think that Prof. Aebischer may have been led to his conclusion by a presumption that from the first moment the *Judicii* was sung, it was accompanied by a dramatic ceremony similar to that observed at Toledo or Mallorca,

---

[7] E. de Coussemaker, *Histoire de l'Harmonie au Moyen Age*, pl. 14; J. Handschin, *Zeitschrift für Musikwissenschaft*, XIII, 122 sqq.; H. Spanke, *Studi Medievali*, 1931, p. 287.
[8] Córdoba, Bibl. Capit., MS 1, fol. 69b.
[9] *La Música española desde la Edad Media hasta nuestros días*, p. 17.
[10] Most musicologists will agree, I think, with Miss Corbin, since it is universally held that previous to the coming of the French ecclesiastics in the eleventh century, Aquitaine notation was not employed in Castile.
[11] 'Le *Cantus Sibyllae*', p. 9.

that is, that someone would dress to impersonate the Sibyl. He is apparently not the only one who has harbored this conviction. Anglès calls the Sibylline text of the tenth century Ripoll manuscript (Barcelona, Ripoll, 106): "per a Catalunya, el drama més antic dels que coneixem" (p. 289). Need it be pointed out that we have no authority for inferring that at Ripoll the words were accompanied by drama? It has already been remarked in the course of this study that in many Spanish churches the verses of the *Judicii* were sung by a group of clerics without any evident attempt at impersonation. There is nothing to indicate that a different procedure was followed at Ripoll.

The Sibyl first appears as a dramatic character in the *Ordo Prophetarum*. The most ancient texts of this play are from Limoges (*ca.* 1096) and Einsiedeln (eleventh to twelfth century). In Spain the first definite evidence of an impersonated Sibyl is given by the fourteenth century Gerona *consueta*. In that instance also she appears in a Prophet Play. The oldest record of an impersonation of the Sibyl *apart* from the Prophet Play is found in the *consueta* of Palma de Mallorca, in the portion of the manuscript written about 1440; but at Palma, too, the longer play of the prophets was sometimes performed. These bits of evidence seem to suggest that the idea of impersonating the Sibyl even when the other prophets did not appear, was derived from the *Ordo Prophetarum*.

Even this latter point, however, is far from established. There remain, for example, certain singularities about the Spanish prophet plays. In them the chant of the Sibyl is always sung in its entirety, whereas in the French plays the Sibyl speaks only a few lines like the other prophets. This results probably from the great popularity of the Sibylline verses in Spain. In that country the verses were chanted in almost every church from a very early date. The question still remains, were they sung with impersonation, apart from the prophet play, before 1400?

The dramatic monologue of the Sibyl, with impersonation of the prophetess, was a tradition in the fifteenth and sixteenth centuries in such cities as Palma, Gerona, Valencia, Toledo, León, and probably Vich and Barcelona; it was no doubt a practice in many other Spanish churches as well. To date no examples of such a custom have been found anywhere outside the Hispanic peninsula.

As the prophet play, and the role of the Erythraean Sibyl in particular, became more popular, other Sibyls began to appear in the religious Christmas plays, notably the prophetess from Tibur, with the charming legend of the *Ara Coeli* and the emperor. The first record of this scene in a dramatic production in Europe is found, I believe, at Barcelona, though probably the scene was dramatized at a much earlier date; the *Ara Coeli* with its spectacular stage equipment had already been adapted for usage in the Valencian Assumption plays by the end of the fourteenth century. It is likely, however, that the Tiburtine Sibyl made her entrance into the plays of the Christmas cycle only when these plays had ceased to be strictly "liturgical".

CONCLUSION

THE immediate origin of the medieval liturgical drama was the custom of trope-singing, a practice which developed, it appears, in the early part of the ninth century. The trope sung for the feast of Easter, *Quem quaeritis in sepulchro, o Christicolae*, was especially dramatic in form, and eventually evolved into a small play. The first record of it as a dramatic performance is found in the *Regularis Concordia*, written about the year 965 for the churches and monasteries of England. The general probabilities are that the piece was brought to England from the continent, perhaps from Fleury or Ghent, but of this there is no proof. It is certain, in any case, that the *Visitatio Sepulchri*, as the new play came to be known, was flourishing in France, England, and Germany by the year 1000. In turn, the success of the Easter performance encouraged the composition of plays for the season of Christmas. The earliest examples of the Christmas and Epiphany plays date back to the eleventh century.

During this period which saw the early development of the liturgical drama, the monasteries and churches of such countries as France, England, Germany, Switzerland, and Italy were in close relationship with one another, and liturgical and literary influences passed back and forth freely between them. To this group must be added Catalonia. Whereas most of the rest of Spain was under Arab control until at least the middle of the eleventh century, the northeastern portion of the peninsula had been reconquered in the days of Charlemagne (768–814); henceforth, until the eleventh or twelfth century, Catalonia was linked ecclesiastically and politically with France rather than with the rest of Spain. Charlemagne brought with him the Roman-French rite. The dioceses of Catalonia were placed under the metropolitan see of Narbonne. When the practice of liturgical plays developed, the important Catalan monastery of Ripoll was not only flourishing and famous for its music school, but was in intimate contact with precisely those French monasteries commonly associated with the early production of these plays. There is no reason, then, why the liturgical drama could not have begun in Catalonia at the same time that it did in France.

Research has indeed shown that this medieval church drama was as popular and widespread in Catalonia as anywhere on the continent. Tropes were a regular part of the liturgy. The Latin Easter play was staged after the third responsory of Matins at Ripoll, Vich, the Seo de Urgel, Gerona, Mallorca, and doubtless elsewhere. The *Peregrinus* was presented at Ripoll and Vich.

In the cathedral of Palma, and at the collegiate church of St. John of Perpignan, clerics attired as the Blessed Mother, the Marys, St. John, and others sang a dramatized version of the *Planctus* after Good Friday Matins.

On the feast of Christmas, liturgical plays were the order of the day at Gerona and Mallorca. In the former city, both at the cathedral and at the church of St. Felix, a *Repraesentatio Partus* was performed during one lesson of Matins and the *Ordo Prophetarum* during another. The Sibyl appeared to sing her prophecy; a dramatic office of an unknown nature took place at Lauds; in the afternoon at Vespers the clerics acted out the martyrdom of St. Stephen. A very similar program was followed at Palma. As for the Sibyl, the prophetess was impersonated in almost every Catalan cathedral.

These are but a few indications of the dramatic activities that marked the liturgy of Catalonia. The majority of these plays are presented or described in fairly late medieval manuscripts, but the Ripoll texts date back to the eleventh and twelfth centuries. Indeed it is probable that the monastery of Santa María de Ripoll played a very important role in the early development and propagation of the liturgical drama. Ripoll was closely linked with St. Martial of Limoges. Generally St. Martial has been considered the disseminator of the Easter trope and play which begins *Ubi est Christus meus*. Actually the version first appears in a manuscript from Ripoll. Since outside of Catalonia this form is very rare, it is quite possible that this particular version was brought from Ripoll to St. Martial instead of vice versa. The merchant scene of the Easter play is also found at Ripoll some one hundred years before it appears elsewhere.

In many ways the Catalan plays complete our knowledge of the liturgical drama of other European countries. Until the present it had been doubted, for example, whether the beautiful prose, *Surgit Christus cum trophaeo*, was ever presented as a little play. The fourteenth century Gerona *consueta* proves that it was, and doubtless many other medieval churches were the scene of a similar performance. The Gerona and Mallorcan *consuetas* also present the first definite examples of dramatization within the Mass which have as yet been found. They verify the statement of Bishop Durandus of Mende that an Easter play was sometimes acted out during the singing of the prose *Victimae paschali laudes* at Mass; incidentally they establish that the Vienne ceremony described by Young (I, 274) was meant to be a play. In view of the French bishop's statement and the evidence afforded by the Catalan manuscripts, this type of performance was probably quite common throughout France and Europe in general. It is noteworthy also that at Mallorca the prose was sung in the vernacular.

Since the number of known texts of the *Procession of Prophets* is so very small, the new information provided by the Catalan codices is particularly welcome. We learn that, at least in the late Middle Ages, St. Augustine himself sometimes appeared in the liturgical play. We also learn that the play was occasionally acted out as one of the nine lessons of Matins. The wording of the Gerona *consueta* and other facts which have been considered make it appear probable that in some churches the pseudo-Augustinian sermon served as the text of the play, and that new verses based upon the sermon were not always written. The curious rubrics found in such manuscripts as the Arles lectionary possibly indicate dramatization. All these factors suggest that the prophet play was more common than has been generally believed.

A valuable description of the manner in which the laments of Good Friday were dramatized in the Middle Ages is given by one of the Mallorcan ceremonials. Another manuscript from Perpignan informs us of a new type of play for the feast of Pentecost. It seems, moreover, that the Pentecost liturgy was frequently dramatized in Catalonia. Perhaps in northern France also, liturgical plays were celebrated occasionally on this day. The same may be said of St. Stephen's day.

The dramatic monologue of the Sibyl raises many questions. Was the same practice traditional in France? No examples of it, with impersonation, have ever been found in that country. What is the exact relationship between this poem and the Procession of Prophets play? In what land was it first sung? Was the legend of the Tiburtine Sibyl, with the emperor and the *Ara Coeli*, dramatized at an early date in other countries of Europe? Did the spectacular type of aerial machinery featured in the Catalan performances also color the religious plays staged elsewhere on the continent?

The region of Castile presents a special problem. While the practice of tropes and the liturgical drama was developing in Catalonia and in the lands to the north during the ninth to the eleventh centuries, Castile was still under Arab domination, and was isolated from these movements. The old Hispanic liturgy, somewhat inexactly called the Mozarabic rite, continued to be observed in this area. The custom of trope-singing was unknown to it. So also, it would appear, was the usage of liturgical plays. In any case, no examples of such plays, or any references to them have ever been discovered in Mozarabic liturgical manuscripts. For these reasons most have held that, if the liturgical drama was practised in medieval Castile, it must have been brought there by the French when the Mozarabic rite was supplanted by the Roman around the year 1080. The contrast between the extraordinary success of the liturgical drama in Catalonia, where the Roman-French rite was known from the year 800, and the surprising scarcity of Latin church plays from Castile, makes this view now almost certain.

The view, however, that the liturgical drama came to Castile on a large scale in the eleventh century is not so certain. Research in Castilian libraries and archives has revealed that, save in a very few instances, the medieval *ordinaria* still extant from this region make no mention of liturgical plays, and references to tropes are equally rare. Since medieval *ordinaria* almost invariably mentioned at least the liturgical Easter play, if the tradition of presenting this play existed (the Catalan *consuetas* are an excellent example of this), the silence of the Castilian manuscripts in this regard is a strong argument that the Latin church plays were not very common in this part of the peninsula. Exception must perhaps be made for the dramatization of the *Quem vidistis* antiphon at Christmas Lauds, and the impersonation of the Sibyl at Christmas Matins.

One possibility which has been suggested, in an attempt to explain this relative failure of the liturgical drama to penetrate Castile, is that the religious plays could have already been at the vernacular stage when they were brought from France. Many considerations give support to such a conjecture, such as the early appearance of the vernacular *Auto de los Reyes Magos* in Toledo, the similarity of this piece to the French vernacular plays which have survived, the declarations of Alfonso the Wise indicating that religious plays were very popular in his kingdom, etc. If this reason is to be invoked to account for the paucity of liturgical plays in Castile, it has most important implications for the history of the medieval drama in France.

APPENDIX

Chapter 2, note 24. The following *Peregrinus* play is found in a thirteenth century Rouen *processionale*, Rouen, Bibl. de la Ville, MS 222 (*olim*, A. 551), fol. 43ᵛ–45. The piece was performed at Vespers of Easter Monday. The text has been previously edited by Young, I, 461.

> Post *Benedicamus* fiat processio ad fontes, ut in die Pasche. Et processione stante in medio nauis ecclesie et cantante psalmum *In exitu*, circa finem psalmi duo clerici de secunda sede induti tunicis et desuper capis in transuersum, portantes baculos et peras in similitudinem Peregrinorum, intrent ecclesiam per dextram portam occidentalem. Et lento pede uenientes usque ad processionem, cum finitus fuerit psalmus, subsistentes in capite processionis incipiant cantare hymnum:

Ihesu, nostra redemptio.[1]

Et cum cantauerint usque ad locum illum, *Nos tuo uultu sa‹ties›*, tunc quidam sacerdos indutus alba et amictu, nudus pedes, crucem ferens in manibus, intret ecclesiam per sinistram portam occidentalem, et ueniens usque ad eos uultu demisso subito stet inter illos et dicat:

> Qui sunt hii sermones quos confertis ad inuicem ambulantes, et estis tristes?

Peregrini quasi admirantes et eum respicientes dicant:

> Tu solus peregrinus es in Iherusalem, et non cognouisti que facta sunt in illa hiis diebus?

Sacerdos interroget:

> Que?

Peregrini respondeant:

> De Ihesu Nazareno, qui fuit uir propheta, potens in opere et sermone coram Deo et omni populo.

Sacerdos utrimque respiciens dicat:

> O stulti et tardi[2] corde ad credendum in omnibus que locuti sunt prophete! Nonne sic oportuit pati Christum, et ita intrare in gloriam suam?

Quibus dictis, statim recedat sacerdos fingens se longius ire, et Peregrini

---
[1] The full text of this hymn may be found in Young, I, 641.
[2] tardi] tradi (MS).

festinanter prosequentes eum detineant quasi ad hospicium inuitantes et trahentes baculum ostendentes castellum, et dicentes:

> Mane nobiscum, quoniam aduesperascit et inclinata est iam dies. Sol uergens ad occasum suadet ut nostrum uelis hospicium; placent enim sermones tui, quos refers de resurrectione magistri nostri.

Et ita cantantes ducant eum usque ad tabernaculum in medio nauis ecclesie in similitudinem castelli Emaus preparatum. Quo cum ascenderint et ad mensam ibi paratam sederint, et Dominus inter eos sedens panem eis fregerit, in fractione panis agnitus ab illis subito recedens ab occulis eorum euanescat. Illi autem quasi stupefacti surgentes cantent uersus processionem *Alleluia*, cum versu *Nonne cor nostrum*. Quo reiterato, uertant se uersus pulpitum, et cantent hunc uersum sequentem:

> Dic nobis, Maria, quid uidisti in uia?

Tunc quidam de maiori sede indutus dalmatica et amictu, et uinctus in modum mulieris caput circumligatus respondeat:

> Angelicos testes, sudarium et uestes.

Tun<c> ostendat et explicet unum syndonem ex una parte loco sudarii, et alium ex altera parte loco uestium; deinde dicat:

> Surrexit Christus, spes nostra: precedet uos in Galileam.

Chorus cantet alios duos uersus sequentes, residuos, et interim recedant Maria et Peregrini, et processio, factis memoriis, redeat in choro, et ibi finiantur Vespere.

Chapter 2, note 33. The following text from a thirteenth century Rouen *graduale* is a good example of a typical Christmas play (Paris, Bibl. Nat., MS lat. 904, Grad. Rothomagense, fol. 11^v–14). The piece was performed, as the passage states, after the *Te Deum* of Matins. The text has been previously edited by Young, II, 16, and others.

> In sancta nocte Natiuitatis Domini post *Te Deum*, Angelus assistet, annunciet Christum natum esse, et hoc dicet:
>
>> Nolite timere, ecce enim euangelizo uobis gaudium magnum, quod erit omni populo, quia natus est uobis hodie Saluator mundi in ciuitate Dauid, et hoc uobis signum: Inuenietis infantem pannis inuolutum et positum in presepio.

Hoc audientes vii. pueri stantes in alto loco dicant:

> Gloria in excelsis Deo, et in terra pax hominibus bone uoluntatis.

Audientes Pastores eant uersus Presepe cantantes hoc responsorium:

> Pax in terris nunciatur,
>   in excelsis gloria.
> Terra <coelo> federatur,
>   mediante gratia.

Mediator, homo, Deus
  descendit in propria,
ut ascendat homo reus
  ad admissa gaudia. Eya! Eya!

Transeamus, uideamus
  uerbum hoc quod factum est;
transeamus ut sciamus
  quod ⟨an⟩nuntiatum est.

Versus: In Iudea puer uagit,
  puer salus populi
quo bellandum se presagit
  uetus hospes seculi.

Accedamus, accedamus
  ad presepe Domini,
et dicamus, ⟨et dicamus:⟩
  Laus fecunde uirgini.

Tunc Pastores gradiantur per chorum, in manibus baculos portantes, et cantantes usque ad Christi Presepe versum:

> Transeamus usque Bethleem, et uideamus hoc uerbum quod factum est, quod fecit Dominus et ostendit nobis.

Illis uenientibus ii. clerici in Presepe cantent versum:

> Quem queritis in presepe, pastores, dicite?

Pastores respondeant:

> Saluatorem Christum Dominum, infantem pannis inuolutum, secundum sermonem angelicum.

Item Obstetrices cortinam aperientes, Puerum demonstrent dicentes versum:

> Adest hic paruulus cum Maria matre sua, de quo dudum uaticinando Ysayas dixerat propheta:

Ostendant Matrem Pueri dicentes:

> Ecce uirgo concipiet et pariet filium; et euntes dicite quia natus est.

Tunc salutent Pastores Uirginem ita dicentes:

Salue, uirgo singularis,
uirgo manens Deum paris
ante secla generatum
  corde Patris.
Adoremus nunc creatum
  carne matris.

Versus:

> Nos, Maria, tua prece
> a peccati purga fece
> nostri cursum incolatus;
> sic dispone
> ut det sua frui natus
> uisione.

Tunc, uiso Puero, Pastores adorent eum. Deinde uertant se ad chorum dicentes:

> Alleluia, alleluia! Iam uere scimus Christum natum in terris, de quo canite omnes cum propheta dicentes.

Postea statim incipiatur Missa, et Pastores regant chorum et cantent *Gloria in excelsis Deo*, et epistolam, et tropa. Et unus Pastorum legat lectionem *Populus gencium* (The *pastores* also sing the gradual and take part in Lauds).

An early and relatively simple form of the Epiphany play is found in an eleventh century *liber responsalis* from the cathedral of Nevers (Paris, Bibl. Mazarine, MS 1708, fol. 81ᵛ). The piece was performed at the conclusion of Matins, before the *Te Deum*. It has been previously published by Young, II, 50.

Finitis lectionibus, iubeat Domnus Presul preparare tres clericos in trium transfiguratione Magorum, quos preparatos terque a presule uocatos ita: *Venite*; pergant ante altare hunc uersum dicentes:

> Stella fulgore nimio rutilat,
> que regem regum natum monstrat,
> quem uenturum olim prophetie signauerant.

Quo finito, uerso eorum uultu ad populum pergant usque ad Regem. Dicant hunc uersum:

> Eamus ergo et inquiramus eum, offerentes ei munera: aurum, thus, et myrram.

Quibus respondens Rex dicat:

> Regem quem queritis, natum esse quo signo didicistis? Si illum regnare creditis, dicite nobis.

At contra ipsi:

> Illum natum esse didicimus in oriente stella monstr⟨an⟩te.

Quo audito, dicat iterum Rex:

> Ite et de puero diligenter inuestigate,
> Et inuentum redeuntes michi renuntiate.

Accepta licentia, pergant:

> Ecce stella in oriente preuisa iterum preueniet.

Vidimus stellam eius in oriente, et agnouimus regem regum natum esse.

Quibus respondeant Custodes ita:

Qui sunt hi qui stella duce, nos adeuntes[3] inaudita ferentes?

At contra ipsi:

Nos sumus, quos cernitis, reges Tarsis et Arabum et Saba dona ferentes Christo, Regi, nato Domino, qui, stella deducente, uenimus adorare.

Ostendentibus illis Imaginem dicant:

Ecce puer ades quem queritis; iam properate, adorate, quia ipse est redemptio uestra.

Quorum Magorum unus offerens aurum dicat;

Salue, Rex seculorum, suscipe nunc aurum.

Et secundus offerens thus dicat:

Tolle thus, tu uerus Deus.

Necnon tercius ‹offerens› mirram dicat:

Mirram, signum sepulture.

His itaque gestis, dicat puer stans in excelso loco:

Impleta sunt omnia que prophetice dicta sunt. Ite, uiam remeantes aliam, ne delatores tanti regis puniendi eritis.

Omnibus peractis, dicat presul *Te Deum laudamus.*

Chapter 2, note 34. The Laon *Ordo Prophetarum* is contained in a thirteenth century troper (Laon, Bibl. de la Ville, MS 263, fol. 147ᵛ–149). It has been published by Young, II, 145, and others.

ORDO PROPHETARUM

Ysaias: barbatus, dalmatica indutus, stola rubea per medium uerticis ante et retro dependens.
Iheremias: semiliter, absque stola.
Daniel: adolescens, ueste splendida indutus.
Moyses: cum dalmatica, barbatus, tabulas legis ferens.
Dauid: regio habitu.
Abacuc: barbatus, curuus, gibosus.
Elisabeth: femineo habitu, pregnans.
Iohannes Baptista: pilosa ueste et longis capillis, barbatus, palmam tenens.
Virgilius: cum cornu et calamo, edera coronatus, scriptorium tenens

---

[3] adeuntes] adientes (MS).

Nabugodonosor: regio habitu, superbo incessu.
Sibilla: ueste feminea, decapillata, edera coronata, insanienti simillima.
Symeon: barbatus, capa serica indutus, palmam tenens.
Balaam: super asinam, curuus, barbatus, palmam tenens, calcaribus urgens.

Gloriosi et famosi regis festum celebrantes gaudeamus.
Cuius ortum, uite portum, nobis datum, predicantes habeamus.
Ecce regem nouam legem dantem orbis circuitu predicamus.

Duo cantores:
Omnes gentes, congaudentes, dent cantus letitie.
Deus homo fit de domo Dauid, natus hodie.

Ad Iudeos:
O Iudei, Uerbum Dei qui negastis hominem,
vestre legis testes regis audite per ordinem.

Ad Paganos:
Et uos gentes non credentes peperisse uirginem,
vestre legis documentis pellite caliginem.

Appellatores:
Isaias, uerum qui scis, veritatem cur non dicis?

Isaias:
Est necesse uirgam Iesse de radice prouehi;
flos deinde surget inde, qui est filius Dei.

Appellatores:
Iste cetus psallat letus; error uetus condempnetur.

Omnis chorus:
Quod Iudea perit rea, hec chorea gratulatur.

Appellatores:
Huc accede, Iheremias; dic de Christo prophetias.

Hieremias:
Sic est, hic est Deus noster.

Duo:
Iste cetus.

Item chorus:
Quod Iudea.

Duo:
Daniel, indica uoce prophetica facta dominica.

Daniel:
Sanctus Sanctorum ueniet, et unctio defitiet (*sic*).

Duo:
Iste cetus.

Chorus:
　Quod Iudea.
Ap‹p›ellatores:
　Dic tu, Moyses, legislator, quis sit Christus et Saluator.
Moises:
　Prophetam accipietis tamquam me hunc audietis.
Duo:
　Iste cetus.
Chorus:
　Quod Iudea.
Ap‹p›ellatores:
　Dic tu, Dauid, de nepote causas que sunt tibi note.
Dauid:
　Universus rex conuersus adorabit Dominum,
　cui futurum seruiturum omne genus hominum.
Duo:
　Iste cetus.
Chorus:
　Quod Iudea.
Appellatores:
　Abacuc, regis celestis nunc ostende quod sis testis.
Abacuc:
　Opus tuum inter duum latus animalium
　ut cognoui, mox expaui metu mirabilium.
Duo:
　Iste cetus.
Chorus:
　Quod Iudea.
Ap‹p›ellatores:
　Illud, Elisabeth, in medium
　de Domino profer eloquium.
Elisabeth:
　Quid est rei quod me mei mater regis uisitat?
　nam ex eo uentre meo letus infans palpitat.
Duo:
　Iste cetus.
Chorus:
　Quod Iudea.
Item duo:
　Da, Baptista uentris cista clausus,
　quos dedisti causa Christi plausus?
　Cui dedisti gaudium,
　profer et testimonium.

Iohannes:
> Venit talis sotularis cuius non sum etiam
> tam benignus ut sim dignus soluere corrigiam.

Duo:
> Iste cetus.

Chorus:
> Quod Iudea.

Duo:
> Maro, uates gentilium, da Christo testimonium.

Maro:
> Ecce polo dimissa sola noua progenies est.

Duo:
> Iste cetus.

Chorus:
> Quod Iudea.

Appellatores reducunt Danielem, et dicunt ad Regem:
> Puerum cum pueris, Nabugodonosor,
> cum in igne uideris, quid dixisti?

Nabugodonosor:
> Tres in igne positi pueri
> quarto gaudent comite liberi.

Duo:
> Iste cetus.

Chorus:
> Quod Iudea.

Ap‹p›ellatores:
> Tu, Sibilla, uates illa,
> dic aduentum iudicis, dic signum iudicii.

Sibilla:
> Iudicii signum: Tellus sudore madescet;
> E celo rex adueniet per secla futurus,
> Scilicet in carne presens, ut iudicet orbem.
> Vnde Deum cernent incredulus atque fidelis
> Celsum cum sanctis, eui iam termino in ipso.

Duo:
> Iste cetus.

Chorus:
> Quod Iudea.

Appellatores:
> Symeon, inter prophetas
> pande nobis quid expectas.

Symeon:
>Vite non spero terminum
>donec uideam Dominum.

Duo:
>Iste cetus.

Chorus:
>Quod Iudea.

Symeon accipiens Puerum dicit:
>Tuum sub pacis tegmine
>seruum dimittis, Domine.

Ap‹p›ellatores:
>Dic, Balaam, ex Iudaica
>oriturum Dominum prosapia.

Balaam:
>Exibit de Iacob rutilans noua stella
>et confringet ducum agmina
>regionis Moab maxima potentia.

Hic ueniat Angelus cum gladio. Balaam tangit Asinam, et illa non procedente, dicit iratus:
>Quid moraris, asina, obstinata bestia?
>Iam scindent calcaria costas et precordia.

Puer sub Asina respondet:
>Angelus cum gladio, quem adstare uideo,
>prohibet ne transeam; timeo ne peream.[4]

Chapter 4, note 51. The copyist of the Madrid manuscript has written the following preface to the work:

Advertencias á la presente copia.

El presente MS titulado *Descripcion de la Sta Iglesia Primada de Toledo*[5] es copiado de un tomo en folio, sin mas epigrafe ni nombre de Autor que como aqui va puesto. En la misma portada tiene una Nota (Original) que dice asi: "Este Libro se ha escrito en obsequio de la Santa Iglesia Primada, y convendrá guardarle en su Biblioteca. *Francisco Antonio de Lorenzana.*"[6]

Este mismo Señor, siendo ya Arzobispo de Toledo se le presto á nuestro Reverendísimo Flórez el año de 1773 para que le desfrurase ó copiase á su gusto ... Antes de morir dicho Reverendísimo se havia empezado á

---

[4] The text is apparently incomplete.
[5] What is said of this treatise is also said of *Las Ceremonias ... de Toledo*.
[6] The note at the beginning of the Toledo manuscript (Toledo, Bibl. Mun., Colección Borbon-Lorenzana, MS 154) is the same, except for the concluding words: "convendrá guardarle en la Biblioteca Arzobispal de Palacio. Francisco Antonio de Lorenzana." Esteve Barba in his *Catálogo de la Colección de Manuscritos Borbon-Lorenzana* lists the manuscript as eighteenth century, and states that the prefatory note was written by Lorenzana himself.

copiar este MS y después del fallecimiento envió su Excelencia el Sr. Arzobispo á recogerle (con otro que va incorporado seguido á este) y haviéndole yo informado á su Excelencia del estado en que quedó la copia, y pedido su venia de si gustaba que se continuase en ella, lo concedió muy gustoso, con todas las amplitudes necesarias. Devolví dicho MS á su Excelencia con las gracias correspondentientes año de 1773. M.N.D.Z.

The description of the Christmas ceremonies is found in the Toledo manuscript on fol. 28^v *sqq.*, in the Madrid copy on p. 30 *sqq.*; I follow here the orthography of the latter:

En los Maytines de la noche de Navidad hay muchas cosas que reparar, y aunque parecer jugeres no lo son, sino profundos misterios. Lo primero toda esta noche se gasta en divinas alabanzas, y se celebran con mayor solemnidad que otra, segun lo hacian los Monges de Cluni, y otros de las Galias .... Lo quarto se advierte el regocijo de los Pastores, y de la Sivila, y para que se entiendan mejor las ceremonias de la Sivila y los Pastores me parece conducense poner al pie de la letra todo lo que se executa, y es lo siguiente.
En la Noche de Navidad, concluidos los Maytines, y entre tanto que se canta el *Te Deum laudamus*, sale de la Sacristia un Colegial Seise vestido de Sibila, al que acompañan dos Colegiales Infantes vestidos con albas y estolas, y cada uno de estos lleva en la mano una espada desnuda, y les acompañan tambien otros dos colegiales con achas encendidas, y todos suben á un tablado, que para el caso se hace debajo del pulpito del Evangelio, desde el qual acabados del todo los Maytines canta la Sibila los versos siguientes:

SIBILA ERITHREA

Quantos aqui sois juntados
ruegos por Dios verdadero,
que oigais del dia postrimero
quando seremos juzgados.
Del cielo de las alturas
un Rey venra perdurable
con poder muy espantable
á juzgar las criaturas.

Nota. Acabado esto los Niños, que estan con las espadas altas dan con ellas tres golpes una con otra, y la capilla de Musica canta en el coro lo siguiente:

Juicio fuerte
sera dado
cruel y de muerte.

Prosigue despues cantando la Sibila los versos siguientes:

> Trompetas y sones tristes
> diran de lo alto del cielo
> levantaos muertos del suelo
> recibireis segun hicisteis.
> Descubrirse han los pecados
> sin que ninguno los hable
> á la pena perdurable
> do iran los tristes culpados.

Concluidas estas coplas canta la Musica el estrivillo *Juicio fuerte*, etc. Prosigue despues la Sibila:

> A la Virgen supliquemos
> que antes de aqueste litijo
> interceda con su hijo
> por que todos nos salvemos.

Canta despues la Musica el estrivillo *Juicio fuerte*, etc. Concluido esto vajan todos los del cabildo y dando una vuelta por dentro del coro, se van. El Colegial Seise que hace el papel de la Sibila Erithrea, va vestido á lo oriental, y entre las cosas de que va adornado lleva en el hombro izquierdo un Relicario en el que hay los versos siguientes:

> Juditii in signum tellus sudore madescet,
> Et Rex eternus summo descendet olimpo
> Scilicet ut carnem, mundumque ut judicet omnem
> Unde Deum fidi, difidentesque videbunt
> Summum cum Sanctis in secli fine sedentem.

Luego comienza la Misa del Gallo, y despues de que el diacono dice *Ite Missa est* salen los Pastores, que son los Colegiales Infantes vestidos de tales con unos capillos de paño blanco, y no se meten todos en la Capilla Mayor. Acabada la Misa se ponen los dos sochantres capas Pluviales blancas, y cantan dos veces la Antiphona siguiente:

> Quem vidistis Pastores? dicite; anunciate nobis in terris quis aparuit? Natum vidimus, et choros Angelorum colaudantes Dominum, Alleluya, alleluya.

Y á la repeticion salen los Pastores de la Capilla mayor y llegan á las rejas de el coro, y haviendo concluido los Sochantres la repeticion de la Antifona cantan los Seises á la puerta del coro lo siguiente:

> Infantem vidimus pannis involutum, et choros Angelorum laudantes Salvatorem.

Entre tanto que los Niños cantan esto llegan á la puerta del coro los Sochantres, como se ha dicho, y cantan estas copillas:

> 1a. Bien vengades Pastores.
> Estrivillo. Que bien vengades.

Despues de cada copla dicen los Pastores con algazara y alegre bulla O! O! O!

    2a. Pastores del ganado
        decidnos buen cuidado.
        Que bien vengades.

    Pastores: O! O! O!

    3a. Pastores donde anduvisteis
        decidnos lo que visteis.
        Que bien vengades.

    Pastores: O! O! O!

Y sin intermisión cantan los Colegiales seises las coplas que se siguen, repitiendo los Sochantres á cada una *Que bien vengades*, y los Pastores: O! O! O!

    1a. Vimos que en Belen Señores
        Nació la Flor de las Flores.

    2a. Esta Flor que hoy es nacida[7]
        nos dará fruto de vida.

    3a. Es un Niño y Rey del cielo
        que hoy ha nacido en el suelo.

    4a. Está entre dos animales.
        cubierto en pobres pañales.

    5a. Virgen y limpia quedó
        la Madre que le parió.

    6a. Al hijo y Madre roguemos
        les plega que nos salvemos.

Concluido todo esto entran los Pastores en el Coro, y se canta un villancico, cuya composicion toca al Maestro de Melodia. Luego se cantan las Laudes, y acabadas las laudes se salen los Pastores á desnudar.

Chapter 4, note 53. In the Arcayos manuscript the passage about the *Sibyl* and the *shepherds* is found on fol. 410–412^v; in the copy written in 1765, on fol. 423^v *sqq*. Since the reading given by Arcayos represents an older form than those which we have previously seen, I reproduce it here in its entirety:

Esta noche siguiente se diçen en esta sancta yglesia de Toledo los Maytines, con mucha sollemnidad . . . tañese a ellos a la hora de las diez, hasta las onçe, tañendo con mucha sollemnidad sus tres claustros y dos esquilones. esta la yglesia muy clara con muchas achas puestas en los postes, y pilares, adonde ay hadieros de hierro fixos. a las onçe se empieçan los Maytines diçiendo primero la antifona *Ave regina coelorum*,

---

[7] In this version the rhyme is true, whereas it is faulty in the Vallejo text.

que esta doctada por el Arçobispo Don Gomez Manrique[8] . . . .
[Despues de cada responsorio] diçen villaçincos (sic) muy graçiosos d'esta fiesta por los cantores . . . .
y acavado el himno[9] sube el preste al aguila y diçe el verso *dominus vobiscum*, y responden los cantores y luego diçe la oration *concede quaesumus* y acavada se baxa al banco y diçe el verso *benedicamus* rreçado y responden[10] los capperos. y mientras el organo diçe el dicho verso, y responden los cantores. y dexan las cappas el preste y raçionero y los capellanes. y luego sale la Sybilla. (There follows at this point the passage quoted above, page 45).
. . . vestidos de angeles con dos espadas desnudas en las manos y quando se acaba cada verso de los infrascriptos tocan los Angeles las espadas. y responden los cantores dentro del choro al fasistor de las gradas del Aguila a canto de organo el verso *Juyçio fuerte sera dado, y muy cruel de muerte*. dice la Sybilla los versos en un tablado pequeño que para este proposito se ha hecho entre los dos choros arrimado a la rrexa del choro mayor, por la parte de afuera, junto al pulpito donde se canta el evangelio y alli esta con ellos el Maestro de cleriçones, *allio nomine* claustrero, que tiene el offiçio de ensayador de la Sybilla y tiene salario, el qual pagua la obra. y dos cleriçones estan delante con dos hachas encendidas y los versos en castellano son los siguientes. y al principio tañen[11] los ministriles, y al fin:

> Quantos aqui sois juntados
> ruego os por Dios verdadero,
> que oigais del dia postrimero
> quando seremos juzgados.

Juyçio fuerte *diçen los cantores*.[12]

> Del çielo de las alturas
> un rey venra perdurable
> en carne muy espantable
> a juzgar las criaturas.

Juyçio fuerte *repiten*.

> Trompetas y sones tristes
> diran del alto del çielo
> levantaos muertos del suelo
> reçibireis segun hiçisteis.

Juyçio fuerte *repiten*.

> Descubrirse han los pecados
> sin que ninguno los hable

[8] 1375-1399.
[9] The *Te Deum*.
[10] responden] responde (MS).
[11] tañen] tañe (MS).
[12] We note that the refrain is repeated more frequently in this version.

> a la penna perdurable
> seran dados los dañados.
>
> Juyçio fuerte *repiten*.
>
> A la Virgen suppliquemos
> que sea en este letijo
> medianera con su hijo
> porque todos nos salvemos.
>
> Juyçio fuerte *repiten*.

Los quales versos diçe la dicha Sybilla desde el dicho lugar en canto llano. y en acavando viene al choro con los dichos angeles y los dos cleriçones con las hachas y delante su Maestro de cleriçones, y un pertiguero, y una guarda. y entran en el choro por la puerta del choro del Arçobispo, por que la puerta del choro del Dean esta çerrada por la gran multitud de gente que ay. y van al sagrario a desnudarse que es de adonde salen adereçados. y luego se empieça la Missa que llaman del gallo . . . . . . Nota que desde el prinçipio desta missa salen del sagrario los cleriçones vestidos de pastores y van al altar mayor por el postigo y estan arriba en lo plano del altar mayor mientras se diçe esta Missa dançando y bailando: y acavada la Missa se empieçan las laudes en el choro a los quales abra tañido el campanero como es costumbre por la señal que le hiçieren quando se dixere el himno *Te Deum laudamus*, con la cuerda del choro. y dicho por el preste *Deus in adiutorium*, desde su silla, se empieça luego la primera antifona que es *Quem vidistis pastores*, y la diçen todos. y luego los cleriçones hechos pastores ministrandolos su Maestro el Claustrero diçen en el choro mayor debaxo de la lampara de plata a canto llano el verso *Infantem vidimus pannis involutum et choros angelorum laudantes Salvatorem*. Luego tornan a deçir en el choro, la antifona toda *Quem vidistis*, y los pastores responden entre los dos choros, debaxo de la lampara de en medio, el verso *Infantem vidimus* todo ut supra. y luego diçen en el choro terçera vez la antifona *Quem vidistis* toda. y responden los pastores desde la puerta del choro del Arçobispo el verso *Infantem*. e luego salen los socapiscoles con las capas de brocado y çetros y llegan a la parte del aguila del choro del Arçobispo y alli los cantores a canto llano les haçen las preguntas siguientes y los socapiscoles aven de las manos a dos de aquellos pastorçicos y preguntanles juntamente con los cantores lo siguiente:

Pregunta:	Bien vengades pastores que bien vengades.
	Pastores do andubistes deçidnos lo que vistes.
Respuesta:	Que bien vengades.
	Pastores del ganado deçidnos buen mandado.

	Que bien vengades. *Respuesta.* *Y a este siempre responden* *los cantores.*
Pastores:	Vimos que en Bethlem señores nasçio la flor de las flores.
Respuesta:	Que bien vengades.
Pastores:	Esta flor que oy ha nasçido nos dara fructo de vida.
Respuesta:	Que bien vengades.
Pastores:	Es un niño y Rey del çielo que oy ha nasçido consuelo.
Respuesta:	Que bien vengades.
	Esta entre dos animales enbuelto en pobres pañales.
Respuesta:	Que bien vengades.
	Virgen y limpia quedo la madre que lo pario.
Respuesta:	Que bien vengades.
	Al hijo y madre roguemos les plega que nos salvemos.
Respuesta:	Que bien vengades.

En acavando de deçir estas coplas, diçen un villançico los pastores dançando, y baylando, entre el aguila, y el banco de los capperos. y le rrepiten y diçen los siguientes uno de ellos al arbritio y voluntad del maestro de cleriçones. y en acavando se empieçan las laudes y se diçen como es costumbre.

Cuerpo de Sant con el chiquiritico
cuerpo de Sant que bonito que es.

El niño recien naçido
que del çielo ha desçendido
y una virgen lo ha parido.
Cuerpo de Sant repiten.

Viene a remediar mill males
aunque naçe entre animales
tray riquezas celestiales.
Cuerpo de Sant.

No vi en mi vida tal cossa,
que si la madre es hermosa,

el niño es como la rosa.
Cuerpo de Sant.

Mas hermoso que las flores,
mas lindo que los albores,
su mirar mata de amores.
Cuerpo de Sant.

Estan lindo y agraçiado
que en quantos dios ha criado
ninguno al pie le ha llegado.
Cuerpo de Sant.

Finis

Vala me Dios que bonito es el niño
nunca se bio çagalejo tal.

En un pobre portalejo
vi nasçido un cagalejo
que a una(?)[13] voz dice el conçejo
nunca se vio çagalejo tal.

Es tan lindo, y tan graçioso
tan vellissimo y hermoso
que en velleça y en reposa
nunca se vio çagalejo tal.

La çagala que le cria
es mas hermosa que el dia,
llamanla Virgen, Maria.
nunca se vio çagalejo tal.

Si el chiquito esta llorando
su madre le esta callando
y los angeles cantando
nunca se vio çagalejo tal.

Por nuestra bien y consuelo
naçe probeçito al yelo
sciendo Dios de tierra y çielo
nunca se vio çagalejo tal.

Finis

otro.

Oy a nascido un çagal,
de tal hermosura lleno
que en el suelo no le ay tal
ni alla en el çielo mas bueno.

---

[13] a una] aunque (copy).

Quando Dios determino
de librar al peccador
vençido de puro amor
a su hijo aeterno dio
y aquesta noche tal
nasce pobre y al sereno
que en el suelo no le ay tal
ni alla en el çielo mas bueno.

Humillose Dios aeterno
forma de siervo tomando
y con esto quita el mando
a la muerte y al Infierno
y esta grande su caudal,
aunque esta puesto en el heno
que en el suelo no le ay tal
ni alla en el çielo mas bueno.

No te espante ver tan chico
al que es grande y poderoso,
ni en ver tan menestroso
al que es tan illustre y rrico;
que aunque pobre, es sin ygual,
y de tantas graçias lleno,
que en el suelo no le ay tal
ni alla en el cielo mas bueno.

Finis

En acavando de deçir uno de los dichos villancicos los pastores, diçen las laudes como es costumbre.

Chapter 4, note 60. The text of the Palencia ceremonial reads as follows:

Sexta lectio erit sermo qui incipit *Inter pressuras*, ubi inducuntur (?) testimonia prophetarum. Responsorium: *Quem uidistis*. Versus, *Dicite*. Responsorium, *O regem celi*. Versus, *Ecce Agnus Dei*. Et notandum quod in sexta lectione quando deuentum fuerit ad uersum ubi dicitur, *Quid Sibilla uaticinauerit*, finito uersu cantentur uersus Sibille, *Judicii signum*. Et cantantur a quatuor uel sex binatim. Post quemlibet uersum repetitur a choro *Judicii signum*. Versibus finitis, legitur residuum lectionis. Responsorium, *Gloria in altissimis*. Versus, *Facta est*, et cantatur a sex. Idem *Gloria Patri*. Sequitur prosula, *Quia Verbum*.

If my reading *inducuntur* is correct, I am not sure exactly what it means in this context. The grounds are insufficient, I believe, for concluding that it implies dramatization.

Chapter 4, note 65. A copy of the missal printed at Toledo in 1499 by Petrus Hagenbach is found at the Biblioteca Nacional in Madrid, Incunables 1137 (*olim* I 978). The rubrics after the Communion of Christmas Mass are as follows:

> Quo finito statim dicantur laudes cum suis antiphonis usque ad versum *Laudate Dominum in sanctis ejus.* Et interim sint parati pueri ad altare maius: induti ad modum pastorum. Et antequam dicatur dictus versus, incipiant cantores antiphonam, scilicet, *Pastores dicite nobis.* Qua finita respondeant pueri antiphonam, *Infantem vidimus.* (The antiphon is repeated in this dialogue form three more times). Quibus finitis cum aliis cantilenis que dicuntur propter gaudium festi, incipiat sacerdos sequentem antiphonam . . . .

Chapter 5, note 27. Fr. Durán Gudiol kindly gave me permission to cite the following passages from his study, *La Música en la Catedral de Huesca (siglos XI-XVII)*, which he was preparing for publication in 1954:

> Sólo dos noticias – y estos del siglo XV – poseemos sobre la escenificación que se hacía el día de San Vicente, martir y oscense. En vista de la ausencia de otros datos, sobretodo del siglo XVI tan minucioso y metódico en las cuentas, cabe suponer que la costumbre se perdió a finales del XV o principios del XVI.
> En 1482, 25 de enero: "Item mandato capituli die al maestro de canto per adiutari per fazer el entremés de sant Vicient pagué (sic) 2 sueldos" (*Mensa Canonicorum*, fol. lxviii^v).
> En 1483, 28 de abril: "Item por mandamiento del capitol die al maestro de canto por adiutori de la representació de sanct Vicent XXIIII sueldos" (*Ibid.*, fol. lxx^v).

> También el día de Pascua se escenificaba algún misterio en la Catedral. Pero sólo ha sido posible encontrar unos pocos datos, aunque significativos. El 26 de abril de 1582, escribe el administrador: "pagué al çapatero çinco pares de çapatos para tres infantes y dos mochachos que representaron el día de Pascua de Resurrección; a VI sueldos por cada par son XXXVI sueldos" (*Libro I Prepositura*).

> Desgraciadamente no poseemos ningún relato de testigo ocular de la representación que tenía lugar en la Catedral la noche de Navidad, como tampoco ha llegado hasta nosotros ninguna de las piezas que se ejecutaban, a no ser el canto de la Sibila . . . . Sin embargo, recorriendo las cuentas de la Prepositura correspondientes a los años del siglo XVI, es fácil formarse una idea aproximada de lo que tenía lugar en las fiestas navideñas. Se ponía en la misma iglesia un escenario de madera con decorados, sobre el que actuaban los infantes y monaguillos de la misma Catedral, convenientemente disfrazados. Los actores – según las noticias proporcionadas por los citados Libros de Prepositura – no sobrepasaron casi nunca el número de seis.

En 1539, 18 de enero, por mandato de los capitulares entregaba el administrador al maestro de capilla Antón Sanchez 22 sueldos "por las barbas, saios y cascabillos que para los mochachos alquiló la noche de navidad" (*Lib. I Prepositura*). Tal es la primera noticia que se ha encontrado sobre estas representaciones. En 1561, 11 de enero, se pagaban al maestro Olorón 24 sueldos "por los aderezos de los infantes la noche de Navidad" (*Lib. I, Prep.*). En la cuenta de los gastos de día del Nacimiento del Señor de 1581 figuran seis pares de zapatos "para los representantes" y 190 sueldos que se daban a un platero siciliano por haver hecho "unos vistidos y cetros y otras cosillas para la representación de la noche de Navidad" (*ibid.*).

La cuenta del tablado la encontramos en las del año 1561, en que el canónigo Forner recibe de Prepositura 8 sueldos que había pagado a "maese Juan fustero por el tablado que hizo la noche de navidad para la fiesta de los infantes" (*ibid.*). En las de 1581, además de la cuenta del carpintero, hay la partida de lo que se pagó a un operario extraordinario, el citado platero de Sicilia: "por mandato de los señores de capítulo dí a un platero siciliano 110 sueldos para hacer una boca de infierno para la representación de la noche de Navidad, más le dí por su trabajo que estuvo diez días o más ocupado en hacello 80 sueldos" (*ibid.*). En esta misma ocasión, pagaron "a un escopetero por los coetes y cluxidores que hizo para la dicha representación 8 reales, y más pagué de encordar las biguelas para la dicha fiesta 8 sueldos" (*ibid.*).

Chapter 5, note 28. The Christmas trope, as it appears in the Zaragoza manuscript, is as follows:

Tunc duo stantes ad altare incipiant versum:

Quem queritis in sepulcro, o Christicole.

Et alii duo stantes in choro respondeant:

Versus: Jhesum Nazarenum crucifixum, o celicole.
Versus: Non est hic; surrexit sicut dixerat.
Ite nunciate quia surrexit, alleluya.
Versus: Ad sepulcrum residens angelus nunciat resurrexisse Christum.
Versus: En ecce completum est illud quod olim ipse per prophetam dixerat ad Patrem taliter inquiens.

In die sancto Pasche, officium: *Resurrexi*.

Chapter 5, note 54. The ceremony of the Boy Bishop perhaps approached closest to genuine drama at Toledo. In this cathedral, as in most places, the *episcopellus* was elected on St. Nicholas Day. A large cloud of some sort would descend from the vaulting of the church, and upon it many *angels*. When the cloud had dropped to a position just over the elected one's head, the *angels* would bestow upon him a miter and other insignia.

In some churches the election of the *episcopellus* was accompanied by the selection of another choir-boy to represent Herod. Such was the practice at Huesca in the seventeenth century. A ceremonial of that time declares: "En este dia (de San Juan) a Visperas se acostumbran hacer una inocentada los muchachos; se hace uno obispo, y otro Herodes" (MS 49). The mention of Herod may indicate that this personage took part in some kind of play, perhaps on Innocents Day, or on the great feast of the Epiphany. In many cities of France during the Middle Ages a public procession was held on January 6th in which a cleric or a choir-boy represented Herod. The usage is described by Jean Mellot ("A Propos du théâtre liturgique de Bourges", *Mélanges . . . offerts à Gustave Cohen*, Nizet, 1950, p. 194):

> Particulièrement célébrée, l'*Epiphanie* était aussi l'occasion de grandes réjouissances. A la cathédrale, pour figurer l'étoile qu'avaient vue les Mages, on promenait, dans toute l'église, un vase contenant trois cierges. Puis un cortège se déroulait en ville. Composée des vicaires et des maîtrises de Saint-Etienne et de Saint-Ursin, l'étrange procession, où un clerc à cheval représentait Hérode, s'arrêtait à tous les carrefours pour donner les différentes phases de la vie du roi de Judée, au milieu des lazzi des jongleurs. Après quoi, on revenait, non sans tumulte, à la "métropole", où, vers 1470, l'habitude se prit de jouer une moralité.

At Gerona the *episcopellus* had a rival in the *abbatellus* from the nearby collegiate church of St. Felix.

In Spain the following documents treat of the Boy Bishop (this list is by no means exhaustive):

Barcelona, Bibl. Capit., MS 77, Consueta Barcinonensis saec. xiv-xv, fol. 364.
— , Bibl. Central, MS 276, Consueta Tarraconensis saec. xiii, fol. 50-50^v.
Gerona, Bibl. Capit., Consueta (1360), fol. 26^v, 114^v–116.
— , Bibl. Capit., Repertori de Pontich, I, fol. 227.
— , Seminary, Consueta eccl. Sancti Felicis, fol. 132^v.
Granada, Las buenas y loables costumbres . . . de Granada.
Huesca, Bibl. Capit., MS 49, Ceremonial saec. xvii.
— , Bibl. Capit., MS 54, Ceremonial (1786), V, pp. 455–457.
Lérida, Bibl. Capit., MS 6, Consueta Leridensis saec. xiv, Sanctorale, fol. 3^v-4.
Madrid, Bibl. Universitaria, MS 149, Ordinarium eccl. Toletanae, fol. 48^v-49.
Palencia, Bibl. Capit., Ordinarium saec. xiv.
Palma de Mallorca, Bibl. Capit., Armario LXXVI, Tabla 2, n. 1, Consueta Maioricensis, fol. 5–6^v, 20^v–21^v.
— , Bibl. Capit., Armario LXXVI, Tabla 1, n. 2, Consueta (1511), fol. 78 *sqq*.
Perpignan, Bibl. Mun., MS 71, Ordinarium Elnense (1380), fol. 11^v.
— , Bibl. Mun., MS 79, Libre de serimonies (St. John of Perpignan), fol. 2–2^v, 15–15^v, 24, 66.
Seo de Urgel, Bibl. Capit., Consueta saec. xv, fol. 208^v.

Toledo, Bibl. Capit., MS 42.29, Ceremonial of Juan Chaves de Arcayos, fol. 414ᵛ, 562–563.
Vich, Bibl. Capit., Consueta Vicensis (1413), fol. 12ᵛ–15.
Zaragoza, Bibl. Capit., MS 41–14, Ceremonial, p. 1043.

Chapter 6, note 18. López writes as follows (pp. 9–11):

> Arrinconada hoy la fiesta en núcleos aldeanos, la representación (del Nacimiento) se efectúa con un primitivismo ingenuo y anacrónico, aunque siempre con íntimo fervor religioso. Se denomina con las nombres de *Pastora, La Cordera, Los Villancicos*. El lugar de representación más común es la misma iglesia . . . . En este caso utilizan las distintas zonas del interior del templo para las distintas escenas, sin utilizar decorado alguno, y tiene lugar la noche del 24 de diciembre antes o después de la llamada Misa del Gallo, formando con ella una unidad semilitúrgica, de tal modo que a veces la misa se intercala entre las distintas escenas del auto . . . .
> Cuando el acto se refiere a la fiesta de la Epifanía, los mozos que hacen de Reyes Magos, se atavían con enaguas almodonadas, con cintas y coronas de cartón dorado; y cabalgando en caballos, se llegan a las puertas de la iglesia. Si la escena exige mutación de lugares, lo ejecutan en distintas partes de la iglesia. A veces la ingenuidad popular conduce a excesos como el de situar el palacio de Herodes en un confesionario. Con un realismo despiadado, los pastores en medio de la iglesia enciendan su fogata, y condimentan sus sopas. Las ofrendas varian según los pueblos. . .
> Los pastores se situan, al principio, junto a las gradas del presbiterio, donde fingen dormir. La Sagrada Familia, ya en imágines, ya en personajes vivos, ocupan un lado del presbiterio. El ángel canta desde el coro, o desde el púlpito . . . .
> Hasta fecha relativamente reciente los textos se han transmitido por tradición oral. Aún hoy en muchos casos no existe copia alguna, y es preciso recogerlo de labios de los más ancianos.

Chapter 7, note 8. In the fifteenth century Vich *consueta*, the passage describing the ceremony which accompanied the Easter trope is found on fol. 53:

> Oratione finita, sex presbyteri induant se in choro cum capis sericis. Quibus indutis, diachonus cum baculo pastorali exeat de sacrario, et ueniat ad altare cum uno socio. Et dicat alta uoce tropum, *Hora est psallite*. Et finito versu redeat incontinenti ad episcopum. Et de illis sex presbiteris qui fuerint induti in choro ueniant quatuor priores ad altare Sancti Petri, et unus illorum in dextro cornu altaris, et alius in sinistro. Et alii duo stent ante altare, qui dicant versum *Ubi est Christus meus?* Et illi qui sunt ad altare dicant *Quem queritis*. Et alii dicant *Ihesum Natzarenum*. Et illi qui sunt ad altare leuent pallium altaris, dicendo versum *Non est hic, surrexit*. Et tunc omnes quatuor debent redire ad chorum cantando *Alleluia, ad sepulcrum*, et alium versum *En ecce completum*

est. Quibus finitis omnes sex presbyteri incipiant submissa uoce, oficium (*sic*) *Resurrexi.*

Chapter 7, note 14. The following passage is taken from the *consueta* written for the monastery of San Juan de las Abadesas in the fifteenth century (Vich, Bibl. Capit., MS 212, fol. 237ᵛ–238):

> Illi duo cantores qui fuerunt ultimi in processione uadant ad altare beate Marie, et ibi cantent tropos, *Quem queritis, etc.* Et alii duo respondeant ad altare beati Johannis, scilicet, illi qui fuerunt primi in processione *Jhesum Nazarenum.* Et iterum alii duo respondeant *Non est hic, surrexit.* Et alii iterum respondeant *Alleluia, ad sepulcrum.* His itaque peractis, reuertantur in chorum, et ibi incipiant officium *Resurrexi.*

The twelfth century *consueta* from the Seo de Urgel refers very briefly to the same custom (Vich, Bibl. Capit., MS 131, fol. 38ᵛ):

> In reditu *Christus resurgens.* Versus *Dicant nunc Iudei* cantetur a duobus ante ianuas. Quo dicto, in introitu dicitur, *Resurrexit Dominus a mortuis.* Tropi etiam dicuntur, scilicet, *Quem queritis in Sepulcro.* Et sic peragitur missa sollempniter et deuotissime.

In speaking of tropes, the author of the fifteenth century Urgel ceremonial constantly employs the vernacular (Seo de Urgel, Bibl. Capit., fol. 70ᵛ):

> Antiphona in introitu, *Resurrexit Dominus.* Et prius sint .vi. bene cantantes qui dicant los trops, scilicet, *Quem queritis, etc.* . . . . Finitis los trops, incipiant officium submissa uoce.

Still in 1527 the ceremony was observed at Urgel (*Ordo supplicationum seu processionum*, fol. 70–71; a copy of this book is found at the Biblioteca Central in Barcelona, 10–11–32; the text is provided with music):

> Et cum in choro fuerint officiatores procedant ad altare maius: et seruetur ordo: qui in die natalis Domini dictum est: et dicat diachonus primo versum:
>
> > Psallite, fratres mei omnes, hora est, eya.
>
> Qui in dextra parte sunt cantent versum:
>
> > Quem queritis in sepulcro, o celicole.
>
> Qui in sinistra sunt dicant versum:
>
> > Jesum Nazarenum queritis crucifixum, o deicole.
>
> Qui ante altare sunt dicant versum:
>
> > Non est hic, surrexit sicut predixerat; ite, nunciate quia surrexit, dicentes.
>
> Iterum qui in dextra sunt dicant versum:

> Alleluya, ad sepulcrum residens angelus nunciat resurrexisse Christum. Ecce completum est illud quod olim ipse per prophetam dixerat ad Patrem taliter inquiens.
>
> Tunc omnes ad chorum redeuntes, submissa uoce cantent misse introitum:
>
> Resurrexi et adhuc tecum sum, alleluya.

In the two Barcelona manuscripts the usual text of the trope is preceded by the rubric: *Versus* (Bibl. Central, M. 298 (39), Cantorale saec. xv, fol. 69^v; M. 299 (40), Cantorale saec. xv, fol. 145).

Chapter 7, note 37. The Vich *consueta* written in the year 1413 states as follows (fol. 52):

> Tertium responsorium *Et ualde mane*. Et reiteretur post *gloria*; et dicitur uerbeta *Christus hodie* cum pneuma. Deinde fiat Oficium de tribus Mariis si voluerint. Quo facto dicat Episcopus uel sacerdos *Te Deum laudamus*.

The words *Deinde* to *sacerdos* have been crossed out in the manuscript. This was probably done at the time when future performance of the liturgical Easter play was prohibited at Vich.

Chapter 7, note 98. The Ascension trope was popular everywhere in Europe. A version of it is found in the eleventh century Ripoll troper (Vich, Bibl. Capit., MS 105, fol. 9^v; essentially the same text is found in MS 106, Troparium Ripollense(?) saec. xii, fol. 63):

> IN ASCENSA DOMINI
>
> Quem creditis super astra ascendisse, o celicole?
> Responsio:
> Ihesum qui surrexit de sepulcro, agnicole.
> Responsio:
> Iam ascendit ut predixit: ascendo ad patrem meum et patrem uestrum, Deum meum et Deum uestrum.
> Responsio:
> Alleluja, regna, terre, gentes, lingue, decantate Domino quem adorant celiciues in paterno solio. Viri Galilei.

The trope sung on the feast of St. John the Baptist is found in MS 105 folio 19^v–20; in MS 106 on folio 71^v:

> Quem creditis natum in orbe, o deicole?
> Iohannem precursorem ortum de sterili, angelo nunciante, o celicole.
> Iam natus est, ut dixit Saluator: Mitto angelum meum ante me qui preparet uiam meam.
> Eia! Psallite, omnes cristicole.

Chapter 9, note 28. The sacristan's *consueta* describes the ceremony in the following fashion (fol. 75–75ᵛ; much the same is found on fol. 8–8ᵛ):

> E lo bosser te carech de hauer un diacha, o preuera si noy haura diacha, quis vestira per Sant Steua, e dar li ha un cruat per sos treballs. E quant lo dit Sant Steua anira al cor y a la processo, aportera un ciri de .iii. onces blanch, e un professonal xich. E lo ragent fera aparellar hun pauallo dels maiors lo pus flach; lo qual quatre preueras aporteran ab capas de xemellot vermell, o morat. E mes fera aparellar duas capes de xemellot vermellas per dos preueras qui acompenyaran lo dit Sant Steua, e dos ciris xichs vermells, hu per caschu dels dits preueras . . . .
> E quant al cor torneran la antifona de *Magnificat*, lo dit Sanct Steua partira de la sacrastia, e anira deuall lo pauallo, e dos preueras al costat, axi com ya es dit, e las trompes deuant, anira al cor, e saguira la processo. E quant seran al dit altar de Sanct Steua, lo dit Sanct Steua se possera deuant lo dit altar ab la cara deuers lo poble, e lo pauallo stera estes . . .
> E los domers encenseran deuant Sant Steua e escorreran encensant la capella . . . .

Chapter 9, note 30. The *consueta de sanctis* describes as follows the ceremonies which took place at Mass on St. Stephen's Day (Sala 1, Armario LXXVI, Tabla II, 1, fol. 17–18ᵛ):

> Et in sacristia sit indutus unus diachonus uestimentis et dalmatica, uelataque facie, et portet cereum album accensum. Et duo clerici cum capis associent eum hinc et inde, portantes cereos accensos. Et quatuor alii presbiteri cum capis portent super ipsum unum pannum deauratum in quatuor baculis. Et omnes sic ornati, exeant de sacristia, post crucem. Et canonicus cum suis ministris subsequitur. Et ueniant omnes usque prope portam chori . . . .
> Ad missam maiorem . . . dicatur tropus a duobus primicheriis, scilicet, *Eya colleuite*. Et triumphetur officium, scilicet, *Etenim sederunt* . . . Et dum subdiachonus ibit ad legendam epistolam, associet eum diachonus facie uelatus, indutus dalmatica et uestimentis, et uadat sub papiliono.

The sacristan's *consueta* adds more details (fol. 76ᵛ), declaring that at the epistle St. Stephen is preceded by "las trompes".

Chapter 9, note 38. The following passage is a part of the description of St. Nicholas Day ceremonies; it is found in the sacristan's *consueta* (fol. 70–70ᵛ):

> E lo ragent es tingut aparellar lo vestiment per lo bisbato, ço es una capeta de las millors, e una tunicella petita e si noy haura tunicella pendran una domatigue de las millors dels fadrins del altar, e un camisnet dels dits fadrins, e un hamit e un sinyel, e la mitra e la crossa . . . .
> E mes fara aparellar a la sacrastia tres capetes, ço es una per lo papa ab camis y una domatigue dels dits fadrins, e la tiara. Les altres duas capas seran per los companyons del papa . . .

E quant comenseran les lisions de morts, lo papa partira de la sacrestia ab sos ministres ab la creu deuant, e anira al cor a la cadira que hauran encortinade. E quant lo terç responsori de morts sera dit, comenseran lo entrames del Bisbato. E quant lo dit entrames sera acabat, lo papa alta voce comensera lo *Te Deum laudamus*.

Chapter 10, note 16.

DE PROCESSIONE IN NOCTE PASCHE ANTE MATUTINUM AD SEPULCHRUM CHRISTI

Die sancto Resurrectionis cum fuerit pulsatum ad Matutinum, antequam populus intret ecclesiam, sacerdos cum cruce et thuribulo apparatus superpelliceo, stolla, et pluuiali, precedentibus cereis accensis et sequente toto clero cum reuerentia, aperto Sepulchro, accipiat Corpus Domini et portet illud in loco sacrarii ubi sacrosanctum Sacramentum seruari consueuit. . . . .
Orationibus finitis, Sacerdos Corpus Domini reuerenter thurificet. Dum predicte orationes dicuntur, duo diaconi parentur cum dalmaticis albis et in ecclesia remaneant. Sacerdos autem paratus vt supra cum toto clero exeat per portam ecclesie minorem, maiori porta clausa relicta, et veniant ad portam maiorem ecclesie cantando responsorium *Dum transisset sabbatum*; et cum illuc peruenerint, sacerdos accedit ad portam clausam; clerus circumstat eum. Responsorium:

> Dum transisset sabbatum, Maria Magdalene, Maria Iacobi, et Salome emerunt aromata, ut uenientes ungerent Iesum, alleluia, alleluia. Versus: Et valde mane una sabbatorum veniunt ad monumentum, orto iam sole. Ut venientes. Gloria Patri, et Filio, et Spiritui Sancto, alleluia.

Et dum peruenerint ad fores ecclesie, completo responsorio cum versu et replica, plebanus vel sacerdos paratus pulsat ad ostium manu vel cum cruce dicens sonora voce in tono lectionis:

> Attollite portas, principes, vestras, et elleuamini porte eternales, et introibit rex glorie.

Et pro ista prima pulsatione illi deintus nihil respondent. Et facto modico interuallo, sacerdos iterum uehementius pulsat ad ostium dicens voce altiori in tono lectionis: *Attollite portas, principes, et cetera*. Et illi deintus nihil respondent. Et tunc sacerdos, modico interuallo facto, iterum in eodem tono sed altius quam secundo pulsans fortiter ostium ecclesie dicit: *Attollite portas, principes, et cetera*. Tunc illi dyaconi deintus statim cantando respondent:

> Quem queritis in sepulchro, Christicole?

Et illi de foris respondent:

> Iesum Nazarenum crucifixum, o celicole.

Et iterum illi deintus respondeant:

> Non est hic, surrexit sicut predixerat; ite, nuntiate quia surrexit a mortuis.

Hoc finito, qui deintus sunt aperiant portam ecclesiae, et omnes ingrediantur. Et iterum dicant qui deintus erant:

> Venite et videte locum ubi positus erat Dominus, alleluia, alleluia.

Et cum fuerint portam ingressi, firment se omnes et diuidant per choros. Tunc plebanus vadat ad Sepulchrum et ponat caput in fenestra Sepulchri; et postea conuersus ad populum dicat voce mediocri: *Surrexit Christus.* Chorus respondeat: *Deo gratias.* Quo dicto, plebanus procedat aliquantulum versus populum, et exaltet vocem altius quam primum et dicat: *Surrexit Christus.* Chorus respondeat: *Deo gratias.* Iterum tertio plebanus procedat versus populum aliquantulum, et exaltata voce adhuc altius quam secundo fecerat et dicat: *Surrexit Christus.* Chorus respondeat: *Deo gratias.* Quo facto, omnes procedant ad Sepulchrum et faciant choros hinc et inde. Tunc plebanus vadit ad ostium Sepulchri et statim retrocedat versus chorum et det pacem primo sacerdoti seu clerico vel Domino terre, si ibi fuerit, et dicat voce submissa: *Surrexit Dominus.* Et ille respondeat: *Deo gratias.* Deinde omnes sibi mutuo dent pacem dicentes: *Surrexit Dominus.* Et ille cui pax datur respondeat: *Deo gratias.* Postmodum vadant omnes ad altare Beate Virginis processionaliter, et coram altari genuflexi sacerdote incipiente antiphonam *Regina celi*, eam totam cantent pro gaudio Resurrectionis Filii sui, Domini Nostri.

Chapter 11, *note* 14. I follow the readings of Constans, but the line division is mine.

> Al yorn del iusivy
> parrà qui aurà fayt servisi.
>
> [Un Rey vendr]à perpetual
> del cel com mas non aytal;
> [del cel] vendrà certanament
> per far del segle iugament.
>   Al yorn . . .
>
> Ans del iusivi tot evant
> parrà una seyal molt gran;
> la terra gitarà suor
> e tremirà de gran paor.
>   Al yorn . . .
>
> Aprés ses badarà molt fort
> don és semblant de greu conort
> e mostrarà ab crits e ab trons
> les ymfernals confusions.
>   Al yorn . . .

Un corn molt trist ressonarà
del cel, quils morts rexedarà;
la luna, el sol, s'escurirà
ny l'estela luyrà.
    Al yorn . . .

Foc dexendrà del cel ardent
e sofre qui és molt pudent.
La terra, mar, tot peryrà;
lo foc, tot quant és, delirà.
    Al yorn . . .

[De] perir serà nostra talent,
ladons nos glatiran les dens.
No yaurà negun que nos plor;
tot lo món serà en tristor.
    Al yorn . . .

[Lad]ons no aurà hom talent
de riquesa d'aur, ne d'argent;
[de] res hom no aurà desir,
mas tant solament de morir.
    Al yorn . . .

Los plans, els pugs, seran egals;
aquí seran los bons, els mals,
los Reys, los comptes, los barons,
de tots lur fayt rendiron.
    Al yorn . . .

Anch no feu hom res tant secret,
ne dix, ne so penset,
que aquí no sia tot clar
ia noy porà hom res celar.
    Al yorn . . .

Los enfants qui nats no seran
layns el ventre cridaran
e diran ab veu molt autament:
"Mercé, ay Deus omnipotent".
    Al yorn . . .

Amats seyors, tan gran dolors
auran ladons los pecadors,
que en ymfern, layns n'yran
i amays d'aquí no exiran.
    Al yorn . . .

Ay cel, seyor, qui mon formet
e pur de la Verge nasquet,
nos gart del peccat criminal
e de la pena ymfernal.
   Al yorn . . .

Ver Fil de Deu tu reclamam
al gran iusivi qu'esperam,
quens acuyles en paradís,
ens garts de la flama d'abís.
   Al yorn . . .

Seyer, dans gaug perpetual,
el teu regne celestial,
e garans de l'enemic felon
e del poder de Faraon.
   Al yorn . . .

E vos, seyors, qui m'escoltats,
lo Fil de la Verge reclamats,
quel nos gart de la mala sort
com així de sobtada mort.
   Al yorn . . .

BIBLIOGRAPHY

THE following bibliography includes not only the manuscripts and early printed works examined as a preparation for this study, but also other medieval liturgical manuscripts which are extant, or may be extant, and which I have been unable to consult. Sources not personally consulted are indicated by a cross (+), those which contain *Quem quaeritis* tropes, liturgical plays or information about them are designated by an asterisk. If manuscripts contain the Sibylline chant, that fact is indicated. Since *evangelaria*, choirbooks of large format, and breviaries which follow the rite of the Roman curia never, or very rarely, speak of liturgical plays, as a general rule I have not examined such codices. The same holds true of liturgical manuscripts written for the Cistercian, Carthusian, Dominican, and Franciscan Orders. If the present whereabouts of an important manuscript is unknown, information which will help identify the work is added, and the source of the reference given. When it is known that a cathedral library possesses no medieval liturgical manuscripts, that fact is mentioned.

Abbreviations

Antiph.	= Antiphonarium		Miss.	= Missale
eccl.	= ecclesia		Proc.	= Processionale
frag.	= fragment		Resp.	= Responsoriale
Grad.	= Graduale		saec.	= saeculum
Lect.	= Lectionarium		s.n.	= without number

MANUSCRIPT SOURCES

ASTORGA
Cathedral
There are no medieval liturgical manuscripts at the cathedral library.

AVILA
Cathedral
MS s.n., Miss. Abulense (Avila), saec. xv.

Biblioteca del Marqués de Piedrasalbas
MS s.n., Miss. Abulense, saec. xvi(?).
MS s.n., Brev. Abulense, saec. xvi(?).

BARCELONA
Archivo de la Corona de Aragón
+Monacales 381, Antiph., saec. xi.
Ripoll 74, Tonale, saec. x.
Ripoll 106, Fol. 92^v: "Judicii signum".
Ripoll 112, Missale, saec. xiv.

Ripoll 117, Tractatus de officiis ecclesiae, saec. xii-xiii.
Ripoll 145, Breviarium, saec. xv.
San Cugat 3, Lectionarium, saec. xi.
San Cugat 20, Consueta, saec. xiv-xv.
San Cugat 29, Miss. Parvum, saec. xv.
San Cugat 46, Consueta saec. xiii. Fol. 59:
"Lectio xii. *Inter Pressuras.* Versus *Judicii signum* dicunt duo fratres intus rexias. Et alii duo in letrilio. Et respondit corus *Judicii signum.* Et post finem lectionis, responsorium."
San Cugat 47, Sacramentarium, saec. xiii.
+San Cugat 56, Lectionarium, saec. xiv.
San Cugat 73, Rituale, saec. xiv.
San Cugat 77, Consueta, saec. xv.
San Cugat 85, Consueta, saec. xvi.
San Cugat 87, Breviarium, saec. xiv-xv.

Biblioteca Central

M. 250, Cantorale ordinis Sancti Jeronimi, saec. xv.
*M. 298 (39), Cantorale, saec. xv.
*M. 299 (40), Cantorale, saec. xv.
M. 301 (659), Psalmi et Antiphonae, saec. xv.
M. 302 (706), Antiph., saec. xiv-xv.
M. 303 (705), Antiph., saec. xiv.
M. 304 (662), Antiph., saec. xiv-xv.
M. 305 (663), Antiph., saec. xv.
M. 306 (784), Antiph., saec. xvi.
M. 307 (648), Graduale.
M. 308 (785), Graduale, saec. xvi.
M. 309 (276), Processionale, saec. xvi.
M. 888, Antiph., saec. xiii.
M. 889, Graduale, saec. xiii.
M. 903, Resp.-Proc. monasticum, saec. xvi.
*M. 911, Troparium-Prosarium Gerundense, saec. xv.
M. 1147, Graduale (Ager), saec. xii.
M. 1327, Cantorale, saec. xv.
M. 1408, Fragmenta Gregoriana, saec. xi-xiii.
M. 1409, Fragmenta Gregoriana, saec. xii-xiii.
M. 1451, Fragmenta Gregoriana, saec. xi-xv.
M. 1463, Antiph. (frag.)., saec. xi.
MS 193, Fragmentos de códices litúrgicos, bíblicos, y sermones, saec. x-xii.
MS 276, Consueta eccl. Tarraconensis, saec. xiv.
MS 322, Miss. eccl. Sancti Eudalis de Ripoll (1565).
MS 619, Antiph. Barcinonense, saec. xiii.
MS 620, Missale, saec. xiv-xv.
MS 621, Missale, saec. xv.
MS 865, Brev. (frag.), saec. xv.
MS 1000, Lect. (Ager), saec. xiii.
MS 1139, Consuetas de Mallorca, saec. xvi-xvii; contains vernacular plays.
MS 1237, Missale, saec. xiv.
MS 1238, Missale, saec. xiv.
MS 1538, Psalterium-Antiphonarium, saec. xiv.
MS 1669, Brev. (frag.), saec. xvi.
MS 1670, Miss. (frag.), saec. xiv.
MS 1672, Cantorale (1619).
MS 1759, Breviarium.
+M. 297, Ceremonial, saec. xvi.
+M. 314, Ordinarium, saec. xiii.
+M. 315, Ordinarium.

(The manuscripts numbered M. 297, M. 314, and M. 315 are listed by F. Pedrell, *Catalèch de la Biblioteca Música de Diputació de Barcelona*, Barcelona, 1908. The distinguished director of the Biblioteca Central, Dr. Felipe Mateu y Llopis, has kindly informed me that the Biblioteca Central never possessed these manuscripts. At the time of the organization of the Music Section of the library, when an inventory was taken of the musical works proceeding from the Carreras Degas collection catalogued by Pedrell, it was noted that several of the manuscripts and printed works listed by Pedrell were missing, among them the three mentioned above. These works never reached the library. Judging by the title of the three manuscripts, they probably contained a summary of liturgical ceremonies rather than musical notation. This would perhaps explain why they were not transferred to the department of music of the Biblioteca Central. It is quite possible that these manuscripts are extant somewhere, and that they contain information about liturgical plays.)

Cathedral

C. 77, Consueta eccl. Barcinonensis, saec. xiv-xv.
+ C. 106 to C. 111, Lectionaria, saec. xiv.
+ C. 116, Miss. Barcinonense, saec. xv.
+ C. 137, Brev. Barcinonense, saec. xv.
+ C. 139, Rituale, saec. xiii-xiv.
+ C. 168, Libri liturgici (frag.).
+ C. 169, Antiphonarium.
+ C. 173 to C. 175, Libri liturgici.
+ MS s.n., Lectionarium, saec. xv.

(Except for the *consueta*, I was not given the opportunity to see the manuscripts at the cathedral.)

Museo Diocesano

+ No. 750, Graduale-Prosarium, saec. xiv-xv.
+ No. 1050, Fragmenta Gregoriana, saec. xi-xiii.
+ No. 1087, Troparium de Granollers, saec. xv.
+ MS s.n., Troparium (frag.), saec. xiv.

(The Museum has not as yet been reorganized since the Civil War, so I was unable to see these manuscripts. Their presence at the Museum was pointed out by Anglès, *El Còdex musical de Las Huelgas*, I, xvii, and *La Música a Catalunya fins al segle XIII*, p. 424.)

Orfeó Català

MS 1, Troparium-Prosarium, saec. xiv.
MS 11, Fragmentos Gregorianos, saec. xii-xvi.
MS s.n., Antiph. (incomplete), saec. xiv-xv.
MS s.n., Proc. Monasterii Sancti Johannis de Abbatissis (1425).
MS s.n., Proc. eccl. Valentinae, saec. xvi.

University of Barcelona

MS 165, Breviarium, saec. xiv.
MS 505, Psalterium-Hymnarium Gerundense, saec. xv.

Miscellanea

+ Bibl. José Maciá: Proc. monasterii Sancti Martini de Gerona saec. xv; described by Anglès, *La Música española desde la Edad Media hasta nuestros días*, pp. 69-70.
+ Carreras Candi i Ca.: Graduale, saec. xi; described by Anglès, *La Música a Catalunya*, p. 144.

+ Private library: Graduale (Vall d'Aran), saec. xi-xii; cited by Anglès, *El Còdex musical de Las Huelgas*, I, xvii.
Santa María del Mar: Consueta eccl. Barcinonensis, saec. xv.

Breda (Gerona)

Villanueva mentions a thirteenth century *consueta* which he consulted at the former Benedictine monastery of San Salvador de Breda (*Viage literario*, XIV, 206-209). The pastor of the Breda church has informed me that he does not know where this manuscript is today.

Burgo de Osma

Cathedral

MS 2A, Brev. Oxomense, saec. xv.
MS 2B, Brev. Oxomense, saec. xv; on fol. 31: "Versus Sibille".
+ MS 78A, Brev. Romanum.
+ MS 78B, Brev. Romanum.
MS 94, Evangelarium, saec. xii.
+ MS 100, De Divinis Officiis, saec. xiii.
MS 102, Ordinarium Oxomense, saec. xv; on fol. 19^v: "In sexta lectione cantetur versus de Sibilla. Audite qui (*sic*) dixerit."
MS 107, Evangelarium, saec. xii.
+ MS 138, De Officio Divino, saec. xiii.
MS 164, Missale, saec. xv.
MS 165, Missale, saec. xii.
MS 167, Epistolarium, saec. xii.

Burgos

Cathedral

MS 14, Regula Sancti Benedicti et Responsoriale, saec. xiv.
MS 16, Epistolarium, saec. xiv-xv.
MS 17, Miss. Burgense, saec. xvi.
MS 18, Brev. et Miss. monasticum, saec. xii-xiii.
MS 29, Brev. Burgense, saec. xv; on fol. 165: "Versus Sibille dicitur a duobus sociis."
+ MS 61, Fragmenta Gregoriana, saec. xiii.

Monastery of Las Huelgas

MS 5, Consueta, saec. xiii-xiv.

Calahorra

Cathedral

MS 17, Brev. Calagurritanum (Calahorra), saec. xiv; lesson vi of Christmas Matins: "Versus Sibille".
MS 18, Brev. Calagurritanum (1500); lesson vi: "Judicii signum".

Cardona (Barcelona)

The twelfth century breviary from San Miguel de Cardona, which was consulted by Villanueva (VI, 93) at the Premonstratensian monastery of Bellpuig de las Avellanas, is apparently now lost.
The *Pretiosa*, or *Caputbrevium*, of the monastery of St. Vincent of Cardona (*ca.* 1307) has been edited by its present possessor, J. Sera Vilaró, in *Estudis Universitaris Catalans*, VIII (1914), 3-63.

Ciudad Rodrigo

Fr. M. Martín, the archivist of the cathedral of this city, has informed me that, except for some fifteenth century choir-books of large format, the chapter library possesses no medieval liturgical manuscripts.

CORDOBA

Cathedral

MS 1, Homiliarium (Burgos), saec. x; chant of the Sibyl, fol. 69b. According to the cathedral archivist, there are no other medieval liturgical manuscripts at the chapter library.

FRANCE

Chantilly (Musée Condé)

MS 1434, Brev. monasterii Sancti Petri de Cardeña, saec. xv.

Paris (Bibl. de l'Arsénal)

MS 105, Brev. eccl. Valentinae, saec. xv; on fol. 29: "Judicii signum".

Paris (Bibl. Nationale)

MS lat. 804, Homiliarium Tarraconense; listed as a Tarragona manuscript by J. Vives, "Manuscritos hispánicos en bibliotecas extranjeras", *Hispania Sacra*, II (1949), 449-457.
MS lat. 891, Epistolarium Gerundense, saec. xii-xiii.
MS lat. 897, Evangelarium Gerundense, saec. xii-xiv.
MS lat. 982, Brev. Hispalense (Seville), saec. xv; on fol. 25: "Judicii signum".
MS lat. 1103, Miss. Gerundense, saec. xiv-xv; listed by Vives as a Gerona manuscript, *op. cit.*
MS lat. 1109, Miss Barcinonense, saec. xv.
MS lat. 1133, Missale ad usum cuiusdam abbatiae ordinis Cluniacensis in Hispania; fol. 126-149, Missale Gerundense; so listed by Vives, *op. cit.*
MS lat. 1309, Brev. Gerundense, saec. xv.
MS lat. 1309A, Brev. Illerdense (Lérida), saec. xv.
MS lat. 1309A², Brev. Illerdense, saec. xv.
MS lat. 5302, Lect., saec. xi; on fol. 82-82^v, the verses of the Sibyl; from Catalonia, according to Anglès, *La Música a Catalunya*, p. 292.
MS lat. 12038, Brev. monasterii Poblet, saec. xiii.
MS lat. 13234, Brev. Hispalense, saec. xv; has the verses of the Sibyl.
MS lat. n. acq. 261, Brev. Burgense, saec. xv.
MS lat. n. acq. 495, Troparium Gerundense, saec. xii.
MS lat. n. acq. 838, Brev. Elnense, saec. xiv.
MS lat. n. acq. 839, Brev. Elnense, saec. xiv.
MS lat. n. acq. 840, Brev. Elnense, saec. xiv.
*MS lat. n. acq. 903, Brev. Vicense, saec. xiv.
MS lat. n. acq. 2190, Brev. Silense (Silos), saec. xiv.
MS lat. n. acq. 2193, Brev. Silense, saec. xiv.
MS lat. n. acq. 2194, Miss. Silense.
*MS esp. 342, Las Buenas y loables costumbres . . . de Granada, saec. xvi.

Perpignan (Bibl. Mun.)

MS 71, Liber Ordinationum et consuetudinum eccl. Elnensis, saec. xiv.
*MS 79, Libre de serimonies (St. John of Perpignan), saec. xiv-xv.

Toulouse (Bibl. Mun.)

MS 124, Ordinarium Elnense (1207-1209).

GERONA

Biblioteca Pública

No. 9/108, Ceremonial Monástico de San Benito de Valladolid, saec. xv.

Cathedral

MS 8 (I-I-1), Lect. Gerundense (sanctorale), saec. xiv.
*MS 9 (I-I-2), Consueta Gerundensis (1360).
MS 14 (I-III-3), Miss. Gerundense.
MS 15 (I-III-4), Miss. Gerundense.
MS 17 (I-III-6), Miss. Gerundense.
MS 48 (I-IV-6), Fragmenta Codicis Juris et rerum liturgicarum.
MS 95 (II-I-17), Brev. Gerundense, saec. xiv.
MS 96 (II-I-18), Brev. Gerundense, saec. xiv.
MS 97 (II-III-1), Brev. Gerundense.
MS 98 (II-III-2), Brev. Parvum, saec. xiii.
MS 99 (II-III-3), Brev. cum hymnario, saec. xiii.
MS 125 (II-III-7), Brev. Gerundense.
MS 126 (II-III-8), Brev. Gerundense.
MS 127 (II-III-9), Missale Gerundense, saec. xiv.
MS s.n., Miss. Gerundense, saec. xiv.
MS s.n., Missale, saec. xvi.
MS s.n., Miss. Sancti Felicis, saec. xvi(?).
MS s.n., Evangelarium, saec. xi-xii.
(Almost all the Gerona breviaries have the Sibylline verses.)

Museo Diocesano

MS s.n., Antiph. Gerundense, saec. xii.

Seminary

*MS s.n., Brev. Gerundense, saec. xv.
MS s.n., Brev. Gerundense, saec. xiv.
*MS s.n., Consueta eccl. Sancti Felicis, saec. xv.
+MS s.n., Lect. Gerundense, saec. xiv.
MS s.n., Miss. Gerundense, saec. xiv.
MS s.n., Miss. Gerundense, saec. xv.

The manuscripts of the church of St. Felix were moved to the Seminary in 1936, and have not since been catalogued. In his valuable *Arqueología litúrgica*, Gudiol describes four St. Felix *consuetas* which he saw about the year 1920. One of his descriptions seems to fit the *consueta* listed above: "Consueta de Sant Felix, Girona, dels temps del abat Francisch Vilella (1425-1461), bellament escrite . . . 405 × 285 mm;" at least 326 folios.

Upon my request, the distinguished archivist of the cathedral of Gerona, J. Marqués, has diligently searched for the remaining three *consuetas*, but reports that he has not been able to find them anywhere in Gerona. Since these *consuetas* most likely speak of liturgical plays, and are probably still extant somewhere, I give here part of Gudiol's description of them:

"Consueta nova sive consuetudo officiorum totius anni sec. observ. sedis Gerund., 36 fol., 305 × 225 mm."

"Consueta, MS de St. Felix de Girona, cod. 17, en paper y pergami, xv, 283 fol."

"Consueta antigua de St. Felix de Girona, pergami, xiv, 112 fol."

In *El Còdex musical de las Huelgas*, I, xvii, Anglès also mentions a fifteenth century "Graduale-Troparium" which he saw at the St. Felix library.

Dreves and Blume (*Analecta hymnica*, XVII, 1894, pp. 32, 43) cite passages from an "Officiarium, MS saec. 16, Cod. Semin. Gerunden. 2309"; Anglès also lists this work (*El Còdex musical de las Huelgas*, I, xvii). According to Fr. Marqués, this manuscript cannot be found.

GRANADA

Cathedral

*No. 17, Sección de Libros, Las Buenas y loables costumbres . . . de Granada, saec. xvi.

Huesca

Cathedral

MS 1, Hymnarium, saec. xi.
MS 2, Brev. monasticum, saec. xi; on fol. 31: "Judicii signum".
MS 3, Lect., saec. xi; fol. 27^v: "Sibillina versibus" (*sic*).
*MS 4, Prosarium-Troparium, saec. xi-xii, 153 fol.
MS 7, Brev. Oscense, saec. xii; almost all medieval Huesca breviaries have the verses of the Sibyl.
MS 8, Brev. Oscense, saec. xii.
MS 11, Miss. Oscense, saec. xii.
MS 12, Breviarium Oscense, saec. xiii.
MS 13, Breviarium Oscense, saec. xiv.
MS 14, Breviarium Oscense, saec. xiv.
MS 16, Missale, saec. xiv.
MS 20, Miss. Oscense, saec. xv.
MS 21, Consueta eccl. Oscensis, saec. xv.
MS 22, Brev. eccl. Valentinae, saec. xv.
MS 23, Brev. eccl. Valentinae, saec. xv.
MS 24, Brev. Oscense, saec. xv.
MS 49, Ceremonial de la Catedral de Huesca (1697).
MS 54, Ceremonial de la Catedral de Huesca (1786).

I use the reference numbers given by the cathedral archivist, Fr. Durán Gudiol, in his article, 'Los Manuscritos de la Catedral de Huesca', *Argensola*, IV, 1953. Two manuscripts listed by R. del Arco, *Revista de Archivos, Bibliotecas, y Museos*, XXV, 1911, 299-300, are no longer at the chapter library: 1) "prosario . . .; es benedictino, a lo menos parece serlo por la prosa de San Benito que contiene, y está señalada para la fiesta de la translación, *in translatione Sci. Benedicti*. Este manuscrito, escrito en pergamino, en 4°, de 190 folios, no debe ser, pues, originario de la catedral, sino de algún monasterio antiguo benedictino de la provincia, tal vez San Juan de la Peña . . . . Parece proceder de los últimos tiempos del siglo XI o comienzos del XII. La notación es aquitana, y su escritura francesa. Termina el prosario con un troparion o kirial, y es uno de los mejores que pueden encontrarse en la Península;" 2) "Libro de liturgia o rúbricas, falta de hojas al principio y al fin; de sentir es, porque es un hermoso ejemplar. Hay 141 folios, escritos a dos columnas en el siglo XII. En folio." Since Del Arco describes these codices minutely, I hardly believe he imagined their existence, as some have thought. These very important manuscripts may still be extant.

Jaca

There are no medieval liturgical manuscripts at the chapter library of Jaca.

León

Cathedral

MS 9, Proc. Legionense, saec. xv.
MS 21, Constitutiones eccl. Legionensis, saec. xiv.
MS 23, Cantorum Liber, saec. xv; text and music of the Sibylline chant, fol. 5-8.
MS 36, Diurnale Legionense.
MS 40, Brev. (frag.).
MS 43, Miss. Legionense, saec. xv.
MS 45, Miss. Legionense, saec. xv.

San Isidoro

MS 5, Miss. Legionense, saec. xii.
MS 12, Brev. et Rituale, saec. xii.
MS 13, Brev. et Rituale, saec. xiii.
MS 36, Breviarium, saec. xv; fol. 110: "Versus Sibille".
+MS 38, Brev. Franciscanum, saec. xv.

+ MS 54, to MS 56, Cantorale, saec. xv.
+ MS 110, Cantorale, saec. xv.
MS 119, Proc. eccl. Sancti Isidori, saec. xv.

LÉRIDA

Cathedral

MS 10 (Roda), Evangelarium, saec. xii.
MS 12 (Roda), Brev. Illerdense, saec. xv; on fol. 27^v: "Versus Sibille".

Seminary

MS 5 (Roda 11), Brev. Illerdense, saec. xii.
MS 6 (Roda 13), Consueta Illerdensis, saec. xiii; reference to the vernacular version of the Sibylline poem on fol. 19^v.
(These manuscripts belong to the cathedral capitular library, and are only temporarily at the Seminary.)

LONDON

British Museum

*Add. MS 30848, Brev. monasterii Sancti Dominici de Silos, saec. xi.
Add. MS 30849, Brev. monasterii Sancti Dominici de Silos, saec. xii.
*Add. MS 30850, Brev. monasterii Sancti Dominici de Silos, saec. xi.
+ Add. MS 30856, Miss. monasterii Sancti Dominici de Silos, saec. xv.
+ Add. MS 34663, Miss. eccl. Valentinae, saec. xv.
Add. MS 38037, Miss. Toletanum, saec. xv.
+ Add. MS 41070, Lect. eccl. Zamora, saec. xiv.
(I have not included in this list any manuscripts of the Mozarabic rite.)

LUGO

Cathedral

+ MS s.n., Brev. Lugo (sanctorale), saec. xiv.
(This is the only medieval liturgical manuscript at the cathedral of Lugo which would be of interest to our inquiry; see A. López, *Estudios crítico-históricos de Galicia*, 1916).

MADRID

Archivo Histórico Nacional

MS 1188 (olim 1078 B), Processionale, saec. xv.
MS 1319 (olim 911 B), Brev. ordinis militiae Sancti Iacobi, saec. xiv; on fol. 22^v: "Incipit Sibilla".

Biblioteca Nacional

MS 116, Miss. (frag.)
MS 136 (olim C 131), Processionale, saec. xiv. Formerly listed as "Tolosana ecclesia cathedralis: Ordinarium precum". González Palencia's statement (*Historia de la literatura española*, p. 94) that this manuscript contains liturgical plays is apparently erroneous.
MS 240, Brev. ordinis militiae Sancti Iacobi de Spata, saec. xv; on fol. 23^v the "Judicii signum".
MS 270, Manuale Missae, saec. xii-xiii.
*MS 288 (olim C 151), Troparium eccl. Siculorum (Sicily), saec. xii.
*MS 289 (olim C 153), Troparium eccl. Siculorum (Sicily), saec. xii.
MS 382, Brev. ordinis militiae Sancti Iacobi de Spata.
MS 557, Diurnale Romanum.
MS 1540 to 1546, Missale Toletanum (1503-18).
MS 4442 to 4444, Ceremonias y Ritual de la Misa.
MS 6086, Brev. Hispalense (Seville), saec. xv.

MS 6087, Breviarium, saec. xv.
MS 6532, Brev. (frag.) saec. xv.
+MS 9719, Missale, saec. xii.
MS 9785, Antiph.-Capitularium, saec. xiv.
MS 13039, Rituale Toletanum.
MS 13050, Noticia de varios breviarios antiguos de España.
MS 13062, Noticia de breviarios.
MS 17843, (tomo xii, no. 8), De Liturgia.
MS 19421, Troparium de Catania, saec. xiii.
M. 1322, Antiph.-Resp., saec. xiv-xv.
M. 1361, Grad.-Antiph., saec. xiv.
Vitr. 4-4, Missale Toletanum.
Vitr. 18-8, Brev. Romanum.
*Vitr. 20-4 (olim C 132), Grad. eccl. Siculorum (Sicily), saec. xii.
Vitr. 20-8, Missale, Sahagún, saec. xi.
Vitr. 21-6, Brev. Franciscanum, saec. xv.
Vitr. 21-8, Rituale et Graduale Romanum.
Vitr. 22-7, Missa Nativitatis Domini, saec. xvi.

Palacio Real
+MS 11.19 Breviarium saec. xiv.
+MS 11.20, Breviarium saec. xiv.
+MS 214 (2 B2), Breviarium Toletanum, saec. xiv.
   (There is no catalogue of the manuscripts of this rich library, and access is not given to the card index.)

Real Academia de la Historia
MS 9, Lect., San Millán de la Cogolla, saec. xii.
MS 18, Missale, San Millán, saec. xii.
MS 36, Ordinarium, San Millán, saec. xiii.
MS 43, Regulae Brev. et Missalis, saec. xv.
MS 45, Missale, San Millán, saec. xii-xiii.
MS 51, Graduale-Troparium, San Millán, saec. xii.
*MS 64 (12-19-4), the Villanueva volume on liturgy.
*MS 75 (2-7-4), Vallejo, *Memorias*.
*MS 444 (11-2-7), Ceremonias particulares de la Santa Yglesia Primada de Toledo (1783).

University of Madrid (Sección de Derecho)
MS 48, Breviarium Toletanum, saec. xvi.
MS 49, Brev. Toletanum, saec. xv.
*MS 149, Ordinarium Toletanum, saec. xv-xvi.

MONTBLANCH (BARCELONA)
Iglesia de Santa Maria
+MS s.n., Resp-Antiph., saec. xiii.
+MS s.n., Antiph., saec. xv.
+MS s.n., Antiph., saec. xv.
+MS s.n., Antiph., saec. xv.

MONSTERRAT
MS 13, Diurnale Monasticum, saec. xiv-xv.
MS 36, Brev. Monasticum, saec. xiv.
MS 46, Ceremoniale Monasticum, saec. xv.
MS 51, Diurnale Monasticum, saec. xvi.
MS 72, Antiph.-Resp., saec. xi.
MS 73, Troparium-Prosarium, saec. xii.
MS 74, Ceremoniale Monasticum, saec. xv.

MS 756, Antiph. et Grad. (frag.), saec. xii-xiv.
MS 760, Antiph. (frag.), saec. xiv-xv.
MS 761, Antiph. (frag.).
MS 780, Missale Mixtum, saec. xv.
MS 794, Fragmenta Liturgica, saec. x-xiii.
MS 795, Fragmenta Liturgica.
MS 799, Fragmenta Liturgica.
MS 837, Antiph., saec. xv.
MS 852, Brevarium, saec. xv.
MS 1009, Brev. (frag.), saec. xiii.
MS 1033, Ordinarium (Servites), saec. xv.
*MS s.n., Brev. Toletanum, saec. xiv.

ORENSE

Cathedral

MS 1, Miss. Auriense (Orense), saec. xv.
MS 9, Brev. Auriense, saec. xv.
MS 10, Brev. Auriense, saec. xv; on fol. 275, "Judicii signum".
MS s.n., Ceremonial antiguo de la Catedral de Orense, saec. xvi-xvii (copied in 1846).

OVIEDO

Cathedral

MS 6, Constitutiones eccl. Ovetensis, saec. xiv.
MS 38, Evangelarium, saec. xv.

PALMA DE MALLORCA

Biblioteca de Casa Vivot

+MS s.n., Breviarium Maioricense, saec. xiii, cited by Pérez Martínez, Lorenzo, 'La Asunción, Titular de la Catedral de Mallorca', *Analecta Sacra Tarraconensia*, XXVIII (1955), 291.

Biblioteca Provincial

+MS s.n., Matutinarium-Responsoriale, saec. xiv.

Cathedral

*Sala 1, Armario LXXVI, Tabla II, 1, Consueta eccl. Maioricensis (consueta de sanctis), saec. xv-xvi.
*Sala 1, Armario LXXVI, Tabla I, 2, Ordinacions fetas per lo ragent de la sacrastia (Sacristan's consueta, 1511).
*MS s.n., Consueta eccl. Maioricensis (consueta de tempore), saec. xiv-xv.
+MS s.n., Hymnarium, saec. xiv-xv.

Museo Diocesano

+MS s.n., Cantorale, saec. xv-xvi.

PALENCIA

Cathedral

MS s.n., Ordinarium eccl. Palentinae, saec. xiv; it refers to the "Judicii signum".
*MS s.n., Ceremonial de la Iglesia de Palencia (by Juan de Arce, 1550).

PAMPLONA

Archivo Provincial de Navarra

MS s.n., Brevarium, saec. xv.
MS s.n., Breviarium.

MS s.n., Consuetudines monasticae.
MS s.n., Antiph.-Hymnarium.
MS s.n., Brev. Cisterciense.
MS s.n., Consuetudines Cistercienses.
MS s.n., Brev. monasticum (Irache), saec. xiii.

Cathedral
MS s.n., Brev. eccl. Pamplona, saec. xiv.
MS s.n., Brev. eccl. Pamplona, saec. xiv.
MS s.n., Breviarium, saec. xiv.
MS s.n., Breviarium, saec. xiv.

PLASENCIA
Cathedral
+ MS s.n., Miss. Placentinum, saec. xvi.

RIPOLL
Museo Folklórico de San Pedro de Ripoll
A. 3, Ordinarium eccl. Sancti Petri de Ripoll, (sanctorale), saec. xv.
A. 4, Grad. (frag.), saec. xiv.

SALAMANCA
Cathedral
There are no medieval liturgical manuscripts at the cathedral.

University
MS 227, Brev. Calagurritanum (Calahorra), saec. xiv; on fol. 102: "Judicii signum".

SAN JUAN DE LAS ABADESAS
+ MS s.n., Consueta monasterii Sancti Johannis de Abbatissis, saec. xiv, 28 × 20 cent., 168 fol.
+ MS s.n., Consueta monasterii Sancti Johannis de Abbatissis (1464).
+ MS s.n., Hymnarium.
+ MS s.n., Fragmenta Gregoriana.
   (These manuscripts have been dispersed since 1936.)

SAN JUAN DE VILATORRADA
+ MS s.n., Cantorale, 1352 (see Anglès, p. 125, n. 1).

SAN LORENZO DEL ESCORIAL
a-III-1, Breviarium, saec. xiv.
a-III-2, Breviarium Dominicanum, saec. xv.
a-III-3, Breviarium Dominicanum, saec. xv.
b-III-20, Brev. Brixiense, saec. xiv.
B-II-2, Diurnale, saec. xvi.
e-IV-10, Brev. monasterii Pinnatensis (St. Juan de la Peña), saec. xiv; on fol. 21^v, the "Judicii signum" as a response to the eighth lesson.
g-IV-29, Brev. monasticum, saec. xiv; on fol. 19^v, the "Judicii signum".
g-IV-40, Brev. Ordinis Sancti Hieronymi, saec. xv.
H-III-11, Breviarium, saec. xii.
i-III-16, Breviarium, saec. xii.
I-II-8, Missale, saec. xiii.
I-II-10, Avicenna et Missale, saec. xii.
I-II-12, Evangelarium, saec. xiv.
I-II-13, Evangelarium, saec. xiv.

I-II-14, Evangelarium, saec. xiv.
I-II-17, Missale, saec. xiv.
L-III-3, Brev. Benedictinum, saec. xii.
P-II-1, Brev. sec. ordinem Sancti Benedicti Vallisoletani, saec. xiv.
P-III-12, Breviarium, saec. xiv.
*P-III-13, Brev. Parisiense, saec. xv.
P-III-14, Brev. Caesaraugustinum (Zaragoza), saec. xiv; on fol. 77^v, the "Judicii signum".
Q-III-3, Liber caeremoniarum Monasterii Montiserrati.
R-III-17, Miss. (frag.), saec. xiii.
T-I-14, Consuetudines cuiusdam monasterii, saec. xi.
Vitr. 2, Liber Missarum (1568).
Vitr. 3, Breviarium, saec. xv.

SAN MILLÁN DE LA COGOLLA
MS s.n., Ceremonial y Misal, saec. xiv.
MS s.n., Ceremonias antiguas de la orden.

SANTIAGO DE COMPOSTELLA
Cathedral
+ *MS s.n., Single folio with Easter play, saec. xii.
*MS s.n., Brev. Compostellanum, saec. xv.

SEGOVIA
Cathedral
MS s.n., Consuetudines eccl. Segobiensis (1484).
MS s.n., Flemish Missal.
MS s.n., Libro de ceremonias.
MS s.n., Fragmentos Gregorianos, saec. xii-xiv.
*MS s.n., Las Buenas y loables costumbres . . . de Granada.

SEO DE URGEL
Cathedral
*MS s.n., Consueta eccl. Urgellensis, saec. xv.
MS s.n., Miss. eccl. Urgellensis, saec. xiv.

SEVILLA
This is the one city of importance whose libraries I did not see. There are several medieval missals, breviaries, a *consueta* of 1552, and other liturgical manuscripts at the cathedral library. However Villanueva saw all these manuscripts, and he does not speak of any liturgical play from Seville. His notes on the liturgy of Seville are found in the manuscript at the Real Academia de la Historia.

SIGÜENZA
Cathedral
MS 17, Tractatus de Officio Divino, saec. xiii.
MS 29, Breviarium, saec. xii.
MS 91, Breviarium, saec. xii.

SILOS
+ MS 9, Antiph. Monasticum (San Salvador de Celanova), saec. xii-xiii.
+ MS 14, Intonarius sec. cons. monasterii Sancti Benedicti Vallisoletani, saec. xv.
+ MS 15, Ceremonial (St. Benedict of Valladolid), saec. xv.
+ MS 16, Antiph. (San Millán?), saec. xv.
+ MS 42, Ceremonial (St. Benedict of Valladolid), saec. xvi.
+ MS 43, Ceremonial, saec. xvi.

Solsona

Cathedral

+MS s.n., Brev. Celsonum (1514).
+MS s.n., Consueta eccl. Celsonae, saec. xv (by Pedro Juan de Lobera).
+MS s.n., Consueta eccl. Celsonae, saec. xvi.

These manuscripts are mentioned by Villanueva, IX, 58-59. The chapter library has not as yet been fully reorganized since the Civil war, and consequently the cathedral archivist was not able to tell me if these manuscripts are still extant.

Tarazona

Cathedral

MS 31, Brev. Tirasonense.
MS 32, Miss. Tirasonense.
MS 80, Miss. Tirasonense.
MS 123, Miss. Tirasonense.
MS 133, Miss. (1461).
MS 135, Missale.
+MS ?, Brev. Calagurritanum (Calahorra).
+MS ?, Brev. Tirasonense.

Tarragona

Archivo Capitular

MS s.n., Missale, saec. xv.
MS s.n., Brev. Tarraconense, saec. xiv.
MS s.n., Rituale, saec. xvi.

Archivo Histórico Archidiocesano

MS 80, Breviarium (Valls), saec. xv.
MS 87, Brev. sec. ordinem Beati Rufi (from Valls), saec. xv; has the "Judicii signum".

Other Tarragona manuscripts, recently mentioned by various writers, could not be located when I was at Tarragona. Anglès (p. 441) speaks of a fourteenth century troper at the second library mentioned above; Gudiol (*Arqueología*) refers to a Tarragona *consueta*, 220 × 145 mm., 156 fol., written in 1441, and a *processionale* of the same century; he consulted the former in the capitular library, and the latter in the diocesan museum. Cordiolani (*Hispania Sacra*, V, 1952, 132) also talks of the *consueta*.

Toledo

Biblioteca Provincial

*MS 154, Ceremonias particulares de la Iglesia de Toledo, saec. xviii.

Cathedral

33.4, Antiph., saec. xiii-xiv.
33.5, Breviarium, saec. xii-xiii.
33.6, Brev. Toletanum, saec. xiv; all the Toledo breviaries with the feast of Christmas have the Sibylline verses.
33.7, Brev. Toletanum, saec. xv.
33.8, Diurnale Toletanum.
33.10 to 33.12, Breviaria.
33.17, Brev. Benedictinum (Italian).
33.20, Lectionarium.
33.24, Antiph. Dominicanum.
34.2, Breviarium, saec. xv.
35.9, Breviarium, saec. xi-xii.
35.10, Breviarium, saec. xii.
37.1, Brev. Franciscanum, saec. xiii.

37.2, Brev. eccl. Augustinae (Italian), saec. xv.
37.4, Brev. Franciscanum, saec. xv.
37.6, Ceremoniale Dominicanum, saec. xiv.
37.10, Brev. Dominicanum, saec. xv.
37.11, Oficios varios.
37.12, Liber Missae.
37.14, Benedictionale.
37.15, Missale.
37.16, Missale.
37.17, Evangelarium.
37.18 to 37.27, Toledo Missals, saec. xii-xv.
38.1, Capitularium et Antiph., saec. xiv.
38.25, Constitutiones Toletanae, saec. xiv.
39.3, Missale, saec. xiv.
+ 39.6, De Officio Divino, saec. xiii.
*42.29, J. Chaves de Arcayos, Toledo Ceremonial, saec. xvi; an eighteenth century copy of Arcayos' manuscript is kept in the chapter room.
44.1, Antiph.-Responsoriale, saec. xi-xii.
44.2, Antiph.-Responsoriale, saec. xii.
44.3, Antiph. (Italian), saec. xiv.
44.6, Lect., saec. xiv (Sibyl).
44.7, Lect., saec. xiv.
44.12, lect., saec. xvi.
44.14, Lect., saec. xvi.
48.5, Lectionarium.
48.11 to 48.13, Lectionaria, saec. xiv.
48.14, Antiph.-Responsoriale.
48.15, Antiph.-Responsoriale.
52.4, Missale.
52.5, Missale.
52.14, Missale Toletanum.
MS s.n., Ceremonial. This manuscript was transferred to the library from the cathedral archives just before I left Toledo, so I did not have time to examine it. In the archives its shelf-mark had been I 3. C. 1. 1. The codex, which was very poorly written, appeared to be a fifteenth century copy of a twelfth century manuscript; it treated of liturgical ceremonies at least incidentally.

Tortosa

Cathedral

MS 10, 11, 29, 34, 41, 56, 82, 140, Missalia, saec. xi-xv.
MS 18, 95, 98, 111, 115, 116, 119, 120, 136, 145, Breviaria eccl. Dertusensis, saec. xiv-xv.
MS 22, Epistolarium, saec. xiv.
MS 44, Consueta eccl. Dertusensis, saec. xv.
MS 54, Epistolarium, saec. xv.
MS 92, 266, 267, 277, Proc. eccl. Dertusensis, saec. xiv.
MS 121, Lectionarium, saec. xiv.
MS 135, Troparium, saec. xii-xiii.
MS 232, Lectionarium.
MS 274bis, Brev. Dertusense, saec. xvi.

Ulla (Gerona)

Villanueva (XV, 22) refers to an important fifteenth century *consueta* which he consulted at Santa María de Ulla. Since this manuscript was very similar "en sus ritos con lo que va notado de la catedral de Gerona", it doubtless spoke of liturgical plays. This codex is no longer at the church of Santa María.

Valencia

Cathedral

MS 60, 75, 77, 85, 94, 105, 116, 125, 161, 164, 202, Valencian missals, saec. xv.
MS 76, Missale (English), saec. xv.
MS 81, Brev. Valentinum, saec. xv; Sibylline verses on fol. 29^v.
MS 189, Brev. Valentinum, saec. xvi.
MS 281, Breviarium (Cartagena), saec. xv; fol. 31^v: "Hic cantentur Versus Sibile, scilicet, unum ad unum".
*MS s.n., Consueta eccl. Valentinae, saec. xvi.

Iglesia de San Juan del Mercado

The archives of this church were destroyed in 1936.

University

MS 726 (olim 351), Breviarium, saec. xv.
MS 728 (olim 354), Antiph.-Hymnarium, saec. xv.
MS 783 (olim 861), Diurnale Benedictinum, saec. xv.
MS 815 (olim 1299), Antiph.-Psalterium, saec. xv.

Valladolid

Cathedral

There are no medieval liturgical munuscripts at the cathedral.

University

MS 206, Constituciones de la Iglesia de Usillos (1588).
MS 389, Constituciones de Santa Maria la Blanca de Toledo, saec. xvi-xvii.

Vich

Cathedral

MS 39 (Secunda Pars, fol. 35 *sqq.*), Ordinarium, saec. xi.
MS 68 to 78, Missalia, saec. xii-xv.
MS 80, 81, 82, 84, 86, 92, Breviaria eccl. Vicensis, saec. xiv-xv; all the Vich breviaries with the feast of Christmas have the Sibylline chant.
MS 83, Brev. Barcinonense, saec. xiv.
MS 85, Brev. Urgellense, saec. xv; has the the "Judicii signum".
*MS 105, Troparium-Prosarium, Ripoll, saec. xi-xii.
*MS 106, Troparium-Prosarium, Ripoll (?), saec. xii-xiii.
MS 116, Responsoriale, saec. xv.
*MS 117, Proc. Vicense, saec. xv.
*MS 118, Proc. monasterii Stagnensis, saec. xiv.
MS 123, Fragmenta cantoralium, saec. xi-xiii.
*MS 131, Consueta eccl. Urgellensis, saec. xii.
*MS 134, (Tertia Pars), Consueta eccl. Vicensis, saec. xiii.
MS 208, Miscellanea liturgica, saec. xv; on fol. 7^v-9, the Sibylline verses in Catalan.
MS 209, Missale Elnense, saec. xiv; on fol. 45, for the feast of Easter, a miniature in many colors depicts the three Marys at the sepulchre; they carry ointment jars, and an angel is showing them a small cross; the latter feature reveals the influence of the *Depositio* and the liturgical drama.
*MS 212, Consueta monasterii Sancti Johannis de Abbatissis, saec. xv.
*MS s.n., Consueta eccl. Vicensis, saec. xv.

Villanueva y Geltru (Barcelona)

Biblioteca Museo Balaguer

+MS 1, Missale, saec. xv.
+MS 2, Missale, saec. xv.
+MS 4, Breviarium Toletanum, saec. xiv.

ZARAGOZA
   Cathedral
   MS 14.13, Liber choralis, saec. xv.
   MS 17.89, Brev. Caesaraugustinum, saec. xv.
   MS 25.27, 25.28, 25.29, Missalia eccl. Caesaraugustinae, saec. xv.
   MS 30.115, 30.118, 30.119, Proc. eccl. Caesaraugustinae, saec. xv-xvi; all have the words and music for the Sibylline chant.
   MS 30.116, Liber choralis.
   MS 30.117, Liber choralis.
   MS 30.120, Liber choralis.
   *MS 31.22, Missale eccl. Beatae Mariae Majoris de Pilari (1422).
   +MS 31.54, Liber choralis, saec. xiv (could not be located).

   Iglesia de Nuestra Señora del Pilar
   *Arm. 2, Cax. 6, lig. 1, no. 18, manuscript containing various consuetas (Granada, Zaragoza, etc.), written about 1606.

INCUNABULA AND EARLY PRINTED BOOKS

BREVIARIES
   Avila, 1551.
   Badajoz, 1529.
   Braga, n.d.
   Burgo de Osma, 1487.
   Burgos, 1538, 1552, n.d.
   Calahorra, 1556.
   Ciudad Rodrigo, 1555.
   Córdoba, 1524.
   Coria, 1559.
   Cuenca, 1538, 1560.
   Elne, 1500.
   Evora, 1548.
   Granada, 1544.
   Huesca, 1505.
   Jaén, 1528.
   Lérida, 1479, 1571.
   Monte Aragón, 1521.
   Monastery of St. Benedict of Valladolid, 1499, 1542.
   Monastery of San Cugat, n.d.
   Orense, 1501, n.d.
   Oviedo, 1556.
   Palencia, n.d.
   Palma de Mallorca, 1506.
   Pamplona, 1551.
   Salamanca, 1541, 1562.
   *Santiago de Compostella, 1497, 1569; only the first of these two breviaries has the Easter play.
   Segovia, 1527.
   Segorbe, 1556.
   Seo de Urgel, 1487.
   Seville, 1521, n.d.
   Sigüenza, 1561.
   Tarazona, 1497, 1529.
   Tarragona, 1484.
   Toledo, 1483, 1492, 1506, 1551.
   Tortosa, 1547.

Tudela, 1554.
Valencia, 1533, 1556.
Vich, 1557.
Zamora, n.d.
Zaragoza, 1479, 1496, 1527, 1544, 1556.

MISSALS

Badajoz, 1529.
Barcelona, 1498, 1521, 1529.
Burgo de Osma, 1561.
Burgos, 1546.
Calahorra, 1554.
Córdoba, 1525, 1561.
Gerona, 1546, 1557.
Huesca, 1488.
León, 1504, 1526.
Monastery of St. Benedict of Valladolid, 1499.
Monte Aragón, 1557, 1559.
Orense, 1494.
Oviedo, 1556.
Palencia, n.d.
Pamplona, 1557.
Segovia, 1500.
Seo de Urgel, 1535.
Seville, 1520, 1537.
Tarragona, 1550.
*Toledo, 1483, 1499, 1500, 1512, 1517, 1539, 1550, 1551.
Valencia, 1492, 1509, 1528, 1533.
Zaragoza, 1498, 1522, 1552.
Zaragoza, (Nuestra Señora del Pilar, 1485.)

ORDINARIA SACRAMENTORUM

Barcelona, 1532, 1569.
Gerona, 1550.
Lérida, 1532.
Order of St. Jerome, 1527.
Palma de Mallorca, 1516.
Seo de Urgel, 1548.
Tarragona, 1530, 1550.
Toledo, 1519.
Tortosa, 1523, 1592.
Valencia, 1527.
Vich, 1547.

PROCESSIONALIA

Barcelona, 1522.
Monastery of St. Benedict of Valladolid, 1500, 1543.
Order of St. Jerome, n.d.
Seo de Urgel, 1527.
Toledo, 1562.

VARIA

Cantorale, Zaragoza, 1553.
Hores de la Setmana Sancta, Valencia, 1494.
*— , Valencia, 1533.
Intonarium Toletanum, 1515.
Passionarium et Matutinale, Siguenza, 1565.

BIBLIOGRAPHY

BOOKS AND ARTICLES

ABADAL Y DE VINYALS, Ramón de, *l'Abat Oliba, Bisbe de Vic, i la seva epoca*, Barcelona, 1948.
AEBISCHER, P., 'Un Ultime écho de la *Procession des Prophètes*: Le *Cant de la Sibilla* de la nuit de Noel à Majorque', *Mélanges d'histoire du théâtre du Moyen-Age et de la Renaissance offerts à Gustave Cohen*, Paris, 1950, pp. 261-270.
AGUILÓ Y FUSTÉR, M., *Catálogo de obras en lengua catalana impresas desde 1474 hasta 1860*, Madrid, 1923.
ALBERS, Bruno, *Consuetudines Monasticae*, 5 vols. Monte Cassino, 1900-12.
ALFONSO X, *Las Siete Partidas*, Paris, 1846.
ALVAREZ ESPINO, Romualdo, *Ensayo histórico-crítico del teatro español, desde su origen hasta nuestros días*, Cadiz, 1876.
ANDRÉ DE FLEURY, *Vita Gauzlini*, ed. by L. Deslisle, in *Mémoires de la Société archéologique de l'Orléanais*, II (1853), 257-322.
ANGLÈS, H., 'El Cant de la Sibila', *Vida Cristiana*, IV (1917), 65-72.
— and José Subirá, *Catálogo musical de la Biblioteca Nacional de Madrid*, 3 vols., Madrid, 1946-51.
— *El Còdex musical de las Huelgas*, 3 vols., Barcelona, 1931.
— 'Epístola farcida del martiri de Sant Esteve', *Vida Cristiana*, IX (1922), 69-75.
— 'Gregorian Chant', *The New Oxford History of Music*, II, London, 1954, 92-127.
— 'Latin Chant before St. Gregory', *The New Oxford History of Music*, II, London, 1954, 58-91.
— *La Música a Catalunya fins al segle XIII*, Barcelona, 1935.
— 'La Música conservada en la Biblioteca Colombina y en la Catedral de Sevilla', *Anuario Musical* (Instituto español de musicología), II (1947), 3-39.
— *La Música en la España de Fernando el Santo y de Alfonso el Sabio*, Madrid, 1943.
— *La Música española desde la edad media hasta nuestros días*, Barcelona, 1941.
— 'La Música medieval en Toledo hasta el siglo XI', *Spanische Forschungen*, VII (1937), 1-69.
— 'La Musique en Catalogne aux Xe et XIe siècles. L'Ecole de Ripoll', in *La Catalogne à l'époque romane*, Paris, 1932, pp. 157 sqq.
ANONYMOUS, *Que es canto gregoriano*, Barcelona, 1905.
ANSENJO BARBIERI, F., *Cancionero musical de los siglos XV y XVI*, Madrid, 1890.
ANZ, H., *Die lateinischen Magierspiele*, Leipzig, 1905.
AUBRUN, Charles, 'Sur les débuts du théâtre en Espagne', *Hommage à Ernest Martinenche*, Paris, 1937, pp. 293-314.
BAIST, G., review of K. A. M. Hartmann's Dissertation, *Uber das altspanische Dreikönigspiel*, in *Zeitschrift für Romanische Philologie*, IV (1880), 443-455.
BAIXAULI, Mariano, 'Las Obras musicales de San Francisco de Borja', *Razon y Fé*, IV (1902), 154-170, 273-283.
BARRERA Y LEIRADO, Cayetano de la, *Catálogo bibliográfico y biográfico del teatro antiguo español, desde sus origenes hasta mediados del siglo XVIII*, Madrid, 1860.
BEER, Rudolph, *Die Handschriften des Klosters Santa Maria de Ripoll*, 2 vols. Vienna, 1907-8.
BÖHME, M., *Das lateinische Weihnachtspiel*, Leipzig, 1917.
BOLEA Y SINTOS, Miguel, *Descripción histórica que de la catedral de Málaga hace su canónigo doctoral*, Málaga, 1894.
BONILLA Y SAN MARTÍN, Adolfo, *Las Bacantes, o del origen del teatro*, Madrid, 1921.
BROOKS, N. C., *The Sepulchre of Christ in Art and Liturgy*, Urbana, 1921.
BURGAS DARNÉS, Agusti, 'La Processó de Pasqua a Figueres', *Vida Cristiana*, IV (1917), 228-231.
CABROL, F., *Les Eglises de Jérusalem: la discipline et la liturgie au quatrième siècle*, Paris, 1895.
CAIMARI, A., 'L'Antiga pietat popular entorn de Nadal', *Analecta Sacra Tarraconensia*, XXVIII (1955), 199-223.
CALMETTE, Joseph, *La Question des Pyrénées et la Marche d'Espagne*, Paris, 1947.
CAÑETE, Miguel, *Discurso acerca del drama religioso español antes y depués de Lope de Vega*, Madrid, 1862; reprinted in *Memorias de la Real Academia española*, I (1870), 368-412.
CHAILLEY, Jacques, 'Un Document nouveau sur la danse ecclésiastique', *Acta musicologica*, XXI (1949).
— 'Le Drame liturgique médiéval à St-Martial de Limoges', *Revue de l'histoire du théâtre*, VII (1955), 127-144.

— 'Les Premiers troubadours et les *versus* de l'école d'Aquitaine', Romania, LXXVI (1955), 212-240.
CHAMBERS, Edmund, *English Literature at the Close of the Middle Ages*, Oxford, 1945.
— *The Medieval Stage*, 2 vols., Oxford, 1903.
CHEVALIER, Ulysse, *Repertorium Hymnologicum: Catalogue des chants, hymnes, proses, séquences, tropes en usage dans l'Eglise latine depuis les origines jusqu'à nos jours*, 6 vols., Louvain and Brussels, 1892-1920.
CIROT, G., 'Pour combler les lacunes de l'histoire du drame religieux en Espagne avant Gómez Manrique', *Bulletin Hispanique*, XLV (1943), 55-62.
COHEN, Gustave, *Histoire de la mise en scène dans le théâtre religieux français du moyen âge*, nouv. éd., Paris, 1951.
— *Le Théâtre en France au moyen âge: I, Le Théâtre religieux*, Paris, 1928.
COLLET, Henri, *Le Mysticisme musical espagnol au XVI siècle*, Paris, 1913.
CONDE DE CEDILLA (López de Ayala Alvarez de Toledo y del Hierro, Jierónimo), 'Toledo en el siglo XVI', *El discurso de recepción en la Real Academia de la Historia*, Madrid, 1901.
CONSTANS, Luis, 'Un "Dies Irae" en romance catalán del siglo XIII', *Cuadernos del Centro de Estudios Comarcales de Bañolas*, August, 1948, pp. 7-11.
CORBIN, Solange, 'Le *Cantus Sibyllae*: Origines et premiers textes', *Revue de musicologie*, XXXI (1952), 1-10.
— *Essai sur la musique religieuse portugaise au Moyen Age, 1100-1385*, Paris, 1952.
— 'L'Office portugais de la sépulture du Christ', *Revue de musicologie*, XXVI (1947), 63-71.
— 'Le Manuscrit 201 d'Orléans, drames liturgiques dits de Fleury', *Romania*, LXXIV (1953), 1-43.
CORDIOLANI, A., 'Inventario de los manuscritos de cómputo eclesiástico conservados en las bibliotecas de Cataluña', *Hispania Sacra*, IV (1951), 359-384, V (1952), 121-164.
CORTÉS, N. A., *El Teatro en Valladolid*, Madrid, 1923.
COSTA I BARRÀS, José Domingo, *Obras*, V, 1866.
COTARELO Y MORI, Emilio, *Teatro español anterior a Lope de Vega. Catálogo de obras dramáticas impresas pero no conocidas hasta el presente, con un apéndice sobre algunas piezas raras o no conocidas de los antiquos teatros francés é italiano*, Madrid, 1902.
COUSSEMAKER, E. de, *Drames liturgiques du Moyen Âge*, Rennes, 1860.
— *Histoire de l'harmonie au Moyen Âge*, Paris, 1852.
CRAIG, Hardin, *English Religious Drama of the Middle Ages*, Oxford, 1955.
CRAWFORD, J. P., 'A Note on the Boy-Bishop in Spain', *Romanic Review*, XII (1921), 146-154.
— *Spanish Drama before Lope de Vega*, rev. ed., University of Pennsylvania Press, 1937.
CREIZENACH, W., *Geschichte des neuren Dramas*, 2d ed., 3 vols., Halle, 1911-23.
DAVID, Pierre, *Etudes historiques sur la Galice et le Portugal du VI au XIIe siècle*, Paris, 1947.
DE BARTHOLOMAEIS, V., *Le Origini della poesia drammatica italiana*, Bologna, [1924].
DEFOURNEAUX, Marcelin, *Les Français en Espagne aux XIe et XIIe siècles*, Paris, 1949.
DEL ARCO, Ricardo, 'El Archivo de la Catedral de Huesca', *Revista de Archivos, Bibliotecas, y Museos*, XXV, (1911), 294-301, 453-462.
— 'Misterios, autos sacramentales y otras fiestas en la Catedral de Huesca', *Revista de Archivos, Bibliotecas, y Museos*, XLI (1920), 263-274.
DELISLE, L., 'Un Livre de choeur normano-sicilien conservé en Espagne', *Journal des Savants*, 1908, 42-49.
DE VITO, Maria, *L'Origine del dramma liturgico (Biblioteca della Rassegna, vol. xxi)*, 1938.
D'OLWER, Nicolas, 'La Littérature latine au Xe siècle', in *La Catalogne à l'époque romane*, Paris, 1932.
DIAZ DE ESCOBAR, N., *Anales del teatro español anteriores al año 1550*, Madrid, 1910.
— and F. DE LA VEGA, *Historia del teatro español*, 2 vols., Barcelona, 1924.
DIAZ DE ESCOVER, N., *El Teatro en Málaga*, Málaga, 1896.
DIAZ-PLAJA, Guillermo, ed. *Historia general de las literaturas hispánicas: I, Desde los orígenes hasta 1400*, Barcelona, 1949.
DREVES, G. M., and C. BLUME, ed., *Analecta Hymnica Medii Aevi*, Leipzig, 1886 sqq.
DU MÉRIL, E., *Origines latines du théâtre moderne*, Paris, 1849.
DURÁN GUDIOL, A., *Los Manuscritos de la catedral de Huesca*, Huesca, 1953; also published in *Argensola*, IV (1953), 293-322.

DURANDUS, G., *Rationale Diuinorum Officiorum*, Strassburg, 1486.
DÜRRE, K., *Die Mercatorszene im lateinisch-liturgischen, altdeutschen und altfranzösischen religiösen Drama*, Göttingen, 1915.
España Sagrada, 51 vols., Madrid, 1747-1879.
ESTEVE BARBA, F., *Catálogo de la colección de manuscritos Borbon-Lorenzana*, Madrid, 1942.
EVANS, J., *Monastic Life at Cluny, 910-1157*, Oxford, 1931.
FÉROTIN, Marius, *Histoire de l'Abbaye de Silos*, Paris, 1897.
FERRERES, Juan, *El Breviario y las nuevas rúbricas*, 2 vols., Madrid, 1914.
FISCHER, L., 'Sahagún und Toledo', *Spanische Forschungen der Görresgesellschaft*. Erste Reihe, III (1931), 286 sqq.
FITZMAURICE-KELLY, J., *A New History of Spanish Literature*, Oxford, 1926.
FOCILLON, Henri, *L'An Mil*, Paris, 1952.
FORD, Jeremiah, *Old Spanish Readings*, New York, 1911.
FRANK, Grace, Introduction. 'Introduction to a Study of the Medieval French Drama', in *Essays and Studies in Honor of Carleton Brown*, New York, 1940.
— *The Medieval French Drama*, Oxford, 1954.
FRERE, W. H., ed. *The Winchester Troper*, London, 1894.
FRONING, R., *Das Drama des Mittelalters*, 3 vols., Stuttgart, 1891.
GARCÍA SORIANO, Justo, *El Teatro universitario y humanístico en España. Estudios sobre el origen de nuestro arte dramático*, Toledo, 1945.
GAUTIER, L., *Histoire de la poésie liturgique au Moyen Age: les Tropes*, Paris, 1886.
GÉROLD, Th., 'Les Drames liturgiques médiévaux en Catalogne', *Revue d'histoire et de philologie religieuse*, 16e année (1936), 429-444.
GILLET, Joseph, 'The *Memorias* of Felipe Fernández Vallejo and the History of the Early Spanish Drama', in *Essays and Studies in Honor of Carleton Brown*, New York, 1940, 264-280.
— 'Danza del Santísimo Nacimiento de Suarez de Robles', *PMLA*, XLIII (1928), 614-634.
GIRBAL, Enrich Claudio, 'Noticias de las antiguas representaciones litúrgicas o autos sacramentales en Gerona', *Revista de Gerona*, V (1881), 182-191.
— 'El Obispillo de Inocentes', *Revista de Gerona*, V (1881), 459-464.
GONZÁLEZ, Raimundo, 'El Teatro religioso en la Edad Media', *Cuidad de Dios*, CXV (1918), 177-185, CXVI (1918), 5-14, CXVII (1919), 89-100.
GONZÁLEZ PALENCIA, A., See Hurtado, J., y González Palencia, A.
GRAF, Arturo, *Studii Drammatici*, Turin, 1878.
GRIERA, A., 'Liturgia popular', *Butlleti de dialectología catalana*, XVIII (1930), 1-98.
GUDIOL, J., *Arqueología litúrgica de la provincia eclesiástica tarragonina*, MS at the Vich chapter library.
— 'El Bispeto', *Lectura popular*, XIV, 355-366.
— 'Catalèg dels manuscrits de Vich', *Butlleti de la Biblioteca de Catalunya*, VI (1920-22), 50-97, VII (1923-27), 60-154, VIII (1928-32), 46-120.
— 'El Drama sagrat a Catalunya', *Gazeta de Vich*, 1924, Nos. 2775-2777.
— 'Els entremesos o oratoris pasquals', *Vida Cristiana*, I (1914), 237-240.
— 'L'evolució litúrgica en la provincia eclesiastica tarragonina', *Vida Cristiana*, XII (1925), 273-282.
— 'La festa de Nadal en els segles XI i XII', *Vida Cristiana*, III (1916), 88-92.
HALLINGER, Kassius, *Gorze-Kluny*, 2 vols., Rome, 1950-51.
HANDSCHIN, J., 'Trope, Sequence, and Conductus', in *The New Oxford History of Music*, II, London, 1954, 128-174.
HARTL, Eduard, *Das Drama des Mittelalters, sein Wesen und sein Werden*, 2 vols., Leipzig, 1937.
HARTMANN, K. A. M. *Uber das altspanische Dreikönigspiel*, Beutzen, 1879.
HAZAÑAS Y LA RUA, Joaquín, *Discurso leido en la Universidad de Sevilla*, Seville, 1907.
HURTADO, J. Y GONZÁLEZ PALENCIA, A., *Historia de la literatura española*, 6th ed., Madrid, 1949.
JIMENEZ DE RADA, Rodrigo, *Rerum in Hispania gestarum chronicon*, ed. Andreas Schottius, S. J., in *Hispaniae Illustratae Scriptores*, II, Frankfort, 1603-8, pp. 25-195.
KEHR, P., *Das Papsttum und der katalanische Prinzipat bis zur Vereinigung mit Aragon*, Berlin, 1926.
KING, Georgiana Goddard, *The Play of the Sibyl Cassandra*, Bryn Mawr, 1921.
LAFUENTE V., *Historia eclesiástica de España*, 4 vols., Barcelona, 1855-59.
LAMARCA, Luis, *El Teatro en Valencia desde su origen hasta nuestros días*, Valencia, 1840.

Lange, C., *Programm*. 'Die lateinischen Osterfeiern' in *Jahresbericht über die Realschule erster Ordnung in Halberstadt*, Programm no. 223, Halberstadt, 1881, pp. 1-35.
— *Die lateinischen Osterfeiern*, Munich, 1887.
Le Lorrain, J., *De l'ancienne coutume de prier debout*, 2 vols., Liège, 1700.
Le Verdier, Pierre, ed. *Mystère de l'Incarnation et Nativité de Notre Seigneur et Rédempteur Jésus-Christ représenté à Rouen en 1474*, Rouen, 1884-86.
Llabres, G., 'Repertorio de *Consuetas* representadas en las iglesias de Mallorca', *Revista de Archivos, Bibliotecas, y Museos*, V (1901), 920-927.
Lopez, Atanasio, *Estudios Critico-históricos de Galicia*, Santiago de Compostella, 1916.
— *La Imprenta en Galicia, siglos XV-XVIII*, Madrid, 1953.
Lopez Ferreiro, Antonio, *Galicia en el último tercio del siglo XV*, 2d ed., La Coruña, 1896.
— *Historia de la Iglesia Catedral de Santiago*, 11 vols., 1898-1909.
Lopez Santos, 'Autos del Nacimiento leoneses', *Archivos leoneses*, I (julio-diciembre, 1947), 7-32.
Lucas Fernández, *Farsas y églogas*, Madrid, 1867.
Martène, E., *De Antiquis Ecclesiae Ritibus*, 4 vols., Venice, 1788.
Massó Torrents, J., *Repertori de l'antiga literatura catalana*, Barcelona, 1932.
Mellot, Jean, 'A Propos du théâtre liturgique de Bourges', *Mélanges d'histoire du théâtre du Moyen-Age et de la Renaissance offerts à Gustave Cohen*, Paris, 1950, pp. 193-198.
Menéndez-Pidal, R., *Cantar de Mío Cid*, I, Madrid, 1908.
— ed. 'Misterio de los Reyes Magos', *Revista de archivos y museos*, Epoca 3, IV (1900).
Mérimée, Henri, *L'Art dramatique à Valencia*, etc., Toulouse, 1913.
Meyer, W., *Fragmenta Burana*, Berlin, 1901.
Migne, J. P., ed. *Patrologiae Cursus Completus: Series Graeca*, 161 vols., Paris, 1857-66.
Migne, J. P., ed. *Patrologiae Cursus Completus: Patrologia Latina*, 221 vols., Paris, 1844-64.
Milá i Fontanals, 'Orígenes del teatro catalán', *Obras Completas*, VI, Barcelona, 1895.
Milchsack, G., *Die Oster- und Passionsspiele. I, Die lateinischen Osterfeiern*, Wolfenbüttel, 1880.
Miralles Sbert, J., *Catálogo del Archivo Capitular de Mallorca*, 3 vols., Palma, Madrid, 1942-3.
Miret i Sans, Joaquim, 'El Sermó de Sant Nicolau', *Revue hispanique*, XXVIII (1913), 390-395.
Moléon, Le Sieur de (Jean Baptiste Le Brun des Marettes), *Voyages liturgiques en France*, Paris, 1718.
Mone, F. J., *Schauspiele des Mittelalters*, 2 vols., Karlsruhe, 1846.
Moraleda y Esteban, Juan, *Los Seises de la Catedral de Toledo. Antiguedad, Vestidos, Música y Danza*, Toledo, 1911.
Moratín, L., *Orígenes del teatro español*, Paris, 1838.
Morel-Fatio, A., and Leo Rouannet, *Le Théâtre espagnol*, Paris, 1900.
Neri, F., 'Le Tradizioni italiane della Sibilla', *Studi Medievali*, IV (1912-13), 213-230.
Noguera, A., *Memoria sobre los cantos, bailes y tocatas populares de la isla de Mallorca*, Palma, 1894.
Nuñez Marquez, *Guía de la S. I. Catedral del Burgo de Osma y Breve Historia del Obispado de Osma*, 1949.
Ortíz de Zúñiga, Diego, *Anales eclesiásticos y seculares de la muy noble y muy leal ciudad de Sevilla*, Madrid, 1677.
Parker, Alexander, 'Notes on the Religious Drama in Medieval Spain and the Origins of the Auto Sacramental', *Modern Language Review*, XXX (1935), 170-182.
Patt, Beatrice, *The Development of the Christmas Play in Spain from the Origins to Lope de Vega*, Bryn Mawr doctoral dissertation (unpublished), 1945.
Pedrell, Felipe, *Cancionero musical popular español*, 2d ed., Barcelona, 1922.
Pedrell, Felipe, *La Festa d'Elche, ou le drame lyrique liturgique espagnole*, Paris, 1906.
Pérez, Florentino, 'San Gregorio VII y la liturgia española', *Liturgia*, III (1948), 105-113, 323-330.
Pérez de Urbel, Justo, *Los Monjes españoles en la Edad Media*, 2 vols., Madrid, 1933-34.
— 'La Regla benedictina y la liturgia española', *Liturgia*, II (1947), 379-389.
— *Sancho el Mayor de Navarra*, Madrid, 1950.
Prado, Germán, 'O Antiguo melodrama pascoal', *Nos*, IX (1932), 78-80.
Pujades, Géronimo, *Crónica universal del Principado de Cataluña, escrita a principios del siglo XVII*, Barcelona, 1830.
Pujol, F., 'El Cant de la Sibilla', *Butlleti del Centre excursionista de Catalunya*, XXIII (1918).

QUADRADO, José, 'Un misterio catalán del siglo xiv', *La Unidad católica*, Palma de Mallorca, 1871; reprinted in Milá y Fontanals, *Obras completas*, VI, 315-323.
RENNERT, Hugo Albert, *The Spanish Stage in the Time of Lope de Vega*, New York, 1909.
REYNIER, G., 'Le Drame religieux en Espagne', *Revue de Paris*, II (1900), 821-872.
RIAÑO, Juan, *Critical and Bibliographical Notes on Early Spanish Music*, London, 1887.
RIPOLLÈS PÉREZ, Vicente, *El Drama Litúrgico*, Valencia, 1928.
ROCHER, Charles, *Les Rapports de l'église du Puy avec la ville de Gérone en Espagne*, Le Puy, 1878.
RODRÍGUEZ, Raimundo, 'El Canto de la Sibila en la Catedral de León', *Archivos leoneses*, I (1947), 9-29.
ROJO, Casiano, and Germán PRADO, *El Canto Mozárabe*, Barcelona, 1929.
ROKSETH, Yvonne, '*Danses cléricales au XIIIe siècle*', in *Mélanges des publications de la Faculté des Lettres de Strasbourg*, Paris, 1947.
ROSA Y LOPEZ, Simón de la, *Los Seises de la Catedral de Sevilla*, Seville, 1904.
ROY, Emile, *Le Mystère de la Passion en France du XIVe au XVIe siècle*, Paris, 1903.
RUIZ I CALONJA, Juan, *Historia de la literatura catalana*, Barcelona, 1954.
RUIZ DE LIHORY, J., *La Música en Valencia, diccionario biográfico y crítico*, Valencia, 1903.
SABLAYROLLES, M., 'A la recherche des manuscrits grégoriens espagnols, *Iter Hispanicum*', in *Sammelbände der Internationalen Musikgesellschaft*, XIII (1911-12), 205-247, 401-432, 509-531.
SACHS, Curt, *Eine Weltgeschichte des Tanzes*, Berlin, 1938; tr. by L. Kerr, *Histoire de la Danse*, Paris, 1938.
SAGRISTÁ, Emilio, *El Enigma de la capilla de la Trinidad*, Castellón de la Plana, 1952.
SANCHEZ ARJONA, José, *Noticias referentes a los anales del teatro en Sevilla, desde Lope de Rueda hasta fines del siglo XVII*, Seville, 1898.
— *El Teatro en Sevilla en los siglos xvi-xvii*, Madrid, 1887.
SANCHIS Y SIVERA, José, *La Catedral de Valencia, guía histórica y artística*, Valencia, 1909.
SANZ Y DIAZ, José, *La Navidad en la literatura nacional del siglo XII al XX*, Barcelona, 1941.
SCHACK, Adolf Friedrich von, *Geschichte der dramatischen Literatur und Kunst in Spanien*, 3 vols., Berlin, 1845-46.
SCHMIDT, Erich, *Die Darstellung des spanischen Dramas vor Lope de Vega*, Berlin, 1935.
SEPET, Marius, *Le Drame chrétien au Moyen Age*, Paris, 1878.
— *Origines catholiques du théâtre moderne*, Paris, [1901].
— *Les Prophètes du Christ*, Paris, 1878.
SERDÁ, Luis, 'Inicios de la liturgia romana en la Cataluña vieja', *Hispania Sacra*, VIII (1955), 387-394.
SERÍS, Homero, *Manual de bibliografía de la literatura española*, Syracuse, 1948.
SERRANO, Luciano, 'Historia de la música de Toledo', *Revista de Archivos, Bibliotecas, y Museos*, X (1907), 219-243.
SERRANO, Luciano, *El Obispado de Burgos y Castilla primativa*, 3 vols., Madrid, 1935.
SHOEMAKER, W. H., *The Multiple Stage in Spain during the Fifteeth and Sixteenth Centuries*, Princeton, 1935.
SIMON-DIAZ, José, *Bibliografía de la literatura hispánica*, 3 vols., Madrid, 1951.
STUDER, Paul, ed. *Le Mystère d'Adam*, Manchester, 1918.
STURDEVANT, Winifred, *The Misterio de los Reyes Magos: Its Position in the Development of the Medieval Legend of the Three Kings* (*John Hopkins Studies in Romance Literatures and Languages*, X), Baltimore and Paris, 1927.
SUBIRÁ, José, *Historia de la música teatral en España*, Madrid, 1945.
THOMAS, L. P., ed. *Le Sponsus*, Paris, 1951.
THOMAS-BOURGEOIS, C. A., 'Le Personnage de la Sybille et la légende de l'Ara Coeli dans une Nativité wallonne', *Revue belge de philologie et d'histoire*, XVIII (1939), 883-912.
TREND, J. B., *The Music of Spanish History to 1600*, Oxford, 1926.
UBIETO ARTETA, Antonio, 'La Introducción del rito romano en Aragón y Navarra', *Hispania Sacra*, I, (1948), 299-324.
VALBUENA PRAT, Angel, *Historia de la literatura española*, 2 vols., 2nd ed., Barcelona, 1946.
— *Literatura dramática española*, Barcelona, 1930.
VALOUS, Guy de, *Le Monachisme clunisien des origines au XVe siècle*, Paris, 1935.
— 'Les Monastères et la pénétration française en Espagne du XIe au XIIIe siècle', *Revue Mabillon*, XXX (1940), 77-97.

VICENTE, Gil, *Obras completas*, Lisbon, 1942-44.
VILLA-AMIL Y CASTRO, *Catálogo de los manuscritos existentes en la biblioteca del Noviciado de la Universidad Central, I, Códices*, Madrid, 1878.
VILLANUEVA, J., *Viage literario a las Iglesias de España*, 22 vols., Madrid, 1803-52.
VIVES, JOSÉ, 'Manuscritos hispánicos en bibliotecas extranjeras', *Hispania Sacra*, II (1949), 449-457.
WARDROPPER, Bruce, *Introducción al teatro religioso del Siglo de Oro (La evolución del auto sacramental: 1500-1648)*, Madrid, 1953.
WRIGHT, Edith, *The Dissemination of the Liturgical Drama in France*, Bryn Mawr, 1936.
YOUNG, Karl, *The Drama of the Medieval Church*, 2 vols., Oxford, 1933.
— 'The Harrowing of Hell in Liturgical Drama', in *Transactions of the Wisconsin Academy of Sciences, Arts, and Letters*, XVI, part II (1909), 889-947.
— 'Officium Pastorum: A Study of the Dramatic Developments within the Liturgy of Christmas', in *Transactions of the Wisconsin Academy of Sciences, Arts, and Letters*, XVII, part I (1912), 299-396.
— 'Ordo Prophetarum', in *Transactions of the Wisconsin Academy of Sciences, Arts, and Letters*, XX (1922), 1-82.
— 'The Origin of the Easter Play', *Publications of the Modern Language Association of America*, XXIX (1914), 1-58.
— 'Some Texts of Liturgical Plays', *Publications of the Modern Language Association of America*, XXIV (1909), 294-331.

INDEX

ABBREVIATIONS: *Proc. Proph.* Processio Prophetarum; *Q. q.* Quem quaeritis; *Rep.* Repraesentatio; *V. S.* Visitatio Sepulchri.
Adam and Eve, 72, 144-5.
Adam novus (liturgical text), 83, 84.
Adoration of the Cross, 8.
Agen, 25.
Ager, 87, 137.
Al iorn del iudici (Sibylline chant in vernacular), 115, 121, 161.
Alba, Duke of, 145.
Alexander II, Pope, 23, 26.
Alfonso VI, 23, 25.
Alfonso X, 30, 43, 73.
Alleluia, ad sepulchrum (antiphon), 53-6, 74-8, 81, 194.
Alleluia, resurrexit Dominus (antiphon), 11, 13.
Almunia, Andreas de, 76.
Alta concinite Christo voce (prose), 55.
Altar: as *praesepe* or *sepulchrum*, 16, 35, 36-7, 54-5, 60-2, 76-7, 84, 92, 93, 96-7, 115-6, 125, 130.
Amiens, 163.
Angels, 9, 12, 36-7, 39-42, 46, 49, 54-5, 58, 59-62, 63-4, 77, 79-81, 83-4, 85, 88-91, 99-100, 105-9, 111, 116, 124, 133-5, 140-3, 144-5, 173-5, 184-5, 190, 192.
Angers, 38.
Apothecary: in *V. S.*, 102-3.
Apothecary's wife and son: in *V.S.*, 102-3.
Apostles, 87, 100, 126, 138, 143, 157-60.
Appellatores: in *Proc. Proph.*, 122, 177-80.
Aquitaine, 22, 23, 34.
Aquitaine notation, 26-7.
Arab domination in medieval Spain, 20, 22, 25, 120, 139.
Aracoeli, 145-6, 162-4, 167.
Arcayos, Juan Chaves de, 31, 37-9, 45-6, 183-8, 192.
Arce, Juan de, 63.
Arles, 155-6.
Ascension trope, 96, 194.
Assumption: tropes and plays, 96-7, 137-8, 143, 145-6, 164, 167.
Auch, 23, 24, 25.
Auto de los Reyes Magos, 20, 30, 70-3.
Autpert, Ambroise, 112.
Avalos, Gaspar de, 63.

Avila, 65.
Ayala, Martin Perez de, 61.
Badajoz, 144.
Balaam: in *Proc. Proph.*, 177-80.
Baldasar, 95.
Barcelona: in metropolitan see of Narbonne, 26.
– Christmas play, 118.
– St. Stephen play, 117-8.
– dramatic Pentecost ceremony, 160.
– *V.S.*, 161.
– *sepulchrum*, 161-2.
– Sibyl plays, 162-4, 167.
– Boy Bishop, 191.
Barbastro, 25.
Baruch: in *Proc. Proph.*, 150.
Beards: worn in liturgical or religious drama, 17, 123, 176-7, 190.
Benedictines, 18, 37, 44; see also Cluny.
Benediktbeuern: liturgical drama at, 71, 82, 103, 122, 155.
Bernard, archbishop of Toledo, 23-5.
Bernard of Agen, 24.
Bethlehem: in Christmas play, 36, 112, 144-5.
Blessed Virgin Mary: in liturgical and religious drama, 58, 61, 96-7, 112-4, 135-8, 143, 144-5, 157-61, 163-4, 174-5.
Bobbio, 28.
Bourges, 28, 36-7, 191.
Boy Bishop, 65-6, 117, 130, 190-2, 195.
Breviary: papal reform of, 4.
– recording liturgical plays, 4.
– with twelve lessons, 52, 69-70.
Braga, 24, 25, 125.
Burgo de Osma, 25, 68, 144.
Burgos, 65, 166.
– Council of, 21.
Byzantine theater, 8.
Cadafalch, 102, 118, 158, 162; see also *tablado*.
Cain and Abel, 72.
Cambrai: liturgical drama, 35, 36, 48, 118-9.
Cañete, Manuel, 31.
Capitular statutes, 5.
Cape: worn by shepherds in Christmas play, 36-7.
Castissimum Mariae Virginis: lesson associated with Gerona Christmas play, 93, 110-4.

INDEX

Centurion: in Easter play, 87-91, 102-3.
Charlemagne, 21, 25-6.
Chaves de Arcayos, see Arcayos.
Child Jesus: represented in Christmas play, 115-6, 144-5.
Christmas Lauds, 15-7, 44, 47-9.
– France, 15-7, 34-9.
– Dax, 34.
– Cambrai, 35.
– Narbonne, 35.
– Pleinpied (Bourges), 36.
– Toledo, 31-4, 37-9, 44, 47-9.
– Valencia, 65.
– Coimbra, 69.
– Gerona, 115-6.
– Palma de Mallorca, 125-6.
Christmas plays and tropes, 14-7, 73.
– Rouen, 111, 173-5.
– Toledo, 31-4, 37-50, 106-4.
– Huesca, 56-7, 190.
– region of Vich, 91-4.
– Gerona, 110-7.
– Barcelona, 117-8, 162-4.
– Palma de Mallorca, 120-30.
– Valencia, 144-56.
– Tarragona, 160.
– province of León, 192.
– see also Christmas Lauds; *Officium Pastorum*; *Pastores, dicite*; *Processio Prophetarum*; *Quem quaeritis in praesepe*.
Christ: in Easter play, 13, 100.
– in *Peregrinus*, 85-6, 103, 172-3.
Christos Paschon: Greek religious play, 8.
Christus hodie surrexit (*verbeta*), 82-3.
Clouds: artificial in church, 144, 145, 157-8.
City of God (St. Augustine), 43, 165.
Clermont-Ferrand, 16, 35, 36, 38.
Cluny, 2, 4, 22 sqq., 28, 52, 67, 69-70, 73.
Coimbra, 25, 69.
Cologne, 38.
Colometa, 144-5, 157-60.
Compostella, 25, 52-6, 65, 66, 68, 75, 97.
Consueta: meaning, 4, 58, 63.
– recording liturgical plays, 2, 4.
– see also *ordinarium*, bibliography.
Coronet: worn by Sibyl, 41.
Corpus Christi, 87, 119, 126.
Creed play, 157-60.
Cross: used in *Depositio* and *Elevatio*, 8-10, 212.
Crown: see diadem.
Cuerpo de Sant (*villancico*), 186.
Cuxa, 28.
Dancing: in liturgical drama, 31-3, 38, 48, 185-6.
Dalmatius, bishop of Compostella, 25.
Daniel: in liturgical drama, 17, 123, 148, 176-7.

David, 123, 146, 149, 176, 178.
Dax: dramatic Lauds at, 34, 36, 48.
Depositio, 8-9, 12, 212.
Diadem or crown: worn in liturgical drama, 123, 129, 130, 138, 140, 142, 143, 145, 146, 157-8, 192.
Dic, impie Zabule, 86.
Directorium: see *ordinarium*.
Disciples: in *Peregrinus*, 85-6, 172-3.
Dove, 144, 157-60.
Drama: definition of, 6.
Dramatization at Mass, 109-10, 132-5.
Durandus, bishop of Mende, 109.
Eamus mirram emere: chant in Easter play, 78, 89, 91.
Earrings: worn by Sibyl, 41.
Easter Monday, 13, 84, 86, 109, 161, 172.
Easter play, 63, 68, 189: see also *Visitatio Sepulchri*.
Easter Tuesday, 133-5.
Einsiedeln, 155, 167.
Elche, 164.
Elevatio, 8-10, 59, 63-4, 142, 212.
Elizabeth: in *Proc. Proph.*, 123, 151, 176, 178.
Elne, 26, 191, 212.
Emmaus: in *Peregrinus*, 13, 86, 173.
Encina, Juan del, 145.
Entramés del bisbató, 130, 196.
Epiphany play, 15, 17, 68, 70-2, 94-5, 158, 175-6; see also Magi, *Ordo Stellae*.
Episcopellus: see Boy Bishop.
Etheria: see *Peregrinatio Etheriae*.
Eusebius of Caesarea, 43, 165.
Facta est cum angelo (antiphon): in Christmas play, 36.
Farsi, 136-7, 160.
Fasi, see *farsi*.
Fasos, see *farsi*.
Fernández Vallejo, see Vallejo.
Fishing, 102, 104.
Fleury, 13, 18-9, 27-8, 67-8, 70; see also St-Benoît-sur-Loire.
France, 2, 4, 8-29, 34-9, 41, 42, 52, 53, 56, 57, 71-3, 157-9, 164, 168-71; see also Cluny, Benedictines, Rouen, Laon, etc.
Fruttuaria: Easter play at, 12.
Gabriel, angel: in liturgical play (?), 112-4.
Galicia, 23, 52-6.
Gandía, V. S. at, 139-43.
Garland: worn in liturgical drama, 39-42, 60-2.
Gascony, 22.
Gaspar, 95.
Gauzlin, abbot of Fleury, 28.
Gerald, 22-3.
Gerbert, 27-8.
Gerona, 2, 97, 98-119.

INDEX

Gerona, in metropolitan see of Narbonne, 26.
– boy bishop, 65, 117, 191.
– *Q. q.* Easter trope, 98.
– *V.S.*, 99-103.
– *Rep. Centurionis*, 102-4.
– *Rep. Thomae*, 102-4.
– *Rep. Mariae Magdalenae*, 102-110.
– *Rep. Partus*, 110-16, 122.
– *Proc. Proph.*, 110-2, 114-5, 155-6.
– dramatic Christmas Lauds, 115-6.
– *Q. q.* Christmas trope, 116.
– *Rep. Sancti Stephani*, 117.
– Sibyl, 111, 115, 167.
– see also St. Felix of Gerona.
Ghent, 13.
Gloria in excelsis Deo (antiphon): in Christmas play, 37, 173.
Gloves: worn by Sibyl, 94.
Gómez Manrique, 184.
Good Friday, 135-7.
Granada, 59-63, 66, 68, 191.
Gregory VII, Pope, 23.
Guadix, 59-63, 66, 68, 135.
Habacuch: in *Proc. Proph.*, 150, 176, 178.
Harrowing of Hell, 142.
Hell, mouth of: stage effect in religious drama, 190.
Herod, 65, 95, 175-6, 191, 192.
Heu, quantus est noster dolor: sung in *V.S.*, 79, 82, 136.
Hodie cantandus est (trope), 92.
Holy Spirit, 144-5, 157-60.
Holy Thursday, 87.
Holy Week, 6-7, 135-7.
Hood: worn by shepherds in Christmas play, 36-7, 44, 182.
(H)*ora est, psallite* (antiphon), 74-5, 76, 77, 92-3, 96, 98.
Horseback: actors on, 64, 191, 192.
Host: used in *Deposito* and *Elevatio*, 8-10.
Huesca, 25, 56-8, 66, 68, 144, 189-90, 191.
Hugh of Cluny, 23, 25, 26.
Impersonation: required for drama, 6, 35.
Improperia, 86, 133-4.
Introit, 11.
Isaac, sacrifice of: dramatized, 119.
Isaias: in *Proc. Proph.*, 17, 146, 148, 156, 176-7.
Jeremias: in *Proc. Proph.*, 17, 146, 148, 156, 176-7.
Italy, 26.
Jaca, 57.
Jérome of Périgueux, 25.
Jerusalem, 144-5.
Jesum quem quaeritis (antiphon), 60-2.
Jeu d'Adam, 72.
Jews: in Easter play, 88.

Jiménez de Rada, 24, 25.
John, prior at St. Cecilia's of Montserrat and abbot of Fleury, 28.
Joseph: play of, 119.
Judicii signum, 42-3, 45-7, 64, 65, 93, 94, 111, 115, 120-1, 162, 165-7; see also Sibyl.
Juicio fuerte (Sibylline chant in vernacular), 40, 45, 181-5.
Klosterneuberg, 82.
Laon, 41, 122, 123, 129, 155, 176-80.
León, 23, 41, 64, 66, 68, 73, 94, 145, 167, 192.
Lérida, 25, 65, 159, 161, 191.
Liber consuetudinum, see *ordinarium*.
Lichtenthal, 105-9.
Lightning, 60.
Limoges: see St.Martial of, St. Augustine of.
Lisieux, 38
Liturgy: meaning, 6-7.
– at Jerusalem in fourth century, 7-8.
Lluchmaior, 125.
Lope de Loaysa, 37.
Lorsch, 28
Lyon, 165.
Magi, 95, 158, 175-6, 192.
Málaga, 65.
Malalas, Johannes, 163.
Manger: depicted or symbolized in Christmas play, 14-7; see also *praesepe*.
Manlleu (Augustinion monastery), 75.
Manuscripts: list of, see bibliography.
– medieval Spanish liturgical, 2, 4, 67, 73, 74.
Mary(s), the, 9, 12, 13.
– Compostella, 54-6.
– Zaragoza, 58.
– Granada and Guadix, 60-2.
– Vich, 77, 82-3, 89-91.
– Ripoll, 78-82.
– Seo de Urgel, 83-4.
– Gerona, 99-103.
– Palma de Mallorca, 130-2, 136-7, 138.
– Gandía, 140-3.
– Valencia, 144.
– Perpignan, 160.
– Barcelona, 161.
Mary Magdalen, 13.
– in *Peregrinus* at Ripoll, 85-6.
– in dramatized *Victimae paschali laudes* at Vich, 86.
– in vernacular Easter play, 89-90.
– at Palma de Mallorca, 132-5, 137.
– in Gerona Easter play, 102-10.
– at Valencia, 144.
– at Rouen, 173.
Mary of James: in Easter play, 89-90.
– in *Planctus*, 137.

Mary of Salome: in Easter play, 89-90.
Mask: see veil.
Mass: dramatic aspects of, 6.
— drama before, 11-2.
Maurice of Limoges, 25.
Melchior, 95.
Melódicos, 33.
Merchant: in Easter play, 13, 79, 81-2, 99-103.
Merchant's wife: In *V.S.*, 102-3.
Merodio, Christoval de, 64.
Miranda, Canon at Compostella, 54.
Moissac, 24, 28, 29.
Montserrat, 66.
Monumentum, 58, 63-4, 87, 90-1, 139-43; see also *sepulchrum*.
Moon: artificial in church plays, 144.
Moosburg, 159.
Moses: in *Proc. Proph.*, 17, 123, 149, 176, 178.
Mozarabic liturgical rite, 2, 20 sqq., 46, 70, 120, 139, 166.
Mozarabic script, 51.
Munster, 38.
Música de aves, 61.
Nabuchodonosor: in *Proc. Proph.*, 17, 115, 152, 177-9.
Nájera, 52.
Narbonne: metropolitan see of Catalonia, 26, 27.
— dramatic Christmas Lauds, 35, 48.
— Sibyl, 43.
— merchant in *V.S.*, 82.
Navarre, 28, 66; see also Sancho the Great.
Necklace: worn by Sibyl, 41.
Nevers, 175-6.
Notker Balbulus, 10.
Nuncium vobis (hymn): in Christmas play, 37.
Obstetrices, 111.
Octavian: in Sibyl play, 162-4, 167.
Odon of Champagne, 22.
Offertory of Mass, 157-8.
Officium Pastorum, 17, 36, 38, 93, 110-1; see also Christmas plays and tropes.
Officium Stellae: see *Ordo Stellae*, Epiphany play.
Ointment jars for Marys, 83-4, 140, 142.
Oliva, abbot of Ripoll, 22, 28.
Oratio Constantini (Eusebius), 43, 165.
Ordinarium: meaning, 4.
— recording liturgical plays, 4, 67-8.
— see also *consueta*, bibliography.
Ordo Prophetarum, 8, 17, 18, 41, 42, 44, 72, 154-6, 163, 165-7.
— Gerona cathedral, 110-2, 114-5.
— St. Felix church, Gerona, 115.
— Palma de Mallorca, 121-4, 138.
— Valencia, 147-56.

Ordo Stellae, 50, 110; see also Epiphany Play.
Orense, 65.
Origny-Sainte-Benoîte, 82.
Oy a nascido un çagal (villancico), 187.
Palencia, 47, 63-4, 65, 68, 93, 121, 144, 188, 191.
Palm: used in dramatic ceremonies, 118-9, 129, 137-8, 140, 142, 176.
Palm Sunday, 6, 142.
Palma de Mallorca, 42, 63, 65, 73, 120-38, 160.
— *Proc. Proph.*, 121-3.
— Sibyl, 120-5, 166-7.
— dramatic Christmas Lauds, 125-6.
— *Q.q.* Christmas trope, 126.
— St. Stephen ceremony, 126, 195.
— St. John ceremony, 128-30.
— boy bishop, 130, 191, 195.
— liturgical Easter plays, 130-5.
— *planctus*, 135-7.
Palometa, 144-5, 157-60.
Paradise, 144-5.
Parvus filius (antiphon): in Christmas play, 37.
Pamplona, 65.
Passion play, 119, 122.
Pastores, dicite, quidnam vidistis (antiphon), 15-7, 36, 65.
— Clermont-Ferrand, 16.
— Dax, 34.
— Cambrai, 35.
— Narbonne, 35.
— Bourges, 37.
— Toledo, 48-9.
— Orense, 65.
— Avila, 65.
— Burgos, 65.
— Palencia, 65.
— Compostella, 65.
— Palma de Mallorca, 125-6.
Pastourelle, 36.
Paterno, 22.
Pendant: worn by Sibyl, 41.
Pentecost, 143-4, 157-60.
Peregrinatio Etheriae, 7.
Perez de Ayala, see Ayala.
Peregrinus, 13, 68, 84-6, 103, 172-3.
Périgueux, 25.
Perpignan: Pentecost play, 157-9.
— *Planctus*, 160.
— boy bishop, 191.
Pierre, bishop of Palencia, 25.
Pierre of Agen, 25.
Pierre of Bourges, 25.
Planctus, 135-7, 160.
Pleinpied (Augustinian monastery), 36, 44.
Poitiers, 56, 75.
Portugal, 68-9, 73.

Praesepe, 14-7, 111, 173.
Prague, 82.
Processio Prophetarum: see *Ordo Prophetarum*.
Prophets, 145-6; see also *Ordo Prophetarum*, pseudo-Augustinian sermon *Contra Iudeos*.
Prosario, 27.
Provençal influence on drama, 87.
Pseudo-Augustinian sermon *Contra Iudeos*, 8, 17, 42, 46-7, 111-2, 114-5, 121-4, 146-56, 165-7; see also Quodvultdeus.
Quem quaeritis in praesepe: in Christmas play, 36, 174.
Quem quaeritis in praesepe: Christmas trope, 14-5.
– Huesca, 56-7, 66.
– Ripoll, 91.
– Vich, 92.
– Santa María del Estany, 92-3.
– San Juan de las Abadesas, 92.
– Seo de Urgel, 93.
– Gerona, 116.
– Palma de Mallorca, 126.
– Zaragoza, 190.
Quem quaeritis in sepulchro: Easter play, see *Visitatio Sepulchri*.
Quem quaeritis in sepulchro: Easter trope, 11, 14, 18, 60.
– Huesca, 57, 66.
– Zaragoza, 57-8, 66.
– Ripoll, 74-5.
– Vich, 76, 192.
– Estany, 77.
– Seo de Urgel, 78, 193.
– San Juan de las Abadesas, 78.
– Gerona, 98.
Quem sine matre (trope), 92.
Quem vates (trope), 92.
Quem vidistis, pastores (antiphon), 15-7, 32, 36, 37, 47, 182, 185.
Qui sunt hi sermones (antiphon): in *Peregrinus*, 85, 172.
Quis revolvet nobis lapidem (antiphon): in *V.S.*, 62, 141-2.
Quodvultdeus, 17, 165.
Raymond of Salvetat, 25.
Regularis Concordia of St. Ethelwold, 12-3, 18.
Reichenau, 27, 28.
Reims, 28.
Repraesentatio Partus, 110-6, 122.
Ripoll, 56, 97, 99, 101.
– medieval cultural and liturgical center, 27-9.
– Q.q. Easter trope, 74-5.
– Q.q. Easter play, 78-82, 91.
– *Peregrinus*, 84-6.
– Q.q. Christmas trope, 91.
– other tropes, 96, 194.

– Sibyl, 165-7.
– see also Oliva, abbot of Ripoll.
Rojas, Anton de, 61, 63.
Roman-French liturgical rite, 2, 20 sqq., 69.
Rouen, 8-9, 15, 17, 41, 43, 45, 110, 111, 114, 122, 123, 129, 155, 164, 172-5.
Rufinus of Aquileia, 159.
Sacristy account books, 5.
Sahagún, 23, 52.
St-Augustin de Limoges, 56.
St. Augustine, 17, 43, 45, 121-2, 165.
St.Benoît-sur-Loire, 11; see also Fleury.
St. Dominic of Silos, 52.
St. Ethelwold, 12-3, 54.
St. Felix of Gerona (collegiate church): Q.q. Easter trope, 98.
– *V.S.*, 101.
– dramatized *Victimae paschali laudes*, 110.
– *Proc. Proph.*, 115.
– *Rep. Partus*, 115.
– Q.q., Christmas trope, 116.
– boy bishop, 117.
St. Francis Borgia, 139-143.
St. Gall, 10, 11, 27-8, 142.
St-Germain-des-Prés, 28.
St. Isidore of Seville, 20.
St. John Baptist: trope, 96.
– in dramatic ceremony of St. John Evangelist, 128-9, 151-2, 176-9, 194.
St. John Evangelist, 13, 65, 96, 128-30, 136-8, 141-2, 149, 154, 159, 160.
St. Joseph, 112, 144-5.
St. Leander, 20.
St-Martial de Limoges, 11, 18, 19, 27-9, 56, 70, 75, 97, 114, 155, 158, 161, 165-7.
St. Nicholas: miracle plays, 18.
St-Orens of Auch, 23, 24, 25.
St. Peter, 13, 104, 137-8, 149, 159.
St-Ruf d'Avignon, 69.
St-Pons de Thomières, 25.
St. Stephen, 65, 96, 117-9, 126-8, 195.
St-Victor (Marseille), 28.
St. Thomas: play of, 102-4.
St. Vincent: play of, 57, 189.
Ste-Foy de Conques, 25.
Salamanca, 65.
Salerno, 154-6.
Salvetat, 23, 25.
San Andrés del Torn (Gerona), 160, 197.
San Benito of Valladolid, 68.
San Jan de Sahagún: see Sahagún.
San Juan de la Peña, 22.
San Juan de las Abadesas: Q.q. Easter trope, 78, 193.
– Q.q. Chrstimas trope, 92.
San Millán de la Cogolla, 52, 68.
San Pedro of Cardeña, 25, 52.

San Quirze de Pedret, 161.
Sancho the Great, 22.
Santa Ana (Barcelona), 162.
Santa Clara of Gandía: see Gandía.
Santa María del Estany, 97.
– Q.q. Easter trope, 77-8.
– Q.q. Christmas trope, 92-3.
– dramatic Assumption trope, 96-7.
Santa María del Mar (Barcelona), 162.
Santa Tecla, 160.
Santiago de Compostella: see Compostella.
Santo Domingo de Silos: see Silos.
Script, French, 25.
Segovia, 25, 59, 66, 68, 105.
Seises, 38, 39, 181-8.
Sens, 10.
Seo de Urgel: in metropolitan see of Narbonne, 26.
– tropers, 27.
– Q.q. Easter trope, 78, 193.
– Q.q. Easter play, 83.
– Q.q. Christmas trope, 93.
– Judicii signum, 94.
– boy bishop, 91.
Sepulchre (sepulchrum), 8-9, 16, 59-62.
– Vich, 83.
– Gerona, 99, 101, 111 (during Christmas play).
– Barcelona, 161-2.
– see also monumentum.
Seven Capital Sins, play of, 119.
Seville, 65, 68, 144.
Shakespeare, 95.
Shepherds, 14-7, 35-8, 65, 111.
– Toledo, 32-9, 44, 45, 48-9, 180-8.
– Dax, 34.
– Cambrai, 35.
– Narbonne, 35.
– Valencia, 145.
– Rouen, 173-5.
Shotgun, 60, 62.
Shrewsbury fragments, 73, 122.
Shroud, 9, 13, 59-61, 173.
Sibyl: Erythraean, 17, 37, 68, 160-1, 165-7.
– Toledo, 39-50, 66, 180-5.
– dress of, 41.
– León, 64, 66.
– Vich, 93.
– Gerona, 111, 115.
– Palma de Mallorca, 121-5.
– Lluchmaior, 125.
– Valencia, 146-56.
– Tarragona, 160.
– San Andrés del Torn (Gerona), 160-1, 197.
– Provence, 161.
– Lérida, 161.
– Santa Ana (Barcelona), 162.

– Rouen, 177-9.
– see also Judicii signum.
Sibyl: Tiburtine, 162-4, 167.
Sicily, 84.
Sigüenza, 24.
Silos, 51-2, 66, 70.
Simeon: in Proc. Proph., 151, 177-80.
Sponsus, 72, 161.
Staff: carried by shepherds in Christmas play, 36-7, 174.
Sulmona, 73, 122.
Sun: artificial in church, 144.
Surgit Christus cum trophaeo (prose): dramatized, 104-9.
Surrexit Dominus de sepulchro (antiphon), 13, 63.
Sword: used in Sibyl ceremony, 39-42, 46, 123, 181-5.
Tablado, 39, 41, 143, 144-5, 181, 189-90; see also cadafalch.
Tarragona, 160, 191.
Temptation of Christ: dramatized, 119.
Toledo: introduction of Roman-French rite, 23 sqq.
– liturgical drama, 30 sqq, 68.
– play of the shepherds, 31-9, 181-8, 189.
– Sibyl, 31, 39-49, 94, 124-5, 166-7, 181-5.
– dove on Pentecost, 144.
– boy bishop, 190-2.
– see also Bernard, archbishop of Toledo.
Toulouse, 136, 160.
Tours, 82, 84, 103, 114, 155.
Transeamus usque Bethlehem (antiphon): in Christmas play, 37, 174.
Trope, 10 sqq., 92, 96-7; see also Quem quaeritis in praesepe (Christmas trope), Quem quaeritis in sepulchro (Easter trope), troper.
Troper: recording liturgical plays, 4.
– not in Castile, 21.
– in Catalonia, 27.
– early at Seo de Urgel, 27.
Trumpet, 60, 62, 64, 102, 124, 195.
Tu solus peregrinus (antiphon): in Peregrinus, 85, 172.
Tutilo: author of tropes, 11, 92.
Ubi est Christus meus (antiphon), 97.
– Compostella, 53-6.
– Ripoll, 74-5, 81-2, 97.
– Vich, 76.
– Santa María del Estany, 77.
– Seo de Urgel, 83.
Ubi est mater nostri Domini (trope), 96-7.
Vala me Dios (villancico), 187.
Valencia, 25, 61, 139-56, 157, 164, 167.
Vallejo, 30-45, 183-8.
Veil or mask: worn in liturgical plays, 83-4, 125-6, 127-9, 130-2, 136, 143, 195.

Venice, 142.
Venite et videte locum (antiphon), 13, 140.
Venite, nolite timere vos: in *V.S.*, 83.
Verbeta, 82, 84, 99, 101, 102-3, 110, 111, 131.
Vercelli, 52.
Vernacular: in liturgical drama, 33, 37-40, 43, 45, 48-9, 121, 132-7, 146, 153, 181-8.
Vernacular religious drama, 70-3, 87-91, 138, 143, 145, 158, 167, 189-92.
Vich, 99, 103, 132, 134.
– in metropolitan see of Narbonne, 26.
– Roman-French rite, 27.
– Gerbert at, 28.
– under bishop Oliva, 28.
– boy bishop, 65.
– *Q.q.* Easter trope, 76, 192.
– *Q.q.* Easter play, 82-3, 194.
– *Peregrinus*, 86.
– *Q.q.* Christmas trope, 92.
– Sibyl, 93, 94, 167.
– St. Stephen play, 96.
– St. John's Day play, 96.
– boy bishop, 192.
Vich y Manrique, 125.
Victimae paschali laudes (sequence): dramatized, 172.
– Compostella, 55.
– Vich, 86, 91.
– Gerona, 99-101, 108-10.
– Palma de Mallorca, 130-2.
– Gandía, 141-2.
Vienne, France, 109.
Villancico, 44, 45, 184-8, 192.
Virgil: in *Proc. Proph.*, 17, 176, 179.
Visitatio Sepulchri, 12 sqq., 17, 18, 50, 67-8.
– Silos, 51-2.
– Compostella, 53-6.
– Granada, 59-63.
– Guadix, 59-63.
– Ripoll, 78-82.
– Vich, 82-3, 194.
– Seo de Urgel, 83-4.
– Gerona, 98-103.
– Gandía, 139-43.
– Barcelona, 161.
Vocatores, 122.
William, Duke of Aquitaine, 22.
Wings, angels with, 133-5, 138, 144.
York: Creed play, 159.
Zacharias, 151.
Zamora, 25.
Zaragoza, 25, 57-9, 65, 66, 68, 105, 190, 192.
Zwickau, 82.